A Critical Bibliography of Writings on Judaism

PART II

David B. Griffiths

Jewish Studies
Volume 2

The Edwin Mellen Press
Lewiston/Queenston
1988

Library of Congress Cataloging-in-Publication Data

Griffiths, David B.
    A critical bibliography of writings on Judaism / David B.
Griffiths.
       p.   cm. -- (Jewish studies ; v. 2)
    ISBN 0-88946-254-2
    1. Judaism--History--Bibliography. 2. Jews--History-
-Bibliography. 3. Holocaust, Jewish (1939-1945)--Bibliography.
I. Title. II. Series: Jewish studies (Lewiston, N.Y.) ; v. 2.
Z6370.G75 1989
[BM155.2]
016.296--dc19   88-30700
                                                            CIP

This is volume 2 in the continuing series
Jewish Studies
Volume 2: Part I ISBN 0-88946-252-2
Volume 2: Part II ISBN 0-88946-257-7
JS Series ISBN 0-88946-251-8

The Edwin Mellen Press

Box 450   Box 67
Lewiston, New York   Queenston, Ontario
USA   14092   CANADA L0S 1L0

Mellen House
Lampeter, Dyfed, Wales
United Kingdom SA48 7DY

Printed in the United States of America

For Gertrude, Jenny, Wendy, Caitlin,
Michael and Michel

ABBREVIATIONS

Q	quarto (25-30 cm high)
F	folio (30 cm high)
D	duodecimo (17-1/2-20 cm high)
O	octavo (20-25 cm)
pa.	paperback
Rpt.	reprint
Biblio.	Bibliography
ibidem.	In the same place
illus.	illustrated
AAJR	American Academy for Jewish Research
AHR	American Historical Review
AJHS	American Jewish Historical Society
AJHSP	American Jewish Historical Society Proceedings
AJHQ	American Jewish Historical Quarterly
AJY	American Jewish Yearbook
CBQ	Catholic Biblical Quarterly
HJ	Historia Judaica
HTR	Harvard Theological Review
HUCA	Hebrew Union College Annual
JBA	Jewish Book Annual
JBL	Journal of Biblical Literature
JHSE	Jewish Historical Society of England

JJS	Journal of Jewish Studies
JNES	Journal of Near Eastern Studies
JPS	Jewish Publication Society of America
JQR	Jewish Quarterly Review
JSS	Jewish Social Studies
JTSA	Jewish Theological Seminary of America
LBIY	Leo Baeck Institute Yearbook
MGWJ	Monatsschrift für Geschichte und Wissenschaft des Judenthums
PAAJR	Proceedings of the American Academy for Jewish Research
REJ	Revue des études juives
SBB	Studies in Bibliography and Booklore
SBL	Society of Biblical Literature
SCM	Student Christian Movement (London)
S.P.C.K.	Society for the Promotion of Christian Knowledge
UAHC	Union of American Hebrew Congregations
YIVO	Yivo Annual of Jewish Social Science/Yivo Institute for Jewish Research
W.Z.O.	World Zionist Organization
Z.O.A.	Zionist Organization of America

TABLE OF CONTENTS

PART V :
MODERN JEWISH HISTORY: TOPICS AND CURRENTS

PART V:

CHAPTER 1:

THE HOLOCAUST

A. Anti—Semitism and the Rise of National Socialism. (For other entries on anti-semitism, see Part II, Chapter 2; Part III, Chapter 2, Section A; Part V, Chapter 3, Section B). In this and the following section note the disagreements between scholars who see the Final Solution as a result of chaotic events and decisions, not a set and coordinated plan (Schleunes, Adam, Broszat, Mommsen, etc.) and scholars who posit a linear connection between early Nazi anti-semitism, Hitler's anti-Jewish phobia and the Extermination (most American and British scholars, Krausnick, Nolte, Bracher, Jackel, Fleming, S. Gordon). One should also ponder differences in the definition of Nazism. Was it a form of Fascism? Should it be classified as a type of *totalitarianism*? And to what extent was *the Jewish Question* at the center of Nazism? A largely unexplored question is the attraction that National Socialism had for a segment of the anti-communist Orthodox Jewish Community, see Schoeps (1970).

> I think of Germany in the night and sleep
> leaves me, I can no longer close my eyes, I
> weep hot tears.
> *H. Heine*

> The most European of all accomplishments,
> that more or less discernible irony with
> which the individual asserts the right to run
> its course independently of the community
> into which he is cast, has completely deserted
> the Germans.
> *W. Benjamin*

> Tod ist ein Meister aus Deutschland.
> *P. Celan*

Adler, H.G. The Jews in Germany. From the Enlightenment to National Socialism. London: University of Notre Dame Press, 1969. Biblio.: p. 143-146.

Adorno, Theodore W., Else Frenkel-Brunswick, D.J. Levinson, and R. Nevitt Sanford. The Authoritarian Personality. (Studies in Prejudice, edited by Max Horkheimer and Samuel H. Flowerman. Sponsored by the American Jewish Committee). N.Y.: Harper & Row, 1950. 990 p. Using empirical techniques, the authors establish a close correlation between deep-rooted personality traits and overt prejudice. The potentially fascist "authoritarian man" combines ideas and skills typical of highly industrialized society with irrational beliefs. The authors argue that the determinants of anti-Semitic opinions and attitudes lie within the individuals who express them.

Arendt, Hannah. The Origins of Totalitarianism. 1951. 2nd rev. ed. Cleveland and N.Y.: The World Pub. Co., 1958. A commanding analysis of the relationship between totalitarianism and 19th-century anti-Semitism, imperialism and the disintegration of the nation-state. Arendt demonstrates the central importance of anti-Semitism, terror and the concentration camps in the Nazi system. The book, Arendt said, "does not really deal with the "origins" of totalitarianism (sic)...but gives a historical account of the elements which crystallized into totalitarianism." (January, 1953, the Review of Politics). See her "Ideologie und Terror," In Offener Horizont. Festschrift für Karl Jaspers (München. R. Piper & Co., 1953), pp. 229-254.

Bein, Alex. "The Jewish Parasite. Note on the Semantics of the Jewish Problem with Special Reference to Germany." LBIY, 9 (1964):3-49.

Bein, Alex. "The Jewish Question in Modern Anti-Semitic Literature. Prelude to the 'Final Solution,'" Dispersion and Unity (Jerusalem), (Winter, 1964): 125-154.

Beradt, Charlotte. The Third Reich of Dreams. With an Essay by Bruno Bettelheim. Chicago: Quadrangle Books, 1968. 177 p. Argues that the degree of Nazi control was so deep that dreams (a sample collected from 1935 to 1945) cautioned compliance rather than resistance.

Bolkosky, Sidney M. The Distorted Image: German Jewish Perception of Germans and Germany 1918-1935. N.Y.: Elsevier Scientific Pub. Co., 1975. Bolkosky argues that "German Jews projected their Old Testament intellectual traditions, their ethics and moral values, onto the external world and made a Germany in their own image." (pp. 188-189). Thus, essentially what German Jews loved in their images of Germans was themselves.

Bramsted, Ernest. "'The Satanic Principle' in History. Lessons of Authoritarian Nationalism." Wiener Library

Bulletin (WLB), 18 (1964): 31, 38 (with references). Comments: WLB, 19 (1965): 12.

Bramsted, Ernest. Goebbels and National Socialist Propaganda, 1925-1945. East Lansing, MI.: Michigan State University Press, 1965. A massive and thorough study of the creator and chief operator of the Nazi propaganda machine.

Butler, Rohan D. The Roots of National Socialism, 1783-1933. 1941. Rpt. N.Y.: Howard Fertig. 1968.

Delm, Ferdinand. "Antisemitismus in German Encyclopedias." WLB, (Autumn, 1967): 31-36.

Einstein, Albert. "Why do They Hate the Jews?" Collier's Magazine (NYC), (November, 26, 1938). Rpt. in Out of My Later Years. N.Y.: Philosophical Library, 1950. pp. 245-253, and in Ideas and Opinions. N.Y.: Crown Pub. Co., 1954. pp. 191-198.

Flannery, Edward H. The Anguish of the Jews. Twenty-three Centuries of Anti-Semitism. Preface by John M. Oesterreicher. N.Y.: Macmillan, 1965. A well-received scholarly study.

Friedlander, Saul. L'Antisemitisme Nazi: Historie d'une psychose collective. Paris: Editions Seuil, 1971. Important, a psychological focus.

Gasman, Daniel. The Scientific Origins of National Socialism: Social Darwinism in Ernest Haeckel and the German Monist League. N.Y.: American Elsevier, 1971.

On the topic of racist-eugenics, see also Poliakov (1971), and Mosse (1978), cited below.

Geoffrey, G. Evangelist of Race, The Germanic Vision of Houston Stewart Chamberlain. N.Y.: Columbia University Press, 1981. A biographical study of the "spiritual father" of the Third Reich.

Glasser, Hermann. The Cultural Roots of National Socialism. trans. with Introd. and Notes by E.A. Menze. Austin, Texas: University of Texas Press, 1978. Glasser studies the interrelationship of literature, media and politics and argues that the German embrace of Nazism was a concluding step in a process of cultural decay.

Isaac, Jules. Jesus and Israel. ed. by Claire H. Bishop. trans. from the French by Sally Gran. N.Y.: Holt, Rinehart & Winston, 1971. A major study on the relationship between Christian anti-Semitism and Nazi anti-Semitism.

Kaltenbrunner, Gerd-Klaus. "Houston Stewart Chamberlain--the Most Germanic of Germans." WLB, (Winter 1967-68): 6-12.

Karbach, Oscar. "The Founder of Political Anti-Semitism: Georg von Schonerer." JSS, (January 1945): 3-30.

Katz, Jacob. From Prejudice to Destruction, Anti-Semitism 1700-1933. Cambridge, Mass: Harvard University Press, 1980. Notes. Index. An outstanding work by a creative historian. Methodologically, Katz does not simply focus on anti-Semitic ideologies but asks "what were the social intentions and political goals that motivated the ideologues to use these ideas, and how did they adapt them to the needs of the situation at each particular time." (p. 9).

Kehr, Helen and Janet Langmaid. The Nazi Era, 1919-1945. A Selected Bibliography of Published Works from the Early Roots to 1980. London: Mansell, 1982. XVI, 621 p. (Cited above, Part I, Chap. I, d).

Kohler, Erich. "The Jews and the Germans." In Studies of the Leo Baeck Institute. ed. by M. Kreuzberger. N.Y.: Ungar, 1967. pp. 17-43.

Kohler, Erich. The Tower and the Abyss. N.Y.: Viking Press, 1967. Develops a theory of literal schizophrenia in relationship to Nazi behaviour.

Laqueur, Walter Z. Young Germany; A History of the German Youth Movement. Introd. by R.H.S. Crossman. N.Y.: Basic Books, 1962. 253 p. An important examination of the non-political "idealist" groups. Cf. G. Mosse (1964, 1970, cited below). New ed. with Introd. by W. Laqueur; (Transaction Books) New Brunswick, N.J. 1984. 253 p. Appendix, Bibliography. Index. The early youth movement included both a volkisch anti-Semite wing out of which National Socialism grew (p. 234, passim) and a left-wing group that later found its way to Social Democracy and Communism. The youth movement produced both open-minded "social courage and responsibility, and a profoundly illiberal outlook." p. 236.

Leschnitzer, Adolf. The Magic Background of Modern anti-Semitism. An Analysis of the German-Jewish Relationship. N.Y.: International Universities Press, 1956. 236 p. A lucid and penetrating analysis, by a German-Jewish professor, of the German-Jewish relationship; and of the paranoid, magical motivations involved in anti-Semitism.

Lestchinsky, Jacob. "Anti-Semitism." In European Ideologies. A Survey of 20th Century Political Ideas. ed. by Felix Gross. N.Y.: Philosophical Library, 1948. pp. 649-673.

Levy, Richard S. The Downfall of the anti-Semitic Political Parties in Imperial Germany. (Yale Historical Pubs., Miscellany #106). New Haven, CT: Yale University Press, 1975. VII, 335 p. Reviewed by Michael A. Meyer, AHR, 82 (Fall 1977): 127. A work of important scholarship, cf. Massing (1949), Pulzer (1964), Schorsch (1972), Tal (1969), Lamberti (1978, cited in Part 5, chap. 3, b). Levy distinguishes between "conventional" political anti-Semitism (the goal was to reverse Emancipation but within the parliamentary framework) and "revolutionary" anti-Semitism (e.g., T. Fritsch). Political anti-Semitism was a failure but there was continuity between the ruthless, nihilistic anti-Semitism of the Nazis and the "revolutionary" anti-Semitism of the Imperial period.

Littell, Franklin H. The Crucifixion of the Jews. N.Y.: Harper & Row, 1975. 153 p. Argues that anti-Semitism is rooted in a spiritualizing tendency within Christianity, an inclination to retreat from history.

Distinguishes theological anti-Semitism, cultured anti-Semitism, intentional anti-Semitism (political).

Low, Alfred D. Jews in the Eyes of the Germans. From the Enlightenment to Imperial Germany. Phila.: Institute for the Study of Human Issues, 1979. 509 p. Notes. Biblio.: p. 462-494. Index. illus. Gathers and analyzes the major sources on the German evaluation of Judaism and Jews in the period between 1750 and 1890. "In the eighteenth and nineteenth centuries German anti-Semitism underwent a radical transformation...To the time-worn religious "justification" of Jew-hatred, it added new dimensions, novel accusations of an economic, social and political, and ultimately "racial" type." Low discusses German literary and political figures, using abundant quotations. He refutes, or qualifies, the judgment that all the great Germans were Jew-haters, e.g., Fichte; and Schopenhauer who had no affection for the Jewish religion "was not a real enemy of the Jews." (p. 326).

Lukacs, Georg. Die Zerstorrung der Vernuft. ("The Destruction of Reason"). Berlin: Spandau, 1962. A brilliant Marxist-influenced analysis of the cult of irrationality in German history; flawed by Stalinist phobias; and stretches the connection between Schopenhauer and Nietzsche, and the Nazis.

Mayer, Milton S. They Thought They Were Free. The Germans, 1933-1945. Chicago: University of Chicago Press, 1955. 345 p. On the attitudes of the "little men" (kleine Leute); by an American journalist, Jewish in faith and of German descent, who spent a year in Kronenberg, after the war, talking with ten Nazi party (1933-1945) members.

Massing, Paul W. Rehearsal for Destruction: A Study of Political anti-Semitism in Imperial Germany. N.Y.: Harper, 1949. 341 p. Rpt. N.Y.: Howard Fertig, 1967. Bibliographical references in the Notes. 12 original documents. Index. This important study of anti-Semitism from 1871-1914 focuses on Stoecker's Christian Social Movement, early racialist anti-Semites, and the reactions of the political parties (of particular interest being the case of the Socialists with their abstract optimism) to anti-Semitism. "The years 1875-1895 were the formative period of all German political anti-Semitism. In the economic transformations and political conflicts of these twenty years anti-Semitism was established as a quasi-automatic group reaction as well as a consciously used instrument of power. The conditions of its growth and its inherent explosive forces had become discernible a generation prior to the Nazi ascent to power." (p. 109).

Meinecke, Friedrich. The German Catastrophe: Reflections and Recollections. trans. from the German (1946). Cambridge, Mass.: Harvard University Press, 1950. Meinecke argues that the Nazis were a fluke or "accident" of history. Cf. Gerhard Ritter, Europa und die deutsche Frage (Munich, 1948). On the problem of German historicism, see Georg Iggers, The German Conception of History (Wesleyan University Press, 1968).

Mosse, George L. "Mystical Origins of National Socialism." Journal of the History of Ideas (January/March 1961): 69-81.

Mosse, George L. The Crisis of German Ideology: Intellectual Origins of the Third Reich. N.Y.: Grosset &

Dunlap, 1964. 373 p. A "milestone" analysis of the Volkish ideology and its development into a political movement. Some of Mosse's judgments appear somewhat overstated. Reviewed by W. Laqueur, N.Y. Review of Books, 3:14 (Jan 14, 1965). On Volkish antimodernity compare F. Stern's insights in The Politics of Cultural Despair (1974), cited below) with Mosse.

Mosse, George L. Germans and Jews; the Right, the Left, and the search for a "Third Force" in pre-Nazi Germany. N.Y.: Howard Fertig, 1970. Notes, Index. Reviewed by Lewis D. Wurgaft, Commentary (October 1970): 94-100. On the role of mass politics after 1870 and the Volkish ideology that nourished the Nazi movement, but also influenced certain Jewish circles see pp. 77-115. See, esp., the original essays, "Culture, Civilization and German Anti-Semitism," and "The Image of the Jew in German Popular Literature: Felix Dahn and Gustav Freytag."

Mosse, George L. The Nationalization of the Masses: Political Symbolism and Mass Movements in Germany from the Napoleonic War through the Third Reich. N.Y.: Howard Fertig, 1975. 252 p. On modern nationalism as a "religious" mass movement with mythic, liturgical, theatrical trappings.

Mosse, George. "German Socialists and the Jewish Question in the Weimar Republic." L.B.I.Y. 16 (1971): 123-151. Cf. D. Niewyk: "The theories of the Left served to betray the Jew at a moment of crisis..." (p. 150).

Mosse, George. _Toward_ _the_ _Final_ _Solution_: _A_ _History_ _of_ _European_ _Racism_. N.Y.: Howard Fertig, 1978. 277 p. A very impressive work, too short to be definitive but excellent as an introduction. Esp. valuable on Gobineau's work (1853-55) in which racism first appears as a system. Mosse views racism not as aberrant but as central to modern European experience.

Niewyk, Donald L. _The_ _Jews_ _in_ _Weimar_ _Germany_. Baton Rouge: Louisiana State University Press, 1980. 299 p. Bibliography, Index. Important material and insight on assimilation, and on anti-Semitism and responses to it. Niewyk attempts to refute the passivity charge. Cf. Wheaton (1969, cited below). Niewyk's earlier study, _Socialist,_ _anti-Semite,_ _and_ _Jew_ (La. State University Press, 1972) documented the anti-anti-Semitism of the Weimar Left. Cf. G. Mosse. More research is needed on the Jews and the Left. See the succinct discussion by S. Aschheim, in chap. 9 of _Brothers_ _and_ _Strangers_ (1982, cited in Part 5, chap. 3:b).

Pinson, Koppel S. ed. _Essays_ _on_ _anti-Semitism_. 1942. 2nd ed. rev. and enl. With a foreword by Salo W. Baron. N.Y.: Conference on Jewish Relations, 1947. 296 p. Includes several penetrating essays, e.g., Hannah Arendt on modern France, Waldemar Gurian on German anti-Semitism, K. Pinson on postwar anti-Semitism.

Pinson, Koppel S. _Modern_ _Germany,_ _Its_ _History_ _and_ _Civilization_. N.Y.: MacMillan, 1954. 637 p. A scholarly account and a well-rounded interpretation.

Poliakov, Leon. _Harvest_ _of_ _Hate_: _The_ _Nazi_ _Program_ _for_ _the_ _Destruction_ _of_ _the_ _Jews_ _of_ _Europe_. trans. from the

French. Syracuse University Press, 1954. By a notable scholar.

Poliakov, Leon. The Aryan Myth: A History of Racist and Nationalist Ideas in Europe. trans. from the French (1971) by Edmund Howard. N.Y.: Basic Books, 1974. 388 p. Argues that Western racism is an offshoot of the Enlightenment assumption of a superior Aryan race, an idea resting upon badly conceived Sanskrit studies and poorly done comparative linguistics.

Poliakov, Leon. The History of anti-Semitism. Vol. 1: From Roman Times to the Court Jews. trans. from the French by Richard Howard. (Littman Library of Jewish Civilization). London: Routledge & Kegan Paul, 1974. Vol. II: From Mohammed to the Marranos. trans. from the French by Natalie Gerardi. Routledge & Kegan Paul, 1974. Vol. III: From Voltaire to Wagner. trans. from the French by Miriam Kochan. Routledge & Kegan Paul, 1975. Pub. in N.Y.: Vanguard Press, 1965, 1973, 1977. Scholarship that is sensitive to the social and psychological factors involved in religious-ethnic hatred. Vol. 3 (582 p. Notes. Index) covers the period from 1700 to 1870. Poliakov does both historical sociology and the history of ideas with citations from many texts, most of them little known (and quite dreadful). Poliakov faults the concept of economic anti-Semitism, ascribing the primary role to theology: "...if contemporaries formed an imaginary image of a Jewish race, they did so because a theologically condemned caste already existed." (p. 458). Argues that the appointment of the Jews as scapegoats was "an essential and specific cause of Christian anti-Semitism..."

Pulzer, Peter G. The Rise of Political anti-Semitism in
Germany and Austria. N.Y.: Wiley, 1964. 365 p. Bibliographical essay. Based on his Ph.D. Dissert. University
of Cambridge, 1960. An important contribution to the
historiography of political anti-Semitism in Central
Europe and a documentation of how the Nazis exploited
the anti-Semitic movement that arose between 1867 and
1918. In the original section on Austria, Pulzer argues
that anti-Semitism flourished there because Liberalism
was unable to resolve nationalist conflicts and meet
economic needs. Reviewed by G.L. Mosse, AHR, 70:772
(April 1965).

Ragins, Sanford. Jewish Responses to anti-Semitism in
Germany, 1870-1914: A Study in the History of Ideas.
(Alumni Series of the Hebrew Union College Press).
Cincinnati: HUC Press and Ktav, 1980. Based on his
Ph.D. Dissert. Brandeis University, 1972, see History,
Modern. p. 3556, Vol. 33/07-A. Dissert. Abstracts
Intern. Compare with I. Schorsch (1972, cited below),
U. Tal (1969, cited below), and M. Lamberti (1978, cited
in Part 5, chap. 3 sec. b).

Reich, Wilhelm. Mass Psychology of Fascism. trans.
from the German by T.P. Wolfe. N.Y.: Orgone Institute
Press, 1946. Rpt. N.Y.: Simon & Schuster, Touchstone
Bks., 1974. Argues that Nazism was rooted in mass
psychology and sexual repression.

Reichman, Eva G. Hostages of Civilization. The Sources
of National Socialist anti-Semitism. London: Gollancz,
1950; Boston: Beacon Press, 1951. 218 p. Bibliography.
A sociological analysis of the causes of anti-Semitism
in modern Germany. The work would be strengthened

through comparative analysis. Reichman argues that the
Holocaust does not prove Emancipation a failure because
modern German hostility reflected old anti-Jewish
stereotypes.

Schmidt H.D. "Anti-Western and Anti-Jewish Tradition in
German Historical Thought." LBI, 4 (1959): 37-60.

Schoeps, Hans-Joachim. Bereit für Deutschland! Der
Patriotismus deutscher Juden und der Nationalsozialismus. Berlin: Haude & Spenersche, 1970. 316 p. Note the
following (quite incredible): "Im Deutschland haben
gerade manche orthodoxen Juden aus ihrer antimarxistis-
chen Gesinnung heraus Bekenntrisse abgelegt wie der
Ansbacher Rabbiner Elie Munk: 'Ich lehne die Lehre des
Marxismus vom judischen Standpunkt aus ab und bekenne
mich zum Nationalsozialismus ohne seine antisemitische
Komponente. Ohne der Antisemitismus wurde der Nationalsozialismus in den uberlieferungstreum Juden seine
treuesten Anhanger finden.'" (p. 12). This question has
been neglected in the literature. But see chap. 9 of
S.Aschheim's Brothers and Strangers (1982), cited in
Part 5, chap. 3:b) and bibliographical notes. In 1933
Schoeps and his Vortrupp attempted "to solve the Jewish
problem within the volkish framework. He submitted a
memorandum to the Nazis defining the Jews as a Stand,
possessed of equal rights and responsibilities within
the Volk. Ostjuden and zionists were excluded..." (p.
299). This attempt to achieve a total Germanization of
Jews through the Volkish ideology was of course a
complete and tragic failure. Only the Zionists--as a
group--understand the nature, intent and depth of the
anti-Semitic animus.

Schorsch, Ismar. _Jewish_ _Reactions_ _to_ _German_ _anti-_
Semitism, _1870-1914._ N.Y. & London: Columbia University
Press, 1972; Phila.: JPS, 1972. (Studies in Jewish
History, Culture, and Institutions, 3). 288 p. Bibliography. A carefully-researched study of the intimate
connection between political pressure and religious
reform in late 19th-century Germany. The constant pressure to convert or to assimilate was the decisive force
shaping the relationship between Jews and religious
tradition. In 1893, assimilation proven ineffectual,
Jews founded a self-defense organization.

Stern, Fritz. _The_ _Politics_ _of_ _Cultural_ _Despair._ _A_ _Study_
_of_ _the_ _Rise_ _of_ _the_ _German_ _Ideology._ Garden City, N.Y.:
Doubleday, 1961; Anchor Books ed., 1965: Berkeley,
University of California Press, 1962. 367 p. From his
Ph.D. Dissert. Columbia University, 1954. A brillant
study of three intellectually shoddy champions of
"Germanic ideology" (although one should not attribute
much homogeneity to this construct), de Lagarde,
Langbehn, and Moeller van den Bruck.

Stern, Fritz. _Gold_ _and_ _Iron_: _Bismarck,_ _Bleichroder,_
and _the_ _Building_ _of_ _the_ _German_ _Empire._ N.Y.: Knopf,.
1977. 620 p. Insight on the anti-Semitic campaign of
the 1870's and a major contribution to the history of
Bismarckian Germany.

Tal, Uriel. _Christians_ _and_ _Jews_ _in_ _Germany;_ _Religion,_
Politics, _and_ _Ideology_ _in_ _the_ _Second_ _Reich,_ _1870-1917._
trans. from the Hebrew by W.J. Jacobs. Ithaca & London:
Cornell University Press, 1969. In this important
study, based on extensive research, Tal argues that the
German Jewish quest for full integration while preserv-

ing Jewish identity, failed because German liberals wanted simply germanization for the Jews, and liberal Protestants wanted the Jews to convert. Cf. I. Schorsch (1972, cited above). Tal makes the very important point that there were two anti-Semitisms during the Second Reich; one, a racialist anti-Semitism was profoundly anti-Christian, although it appropriated and reshaped Christian images; and the other anti-Semitism was Christian-based and wide-spread among the clergy.

Tal, Uriel. "Violence and Jew in Nazi Ideology" In Violence and Defense in the Jewish Experience. ed. by Salo W. Baron and George S. Wise. Phila.: JPS, 1977. pp. 205-223.

Trachtenberg, Joshua. The Devil and the Jews: The Medieval Conception of the Jew and its Relation to Modern anti-Semitism. New Haven, CT: Yale University Press, 1943. 279 p. Rpt. N.Y.: Meridian Books, 1961. Argues that the negative image of the Jew has its pyschological origins in medieval Christian super-stition.

Vago, Bela and George L. Mose. eds. Jews and non-Jews in Eastern Europe, 1918-1945. N.Y.: Halstead, 1974; Jerusalem: Keter Pub. Co., 1974. Includes 17 learned essays on the perception of the Jew in the inter-War period. Nationalism in eastern Europe "left the Jew out in the cold," but except for the case of Hungary racism had little power "until Germany began to apply pressure on the East European nations to adopt a racist policy." (Preface, XVI).

Viereck, Peter. Metapolitics: The Roots of the Nazi Mind. N.Y.: Capricorn Books, 1961. First pub. in 1941 under the subtitle: From the Romantics to Hitler. Cf. Hans Kohn, The Mind of Germany: The Education of a Nation. (N.Y.: Scribner's, 1960).

Whiteside, Andrew G. Austrian National Socialism before 1913. The Hague: Nijhoff, 1962. 143 p. Described by L. Dawidowicz as "a good analysis of a proto-Nazi movement from the perspective of the Czech-German nationality conflict within the Hapsburg Empire." (1981, p. 155; cited below, sect. C, 1).

Whiteside, Andrew G. The Socialism of Fools. Georg Ritter von Schonerer and Austrian Pan-Germanism. Berkeley, Ca: University of California Press, 1975. 404 p. A study of the pan-German "radical right" in Austria, 1881-1907; a detailed contribution to the pre-history of Nazism.

Wheaton, Eliot B. Prelude to Calamity. The Nazi Revolution, 1933-35; with a background survey of the Weimar era. Garden City, N.Y.: Doubleday, 1968; London: Gollancz, 1969. 523 p. Includes maps. A useful, detailed summary; mainly political in focus.

Zisenwine, David W. ed. Anti-Semitism in Europe; Sources of the Holocaust. Introd. by Robert Chazan. (The Jewish Concepts Issues Series). N.Y.: Behrman House, 1977. 110 p. A collection of primary sources from the 17th century to the Nazi era. Bibliography.

Zuckerman, Nathan. ed. The Wine of Violence. An Anthology on Anti-Semitism. N.Y.: Association Press,

1947. 362 p. Bibliography. Topic Readings include: "The problem of anti-Semitism", "Techniques of ...," "Alleged causes of..." The material included (uneven and often incomplete) ranges from one or two lines to 13 pages.

A Note on Anti-Semitism and the "Elders of Zion."

Bernstein, Herman. The Truth about "The Protocols of Zion"; A Complete Exposure. N.Y.: Covici, 1935. 296 p. New ed. with Introd. by Norman Cohn. N.Y.: Ktav, 1972.

Cohn Norman. Warrant for Genocide: The Myth of the Jewish World Conspiracy and the Protocols of the Elders of Zion. N.Y.: Harper and Row, 1967. 303 p. Torchbook ed., 1969. Biblio.: p. 289-296. Torchbook ed., 1969. 1969 ed. Rpt. with New Foreword (Brown Judaica Studies, 23) Chico, CA. An eloquent, scholarly investigation of the roots of Nazi anti-Semitism and of the fabrication and dissemination of "The Protocols." Cohn argues that Nazi racialism was a secularized form of medieval, demo-nological anti-Semitic superstition. Reviewed by Walter Laqueur, Commentary, 44:80 (July 1967). Cohen is author of the brilliant, The Pursuit of the Millennium (London: Secker & Warburg, 1957).

Curtiss, John S. An Appraisal of the Protocols of Zion. N.Y.: Columbia University Press, 1942. 118 p. A competent, critical analysis of the infamous forgeries.

Curtiss, John S. "A Historian Analyzes the Protocols." Contemporary Jewish Record, (Feb. 1942): 51-70.

Rollin, H. L. Apocalypse de notre temps: les lessons de la propagande allemande d'apres des documents inedits. Paris, 1939. Regarded as an important work of original scholarship. This exposure of the Protocols was confiscated and destroyed by the Nazis.

Rollin, H. L. "The Truth about the 'Protocols.'" WLB, I (1947): 30, with bibliography.

Vishnaiak, Karl. "New Studies of the `Elders of Zion.'" YIVO Annual, 11-111 (1947-1948): 140-145. A review of Rollin and Curtiss.

B. The Nazi Regime.

They said (*Nazism*) was the end of the
world. And it was.
H. Syberberg

Das Ende des deutschen Judentums ist gekommen.
L. Baeck, 1933.

The word expired when that world awoke.
K. Krauss, 1933.

Abel, Theodore. The Nazi Movement. Why Hitler Came to
Power. N.J.: Prentice-Hall, 1938. 323 p. N.Y.:
Atherton, 1966. Based on 581 Nazi autobiographies.
Abel sought to understand the motives of the "ordinary"
Nazi, before 1933. Includes a chronology of the Hitler
movement, p. 310.

Adam, Uwe Dietrich. Judenpolitik im Dritten Reich.
Dusseldorf, 1972.

Allen, William S. The Nazi Seizure of Power: The
Experience of a Single Town, 1933-1935. Chicago:
Quadrangle, 1965. 345 p. Bibliographical Notes. Chapter
I gives a vivid description of the climate of opinion.
Now see the revised ed. N.Y.: Franklin Watts, 1984. 388
p. Preface to the Revised Edition. Appendices, Notes.
Index. A well-received study, widely read in college
history courses. The rev. ed. makes use of new archival
materials. The methodological question would be: how
representative Northeim (called "Thalburg" in the first
ed.) was of the larger cities. The town was primarily
middle-class and overwhelmingly Lutheran. According to
the 1932 census there were 120 Jews in Northeim out of a

population of 10,000. The Jews were "well-assimilated" and there was "very little" anti-Semitism until the Nazi power takeover. Allen makes an important contribution toward the comprehension of Nazism by detailing how a local party organization arose and functioned. His work should be read together with the important study of regional organization done by Jeremy Noakes, The Nazi Party in Lower Saxony: 1921-1933 (Oxford University Press, 1971). The Nazi rise to power, Allen writes, "was not some mysterious plague that could creep up again with little warning. Analyzed in detail, the Nazi victory is quite explicable as a consequence of clever (but comprehensible) techniques under conditions that were terribly conducive to their success (but which were also avoidable)." Preface to Revised Edition, XVIII.

Anatomy of the SS State. trans. from the German (1965) by Richard Barry, et al. Introd. by Elizabeth Wiskemann. N.Y.: Walker & Co., 1968. Includes Glossary, "Dramatis personae," Chronology, Select Bibliography, Index. See: H. Krausnik, "The Persecution of the Jews," H. Buchheim, "The SS-Instrument of Domination," and "Command and Compliance," M. Broszat, "The Concentration Camps 1933-45."

Astor, Gerald. The Life and Times of Dr. Joseph Mengele. N.Y.: Donald I. Fine, 1986. 305 p. Astor's evidence supports Arendt's thesis on the "banality" of the war criminals. Mengele, the evil doctor of Auschwitz, was "not a TV type homicidal maniac..." "Mengele was part of the mainstream of his nation and its prevailing moods..."

Baird, Jay W. The Mythical World of Nazi War Propaganda, 1939-1945. Minneapolis: University of Minnesota Press, 1974. Biblio.: pp. 311-322. Nazi propaganda was unique in its merger of irrational myth (ethos based on race) with traditional German nationalism.

Baum, Rainer C. The Holocaust and the German Elite: National Suicide in Germany, 1871-1945. London, Croom Helm, 1981. 374 p. Towowa, N.J.: Rowman & Littlefield, 1981. An intellectually exciting work that manifests real research but it is also replete with sociological jargon and generalization. Argues that the Jewish question was a "sideshow" to the Nazi elite, whose main interest was in the construction of Empire. Relates German passivity to confusion of values and social disintegration.

Binion, Rudolph. Hitler among the Germans. N.Y.: American Elsevier, 1976. 207 p. Argues that Hitler's charismatic power resulted from the merger of his personal trauma and obsessions (including a "castration complex") with "the national traumatic need." For another example of the psychohistorical approach, see Peter Loewenberg, "The Psychohistorical Origins of the Nazi Youth Cohort." AHR, 76 (December 1971): 1457-1502.

Bracher, Karl Dietrich. The German Dictatorship: The Origins, Structure, and Effects of National Socialism. trans. from the German by Jean Steinberg. N.Y.: Praeger, 1970. 685 p. An outstanding comprehensive study. Nazism had three Ideological principles: anti-Semitism, the Fuhrer principle, and Lebensraum (racial imperialism).

Browning, Christopher R. The Final Solution and the German Foreign Office; A Study of Referat D III of Abteilung Deutschland 1940-43. N.Y.: Holmes & Meier, 1978. A scholarly case study of the German Foreign Office, specifically of the "Jewish desk." According to Browning, the "Final solution" was not ordained from 1933 but evolved out of the competition for favour between different bureaucratic and party agencies.

Broszat, Martin. National Socialism, 1918-1933. Santa Barbara, Ca: Clio Press, 1967. By a major specialist.

Broszat, Martin. "Hitler and the Genesis of the 'Final Solution': an Assessment of David Irving's Theses." Yad Vashem, 13 (1979)" 73-123. A balanced critique, see Irving (cited below), G. Fleming (cited below).

Buchheim, Hans. The Third Reich. Its Beginnings, Its Development, Its End. London: Wolff, 1961.

Buchheim, Hans. Totalitarian Rule: Its Nature and Characteristics. trans. from the German (Totalitare Herrschaft, 1962) by Ruth Hein, with annotations by Kurt P. Tauber and R. Hein. Middletown, Conn.: Wesleyan University Press, 1968. 112 p. Bibliography. Follows a holistic approach, regards the Nazi and Stalinist regimes as the only true totalitarian systems. Cf. Carl J. Friedrich. ed. with Introd. Totalitarianism. N.Y.: Grosset & Dunlap, 1954, 1964. X, 386 p.

Bullock, Alan. Hitler: A Study in Tyranny. 1954. rev. ed. N.Y.: Harper and Row, 1964. 848 p. A standard work, scholarly, careful, comprehensive; but Bullock's methodological imagination is limited and perspectives from other disciplines are not used.

Colodner, Solomon. "Jewish Education under National socialism." Yad Vashem Studies, 3 (1959): 161-180. See also: Maurice Friedman, Martin Buber's Life and Work. The Middle Years 1923-1945 (N.Y.: E.P. Dutton, 1983), chap. 11, "Jewish Education as Spiritual Resistance," pp. 198-222.

Daim, Wilfred. Der Mann, der Hitler die Ideen gab. (Institute fuer Politische Psychologie, Wien). München: Isar, 1958. Contains rather tenous arguments linking Nazi leadership fixations and Nazi prejudice with Oedipal fantasies.

DeLarue, Jacques. The Gestapo: A History of Horror. trans. from the French. N.Y.: William Morrow & Co., 1964. Frequently cited in the literature.

Dicks, Henry. Licensed Mass Murder: A Social-Psychological Study of some SS Killers. N.Y.: Basic Books, 1972.

Documents on Nazism, 1919-1945. ed. and with an Introd. by J. Noakes and G. Pridham. London: Jonathan Cape, 1974. Includes Select Bibliography, list of sources, name Index.

Erikson, Erik. "The Legend of Hitler's Childhood." In Childhood and Society. N.Y.: Norton, 1950; 2nd rev. and enl. ed. Norton, 1963. pp. 326-358. "Strong eras and strong countries assimilate the contributions of strong

Jews...In times of collective anxiety, however, the very suggestion of relativity is resented..." pp. 356-357.

Esh, Shaul. "Words and Their Meaning: 25 Examples of Nazi-Idiom." Yad Vashem Studies 5 (1963). And see further A. Rosenfeld, A Double Dying (Indiana University Press, 1980), chap. 7, "Immolation of the Word." Also see: Nachman Blumenthal, "On the Nazi Vocabulary," "Action," and "From the Nazi Vocabulary," Yad Vashem Studies, I, 4, 6, (1957, 1960, 1967); and see Heinz Paechter, Nazi-Deutsch: A Glossary of Contemporary German Usage (N.Y.: Ungar, 1944).

Feig, Konnilyn G. Hitler's Death Camps: The Sanity of Madness. London: Homes & Meier, 1981. 547 p. A detailed, mammoth study of the 19 infamous camps, class-ified by types. Includes a preface that discusses causality and a final section on post-Holocaust questions. Extensive bibliography.

Fest, Joachim C. The Face of the Third Reich: Portraits of the Nazi Leadership. N.Y.: Pantheon, 1970. 402 p. trans. from the German (1963) by Michael Bullock. A comprehensive synthesis that coordinates character-analysis with historical detail.

Fest, Joachim C. Hitler. trans. from the German By Richard and Clara Winston. N.Y.: Harcourt Brace, Jovan-ovich, 1974. 844 p. This massive biography supplements the work by A. Bullock (cited above) and in some respects is superior.

Fleming, Gerald. Hitler and the Final Solution. With an Introd. by Saul Friedlander. A trans. of Hitler und die Endlösung (1982). Berkeley and L. A.: University of California Press, 1984. 219 p. Appendix, Select Bibliography, Acknowledgements, Index. Based on wide and thorough archival research. Rejects the view that Hitler did not plan and order the Final Solution.

Fromm, Erich. "Psychology of Nazism." In Escape from Freedom, 1942. N.Y.: Holt, Rinehart & Winston, 1961. pp. 207-239. Cf. Reich (1946, cited above), Adorno (1950, cited above), Merkl (1975, cited above).

Gilbert, G.M. Nuremberg Diary. N.Y.: Farrar, Straus, 1947. 471 p. Contains a mass of quotations that provide insight into the Nazi mentality.

Gilbert, G.M. Psychology of Dictatorship. N.Y.: Ronald Press, 1950. 327 p. Gilbert, the court psychiatrist at the Nuremberg trials, interviewed 21 of the Nazis under trial.

Goldston, Robert C. The Life and Death of Nazi Germany. Indianapolis: Bobbs-Merrill, 1967. 224 p. illus., by Donald Carrick. Composed for a high-school readership; detailed, concise, and clearly written.

Gordon, Harold J. Jr. Hitler and the Beer Hall Putsch. Princeton, N.J.: Princeton University Press, 1972. 666 p. Includes annotated bibliography. On the Nazi-led "Patriotic Movement" and its bid for power in Bavaria in 1923. The Putsch was beneficial to the Nazi party and the starting point for Hitler's career.

Gordon, Sarah. Hitler, Germans and the "Jewish
Question." Princeton, N.J.: Princeton University
Press, 1984. 412 p. Notes. Biblio. p. 389-405. Tables.
Index. A clearly written and analytically differentiated sociological study. Uses Merkl (cited below)
extensively. Draws on archival materials, including
Gestapo files for the Government district Dusseldorf and
using this material revises somewhat the image of the
extent and range of German opposition (including that
within the Nazi party) to Nazi racist legislation and
policies. The somewhat startling results of her
research on German opposition are present in chapters 7-
9. The data presented is very important but some of her
judgments may be challenged, e.g., "a large segment of
the public appears to have opposed Kristallnach..." (p.
252). Gordon cites about 3,000 cases of Germans (out of
a population of about 60 million) arrested for violating
race laws or aiding Jews. The author challenges the
middle-class origins theory, aruging that the Nazi party
was a "catchall" party for people disaffected with other
options (chap. 2). There were more rabid anti-Semites
among Protestants and members of some middle-class occu-
pations than other groups. However, the opponents of
Nazism were overrepresented by independents and white-
collar (esp. upper levels) workers and underrepresented
by blue-collar (esp. urban) workers. Gordon argues that
the timing of the persecution of the Jews and the extermination policies (cf. Broszat, Schleunes) were decided
by Hitler "because this was a logical consequence of his
ethnic theory." (p. 300). Gordon claims that anti-
Semitism served basic functions in the Nazi state "but
it was not logically necessary to Nazism." (p. 311).
This could be held in the case of Italian fascism but it
is a hollow point here since Hitler's central obsession

was anti-Semitism and he "for all practical purposes was the state..." (p. 315).

Gross, Leonard. The Last Jews in Berlin. N.Y.: Simon and Schuster, 1983. 349 p. Contains valuable material gathered from interviews but lacks rigorous analysis.

Grunberger, Richard. A Social History of the Third Reich. The 12 Year Reich. London: Weidenfeld & Nicolson, 1971. Includes "suggested further reading," References, Glossary, Index. See, esp., chap. 20, "Nazi Speech," and chap. 30, "The Jews."

Haffner, Sebastian. The Meaning of Hitler. Hitler's Use of Power: His Successes and Failures. N.Y.: Macmillan, 1979. Critically discussed in S. Gordon (1984).

Hale, Oron J. The Captive Press in the Third Reich. Princeton, N.J.: Princeton University Press, 1964. 353 p. Bibliography. A valuable study of the Nazi publishing industry and of Max Amann, publisher of the Volkischer Beobachter, but one regrets the narrow limitations of the book. The reality of anti-Semitism and the content of what was suppressed are not adequately covered.

Heiden, Konrad. Der Fuehrer: Hitler's Rise to Power. trans. from the German by Ralph Manheim. Boston: Houghton Mifflin, 1944. This biographical study, to 1934, still has merit although superseded by A. Bullock (1964, cited above) and J. Fest (1974, cited above).

Hinz, Bertold. Art in the Third Reich. trans. from the German by Robert and Rita Kimber. N.Y.: Pantheon, 1980. 268 p. Bibliography. ca. 160 illus., Index. A critical social-historical approach and focus; the problem for defining fascist aesthetics remains unclarified.

Hitler's Mein Kampf. trans. by Ralph Manheim. London: Hutchinson, 1969.

Hoess, Rudolf. Commandant of Auschwitz. The Autobiography of Rudolf Hoess. Introd. by Lord Russell of Liverpool. trans. from the German by Constantine Fitz-Gibbon. London: Weidenfeld and Nicolson, 1959; Cleveland: World Pub. Co., 1959, 2nd ed. 1960. 285 p. Written in Cracow prison in 1947, first pub. in a Polish translation, 1951. The German text of 1958 has a scholarly introd. by M. Broszat. A grim and terrible document of the Nazi mentality and period. See J. Tenebaum, "Auschwitz in Retrospect..." JSS (July-Oct. 1953): 203-236. In his banal and appalling platitudes, Hoess fits the image of Eichmann as drawn by H. Arendt.

Homze, Edward L. Foreign Labor in Nazi Germany. Princeton, N.J.: Princeton University Press, 1966. 350 p. Bibliographical essay. A study, based on captured German documents, of the Nazi foreign labor (ca. 8 million people were involved) program. At times the discussion is naive and the picture of "The 'Untermensch' philosophy in Action" is highly inadequate.

Irving, David. Hitler's War. N.Y.: Basic Books, 1977. 926 p. Reflects a great deal of research and an intense but rather erratic energy. Irving's contention that it was Himmler and not Hitler that was responsible for the extermination policies has been rejected by qualified scholars. That Irving is an "apologist" for Hitler (so L. Dawidowicz) is surely overstatement but his contention that Hitler was unaware of the Final Solution up to 1943 "goes against all evidence." (Saul Friedlander, Introd. to G. Fleming, Hitler and the Final Solution (1984, cited above, XXVIII).

Jackel, Eberhard. Hitler's Weltanschauung: A Blueprint for Power. Middletown, Conn.: Wesleyan University Press, 1974. 140 p. trans. from the German by Herbert Arnold. Argues that Hitler had definite principles and a world-view, i.e., expansion of territory and destruction of the Jews. Reviewed by G. Barraclough, N.Y. Review of Books, 19:32 (Nov. 2, 1972).

Kershaw, Ian. Popular Opinion and Political Dissent in the Third Reich: Bavaria, 1933-1945 N.Y.: Oxford University Press, 1983. Important scholarship, cf. S. Gordon (1984), W. Allen (1984), J. Noakes (1971).

Koehl, Robert L. RKFDV: German Resettlement and Population Policy, 1939-1945. Cambridge, Mass.: Harvard University Press, 1957. Bibliographical references, Appendix: A Note on the Documentation, Glossary, Documents and Decrees, Index. Based largely on unpublished materials gathered for the Nuremberg trials. A study of the Germany agency (Reich Commission for the Strengthening of Germandom) responsible for the task of "fighting the biological war of population on German's frontiers." The RKFDV was "imperialism via demography." The Nazis were characterized by their "gangland character," their irrationality, "infernal activism" and commitment to brute force.

Koehl, Robert L. "Feudal Aspects of National Socialism." American Political Science Review, 54 (December 1960): 921-933.

Lane, Barbara Miller and Leila J. Rupp. eds. Nazi Ideology before 1933. A Documentation. Austin & London: University of Texas Press, 1978. 26 selected and trans. documents with Introd. Includes Appendix, Biographies, Notes, Index.

Langer, Walter C. The Mind of Adolf Hitler: The Secret Wartime Report. Foreword by William L. Langer; afterword by Robert G.L. Waite. N.Y.: Basic Books, 1972. 269 p. A war-time psychological profile of Hitler as a neurotic psychopath with schizophrenic aspects. Early psychohistory and perceptive but the historical context is slighted. See L. Dawidowicz (1981, 38ff, cited below).

Lesser, Jonas. Germany the Symbol and the Deed. N.Y.: Thomas Yoseloff, 1965. 601 p. A heavy indictment ("the deed") but also documents the range and depth of dissent.

Mau, Hermann and Helmut Krausnik. German History 1933-1945: An Assessment by German Historians. trans. from the German by Andrew and Eva Wilson. London: Wolff, 1959. 157 p. An incise analysis by two historians of the Institute for Contemporary History in Munich.

Manvell, Roger and Heinrich Fraenkel. The Incomparable Crime: Mass Extermination in the Twentieth Century: the legacy of guilt. London: Heinemann, 1967. 339 p. Based entirely on secondary sources, characterized by superficial descriptions and written in weak prose.

McRandle, James Harrington. The Track of the Wolf, Essays on National Socialism and Its Leader. Evanston, Ill.: Northwestern University Press, 1965. Includes five essays: The Track of the Wolf, The German Revolution, Warrior and Worker, The Ideologist, The Suicide. The methodology is shaky and McRandle makes extreme statements.

Merkl, Peter H. Political Violence under the Swastika, 581 Early Nazis. Princeton, N.J.: Princeton University Press, 1975. 735 p. Appendices. Bibliography. Merkl's work, based on Abel's study (1938), advances understanding of the social dynamics of the early Nazi movement. The Nazis were not mainly motivated by Ideology but by "virulent prejudice and a desire for fighting." (p. 697). While Merkl finds "lower middle-class revolt" explanations too simple, he can still argue that: "there were obviously highly differentiated motive forces at work which had few common denominators except for frustrated upward mobility and an in-between or misfit status between the two powerful camps of the liberal bourgeoisie and the organized working class." (p. 668). But see the important study by Max H. Kele, Nazis and Workers: National Socialist Appeals to German Labor, 1919-1933. (University of North Carolina Press, 1972); Kele shows how Hitler manipulated the Left wing of the Nazi party which had ties with the working classes.

Mommsen, Hans. "Die Realisierung des Utopischen: Die 'Endlosung' der Judenfrage im Dritten Reich,' Geschichte und Gesellschaft, 9:3 (1983): 381-417. And see Mommsen's Hitlers Stellung im nationalsozialistischen Herrschaftssystem. (Stuttgart, 1981).

Mosse, George L. ed. Nazi Culture. Intellectual, Cultural and Social Life in the Third Reich. N.Y.: Grosset & Dunlap, 1966. 386 p. A comprehensive "collection of materials intended to show what life was like under Hitler..." Specific introductions and a general introduction by Mosse.

Mosse, George L. Nazism: A Historical and Comparative Analysis of National Socialism: An Interview with Michael A. Ledeen. (Issues in Contemporary Civilization). New Brunswick, N.J.: Transaction Books, 1979. No Index. no Bibliography. 134 p. The title is somewhat incorrect, this is the transcription of a conversation.

Naumann, Bernd. Auschwitz: A Report on the Proceedings Against Robert Ludwig Mulka and Others Before the Court at Frankfurt. trans. from the German by Jean Steinberg. Introd. by Hannah Arendt. N.Y..: Praeger, 1966. An account of the legal proceedings of the "Auschwitz Trial" of 1965, conducted under the penal code of 1871. It was inevitable that "neither the judges nor the jury found the truth" (Arendt) because that code did not recognize murder as a governmental institution.

Neumann, Franz. Behemoth: The Structure and Practice of National Socialism. 1942. 532 p. N.Y.: Harper and Row (Torchbook), 1966. The best of the philosophical Marxist interpretations; erudite but doctrinaire, and mistaken in the assumption that there is a Model of/for Fascism per se.

Nolte, Ernst. Three Faces of Facism: Action Française, Italian Fascism, National Socialism. trans. from the German (1963) by Leila Vennewitz. N.Y.: Holt, Rinehart and Winston, 1966. Exhibits philosophic range but Part 5: "Fascism as a metapolitical phenomenon" is obscure and replete with jargon. Nolte views Nasizm as an anti-modernist movement. Scholarly notes, pp. 463-546.

Nyomarkay, Joseph. Charisma and Factionalism in the Nazi Party. Minneapolis: University of Minnesota Press, 1967. 161 p. A highly specialized and technical analysis of interparty disputes in relationship to the charisma of Hitler, the sole source of political legitimacy. Hitler was adept at exploiting this factionalism. This monograph would have been stronger had it drawn from Laqueur (1962, cited above) and Mosse (1964, cited above).

O'Neill, Robert J. The German Army and the Nazi Party, 1933-1939. Foreword by Sir Basil Liddell Hart. N.Y.: Heinemann, 1966. 286 p. Annotated Bibliography. Index. An instructive account of the tension between Hitler and the Generals and of how the military gradually became his tool.

Orlow, Dietrich. The History of the Nazi Party, 1919-1933. Pittsburgh: University of Pittsburgh Press, 1969. By the author of The Nazis in the Balkans (University of Pittsburgh, 1968). The standard study of the development and structure of the NSDAP. Based on primary sources. Bibliographical essay. But downgrades ideology and the discussion of anti-Semitism is minimal.

Peterson, E.N. "The Bureaucracy and the Nazi Party." Review of Politics, 28 (April 1966): 172-192.

Pridham, G. Hitler's Rise to Power: The Nazi Movement in Bavaria 1923-1933. London: Hart-Davis, MacGibbon, 1973.

Pryce-Jones, David. <u>Paris</u> <u>in</u> <u>the</u> <u>Third</u> <u>Reich</u>: <u>A</u> <u>History</u>
<u>of</u> <u>the</u> <u>German</u> <u>Occupation,</u> <u>1940-1944</u>. London: Collins,
1981. X, 294 p. Includes notes, illus., Index. A high-
level, popular narrative history with over 100 photos;
the focus is on French politics and Parisian life, June
13, 1940-July 1944. The question as to why France was
the leading case/example of collaboration remains
unanswered. Cf. Gerald Walter, <u>Paris</u> <u>under</u> <u>the</u> <u>Occupa-</u>
<u>tion</u>. trans. from the French by Tony White (N.Y.: The
Orion Press, 1960). A study based on "the occupied
press" of Paris.

Reitlinger, Gerald. <u>The</u> <u>SS</u> <u>Alibi</u> <u>of</u> <u>a</u> <u>Nation</u> <u>1932-1945</u>.
N.Y.: Viking Press, 1957. 502 p. Bibliography, maps,
List of important persons, Index. The authoritative
history. Now also consult Charles W. Sydnor, Jr.,
<u>Soldiers</u> <u>of</u> <u>Destruction</u>: <u>The</u> <u>SS</u> <u>Death's</u> <u>Head</u> <u>Division</u>
<u>1933-1945</u>. Princeton, N.J.: Princeton University
Press, 1977. 371 p. Bibliography, maps. illus., Index.
And see the monumental, documented study by Heinz Hohne,
<u>The</u> <u>Order</u> <u>of</u> <u>the</u> <u>Death's</u> <u>Head</u>: <u>the</u> <u>Story</u> <u>of</u> <u>Hitler's</u> <u>SS</u>.
trans. from the German by Richard Barry. (Rutherford,
N.J.: Coward, MaCann; N.Y.: Ballantine, 1971, 690 p.)

Remak, Joachin. ed. <u>The</u> <u>Nazi</u> <u>Years.</u> <u>A</u> <u>Documentary</u>
<u>History</u>. Englewood Cliffs, N.J.: Prentice-Hall, 1969.
Short selections with Introductions. No bibliography.

Rich, Norman. <u>Hitler's</u> <u>War</u> <u>Aims</u>. Vol. I: <u>Ideology,</u> <u>the</u>
<u>Nazi</u> <u>State,</u> <u>and</u> <u>the</u> <u>Course</u> <u>of</u> <u>Expansion</u>. N.Y.: W.W.
Norton, 1973. 352 p. Vol. II: <u>The</u> <u>Establishment</u> <u>of</u> <u>the</u>
<u>New</u> <u>Order</u>. N.Y.: W.W. Norton, 1974. In Vol. I, Rich
studies the nexus between Nazi ideas and actions,

arguing that Hitler remained basically true to the aims expressed in Mein Kampf. Vol II is a solidly researched administrative history of Nazi rule in the occupied countries.

Sauer, Wolfgang. "National Socialism: totalitarianism or Fascism?" AHR, 72 (July 1967): 404-424. Sauer calls for a socioeconomic theory of fascism, and asks if perhaps the Nazis were not motivated by having been the "losers of the industrial revolution."

Schleunes, Karl A. The Twisted Road to Auschwitz, Nazi Policy Toward German Jews 1933-1939. Urbana, Ill.: University of Illinois Press, 1979. 280 p. Biblio.: p. 263-275. This thoroughly researched and well-written study (from his Ph.D. Dissert. University of Minnesota, 1966) confronts the basic centrality of hatred, phobia and anti-Semitism in Nazism. But Schleunes argues that the Nazis "stumbled" toward the 'Final Solution'; it was not the product of a single or set design. Cf. Browning (1978, cited above). "Germany's real misfortune was the fact that her quest for identity coincided with a period of severe economic dislocation. Economic crisis brought to the surface the older anti-Jewish prejudices and helped create the climate in which these prejudices found a new footing in Racism." (p. 23). Cf. Massing (1949, cited above).

Schoenbaum, D. Hitler's Social Revolution: Class and Status in Nazi Germany 1933-1939. Garden City, N.Y.: Doubleday, 1966. 366 p. Bibliography, Index. A major social-economic history that details the impact of the regime on various social groups. Argues that the Third Reich was an extension of German history. Contrast:

Meinecke (1946, cited above), Ritter (1948, cited above).

Sereny, Gitta. Into That Darkness: From Mercy Killing to Mass Murder. N.Y.: McGraw Hill, 1974. A grim and depressing story is told in this brave book based on extensive talks with Stangl, a "commonplace" individual who went from the euthanasia program to commander of Treblinka.

Shirer, William. The Rise and Fall of the Third Reich. A History of Nazi Germany. N.Y.: Simon and Schuster, 1960. 1245 p. A vast, comprehensive and erudite reconstruction but Shirer is sometimes simplistic in analysis, e.g., on the question of the "roots" of the Third Reich. Reviewed by Terence Prittie, The Atlantic, 206:106 (December 1960): 106-110.

Smith, Bradley F. Heinrich Himmler: A Nazi in the Making, 1900-1926. Stanford, Ca: Hoover Institution Press, 1971. The early life of a cruel bloodthirsty Nazi who was "the obedient son of a typical Bourgeois family" with social ambitions and a strict morality. Smith uses important personal evidence of letters and family documents. Surpasses R. Manvel and H. Fraenkel's Heinrich Himmler (Putnam, 1965).

Smith, Bradley F. "Two Alibis for the Inhumanities..." German Studies Review, 1:3 (October 1978): 327-335. A critique of the so-called "revisionist" works on Nazism.

Speer, Albert. Inside the Third Reich Memoirs. Introd. by Eugene Davidson. N.Y.: Macmillan, 1970. 596 p. Speer was part of Hitler's inner circle, his architect and later his armaments minister. Written in Spandau prison. These Memoirs must be used with caution. See: L. Dawidowicz, Commentary (Nov. 1970): 85-100.

Speer, Albert. Infiltration: The SS and German Armament. trans. by Joachim Neugroshel. N.Y.: Macmillan, 1981. 384 p. On the efforts of the SS to control the armament industry vs. Speer's advocacy of private management. According to Speer, he urged the use of skilled Jewish labor. Reviewed by W. Laqueur, N.Y. Times Book Review (Oct. 4, 1981).

Stein, George H. The Waffen SS: Hitler's Elite Guard at War, 1939-1945. Ithaca, N.Y.: Cornell University Press, 1966. 330 p. maps, illus., Bibliography. This is probably the definitive work but see the review by G. Reitlinger, N.Y. Times Book Review (March 20, 1966).

Steinert, Marlis G. Hitler's War and the Germans. Public Mood and Attitude during the Second World War. ed. and trans. from the German by Thomas E.J. de Witt. Athens, Ohio: Ohio University Press, 1977. 783 p. Bibliography. Based largely on documents of the Internal Security branch of the SS. Information on the changing moods of the German people, insight on the role of propaganda and the function of public opinion in a totalitarian state.

Stephenson, Jill. The Nazi Organization of Women. London: Croom Helm, 1981. 246 p. Glossary, Bibliography, Index. An organizational study of the NSF (Nazi Women's Group), mainly during the years 1933-1934. See also her instructive: Women in Nazi Society (Harper, 1976).

Thalmann, Rita and Emmanuel Feinerman. Crystal Night, 9-10 November 1938. London: Thames & Hudson, 1974. 192 p. A documentary study of the first "modern" (i.e., technologically sophisticated) pogrom.

Toland, John. Adolf Hitler. N.Y.: Random House, Ballantine Books, 1977; Doubleday, 1976. 1035 p. Includes Glossary, Sources, Notes, Maps & Tables, Index. The bibliography is adequate but not extensive. Based on vast and careful research, rich in fact and interesting prose. Toland had "no thesis." This is a conventional narrative biography, a genuine contribution but not the equal of A. Bullock (1964) or J. Fest (1974). "Deprived of heaven, Adolf Hitler chose hell--if, indeed, he knew the difference between the two. To the end, obsessed by his dream of cleansing Europe of Jews, he remained a Knight of the Hakenkreuz (swastika), a warped archangel, a hybrid of Prometheus and Lucifer." (XI).

Weinreich, Max. Hitler's Professors. The Part of Scholarship in Germany's Crimes Against the Jewish People. N.Y.: Yivo, 1946. 291 p. Facsimiles of Excerpts. Indices. The very angry and distressing story of the German scholars who worked closely with the murderers of the Jewish people; esp. disturbing is the account of Gerhard Kittel, prof. of theology at Tübingen, and son of the famous biblical scholar, R. Kittel. (pp. 40-43).

Weinstein, Fred. The Dynamics of Nazism: Leadership, Ideology, and the Holocaust. (Studies in social discontinuity) N.Y.: Academic Press, 1980. 168 p. Contains a trenchant and heated critique of previous historical studies of Nazism but Weinstein's methodological recommendation, the integration of psychoanalysis and sociology, remains unconvincing.

Wistrich, Robert S. Who's Who in Nazi Germany. N.Y.: Macmillan, 1982. 359 p. 350 short biographies of people significantly associated with the Nazi period, including Jews and anti-Nazi figures.

C. Jewish History in the Nazi Era.

1. General Historical Studies. Essay and Document Collections.

Arad, Yitzhak, Yisrael Gutman, Abraham Margaliot. eds. Documents on the Holocaust; Selected Sources on the Destruction of the Jews of Germany and Austria, Poland, and the Soviet Union. N.Y.: Ktav, in association with Yad Vashem and the Anti-Defamation League, 1982. 504 p. illus. Includes over 200 documents.

Dawidowicz, Lucy S. "Towards a History of the Holocaust." Commentary, 47 (4 April 1969): 51-56. A historiographical essay, including a critical survey of research projects.

Dawidowicz, Lucy S. The War Against the Jews, 1933-1945. N.Y.: Holt, Rinehart & Winston, 1975. 460 p. maps. London: Weidenfeld, 1975. Toronto: Bantam paperback, 1976. Biblio.: p. 437-450. Outstanding work that complements Reitlinger (1953) and Hilberg (1951). Corrects Hilberg through extensive use of Jewish sources and presents a more balanced view of the Jewish Councils, see pp. 233-241.

Dawidowicz, Lucy S. ed. with introductions and notes. A Holocaust Reader. "Introduction: On Studying Holocaust Documents." (pp. 1-21). (Library of Jewish Studies) N.Y.: Behrman House, 1976. 397 p. maps. Biblio.: p. 383-386. Sources. p. 387-391. All the documents (except one by K. Gerstein) are contemporary with the events they describe.

Dawidowicz, Lucy S. The Jewish Presence: Essays on Identity and History. N.Y.: Holt, Rinehart and Winston, 1977. 308 p. Includes essays on the Holocaust.

Dawidowicz, Lucy S. "Lies About the Holocaust." Commentary, 70 (Dec. 1980): 31-37. On so-called "Revisionist" attempts (cf. Butz) to erase the past.

Dawidowicz, Lucy S. The Holocaust and the Historians. Cambridge, Mass.: & London, Eng.: Harvard University Press, 1981. 187 p. Six essays dealing with the failure of many historians in different countries honestly to and fully confront the reality of the Holocaust.

Friedlander, Albert H. ed. with Introd. Out of the Whirlwind; A Reader of Holocaust Literature. Garden City: Doubleday, 1969. 536 p. Includes bibliographical footnotes and goes with a discussion guide by Jack D. Spiro. Illus. by Jacob Landau. Discussed in Section F. Part 1.

Friedlander, Albert H. Leo Baeck, Teacher of Theresienstadt. N.Y.: Holt, Rinehart & Winston, 1968. 294 p.
See, below, L. Baker.

Friedlander, Henry. On the Holocaust: A Critique of the
Treatment of the Holocaust in History Textbooks
Accompanied by an Annotated Bibliography. N.Y.: Anti-
Defamation League of B'nai B'rith, 1972.

Friedlander, Henry. with Sybil Milton. eds. The Holocaust: Ideology, Bureaucracy, and Genocide--the San Jose
Papers. Millwood, N.Y.: Kraus International Publications, 1980. Includes papers by P. Merkl, H. Feingold,
A. Beyerchen, F. Ringen.

Friedman, Philip. Road to Extinction: Essays on the
Holocaust. ed. by Ada June Friedman. Introduction by
Salo W. Baron. (Conference on Jewish Studies).
Phila.: JPS, 1980. Q. 610 p. Lucid, scholarly and
important essays (see, e.g., "The Jewish Ghettos of the
Nazi Era." (JSS, 1954), "The Jewish Badge and the Yellow
Star in the Nazi Era." (HJ, 1955), etc. By "the father
of the Jewish Holocaust literature."

Gilbert, Martin. The Holocaust. N.Y.: Holt, Rinehart
and Winston, 1986. 830 p. Comprehensive scholarship
using diaries, allied documents, German communications.

Gutman, Yisrael and Livia Rothkirchen. eds. The
Catastrophe of European Jewry: Antecedents, History,
Reflections: Selected Papers. Jerusalem: Yad Vashem,
1976.

Heller, Celia S. On the Edge of Destruction. Jews of
Poland Between the two World Wars. N.Y.: Columbia
University Press, 1977. 369 p. Notes, 301-355. illus.
Index. Historical sociology done with confidence and
clarity. Based on a review of the extensive interwar
literature in Yiddish, Polish, Hebrew; and on interviews
with survivors, census data, the Jewish daily press (in
Polish and Yiddish) and autobiographical documents
recovered after the war.

Hilberg, Raul. The Destruction of the European Jews.
Chicago: Quadrangle Books, 1961. Q. 788 p. maps. A
massive and detailed study based on German sources.
Often regarded as the "definitive scholarly" work, but
he lacked knowledge of Jewish sources (see critique in
Dawidowicz, 1981). Hilberg blamed "Jewish ghetto
history" for the "passivity" of the Jews. The reaction
to this view (sparked to some considerable extent by the
Eichmann trial) has been very strong - see, e.g., Y.
Suhl (1967), L. Steinberg (1978), etc. (cited below
section D).

Hilberg, Raul. ed. with commentary. Documents of
Destruction: Germany and Jewry, 1933-1945. Quadrangle
Books, 1971. 242 p.

"Holocaust." EJ, 8:832-906.

Kenrick, Donald and Grattan Puxon. The Destiny of
Europe's Gypsies. N.Y.: Basic Books, 1972. 256 p. In
some respects the fate of the Gypsies followed the same
pattern as that of the Jews: hostility, restrictive
legislation, deportation, extermination. But directives
against the Gypsies were not always applied with the

same ruthlessness; and the policies toward them indicated "the lack of sincerity with which the Nazis
regarded their own racial theories." See, Philip
Friedman, "The Extermination of the Gypsies: Nazi Genocide of an Aryan People." In Roads to Extinction:
Essays on the Holocaust (1980, cited above), pp. 381-86.
See also: Dora E. Yates. "Hitler and the Gypsies, The
Fate of Europe's Oldest Aryans." Commentary, (Nov.
1949): 455-59.

Korman, Gerd. ed. Hunter and Hunted; Human History of
the Holocaust. (The B'nai B'rith Jewish Heritage
Classics). N.Y.: Viking Press, 1973. 320 p. Biblio.: p.
309. Personal documents.

Korman, Gerd. "The Holocaust in American Historical
Writing." Societas, 2 (Summer 1957) 251-70. Note the
discussion of the word "Holocaust"--it came into use in
1957 to describe what had happened (and as unique) to
Eastern European Jews.

Meltzer, Milton. Never to Forget: the Jews of the
Holocaust. N.Y.: Harper & Row, 1976. 217 p. Biblio.:
pp. 201-207. Consists of eye-witness accounts.

Pilch, Judah. ed. The Jewish Catastrophe in Europe.
("Prepared by the National Curriculum Research Institute
of the American Association for Jewish Education").
N.Y.: American Association for Jewish Education, 1968.
Q. 230 p. illus.. Includes bibliographical references.

Poliakov, Leon. Harvest of Hate: The Nazi Program for
the Destruction of the Jews of Europe. trans. from the
French by Albert J. George. Foreword by Reinhold

Niebuhr. (Sponsored by the Am. Jewish Com.). ed. by Martin Greenberg. Syracuse, N.Y.: Syracuse University Press, 1954. 338 p. The first scholarly survey of the Catastrophe as a whole by the head of the Centre de Documentation Juive Contemporaine (Paris).

Reitlinger, Gerald. The Final Solution: The Attempt to Exterminate the Jews of Europe. 1939-1945. N.Y.: Beechhurst Press, 1953, London: Vallentine, 1953. 622 p. maps. Rpt. N.Y.: A.S. Barnes (Perpetua Books), 1961. The first comprehensive detailed study.

Robinson, Jacob. ed. and comp. The Holocaust and After: Sources and Literature in English. Assisted by Mrs. Philip Friedman. (Yad Vashem Martyrs' and Heroes' Memorial Authority, Jerusalem. Yivo Institute for Jewish Research, N.Y. Joint Documentary Projects. Bibliographical Series, no. 12) Jerusalem: Israel Universities Press, 1973. Very useful.

Robinson, Jacob. and Philip Friedman. Guide to Jewish History under Nazi Impact. Forewords by Benzion Dinur and Salo W. Baron. N.Y.: Ktav, 1974. Q. XXXI, 425 p.

Szajkowski, Zosa. An Illustrated source Book on the Holocaust. Vol. I. N.Y.: Ktav, 1977. F. illus.

2. The Fate of Jewish Peoples in the Nazi Era.

Apenszlak, Jakob, et al. eds. The Black Book of Polish Jewry; An Account of the Martyrdom of Polish Jewry under the Nazi Occupation. (spons. by Mrs. Eleanor Roosevelt and others) N.Y.: American Representation of Polish Jews, Roy Pubs. 1943. O. XVI, 343 p. illus.

Arad, Yitzhak. Ghetto in Flames: The Struggle and Destruction of the Jews in Vilna in the Holocaust. N.Y.: Ktav (with Yad Vashem), 1981. 500 p. illus.

Baker, Leonard. Days of Sorrow and Pain; Leo Baeck and the Berlin Jews. N.Y.: Macmillan, 1978. Q. 396 p. Sources, Notes, Index. illus. A well-researched biographical study focusing on Baeck's leadership of the German Jewish community. The title is from a letter written by Baeck before he was arrested (that happened five times). Baeck became president of the Reichsvertretung in Sept. 1933. This organization was responsible for Jewish welfare, education, emigration; and it had to deal with the Nazi government. Baeck consistently showed great courage and dignity in dealing with the Gestapo. His plan for German Jewry was for emigration, esp. of the young, and for strengthening the cultural and spiritual life of the Jews who remained. In 1933 there were between 500,000 and 600,000 Jews in Germany, less than one percent of the population. By the end of .1938 one-third of the Jews had emigrated; after Kristallnacht (Nov. 9, 1938) until Sept. 1939 another third of German Jewry emigrated. After Kristallnacht the Nazis reconstituted the Reichsvertretung (now called the Reichsvereinigung) under their direct control. Baker challenges the charge (which "hangs over this period") of R. Hilberg (adopted by H. Arendt, see below) that the "Germans controlled the Jewish leadership and that leadership, in turn, controlled the Jewish community." (Hilberg, Destruction...pp. 124-25.). But

the interpretation of this painful matter is still open.
The Jewish organizations cooperated fully with the
German deportation orders of Oct. 1941. (see pp. 270-
273). Of course, Jewish officials who had not cooperated would have been imprisoned or shot, and the
officials knew that they could act in a humane way as
against the brutality of the Gestapo. (see Part 4,
below; and section d, below).

According to Baker (p. 311), Baeck said after the war
that he had learned of Auschwitz in August 1943. He
decided that "no one should know." That decision led to
later criticism of Baeck, e.g., Paul Tillich said that
"the full existential truth should always be made available..." (quoted in Baker, p. 311, no source given: the
source is an interview with A.H. Friedlander (cited in
1969, p. 47)). H. Arendt in her controversial Eichmann
in Jerusalem (rev. ed., 1963, p. 119) was also critical
of Baeck. Arendt was bitterly attacked for her
criticism of the role of the Jewish Councils and for her
statements about Baeck (one sentence about him was
dropped from the rev. ed.). A basic primary source is
H.G. Adler's Theresienstadt 1941-1945 (Tübingen, 1945).
Adler was confined in the camp and knew Baeck. He was
critical of Baeck's decision. Albert H. Friedlander in
his Leo Baeck, Teacher of Theresienstadt (N.Y.: Holt,
Rinehart & Winston, 1968) defends Baeck but also adds:
"With what we know now, it is not unreasonable to feel
.that Baeck's judgment faltered here." (p. 48). Friedlander suggests that Baeck was worried about the
accuracy of the information and feared the spread of
rumor. Baker's discussion (pp. 311-312) of this painful
subject is analytically unsatisfactory. In his detailed
comprehensive study of Jewish resistance, the French

Jewish scholar L. Steinberg says of Baeck's not sharing
his knowledge: "...and here it might be said that if
they had known what fate awaited them many of them might
have escaped..." But Steinberg then confuses things by
declaring, "but the eminent Rabbi...reasoned that since
his fellow Jews were doomed in any case, it was better
to spare them mental anguish..." (1978, corr. ed., cited
below, p. 12). But how was Baeck to know that they
"were doomed in any case..."? Escape from Theresienstadt was not impossible, see Steinberg, p. 45 on W.
Scharff and Francia Grun. On the other hand neither
Baker nor Steinberg mention the fact that Baeck may have
been shot if he had shared his information. That was
the fate of Paul Eppstein, former executive director of
the Reichsvereinigung. Baeck had disagreed with
Eppstein on the issue of cooperation with the Nazis.
Arendt (p. 64, p. 120, by implication) pictures Eppstein
as completely under Eichmann's control. One must be
cautious and nuanced in discussing this situation and
in evaluating the behaviour of the Jewish Councils.
Human responses to concrete crisis situations are not
predictable and <u>Hinterher</u> <u>ist</u> <u>es</u> <u>leicht,</u> <u>weise</u> <u>zu</u>
<u>erscheinen</u>.

Bauer, Yehuda. <u>The</u> <u>Holocaust</u> <u>in</u> <u>Historical</u> <u>Perspective</u>.
Seattle: University of Washington Press, 1978. D. 181 p.
Notes. Index. In four parts: "The Holocaust and
American Jewry." "Against Mystification: The Holocaust
as a Historical Phenomenon." "Jew and Gentile: The Holocaust and After." "The Mission of Joel Brand." Bauer
pays attention to detail and presents a differentiated
analysis. He distinguishes Holocaust and genocide, the
policy intended for the Slavic peoples, destruction of
nationality and leadership, leaving a subject, slave

people). The Nazi intent to destroy all Jews was Holocaust (this developed in stages boycott-pogrom). The
one constant idea was that no Jews were to remain in
Germany. Bauer distinguishes knowledge of Nazi intent
from belief, the Jews knew but refused to believe, this
refusal was related to fear and to the sense that nothing could be done.

Boas, Jacob (Jack). The Jews of Germany: Self-Percep-
tions in the Nazi era as reflected in German Jewish
Press, 1933-1938. Ph.D., 1977, University of
California, Riverside. See History. Europe, p. 7503,
vol. 38/12, Diss. Abstract Int'l.

Brahm, Randolph L. ed. The Destruction of Hungarian
Jewry: A Documentary Account. 2 vols. N.Y.: World
Federation of Hungarian Jews, 1963. Includes photosta-
tic reproductions of the original German documents,
synopses and affidavits in English.

Brahm, Randolph L. ed. Jewish Leadership during the
Nazi Era (Social Science Monographs and Institute for
Holocaust studies of The City University of New York)
N.Y.: Columbia University Press, 1985. XIV, 154 p.
Five essays on leadership in the U.S. (D. Wyman),
Britain (B. Wasserstein), the Yishu, Switzerland, and
Latin America.

Brahm, Randolph L. The Hungarian Jewish Catastrophe; A
Selective and Annotated Bibliography. N.Y.: Yivo Institute (with Yad Vashem), 1962. XXV, 86 p.

Brahm, Randolph L. The Politics of Genocide; the
Holocaust in Hungary. 2 vols. N.Y.: Columbia University

Press, 1981. XLIII, 594 p; 595 p. illus. maps. The authoritative research.

Chary, Frederick B. <u>Bulgarian</u> <u>Jews</u> <u>and</u> <u>the</u> <u>Final</u> <u>Solution,</u> <u>1940-1944</u>. Pittsburgh: University of Pittsburgh Press, 1972. Based on extensive research, Chary's work fills a gap in knowledge of the Catastrophe. "The justification for studying the application of the Nazi Final Solution to the Bulgarian Jews lies in the rather startling observation that more Jews were living in Bulgaria after World War II than before." (XIII). The most important factor accounting for the Bulgarian hesitation in implementing the deportation orders was the turn in the war after Stalingrad. But also significant was Jewish resistance, the support given Jews by powerful Bulgarians, and the sympathy of the Bulgarian Church for the plight of the Jews.

Fein, Helen. <u>Accounting</u> <u>for</u> <u>Genocide</u>: <u>National</u> <u>Responses</u> <u>and</u> <u>Jewish</u> <u>Victimization</u> <u>During</u> <u>the</u> <u>Holocaust</u>. N.Y.: The Free Press, 1979. XXI, 468 p. Biblio.: p. 409-449. Figures, Maps, Tables, Appendices. Index. An analytical study of correlations between victimization and national response, including awareness of the international power situation. Concludes that survival was highest where anti-Semitism was low, SS control was low, and where there was local Church opposition.

Fenyo, Mario D. <u>Hitler,</u> <u>Horthy,</u> <u>and</u> <u>Hungary;</u> <u>German-Hungarian</u> <u>Relations,</u> <u>1941-1944</u>. (Yale Russian and East European Studies, 11). New Haven, CT.: Yale University Press, 1972. Q. 279 p.

Gilbert, Martin. The Macmillan Atlas of the Holocaust. N.Y.: Macmillan, 1982. Q. 256 p. Includes 316 maps with descriptive data. And vide Gilbert, The Holocaust (1986, cited above).

Gross, Leonard. The Last Jews in Berlin. N.Y.: Simon & Schuster, 1982. 349 p. Based on interviews, journalistic.

Gutman, Yisrael. The Jews of Warsaw, 1939-1943: Ghetto, Underground, Revolt. trans. by Ina Friedman. Blooming-ton: Indiana University Press, 1982. A careful, well-focused and scholarly study of the Jews under German occupation, based on German, Polish and Jewish sources.

Gutman, Yisrael and Cynthia Haft. eds. Patterns of Jewish Leadership in Nazi Europe, 1933-1945: Proceedings of the Third Yad Vashem Intern. Historical Conference, Jerusalem, April 4-7, 1977. trans. by Dina Cohen, et al. Jerusalem, Yad Vashem, 1979. O. 419 p.

Handler, Andrew. ed. and trans. with Introd. and notes. The Holocaust in Hungary; An Anthology of Jewish Response. (Judaic studies series). University of Ala.: The University of Alabama Press, 1982. 162 p.

Hanusiak, Michael. Lest We Forget. Toronto: Progress Books, 1976. On atrocities in the Ukraine during the German occupation. Insufficient research has been done on Ukrainian Jewish history and on Ukrainian-Jewish relations during the Catastrophe. See: Philip Friedman, "Ukrainian-Jewish Relations During the Occupation." In Roads to Extinction (1980, cited above), pp. 176-208.

Huttenbach, Henry R. The Destruction of the Jewish Community of Worms, 1933-1945; A Study of the Holocaust Experience in Germany. N.Y.: The Memorial Committee of Jewish Victims of Nazism from Worms, 1981. 245 p.

Jong, Louis de. "The Netherlands and Auschwitz: Why Were the Reports of Mass Killings So Widely Disbelieved?" In Imposed Jewish Governing Bodies under Nazi Rule. N.Y.: YIVO, 1972.

Katz, Robert. Black Sabbath; A Journey through a Crime against Humanity. N.Y.: MacMillan, 1969, 398 p. Biblio.: p. 382-88. An account of the Oct. 16, 1943 roundup and deportation of more than one thousand Italian Jews. The evidence permits a "nearly complete record of the whole complex affair." (XVI). Katz also uses the event in Rome to discuss the problem of Jewish collaboration (cf. Arendt, Robinson, Trunk, etc.). He argues that Italian Jewry was part of the oppressive Western "imperialist" social system that ultimately produced Auschwitz. The implicit historicism in the overgeneralization does not command assent. And Katz contends that Italian Jewry's ruling Class-Fascist until 1938 was willing to sacrifice the many to save the few "in order that their institutions might survive."

Katzburg, Nathaniel. Hungary and the Jews; Policy and Legislation, 1920-1943. Ramat Gan, Bar: Bar-Ilan University, 1981. 299 p.

Kochan, Lionel. Pogrom, 10 November 1938. London: Andre Deutsch, 1957. 159 p. Includes Bibliography and Index. A study of the first modern, technically sophisticated pogrom that destroyed organized Jewish life in Germany.

Kugelmass, Jack and Jonathan Boyarin. trans. and ed. From a Ruined Garden: The Memorial Books of Polish Jewry. With geographical Index and Bibliography by Zachary M. Baker. N.Y.: Schocken Books, 1983. 375 p. illus. A source Introduction that contains absorbing and poignant documents.

Levy, Claude and Paul Tilard. Betrayal at the Vel d'Hiv. N.Y.: Hill & Wang, 1969. On the "roundup" of Jews in Paris and their brutal internment.

Marrus, Michael R. and Robert O. Paxton. Vichy France and the Jews. N.Y.: Basic Books, 1981. An impressive, scholarly study that uses newly available German sources. Shows that Vichy introduced anti-Jewish measures independently of Nazi pressures. 7600 Jews were sent "to the East," and about 3% returned. See also, Robert O. Paxton, Vichy France (Columbia University Press, 1982).

Michaelis, Meir. Mussolini and the Jews; German-Italian Relations and the Jewish Question in Italy, 1922-1945. Oxford: The Institute of Jewish Affairs; (Clarendon Press Bk.) 1978. 472 p. Oxford University. Biblio.: P. 432-62. Argues that the Fascist anti-Jewish policy was shaped by the exigencies of the Rome-Berlin alliance. There was no "Jewish problem" in Italy until that alliance was formed. Italian anti-Semitism was not a logical consequence of the Italian fascist creed (although the drive toward monolithic unity was threatening to Jews) but was the consequence of the Rome-Berlin Axis.

Orenstein, Benjamin. The Ghetto and the Annihilation of Polish Jews in the Nazi Epoch. Ph.D. 1956, University of Montreal. Montreal. Quebec.

Poliakov, Leon, and Jacques Sabille. Jews under the Italian Occupation. Paris: Editions du Centre de Documentation Juive Contemporaine, 1955. Text and documents on Italian Jewish policy in the occupied territories. The Italians refused to implement Nazi anti-Jewish measures. Poliakov covers occupied France, Sabille covers Croatia and Greece.

Presser, Jacob. The Destruction of the Dutch Jews. trans. from the Dutch by Arnold Pomerans. N.Y.: E.P. Dutton, 1969. 556 p. illus. Pub. in London under the title: Ashes in the Wind; the Destruction of Dutch Jewry (Souvenir, 1968). The author, a novelist who survived the Occupation by hiding, has written a detailed narrative history of Jewish fate in Holland.

Ringelblum, Emanuel. Polish-Jewish Relations during the Second World War. ed. and annot. by Joseph Kermish and Shmuel Krakowski. Introd. by Joseph Kermish. trans. from the Polish by D. Allon, D. Dabrowska, D. Keren. N.Y.: Howard Fertig, 1976. XXXIX, 330 p. Jerusalem, 1974. And vide: Joseph Kermish, "Emmanuel Ringelblum's Notes Hitherto Unpublished," Yad Vashem Studies, 7 (Jerusalem, 1968): 173-183.

Rosenkranz, Herbert. "The Anschluss and the Tragedy of Austrian Jewry 1938-1945." In The Jews of Austria: Essays on their Life, History and Destruction. ed. by

Josef Frankel. London: Vallentine, Mitchell, 1967. 585 p., pp. 479-546.

Roth, Cecil. "The Last Days of Jewish Salonica. What happened to a 450-year old Civilization." Commentary, 10: I (July 1950): 49-55.

Trunk, Isaiah. Judenrat: The Jewish Councils in Eastern Europe under Nazi Occupation. N.Y.: Macmillan, 1972. XXXV, 664 p. illus. Introd. by Jacob Robinson. An outstanding work of careful scholarship; the first comprehensive study. Using archival material and personal data, Trunk covers 405 Councils. He concludes that "the entire Council phenomenon cannot be analysed in general terms." They were not homogeneous in their internal, geo-demographic, and economic structures. Granted: but Trunk appears equivocal on the moral issue, i.e., Rabbinic law forbids giving up some innocent people in order to save others. See also: Imposed Jewish Governing Bodies under Nazi Rule: YIVO Colloquium Dec. 2-5, 1967 (N.Y.: YIVO Institute for Jewish Research, 1972; in Eng. and Yiddish). And see: Philip Friedman, "Pseudo-Saviors in the Polish Ghettos: Mordechai Chaim Rumkowski of Lodz," "The Messianic Complex of a Nazi Collaborator in a Ghetto: Moses Merin of Sosnowiec," "Jacob Gens: "Commandant" of the Vilna Ghetto," and "Preliminary and Methodological Aspects of Research on the Judenrat." chaps. 12, 13, 14 and 22 of Roads to Extinction (1980, cited above).

Trunk, Isaiah. Jewish Responses... (1979, cited below, 4)

Tushnet, Leonard. The Pavement of Hell. N.Y.: St.
Martin's Press, 1972. A study of the "leaders" of the
Warsaw ghetto (Czerniakow), the ghetto of Lodz
(Rumkowski) and the ghetto of Vilna (Gens). These men
"had good intentions. Their feet laid hold on Hell, but
the paths that led to the death camps...were not of
their making." (XI). For bibliography on the Judenrat,
see Yad Vashem Studies, 10 (1974).

3. The Churches and the Jews. The Allies and the Jews.

There is now a scholarly consensus on the Vatican and the Jews: it is a critical one (see C. Falconi, S. Friedlander, G. Levy, J. Morley, G. Zahn). But R. Hochhoth's image of Pius XII--while founded on historical data--is surely overdrawn; and one must recall the 1937 encyclical "With Burning Sorrow" by Pius XI. Also the Vatican did intervene (albeit discretely) on behalf of Jews in Hungary and Slovakia, did encourage prelates to help Jews, did offer some facilities in Rome for the endangered (but did not forcefully and publically condemn the action against the Roman Jews). The rough consensus on the Vatican does not extend to the Church The attitude of Church leaders and prelates differed profoundly, ranging from ugly anti—Semitism to self-sacrifice. On the Allies and the Jews, the recent major works include D. Wyman, H. Feingold, B. Wasserstein. For additional entries on both topics see sec. D:4.

Eckardt, Roy A. <u>Elder</u> <u>and</u> <u>Younger</u> <u>Brothers</u>: <u>The</u> <u>Encounter</u> <u>of</u> <u>Jews</u> <u>and</u> <u>Christians</u>. N.Y.: Scribner, 1967. XX, 188 p.

Falconi, Carlo. <u>The</u> <u>Silence</u> <u>of</u> <u>Pius</u> <u>XII</u>. trans. from the Italian by Bernard Wall. N.Y.: Little, Brown, 1970. 430 p. Biblio.: pp. 419-22. Appendices, Index. On the basis of archival research, especially Polish and Yugoslav documents, Falconi concludes that the Vatican was well-informed about the "Final Solution." The Pope

was silent because of his pessimistic prediction about
the Catholic response, particularly that of the German
Catholics. He also feared that public protest would
strengthen Communism and thus endanger the Church.
Other factors were the Pope's naive trust in diplomacy
and his Germanophilia.

Feingold, Henry L. The Politics of Rescue: The Roosevelt Administration and the Holocaust, 1938-1945. New
Brunswick: Rutgers University Press, 1970. 394 p. The
standard scholarly study. Reviewed by F.A. Lazin, "Put
Not Your Faith in Princes," Judaism, (Winter 1977): 505-
7. Rpt. with New Preface, and new chapter, "Guilt for
the Holocaust." N.Y.: Holocaust Library, 1980.

Friedlander, Saul. Pius XII and the Third Reich, A
Documentation. trans. from the French and German by
Charles Fullman. N.Y.: Knopf, 1966. Primarily an
analysis of documents, most of them German. No definitive conclusions can be reached without use of Vatican
sources. Regarding his study as incomplete, Friedlander
makes two assertions: the Pope had a strong German bias,
and he feared Bolshevism more than Nazism.

Gilbert, Martin. Auschwitz and the Allies. N.Y.: Holt,
Rinehart & Winston, 1981. Q. 368 p. plates. maps. This
study of how the Allies responded--or failed to
respond--to information about Auschwitz is based on
previously unpublished materials, including Churchill's
secret wartime papers. See also: David S. Wyman, "Why
Auschwitz Was Never Bombed," Commentary, 65:5 (May
1978): 37-46. Wyman uses previously unexamined archival
sources. The proposals to bomb were rejected as
militarily "impracticable" and of "doubtful efficacy."

Wyman considers these reasons invalid: "That the terrible plight of the Jews did not merit any active response remains a source of wonder and a lesson even today." (p. 46). The materials in this article are contained in Wyman's book (1984, cited below).

Gutteridge, Richard. Open Thy Mouth for the Dumb. The German Evangelical Church and the Jews, 1879-1950. Oxford: Blackwell, 1976. N.Y.: Harper, 1976. 374 p. Biblio.: pp. 358-370. A basic study.

Judaism and Christianity under the impact of National Socialism (1919-1945). (Symposium Papers, The Historical Society of Israel, June 1982). Jerusalem, 1982. 484 p. Includes studies by Michaelis (Italy), Comway (Catholicism), A.A. Cohen, Littel, Tal, Marrus (French Churches), Rothkirchen (Churches and Slovakia), Ettinger (Anti-semitism), J. Katz.

Lapide, Pinchas E. The Last Three Popes and the Jews. London: Souvenir Press, 1967. 384 p. Lapide argues that the Vatican saved 860,000 Jews from the Nazis.

Laqueur, Walter A. The Terrible Secret; Suppression of the Truth about Hitler's "Final Solution." N.Y.: Little, Brown, 1981. 262 p. On the terrible "failure to read correctly the signs" and respond to information about the Holocaust.

Lewy, Guenter. The Catholic Church and Nazi Germany. N.Y.: McGraw Hill, 1964. 416 p. Friedlander's main concern was with the Pope's attitude toward the Third Reich; Lewy's principal focus is on the policy of the Church in Germany. He makes two points: the Nazi

assault upon the Jews was "conditioned by centuries of
Christian hostility to Jews," and Pius XII was strongly
influenced by his "constituency," the German Catholics.
Cf. Edgar Alexander, Hitler and the Pope, Pius XII and
the Jews. N.Y.: Thomas Nelson, 1964. On the German
Protestant Church struggle, see John S. Conway, The Nazi
Persecution of the Churches, 1933-1945 (London: Weiden-
feld & Nicolson, 1968), XXXI, 474 p. Also: Franklin H.
Little, The German Phoenix; Men and Movements in the
Church in Germany. (N.Y.: Doubleday & Co., 1960), 226
p., and Eberhard Bethge, Dietrich Bonhoeffer. (Munich,
1966).

Lipstadt, Deborah E. Beyond Belief. The American Press
and the Coming of the Holocaust 1933-1945. New York:
The Free Press, 1986. 370 p. Documentary and bibliographical Notes, pp. 279-357. Index. Detailed, disturbing
evidence on how reporters, editors and publishers failed
their mandate: "They lamented what was happening, condemned the perpetrators, and then returned to their
practice of burying the information." (p. 275). Ultimately 'the press was as culpable as the Allied
governments, among whom existed "A real antipathy toward
Jews..." (p. 277). But Lipstadt's deepest worry is that
their ability "of reports of extreme persecution and
even mass murder in foreign lands to prompt us to act
almost guarantees that the cycle of horror which was
initiated by the Holocaust will continue." (p. 278).

Little, Franklin H. and Hubert G. Locke. eds. The
German Church Struggle and the Holocaust. (Papers from
the Intern. Scholars' Conference, 1st, Wayne State
University project on the History of the Church and the
Holocaust). Detroit: Wayne State University Press,

1974. 328 p. Includes bibliographical notes. Part I:
Introduction and Historical Background. II: Historical
Political Considerations. III: Theological Implica-
tions. IV: Personal Reflections.

Morley, John F. Vatican Diplomacy and the Jews during
the Holocaust, 1939-1945. N.Y.: Ktav, 1980. 327 p.
Biblio.: p. 267-274. Argues that Vatican diplomacy
"betrayed the ideals it had set for itself" by making
"diplomatic presence" and "relations with Germany and
the other states" more important than defense of the
Jews. (p. 207). Makes extensive use of Vatican sources.

Morse, Arthur D. While Six Million Died: A Chronicle of
American Apathy. N.Y.: Random House, 1968. 420 p.
Morse, a professional journalist, was the first to
publish sections from State Department archives on
immigration and rescue. He quotes from I. Katznelson's
Vittel Diary: "Sure enough, the nations did not interfere, nor did they protest...never a murmur. It was as
if the leaders of the nations were afraid that the
killings might stop." Full of justified, righteous
anger; but a more differentiated analysis is needed.

Nawyn, William E. American Protestantism's Response to
Germany's Jews and Refugees, 1933-1941. (Studies in
American History and Culture, 30). Ann Arbor, Mich.:
UMI Research, 1981. Comprehensive research that reveals
a general failure to secure havens for the refugees.

Penkower, Monty Noam. The Jews were Expendable: Free
World Diplomacy and the Holocaust. Champaign, Ill.:
University of Illinois Press, 1983. 429 p.

Ross, Robert W. So It Was True; The American Protestant
Press and the Nazi Persecution of the Jews. Minn.:
University of Minnesota Press, 1980. 374 p. Includes
Notes, Bibliography, Index. Attacks the Protestant
press (57 papers were studied) for its silence while
Jews were "made victims of unchristian policies perpe-
trated by nominal Christians" (p. 263).

Scharf, Andrew. The British Press and the Jews under
Nazi Rule. N.Y.: Oxford University Press, 1964.
Includes Register. Bibliography, Index. Scharf
concludes that the attitudes expressed in the newspapers were contradictory.

Wasserstein, Bernard. Britain and the Jews of Europe,
1939-1945. N.Y.: Oxford University Press, 1979; Oxford:
Clarendon Press, (Instit. of Jewish Affairs) 1979. 389
p. A well-researched and important contribution with
disconcerting conclusions. The British record in
helping endangered Jewry was "unimpressive" and British
policy was lacking in empathy and flexibility. And it
was incorrect in the assumption that direct aid to the
Jews was inconsistent with war priorities.

Wyman, David S. The Abandonment of the Jews. America
and the Holocaust 1941-1945. N.Y.: Pantheon Books,
1984. 444 p. Appendix A, B, Notes. Biblio.: p. 421-432.
Meticulous and comprehensive research. Documents the
lack of a decisive response, see pp. 331-340, "What
Might Have Been Done." "It was not a lack of workable
plans that stood in the way of saving many thousands
more European Jews. Nor was it insufficient shipping,
the threat of infiltration by subversive agents, or the
possibility that rescue projects would hamper the war

effort. The real obstacle was the absence of a strong desire to rescue Jews." (p. 339).

Zahn, Gordon C. <u>German</u> <u>Catholics</u> <u>and</u> <u>Hitler's</u> <u>Wars;</u> <u>A</u> <u>Study</u> <u>in</u> <u>Social</u> <u>Control</u>. N.Y. Sheed, 1962. 232 p. Important for the debate on the Vatican and the Holocaust.

4. Interpretations of the Holocaust. Introductory Note.

The range of interpretation in this section includes the question of the possibility of interpretation itself. Past catastrophes in Jewish history (the Fall of the Temple, the Crusades, the Expulsion of 1492, the pogroms of 1648, 1881-1882) have been comprehended within Jewish belief and liturgy. But the Holocaust challenges the very continuity of Jewish tradition, questions traditional ideas of Deity and threatens the coherence of language. There are several responses to this situation. R. Rubenstein develops an image of the death of God, Berkovits suggests that God is hidden, E. Fackenheim argues for a personally authenticated Jewish existentialism, with a strong affirmation of the new Israel. E. Wiesel affirms the need to bear witness through narrative. A. Cohen thinks a new theological language with a new image of God is the only response to the tremendum of the death camps. There are other views; and see section E and section F.

Arendt, Hannah. Eichmann in Jerusalem: A Report on the Banality of Evil. N.Y.: Viking (Compass) Books, 1963. 275 p. A report on the Jerusalem trial done for the New Yorker and published by it in serial form. The work provoked huge controversy and there is a large bibliography on the book and reactions to it. Her phrase "banality of evil" (now a fixed part of the language) was widely misunderstood. Eichmann represented a Totalitarian type: the bland indifferent killer, bureaucratic technician, whose only loyalty was to his Orders. His actions were not banal or ordinary. But he could talk only in jargon, and he could not think. He committed murder without personal feeling or motive. He "never realized what he was doing" and thus was more terrifying and dangerous than the demonic killer. Stephen J. Whitfield in his Into the Dark. Hannah Arendt and Totalitarianism argues that "no interpretation of Eichmann himself has yet displaced Arendt's extraordinary portrayal." (Phila.: Temple University Press, 1980, p. 24, and see the Bibliography in this intelligent and fair-minded study). Arendt was also attacked (and bitterly) for her views on the Jewish Councils. Her views depended upon Hilberg and were formulated before much information on the Councils was available. Her sensitivity to the moral issue remains but her evaluation must be revised in light of the research done by Trunk, Yad Vashem, Dawidowicz, and others. For information on the severe reactions to Arendt within the American Jewish community and her responses, see Elizabeth Young-Bruehl; Hannah Arendt; For Love of the World (Yale University Press, 1982); XXV, and see Anthony Heilbut, Exiled in Paradise; German Refugee Artists and Intellectuals in America from the 1930's to the Present. (N.Y.: Viking Press, 1983).

Berkovits, Eliezer. Faith after the Holocaust. N.Y.: Ktav, 1973. Notes. 180 p. No bibliography. Index. By an Orthodox theologian who sets the Holocaust experience within the history of Jewish suffering and survival and Jewish hope (modern Israel). Berkovits uses an image of the "hiddenness of God" to comprehend the Holocaust. He gives a badly oversimplified account of anti-Semitism, i.e., positing "a straight line" from the

4th century to the Holocaust: "What was started at the Council of Nicea was duly completed in the concentration camps and the crematoria." (p. 41). The view is not uncommon but distorts the issues on both ends, i.e., the early Church and the Jews, and the terrible newness in Nazi racism.

Berkovits, Eliezer. With God in Hell: Judaism in the Ghettos and Deathcamps. N.Y.: Sanhedrin Press, 1979. Bibliographical references. pp. 159-166.

Bettelheim, Bruno. The Informed Heart: Autonomy in a Mass Age. Glencoe, Ill.: The Free Press, 1960. 309 p. A highly influential but conceptually flawed interpretation of Jewish responses in the camps, based on Bettelheim's experience in Buchenwald from 1938 to 1939. Argues that prisoners became "incompetent children" who "psychologically speaking...committed suicide by submitting to death without resistance." (p. 251). One must not dismiss the insight in this analysis. But Bettelheim is too confident in his notions of what constitutes identity, and the 'sick' vs. the 'healthy.' He thinks a notion of Jewish self-hatred "explains" the inability of Jews to survive. The assimilated Jew has identified with the values of the majority culture. These values disintegrated in the camps. Thus the Jew was left with no inner center and consequently identified with the enemy, "delusionally" destroying them (the Nazis) by their (the Jews) death. Analytically the problem with this is that it reduces the historical particularity of the Holocaust to a social-psychological "law" of behaviour. And Bettelheim "is quicker to blame than to understand the transformed heart that often resulted from daily proximity to the gas chambers." (L. Langer, 1982, cited below. p. 32 and ff.).

Borowitz, Eugene B. How Can a Jew Speak of Faith today? Phila.: The Westminster Press, 1969. 221 p.

Borowitz, Eugene B. Modern Theories of Judaism. N.Y.: Behrman House, 1980.

Brenner, Reeve Robert. The Faith and Doubt of Holocaust Survivors. N.Y.: The Free Press, 1980. 266 p. An original empirical study that attempts to measure the impact of the Holocaust (defined as experience in a camp) upon the religious beliefs and practices of survivors (1,000 people living in Israel were selected, 708 responded). The findings are complicated: many variables are involved; but 53% asserted that the Holocaust had altered their faith in God and of these 72% turned away from faith in Deity, the remaining 28% were brought "nearer" to Deity. Also of great interest is Brenner's finding that the survivors gave "an emphatic no" to the question: "Was the State (of Israel) worth the price of the Holocaust?"

Cargas, Harry James. A Christian Response to the Holocaust. Foreword by Elie Wiesel. Denver, Colo.: Stonehenge Books, 1981. 203 p. Biblio.: p. 189-203.

Cargas, Harry James. ed. When God and Man Failed; non-Jewish views of the Holocaust. N.Y.: Macmillan, 1981. 238 p. Biblio.: pp. 220-238.

Cohen, Arthur A. The Tremendum. A Theological Interpretation of the Holocaust. N.Y.: Crossroad Pub. Co.,

1981. Foreword by David Tracy. 110 p. no bibliography. no index. Searching and subtle reflection on the problem of evil, and the traditional notion of Deity redefined in light of the _tremendum_ of the death camps. But Cohen's suggestions for a new image of Deity are much too vague (C. Hartshorne—while overly schematic—would have been of use here) and will satisfy neither the traditional theist nor a naturalist or pantheist. Cohen writes: "God is not the strategist of our particu- larities or of our historical condition, but rather the mystery of our futurity..." This echoes Whitehead and is understandable but what can one make of the continua- tion:"... the immensity whose reality is our prefigura- tion, and a phors for our language and distortion, whose plenitude and unfolding are the hope of our futurity..." (this echoes Fuerbach and is quite unacceptable). But Cohen's project to "limn" the _tremendum_ by interpreta- tion shows conceptual courage, agility with concepts, and bursts of eloquence. But also some of the termin- ology is obscure, inflated and misleading, e.g., what does one do with "the chthonic vitalities of our blood..." (p. 101, Jewish D.H. Lawrence?) or of the image of Torah as "a nexus of conformance between the modalities of divine egoity and the human person." (p. 100). Cohen's central point is that the _tremendum_ is a "new event," severed from traditional rationality and moral discourse (cf. Berkovits, E. Wiesel, D. Roskies, A. Mintz, Rubenstein, G. Steiner, etc.).   Cohen then proposes the formidable task of forging a new theologi- cal language that can "make clear the theological relevance of the holocaustal caesura." (p. 83).

Des Pres, Terrence. _The_ _Survivor_: _An_ _Anatomy_ _of_ _Life_ _in_ _the_ _Death_ _Camps_. N.Y.: Oxford University Press, 1976.

218 p. Biblio.: pp. 211-18. An analysis of survival literature and the behavior of survivors who experienced existence at its extreme limit.

Eckardt, A. Roy with Alice L. Eckardt. Long Night's Journey into Day: Life and Faith after the Holocaust. Detroit: Wayne State University Press, 1982. Biblio.: pp. 171-195.

Esh, Shaul. "The Dignity of the Destroyed: Towards a Definition of the Period of the Holocaust." Judaism, 11: 2 (Spring 1962): 99-111.

Fackenheim, Emil. "Jewish Faith and the Holocaust. A Fragment." Commentary, 46:I (August 1968): 30-36.

Fackenheim, Emil. God's Presence in History: Jewish Affirmations and Philosophical Reflections. (The Deems lectures, 1968). N.Y.: N.Y. University Press, 1970. 104 p. N.Y.: Harper Torchbook, 1972.

Fackenheim, Emil. The Jewish Return into History: Reflections in the Age of Auschwitz and a New Jerusalem. N.Y.: Schocken Books, 1978. 296 p. Fackenheim, a major philosophical theologian and a Kant and Hegel scholar (see, e.g., The Religious Dimension in Hegel's Thought, Ind. University Press, 1968) argues that the Holocaust demands that Jews reaffirm their Jewishness, thus defeating the aims of Hitler. See also: Quest for Past and Future; Essays in Jewish Theology (Ind. University Press, 1968).

Fackenheim, Emil. To Mend the World: Foundations of Future Jewish Thought. N.Y.: Schocken Books, 1982. Searching reflection; recommended.

Fiorenza, Elisabeth S. and David Tracy. eds. The Holocaust as Interruption. (Concilium) Edinburgh: T. & T. Clark Ltd., 1984. 88 p.

Fleischner, Eva. ed. Auschwitz, Beginning of a New Era? Reflections on the Holocaust. (Papers given at the International Symposium on the Holocaust, held at the Cathedral of Saint John the Divine, N.Y. City, June 3-6, 1974).

Frankl, Viktor E. See Original Testimony section.

Friedlander, Saul. "Some Aspects of the Historical Significance of the Holocaust." Jerusalem Quarterly, I:I (Fall 1976): 36-59. Described by U. Tal as a major contribution to "the study of mass movements and genocide."

Ginzel, Gunther B. ed. Auschwitz als Herausforderung für Juden und Christen. Heidelberg: Lambert Schneider. 1980.

Gouri, Haim. The Glass Cage: Journal of the Eichmann Trial. N.Y.: Orion, 1964. By the Israeli novelist, poet, and journalist. Cf. the account by Arendt (cited above); on Gouri, see below, section f,3.

Jaspers, Karl. The Question of German Guilt. trans. from the German. N.Y.: Dial Press, 1947. By one of the greatest modern German philosophers. Jaspers was a close friend of H. Arendt and married to a Jew; unlike M. Heidegger he was never sympathetic to the Nazis.

Katz, Steven T. "Jewish Faith after the Holocaust: Four Approaches." EJ Yearbook 1975-76. Jerusalem: Keter, 1976. pp. 92-105, Notes, pp. 104-105. A lucid discussion of R. Rubenstein, E. Fackenheim, Ignaz Maybaum, E. Berkovits.

Kren, George M. and Leon Rappoport. The Holocaust and the Crisis of Human Behavior. N.Y.: Homes & Meier, 1980. 176 p. Includes Notes and Bibliographic Essay. The authors view the Holocaust as a unique crisis in values and behavior.

Lookstein, Haskel. Were We Our Brothers' Keepers? The Public Response of American Jews to the Holocaust 1938-1944. Foreword by Elie Wiesel. N.Y.: Hartmore House, 1985. 287 p. Selected Bibliography. Index. A generally depressing account: "The Final Solution may have been unstoppable by American Jewry, but it should have been unbearable for them. And it wasn't" (p. 216).

Maybaum, Ignaz. The Face of God After Auschwitz. Amsterdam: Polak and Van Gennep Ltd., 1965. 265 p.

Milgram, Stanley. Obedience to Authority; An Experimental View. London, Tavistock, N.Y.: Harper, 224 p. 1974. The implications in this study of "ordinary" people in relationship to authority are devasting. Cf. H. Arendt's thesis in Eichmann in Jerusalem.

Neher, Andre. The Exile of the Word, From the Silence of the Bible to the Silence of Auschwitz. trans. from the French by David Maisel. Phila.: JPS, 1981. 246 p.

Podhoretz, Norman. "Hannah Arendt on Eichmann: a Study in the Perversity of Brilliance." Commentary, 36:3 (Sept. 1963): 201-208. A very heated attack by the editor of Commentary. Podhoretz calls for an end to debate about the "Final Solution": "Murderers with the power to murder descended upon a defenseless people and murdered a large part of it. What else is there to say?"

Poliakov, Leon. "The Eichmann Trial." Commentary, 43 (January 1967): 86-90.

Robinson, Jacob. And the Crooked shall be Made Straight: The Eichmann Trial, The Jewish Catastrophe, and Hannah Arendt's Narrative. N.Y.: Macmillan, 1965. 406 p. A detailed attack on Arendt's Eichmann in Jerusalem, concentrating on specific mistakes of fact. Overzealous but contains good notes and bibliography. For Arendt's response, see: "'The Formidable Dr. Robinson': A Reply." The New York Review of Books (Jan. 20, 1966), Rpt. in The Jewish as Pariah, ed. by Ron Feldman (Grove Press, 1978), pp. 263-264; and see: Gideon Hausner, Justice in Jerusalem. N.Y.: Harper & Row, 1966. 528 p. illus. By the Israeli prosecutor. Arendt accused Robinson of simply restating the views of Hausner.

Robinson, Jacob L. Psychoanalysis in a Vacuum: Bruno Bettelheim and the Holocaust. N.Y.: YIVO, 1970. A polemical pamphlet. Argues that: "The (i.e., Bettelheim's) attempt to submerge the extermination of the

Jews into some larger context and to present it not as murder of the Jewish people but as one of many victims of totalitarianism is in line with widely used terminology of concealing the specific nature of the Holocaust during and after the war." One should note that Bettelheim seems to have altered his views somewhat in later studies; see: Surviving and Other Essays (N.Y.: Knopf, 1979).

Rosenbaum, Irving J. The Holocaust and Halakhah. (The Library of Jewish Law and Ethics, ed. by Norman Lamm). N.Y.: Ktav, 1976. 177 p. An account of "theological heroism" during the Catastrophe.

Rubenstein, Richard L. After Auschwitz; Radical Theology and Contemporary Judaism. N.Y.: The Bobbs-Merrill, 1966. 287 p. See chap. I: "Religion and the Origins of the Death Camps, A Psychoanalytic Interpretation." pp. 1-44. Rubenstein suggests that the origins of Nazism and the death camps (anus mundi) can be explicated in terms of the Christian image of the Jew as deicide, Judas, Devil, witch; the Freudian notions of "the return of the repressed" and anal regression, and the notion in Dostoyevski that "if God does not exist, all things are permitted." This is a big order, and Rubenstein is more suggestive than cogent.

Rubenstein, Richard L. The Cunning of History; Mass Death and the American Future. N.Y.: Harper & Row, 1975. 113 p. Stimulating but contains extreme generalizations. Claims that "the secularization process" that led to the society of "total dominance" was "the outcome of the biblical tradition." "Nor can we ignore the biblical roots of the hideous Nazi caricature of the

Chosen People doctrine..." Argues that the Holocaust is
the "rational end product of the deadening of life in a
machine civilization. It was a rationalized way of
dealing with an unwanted surplus population: and it
succeeded." And in a very alarming statement, Rubenstein says that the future may learn its lesson not from
Nuremberg but from Auschwitz.

Ryan, Michael D. ed. Human Responses to the Holocaust;
Perpetrators and Victims, Bystanders and Resisters.
Papers of the 1979 Bernhard E. Olson Scholar's Confer-
ence on the Church Struggle and the Holocaust; sponsored
by the Nat'l conference of Christians and Jews. (Texts
and Studies in Religion, v.9). N.Y.: The Edwin Mellen
Press, 1981. 278 p. Introduction by M. Ryan. In 3
parts: "Perpetrators and Victims," "Bystanders and
Resisters," "Post-Holocaust Theological and Ethical
Reflections." Includes a "Bibliography of Periodicals:
The Holocaust, 1939-1945," by Gayle M. Woodman. In-
cludes (and why?) very painful photographs of Bergen
Belsen. The essays are uneven in quality, see those by
Robert G.L. Waite, Henry Friedlander, Henry L. Feingold,
Robert McAfee Brown, Jacob B. Agus, etc.

Stein, André. Broken Silence Dialogues from the Edge.
Toronto: Lester and Orpen Dennys, 1984. Stein was born
in Budapest in 1936; he now teaches sociology at the
University of Toronto. Contents: "To the Reader,
Prologue, dialogue with a Torturer... with a victim...
with a Spectator... with a Survivor... with a Boy to the
Angels of Life."

Tal, Uriel, "Excursus on the Term: Shoah," Shoah: A Review of Holocaust Studies and commemorations. I:4 (1979): 10-11.

Trunk, Isaiah. Jewish Responses to Nazi Persecution; Collective and Individual Behavior in Extremis. N.Y.: Stein and Day, 1979. Q. 371 p. glossary. Notes. Indices. maps. illus. By an outstanding scholar, author of Judenrat...(1972, cited above, chap. 1:2). In 2 Parts: 1. "Historical Antecedents," "Response to the Nazis." (Discussed in moral, cultural, political-economic terms). Part 2 includes 62 eyewitness accounts, published for the first time in English (Part of the Eyewitness testimonies collection of YIVO). Objects to the notion of Jewish passivity by citing the brutal terror used in the "Resettlements" (p. 53) and insists that "most Jews did not know exactly what ultimate fate the Nazis were preparing for them." (p. 52).

Wiesel, Elie. (see sec. F,3, below).

Zimmels, H.J. The Echo of the Nazi Holocaust in Rabbinic Literature. Ireland, privately printed. 1975.

D. Resistance. Rescue. The Refugee.

1. Jewish Resistance.

Ainsztein, Reuben. Jewish Resistance in Nazi-Occupied Eastern Europe: with a historical survey of the Jew as fighter and soldier in the Diaspora. London: Paul Elek, 1974. 969 pages of material and much of it challenges the "passivity" image as developed in R. Hilberg and others. Cf. I. Steinberg (cited below). It is difficult to sustain the charge of Jewish passivity/ghetto mentality in terms of comparative data, i.e., non-Jewish groups held up to Nazi terror (esp. in occupied E. Europe) no better than did the Jews.

Ainsztein, Reuben. The Warsaw Ghetto Revolt. N.Y.: The Holocaust Library, Schocken Books, 1979. 238 p. illus. The best analysis of the military aspect of the revolt is by S. Krakowski (1984, cited below). The Stroop Report (N.Y.: Pantheon, 1979) presents the German account of the Warsaw Revolt.

Airel, Joseph. "Jewish Self-Defence and Resistance in France during World War II." Yad Vashem Studies, 6 (1967): 221-250.

Arad, Yitzhak. Ghetto in Flames. The Struggle and Destruction of the Jews in Vilna in the Holocaust.

Jerusalem, 1980; N.Y.: Ktav (with Yad Vashem) 1981. 500 p. illus.

Arad, Yitzhak. The Partisan. From the Valley of Death to Mt. Zion. N.Y.: Holocaust Library, Schocken Books, 1979. 241 p. illus.

Artrom, B. Diari. Milan: Centro di documentazione Ebraica Contemporanea, 1960. (Italian) The diaries of an Italian Jewish partisan.

Banasiewicz, Czeslaw A. comp. and ed. The Warsaw Ghetto. N.Y.: Yoseloff, 1968. 111 p. Drawings by Jozef Kaliszan.

Barkai, Meyer. ed. and trans. The Fighting Ghettos. ed. by Issac Zuckerman and Moshe Basak. Phila.: Lippincott, 1962. 407 p.

Bauer, Yehuda. They Chose Life: Jewish Resistance in the Holocaust. N.Y.: American Jewish Committee; Jerusalem: The Hebrew University Press, 1973.

Bauer, Yehuda. The Jewish Emergence from Powerlessness. Toronto: University of Toronto Press, 1979, 89 p. (pa.). Argues (contra Hilberg) that the lack of Jewish armed resistance did not reflect ghetto passivity but the fact that Jews lacked arms and support from the larger environment. But about 5,000 Jewish fighters were active in central Poland under the Occupation, there were three armed rebellions and four attempted rebellions in the ghettoes, and six rebellions in the death camps.

Bauer, Yehuda. A History of the Holocaust. N.Y.: Franklin Watts, 1982. See chap. XI: "Resistance," pp. 245-277. "The main expression of Jewish resistance could not be armed...There were no arms; the nearby population was largely indifferent or hostile...Armed resistance is a marginal comment on the Holocaust, but it is written in very large letters indeed." (p. 177).

Bor, Joseph. The Terezin Requiem. (1963, cited below, sect. e).

Borzykowski, Tienia. (1972, cited below, sec. e).

Cavaglione, P. Levi. Guerriglia nei Castelli Romani. Rome, 1945. An account by an Italian Jewish partisan.

Cholawski, Shalom. Soldiers from the Ghetto. N.Y.: Herzl Press, 1981. Based on personal experience.

Dawidowicz, Lucy. "The Holocaust as Historical Record." In Dimensions of the Holocaust. Northwestern, Ill.: Northwestern University Press, 1977. On the archives and records kept by Jews in the ghettoes.

Dawidowicz, Lucy. ed. A Holocaust Reader. (cited in Part 3). See chap. 9: "Resistance: The Ordeal of Desperation." pp. 329-380.

Donat, Alexander. "Last Days in the Warsaw Ghetto." Commentary, 35 (May 1963): 382-389. A vivid first-hand account. Donat's Holocaust Kingdom is cited in Part 5.

434

Elkins, Michael. *Forged in Fury*. N.Y.: Ballantine Books, 1971. 312 p. Biblio.: p. 307-312. On Jewish resistance, underground movements.

Friedman, Kalmon. "In the Warsaw Ghetto in Its Dying Days." *Vad Vashem Bulletin*. (October 1963): 24-30.

Friedman, Philip. ed. *Martyrs and Fighters, The Epic of the Warsaw Ghetto*. (Sponsored by the Club of Polish Jews, N.Y.). N.Y.: Praeger, 1954. 325 p. trans from Polish, Yiddish, German and French originals by D. Chazen. Illus. by Luba Gurdus. Includes Bibliography, Acknowledgements, Index. Short selections largely from diaries and memoirs. Friedman (d. 1960) was director of the Bibliographical series of the Joint Documentary Projects of VIVO and Yad Vashem.

Friedman, Philip. "Jewish Resistance to Nazism." (Part 2 of "Prel. and Meth. Problems of the Research on the Jewish Catastrophe in the Nazi period). *Yad Vashem Studies*, II, (1958): 113-31. A conference paper pub. in *European Resistance Movements* (1964, cited below). Rpt. in *Roads to Extinction* (1980, cited in Part 3), pp. 387-408. One of the first significant studies, see bibliographical notes. Friedman confronts the problems of political bias, source accuracy, perspective. "There is no point in a quantitative evaluation of Resistance. We must explore the problem in depth and perceive the internal differentiation within each question..." p. 131.

Garlinski, Jozef. *Fighting Auschwitz: The Resistance Movement in the Concentration Camp*. London: Julian Friedmann Pubs. Ltd, 1974. 327 p. illus, maps.

Goldstein, Bernard. (cited below, sec. e).

Gutman, Yisrael. The Jews of Warsaw...(cited above, sec. b).

Handlin, Oscar. "Jewish Resistance to the Nazis." Commentary, 34 (November 1962): 398-405.

Hilberg, Raul. The Destruction of the European Jews. (1961, discussed in sect. c). Hilberg's account of the Warsaw rising (vide pp. 322-327) was largely based on German sources.

Jewish Resistance during the Holocaust. Jerusalem: Yad Vashem, 1971. Papers from the Conference on manifesta-tions of Jewish Resistance held in Jerusalem, April 7-11, 1968. Attempts to counter the "passivity" image: there was "considerable resistance and there was a will to survive."

Kahn, Leon: No time to Mourn, A True Story of a Jewish Partisan Fighter. Vancouver, B.C.: Laurelton Press, 1978. A powerful personal memoir.

Katz, Alfred. Poland's Ghettoes at War. N.Y.: Twayne Press, 1970. Biblio.: p. 161-170.

Kermish, Joseph. "First Stirrings." In Hunter and Hunted. (1973, cited in Part 3, a), pp. 209-230. On the Warsaw rising.

Kohn, Nahum and Howard Roiter. A Voice from the Forest, Memoirs of a Jewish Partisan. N.Y.: The Holocaust

Library, 1980. Kohn was a leader of 18 Jewish fighters (almost all perished). Then he fought in the anti-Fascist Ukrainian group led by Felyuk and finally he was in the group of Medvedev.

Kowalski, Isaac. A Secret Press in Nazi Europe: The Story of a Jewish United Partisan Organization. N.Y.: Central Guide, 1969. 416 p. On the anti-Nazi press in the Vilna area.

Krakowski, Shmuel. The War of the Doomed; Jewish Armed Resistance in Poland, 1942-1944. trans. from the Hebrew by Orah Blaustein. Foreword by Yehuda Bauer. N.Y.: Holmes & Meier, 1984. 340 p. Biblio.: p. 326-327. Index. A first-rate scholarly study based on German, Yiddish, Polish and Russian sources and using interviews with about 500 survivors. Corrects the image of the Jew as passive victim (cf. Hilberg); the results of resistance were "scanty" and "modest" but no other resistance movement faced the isolation and terror that the Jewish people experienced. Despite incredible objective difficulties the Jewish resistance sheltered at least 3,000 defenseless people and contributed to the armed struggle against the Germans.

Kurzman, Dan. The Bravest Battle: The Twenty-Eight Days of the Warsaw Ghetto Uprising. N.Y.: Putnam's Sons, 1976. A popularly written account with Epilogue, Notes. Bibliography. On the day before Passover, April 19, 1943, about 1,500 poorly armed Jews struck at the might of the SS and the Waffen SS. For a more detailed, scholarly account see S. Krakowski (1984, above). (The fighting went on until September).

Lubetkin, Ziviah (Tsivia). "Last Days of the Warsaw Ghetto." Commentary, 3:5 (May 1947): 401-411. A personal account by the "Mother of the ghetto" and a strong personality in the resistance movement. Her full record was published in Hebrew in 1947 and in German in 1950.

Mark, Ber (Bernard). Uprising in the Warsaw Ghetto. N..Y.: Schocken Books, 1975. 209 p. trans. from the Polish by Gershon Freidlin. A detailed history but unreliable in part (see the critique in Dawidowicz, 1981, cited above, pp. 170, 25, 26-171n45,46).

Meed, Vladka (cited below, sec e.).

Opfer, Dalia. "The Rescue of European Jewry and Illegal Immigration to Palestine in 1940 - Prospects and Reality: Berthold Storfer and the Mossad Le 'Aliyah Bet.'" Modern Judaism (Johns Hopkins University). 4:2 (May 1984): 159-181. Storfer, who considered himself simply an honest businessman, operated under Nazi supervision; his operation was opposed by the Mossad. Between 1933 and 1939, 100,000 Jews escaped to Palestine. Storfer's operation rescued 3,500.

Rashke, Richard. Escape from Sobibor. Boston: Houghton Mifflin, 1982. 399 p. Based on the testimony of 18 survivors. See S. Krakowski (1984).

Ravine, Jacques. La Résistance organisée des Juifs en France, 1940-1944. Paris: Juillard, 1973. The most recent comprehensive study. Ravine was active in the Resistance and a founder of "Solidarité."

Ringelblum, Emmanuel. Notes from the Warsaw Ghetto: The Journal of Emmanuel Ringelblum. ed. and trans. by Jacob Sloan. N.Y.: McGraw-Hill, 1958. XXVII, 369 p. The Yiddish diary of a Jewish historian who kept an underground archive during the period of the Warsaw ghetto. Very valuable source. Cited in section following and in Part 5.

Robinson, Jacob. And the Crooked shall be Made Straight...(1965, cited in Part 3, c). See pp. 213-226 on resistance. "The overriding purpose of Jewish activity everywhere in nazi Europe was survival with dignity." (p. 225).

Robinson, Jacob. ed. and comp. The Holocaust and After...(cited in Part 3, a). See for literature on resistance.

Rose, Lessha. The Tulips are Red. N.Y.: A.S. Barnes, 1978. 275 p. illus.

Rosenbaum, Irving J. The Holocaust and Halahkad. (cited in Part 3,d). See for the question of "spiritual" resistance.

Schner, Zvi. "On documentation projects as an expression of Jewish steadfastness in the Holocaust." In Jewish Resistance... (1971, cited above), pp. 191-201.

Sobibor, Martyrdom and Revolt. (Documents and Testimonies Presented by Miriam Novitch). Preface by Leon Poliakov. N.Y.: The Holocaust Library, 1980. On Oct. 14, 1943 about 600 prisoners revolted; c. 300 reached the forest, and thirty-five people survived. See Rashke

(1982, above) and S.Krakowski (1984, cited above), pp. 244-249, "On the whole, the names of twenty Sobibor rebels who lived to see the fall of Hitler are known." (p. 249).

Spiritual Resistance: Art from the concentration Camps, 1942-1945. Phila.: JPS, 1981. 240 p. 85 plates. A collection of art works prepared by the Union of American Hebrew congregations. The art works were rescued by the Ghetto Fighters' Kibbutz. The vol. includes essays by M. Novitch. L. Dawidowicz, T.L. Freudenheim.

Steinberg, Lucien. Not as a Lamb. The Jews against Hitler. trans. from the French (La Revolte des Justes (Paris, 1970) by Marion Hunter. Farnsborough, Eng.: Saxon House, 1974. 358 p. Corrected ed. pub. under the title: The Jews Against Hitler. London and N.Y.: Gordon & Cremonesi, 1978. 358 p. Sources. Index. Based on extensive research, archival collections in 12 countries, interviews, secondary materials; the most comprehensive study available. Steinberg's conclusions about resistance and survival support the position of the critics of the Judenrate. He does not explicitly state this, and he is writing before the massive scholarship of I. Trunk. The Jews in Europe were condemned to death. The only hope for survival "was by disobeying the orders of the German occupying forces. This disobedience could take many different forms; armed resistance was only one of them...refusing to wear the yellow star, refusing to go to the assembly points, refusing to live in the ghettos." (p.5). Apart from the case of armed resistance (which was very difficult) Jewish survival was greater when Jews refused to obey

Nazi orders. For example, only one Jew survived out of 33,000 when the Germans entered Kiev, but half the refugees who hid in the swamps of White Russia, under the help of the Jewish resistance fighters, survived. Jewish resistance proved that "resistance alone can save." (p. 339).

Suhl, Yuri. ed. and trans. They Fought Back, The Story of Jewish Resistance in Nazi Europe. Phila.: JPS, 1967. 327 p. Rpt. N.Y.: Schocken Books, 1975. 327 p. illus. (pa.). Information on resistance in Eastern Europe, Italy, France, Berlin and a contribution to the debate about the "passivity" of the Jews. According to Dawidowicz (1981, cited above, p. 172), this is "...an altogether tendentious work which follows the orthodox Communist position on resistance."

Syrkin, Marie. Blessed is the Match; The Story of Jewish Resistance. (Hillel Library) Phila.: JPS, 1947; N.Y.: Knopf, 1947. 361 p. London: Gollancz, 1948. 254 p. See also Syrkin's critique of H. Arendt's Eichmann in Jersualem, "Miss Arendt Surveys the Holocaust." Jewish Frontier, 30 (May 1963): 7-14.

Szajkowski, Zora. "Western Jewish Aid and Intercession for Polish Jewry, 1919-1939." In Studies on Polish Jewry...(cited above).

Szner, Z. ed. Extermination and Resistance. Vol. I. Haifa: Ghetto Fighters House, 1958.

Yad Vashem Studies on the European Jewish Catastrophe and Resistance. Vol. 10. ed. by Livia Rothirchen. Jerusalem: Yad Vashem, 1974, N.Y.: Ktav, 1975. 326 p.

Contains an index to Vols. 1-X. For items on Jewish resistance, see Verena Wahlen, comp. "Select Bibliography on Judenrate Under Nazi Rule," pp. 227-294. Includes 214 items.

Zuckerman, Isaac, ed. The Fighting Ghettos. N.Y.: Belmont-Tower, 1971.

Zylberg Berg, Michael. A Warsaw Diary, 1939-1945. London: Vallentine, Mitchell, 1969. 220 p. illus. Orign. pub. in Yiddish in the Jewish Daily Forward (NYC). Biblio.: p. 213-214.

2. General Resistance and Rescue Efforts.

Anger, Per. With Raoul Wallenberg in Budapest: Memories of the War Years in Hungary. trans. from the Swedish by David M. Paul and Margareta Paul. N.Y.: Holocaust Library, Schocken Books, 1981. 191 p. Biblio.: p. 183-184. A personal account of the Swedish diplomat who saved thousands of Hungarian Jews. He disappeared in Russia in 1945.

Armstrong. John A. ed. Soviet Partisans in World War II. Foreword by Philip E. Mosley. Madison. Wis.: University of Wisconsin Press, 1964. 792 pp. maps. The activity of Russian Jewish partisans as controlled by Soviet strategy. See also Schwarz (1949, cited below), Kahn (1978, cited above), Kohn (1980, cited above).

Bauer, Yehuda. My Brother's Keeper; A history of the American Jewish Joint Distribution Committee, 1929-1939. Phila.: JPS, 1974. 350 p. On American Jewry and rescue efforts.

Bierman, John. Righteous Gentile: The Story of Raoul Wallenberg, Missing Hero of the Holocaust. N.Y.: Viking Press, 1981. 218 p. There is a sizeable literature now on Wallenberg, see K. Marton, Wallenberg (N.Y.: Random House, 1982); F.E. Werberg, Lost Hero (N.Y.: McGraw Hill, 1982).

Bliss, Andreas. A Million Jews to Save; Check to the Final Solution. N.Y.: A.S. Barnes, 1975. 271 p.

Druks, Herbert. The Failure to Rescue. N.Y.: Robert Speller & Sons, 1977.

Foot, Michael R.D. Resistance, An Analysis of European Resistance of Nazism, 1940-1945. London: Eyre Methuen, 1976. 341 p. N.Y.: McGraw Hill, 1977. 346 p. A scholarly ("with many aphoristic compressions") analysis of "the whole field of wartime resistance to the Nazis in Europe." On the Warsaw ghetto uprising, Foot writes: "Those twenty-eight days of absolutely hopeless, absolutely heroic revolt provide a passionate denial of that other popular stereotype, of Jews who shambled off unprotesting to the slaughterhouse." (p. 294). Estimates that about half a million Jews were saved: "Tremendous efforts were made to save Jews, many of them by Jews, many of them by resisters; but their rescue is not the brightest page in resistance history." (p. 312).

European Resistance Movements, 1939-1945: Proceedings of the Second Intern. Conference on the History of Resistance Movements. N.Y.: MacMillan; Oxford: Pergamon Press, 1964. XIIII, 633 p. illus. The Milan conference, 26-29 Mar. 1961 (sponsored by the inter. comm. for the teaching of hist. and organized by the Istituto nazionale per la storia del movimento di liberazione in Italia).

Friedman, Philip. _Their Brothers' Keepers: The Christian Heroes and Heroines Who Helped the Oppressed Escape the Nazi Terror_. Foreword by John A. O'Brien. N.Y.: Crown Press, 1957. 224 p. Rpt. 1978. Includes almost 40 pages of sources and references.

Friedman, Philip. "Righteous Gentiles in the Nazi Era." First pub. in Yiddish in 1955. Rpt. in _Roads to Extinction_...(1980, cited above). pp. 409-421.

Gutman, Yisrael. and E. Zuroff. eds. _Rescue Attempts during the Holocaust: Proceedings of the Second Yad Vashem Intern. Historical Conference_. Jerusalem: Yad Vashem, 1977. Includes important essays, some are cited below.

Hadar, Alizia R. with Aubrey Kaufmann. _The Princess Einasari_. London: Heinemann, 1963. 217 p. On the rescue of Jewish children.

Hawes, Stephen and Ralph White. eds. _Resistance in Europe, 1939-1945: Based on The Proceedings of a Symposium Held at the University of Salford, March 1973_. London: A. Lane, 1975.

Heimler, Eugene. ed. _Resistance against Tyranny; A Symposium_. London: Routledge & Kegan Paul, 1966. 168 p.

A collection of uneven essays; see, esp., Zagorski on the Polish resistance.

Hellman, Peter. Avenue of the Righteous. Portraits in Uncommon Courage of Christians and the Jews they saved from Hitler. N.Y.: Atheneum, 1980. 267 p. No Bibliography. No Index. Consists of four life stories.

Keneally, Thomas. Schindler's Ark. London: Hodder and Stoughton, 1982. A documentary account (in fictionalized form) of an eccentric German industrialist who saved Jewish lives.

Kluger, Ruth and Peggy Mann. The Last Escape; the Launching of the Largest Secret Rescue Movement of All Time. London: Gollancz, 1974. 518 p. illus. On the rescue of Jews through a route in Rumania.

Laska, Vera. ed. with an Introduction. Women in the Resistance and in the Holocaust. The Voices of Eyewitnesses. Foreword by Simon Wiesenthal. (Contributions in Women's Studies, 37). Westport, Conn.: Greenwood Press, 1983. 330 p. Biblio.: p. 303-314. Index. Illus. Part I. Women in the Resistance. Part II. Women in concentration Camps. Part III. Women in Hiding. Epilogue.

Michel, Henri. The Shadow War, European Resistance, 1939-1945. trans. from the French by F. Richard Barry. N.Y.: Harper & Row, 1972. 416 p. Biblio.: pp. 385-399. Michel, a leading scholar on resistance, makes two points that should be quoted: "As far as the Allies were concerned, they refused to aid the Jews as such; they would give assistance to Poles or Frenchmen, but not to some mythical Jewish nation; they missed many opportunities of saving groups of Jews from genocide." (p. 180).

And: Jews in the resistance "participated as Frenchmen, or communists, and rarely as Jews." (pp. 178-179).

Seth, Ronald. The Undaunted; The Story of Resistance in Western Europe. London: Muller, 1956; N.Y.: Philosophical Library, 1956. 327 p. plates.

Schwarz, Solomon M. "The Soviet Partisans and the Jews." Modern Review (N.Y.), (January 1949): 387-400. The growth of anti-Semitism in the occupied territories inhibited the use of the theme in Soviet partisan propaganda.

Silkinson, James D. The Intellectual Resistance in Europe. Cambridge, Mass.: Harvard University Press, 1981. 358 p. Notes. Selected Bibliography. Index. An intellectual and social history based on published works and journalist sources. Introduction. Conclusion: The Resistance Legacy. 1. France. 2. Germany. 3. Italy. Fascinating and eloquent but little recognition is given to the Jewish situation and anti-Semitism.

Wyman, David S. The Abandonment of the Jews...1984. cited above, sec. C:3.

3. Rescue and Resistance: By Country. See J. Litvak, "Holocaust, Rescue From." EJ, Vol. 8, 905-10, and H. Fein, Accounting for Genocide (1979, cited above, Part III, sec. B).

AUSTRIA

Engel-Janosi, F.   "Remarks on the Austrian Resistance."
Journal of Central European Affairs, 13 (1953).

Frankel, Josef.   ed. The Jews of Austria: Essays on
Their Life, History, and Destruction.   London:
Valentine, Mitchell, 1967. 585 p.

Zahn, Gordon C.   In Solitary Witness: The Life and Death
of Franz Jagerstatter.   N.Y.: Holt, Rinehart and
Winston, 1964. 277 p. illus.   A moving account of the
Austrian Catholic "peasant" who was beheaded for refusing to serve in the German army.

BALTIC STATES

Dallin, Alexander.   German Rule in Russia, 1941-1945, A
Study of Occupational Policies.   London: Macmillan,
1957. XX, 695 p. maps.   The major scholarly study.

Gilboa, Yehoshua A.   The Black Years of Soviet Jewry,
1939-1953.   trans. from the Hebrew by Yosel Schachter
and Dov Ben-Abba.   Boston: Little, Brown, 1971. 418 p.

Hirszowica, Lukasz.   ed. "The Soviet Union and the Jews
during World War II: British Foreign Office Documents,"
Soviet Jewish Affairs, 3 (1963): 104-119.

BELGIUM

Bernard, Henri. La résistance, 1940-1945. 2nd ed. Brussels: La renaissance du livre, n.d. (ca. 1969).

Le Comité de défense des juifs en Belgique, 1942-1944. Brussels: Editions de l' Université de Bruxelles, 1973. The CDJ opposed the Belgium Judenrat, warned Jews, threatened collaborators. With the cooperation of state and church authorities, they helped save over half of the Jews of Belgium.

Flinker, Moshe. Young Moshe's Diary; The Spiritual Torment of a Jewish Boy in Nazi Europe. Jerusalem, Yad Vashem, 1966, 1971. 126 p. illus. Introds. by Shaul Esh and Geoffrey Wigoder.

Gutfreind, Jacob. "The Jewish Resistance Movement in Belgium." In They Fought Back. ed. by Yuri Suhl. N.Y.: Crown, 1967.

Steinberg, Lucien. "Jewish Rescue Activities in Belgium and France." In Rescue Attempts during the Holocaust...(1977, cited above).

BULGARIA

Chary, Frederick B. The Bulgarian Jews and the Final Solution (1972, cited above, sec. 2).

Nizani, Yaacov. "Fighter of the Jewish Underground in Bulgaria." Yad Vashem Bulletin, 8-9 (1961): 35-36.

Oren, Nissan. "The Bulgarian Exception: A Reassessment of the Salvation of the Jewish Community." Yad Vashem Studies, 7 (1968): 83-106.

Yulzari, Matei. "The Bulgarian Jews in the Resistance Movement." In They Fought Back (1967, cited above).

CROATIA-YUGOSLAVIA

Carpi, Daniel. "The Rescue of Jews in the Italian Zone of Occupied Croatia." In Rescue Attempts...(1977, cited above).

Donlagic, A. Yugoslavia in the Second World War. trans. by Lovett F. Edwards. Belgrade: Medin-Arodna Stampa-Interpress, 1967.

Sabille, Jacques. "Attitude of the Italians to the Persecuted Jews in Croatia." In Jews under the Italian Occupation. ed. by L. Poliakov and J. Sabille. Paris: Editions du centre, 1955.

CZECHOSLOVAKIA

Mastny, Vojtech. The Czechs under Nazi Rule: The Failure of National Resistance, 1939-1942. (Columbia University East Central European Studies). N.Y.: Columbia University Press, 1971. 274 p.

DENMARK

Flender, Harold. Rescue in Denmark. N.Y.: Simon & Schuster, 1963. 281 p. illus.; London: W.H. Allen, 1963. 224 p. illus. A straightforward account of Danish resistance.

Yahil, Leni. The Rescue of Danish Jewry: Test of a Democracy. trans. from the Hebrew by Morris Gradel. Phila.: JPS, 1969. XX, 536 p. A comprehensive and analytic study of the rescue of Danish Jewry. Yahil writes that "for the Danes national consciousness and democratic consciousness are one and the same... The struggle of the Danish people for its national existence during the occupation therefore included the struggle for the equal rights of the Jew." This is the definitive work.

FRANCE (and see Ravine, Steinberg, section a).

Ariel, Joseph. "Jewish Self-Defense and Resistance in France..." Yad Vashem Studies, 6 (1967): 221-250.

Avni, Haim. "The Zionist Underground in Holland and France and the Escape to Spain." In Rescue Attempts... (1977, cited above).

Diamant, Zanuel. "Jewish Refugees on the French Riviera." YIVO Annual of Jewish Social Science. 8 (1953): 264-280.

Fabré, Emile C. ed. <u>God's</u> <u>Underground</u>. coll. by J.M. d'Aubigne and V. Mouchon. trans. from the French by W. Nottingham and P. Nottingham. Introd. by Marc Boegner and a chap. on CIMADE today. St. Louis, Mo.: Bethany Press, 1970. 238 p. The story of the remarkable "rescue machine," the Cimade. Founded (1939) by women and led by women it enabled Jews to escape into Switzerland from Southern France.

Hallie, Philip. <u>Lest</u> <u>Innocent</u> <u>Blood</u> <u>be</u> <u>Shed;</u> <u>The</u> <u>Story</u> <u>of</u> <u>the</u> <u>Village</u> <u>of</u> <u>Le</u> <u>Chambon</u> <u>and</u> <u>How</u> <u>Goodness</u> <u>Happened</u> <u>There</u>. N.Y.: Harper & Row, 1979. 304 p. plates. A study of the French village of "safe houses" for Jewish refugees and a portrait of André Trogme, the Protestant "Soul of Le Chambon." Hallie's work is based on extensive interviews and gives a picture of rare moral courage.

Kedward, Harry R. <u>Resistance</u> <u>in</u> <u>Vichy</u> <u>France;</u> <u>A</u> <u>Study</u> <u>of</u> <u>Ideas</u> <u>and</u> <u>Motivation</u> <u>in</u> <u>the</u> <u>Southern</u> <u>Zone,</u> <u>1940-1942</u>. Oxford University Press, 1977. 311 p. maps. Index. Biblio.: p. 286-291. Comprehensive, scholarly, readable.

Kieval, Hille. "Legality and Resistance in Vichy France: The Rescue of Jewish Children." <u>Proceedings</u> <u>of</u> <u>the</u> <u>American</u> <u>Philosophical</u> <u>Society</u>. 124:5 (October 1980): 342-50, 360-61.

Knout, David. <u>Contribution</u> <u>à</u> <u>l'histoire</u> <u>de</u> <u>la</u> <u>résistance</u> <u>juive</u> <u>en</u> <u>France,</u> <u>1940-44</u>. Paris, 1947.

Latour, Amy. <u>La</u> <u>résistance</u> <u>juive</u> <u>en</u> <u>France,</u> <u>1940-1944</u>. Paris: Stock, 1970.

Leboucher, Fernande. _The_ _Incredible_ _Mission_ _of_ _Father_
Benoit. trans. by J. F. Bernard. London: Kimber, 1970.
The drama of a French Franciscan priest who saved
thousands of Jews in France and Italy.

Lowrie, Donald. "Chambon-Sur-Lignon." In _Anthology_ _of_
Holocaust _Literature_. ed. by Jacob Glatstein, et al.
Phila.: JPS, 1968.

Marrus, Michael R. and Robert O. Paxton. _Vichy_ _France_
and _the_ _Jews_. N.Y.: Basic Books, 1981.

Poliakov, Leon. "Jewish Resistance in France." _YIVO_
Annual _of_ _Jewish_ _Social_ _Science_, 8 (1953).

Steinberg, Lucien. "Jewish Rescue Activities in Belgium
and France." In _Rescue_ _Attempts_...(1979, cited above).

GERMANY ("The Germans have been the least effective
        rebels against authority in modern history..."
        W. Laqueur (1964).)

Adreas-Friedrich, Ruth. _Berlin_ _Underground,_ _1938-1945_.
trans. from the German by Barrows Mussey, with an
Introductory note by Joel Sayre. N.Y.: Holt, 1947,
XIV, 312 p. Toronto: Oxford University Press, 1947;
London: Latimer, 1948. 256 p.

Ball-Kaduri, K. Yaakov. "The National Representation of
Jews in Germany; obstacles and accomplishments at its
establishment." _Yad_ _Vashem_ _Studies_, 2 (1958): 159-178.

Bethge, Eberhard. Dietrich Bonhoeffer, Man of Vision, Man of courage. trans. from the German (1967) by Eric Mosbacher (et al.) under the editorship of Edwin Robertson. N.Y.: Harper & Row, 1970. XXIV, 867 p.

Conway, John S. The Nazi Persecution of the Churches, 1933-1945. London: Weidenfeld & Nicolson, 1968. Includes Biographical Notes, Notes, Appendices and Bibliography. Contains a discussion of resistance. Conway made use of Nazi archival materials and papers.

Edelheim-Muhsam, Margaret T. "Reactions of the Jewish Press to the Nazi Challenge." LBIY, 5 (1950): 308-329.

Eschwege, Hemut. "Resistance of German Jews against the Nazi Regime." LIBY, 15 (1970): 143-182.

Esh, Shaul. "The establishment of the "Reichsvereinigung der Juden in Deutschland" and its main activities." Yad Vashem Studies, 7 (1968): 19-38.

Friedlander, Saul. Kurt Gerstein, The Ambiguity of Good. trans. from the French and German by Charles Fullman. N.Y.: Knopf, 1969. Gerstein (1905-1945) opposed Nazi policy toward the Confessional Church and was arrested in 1936 and again in 1938 and sent briefly to a camp. He was reinstated in the party in 1940. Gerstein was deeply troubled by the euthanasia policies of 1940-1941 and joined the Waffen SS to determine what was happening. He then led an almost suicidal double-life in the SS "Institute of Hygiene" in efforts to alert others to Nazi atrocity. But the "others" remained passive spectators and "Gerstein...was caught up in the wheels of the machine he was trying to halt."

(p. 161). "However, what lends Gerstein's tragic fate its unique character and full magnitude is the complete passivity of the "others"...So much of Gerstein's tragedy lay in the loneliness of his action." (p. 227-228). (He died in a French prison, either by his own hand or killed by members of the resistance).

Gallin, Mother Mary Alice. German Resistance to...Hitler: Ethical and Religious Factors. Washington, D.C.: The Catholic University of America, 1962. 259 p. Gordon, Sarah. Hitler, Germans and the "Jewish Question." (cited above) See chap. 7-9.

Graml, Hermann, et al. The German Resistance to Hitler. trans. from the German by Peter and Betty Ross. Introd. by F.L. Carsten. London: Batsford, 1970; L.A. and Berkeley: University of California Press, 1970. XXI, 281 p.

Hoffmann, Peter. Widerstand, Staatsreich, Attentat: Der Kampf der Opposition gegen Hitler. Munich: Piper, 1969. Considered the best study.

Jansen, Jon B. (pseud) and Stefan Weyl. The Silent War. The Underground Movement in Germany. trans. by Anna Caples. Foreword by Reinhold Niebuhr. Phila.: J.B. Lippincott Co., 1943.

Joffroy, Pierre. A Spy for God: The Ordeal of Kurt Gerstein. trans. from the French (1969) by Norman Denny. N.Y.: Harcourt Brace Jovanovich, 1971. 319 p. A sympathetic biography that supplements the work by Friedlander.

Leber, Annedore. comp. Conscience in Revolt: Sixty-
four Stories of Resistance in Germany, 1933-45. trans.
from the German by Rosemary O'Neill. Introd. by Robert
Birley. London: Vallentine, Mitchell, 1957. XXVI, 270
p. illus.

Leuner, Heinz David. When compassion was a Crime:
Germany's Silent Heroes, 1933-1945. London: Wolff,
1966. Used by S. Gordon (1984, cited above).

Lewy, G. The Catholic Church and Nazi Germany. (1964,
cited above: Part 3,c). Gordon (1984, pp. 249-54) cites
action by clergymen and lay church members that defied
the Nazis but Gordon admits that "the institution itself
failed to imitate their heroism" (p. 254).

Littel, Franklin and Hubert G. Locke. eds. The German
Church Struggle and the Holocaust. (1974, cited above).
See the essays in Part II, e.g., "The German State and
Protestant Elites," and "Problems of Resistance in
National Socialist Germany."

Margaliot, Abraham. "The Problem of Rescue of German
Jewry during the years 1933-30. The Reasons for the
Delay in Their Emigration from the Third Reich." In
Rescue Attempts...(1977, cited above).

Paucker, Arnold, and Lucien Steinberg. "Some Notes on
Resistance." LBIY, 16 (1971): 239-248.

Prittie, Terence, C.F. Germans Against Hitler. Foreword by Hugh Trevor-Roper. N.Y.: Little, 1964. 291 p.

Rittner, Gerhard. The German Resistance: Carl Goerdeler's Struggle against Tyranny. trans by R.T. Clark. London: George Allen and Unwin, 1958. N.Y.: Praeger, 1959. 330 p. Standard work, but overly sympathetic to Goerdeler.

Roon, Gervan. German Resistance to Hitler: Count von Moltke and the Kreisau Circle. trans. from the German by Peter Ludlow. London: van Norstrand-Reinhold, 1971. 400 p. illus. See von Oppen (cited below).

Rothfels, Hans. The German Opposition to Hitler: An appraisal. trans. from the German by L. Wilson. Chicago: Regnery, 1948. 9-172 p. 2nd rev. ed. 1962. On the July 1944 attempt to kill Hitler. A more popularly written account is The Men Who Tried to Kill Hitler by R. Manvell and H. Fraenkel (N.Y.: Coward McCann, 1964).

Scholl, Inge. Students against Tyranny: The Resistance of the White Rose, Munich 1942-1943. Middletown, Conn.: Wesleyan University Press, 1965. Their rationale: "We must do it for the sake of life itself--no one can absolve us of this responsibility." They distrbuted leaflets, were caught and beheaded for treason in 1943.

Spangenthal, Max. "The Jewish Question and the German Resistance Movement." Yad Vashem Bulletin 19 (1966): 60-63.

von Oppen, Beate Ruhm. "Helmuth James von Moltke: A Christian witness." In Human Responses to the Holocaust (cited above c:4), pp. 145-167. Includes letters by von Moltke (hanged in Berlin, Jan. 1945).

Werner, Alfred. "The Junker Plot to Kill Hitler. The dying Gesture of a Class." Commentary, (July 1947): 37-42.

Zassenhaus, Hiltgunt. Walls, Resisting the Third Reich, One Woman's Story. Boston: Beacon Press, 1974.

GREAT BRITAIN

Katzburg, Nathaniel. "British Policy on Immigration to Palestine during World War II." In Rescue Attempts...((1977, cited above).

Scharf, Andrew. The British Press and Jews under Nazi Rule. (1954, cited above. Part 3, section c).

Sherman. A.J. Island Refuge: Britain and Refugees from the Third Reich, 1933-1939. London: Elek, 1973; L.A.: University of California Press, 1973. 291 p.

Vago, Bela. "The British Government and the Fate of Hungarian Jewry in 1944." In Rescue Attempts... (1977, cited above).

Wasserstein, Bernard. Britain and the Jews of Europe, 1939-1945. (1979, cited above). The British record in helping Jews was "unimpressive."

Yahil, Leni, "Select British Documents on the Illegal Immigration to Palestine." Yad Vashem Studies, 10 (1974): 241-276.

GREECE

Avni, Haim. "Spanish Nationals in Greece and their Fate during the Holocaust." Yad Vashem on the European Jewish Catastrophe and Resistance. Vol. 8. Jerusalem, 1970.

Eck, Nathan. "New Light on the Charges against the Last Chief Rabbi of Salonika." Yad Vashem Bulletin, 17 (1965): 9-15.

Kabeli, Isaac. "The Resistance of the Greek Jews." YIVO, 8 (1953): 281-288.

Tsatou, Jeanne. (Ioanna) The Sword's Fierce Edge: A Journal of the Occupation of Greece, 1941-1944. trans. from the Greek by Jean Demos. Nashville, Tn.: Vanderbilt University Press, 1969. 131 p. illus.

HUNGARY

Braham, Randolph L. "The role of the Jewish Council in Hungary: A Tentative Assessment." Yad Vashem Studies, 10 (1974): 69-110.

Goldfarb, Zvi. "On 'Hehalutz' Resistance in Hungary." In Extermination and Resistance. ed. by members of Kibbutz Lohamei Hagettaot. Israel: Kibbutz Lohamei Hagettaot, 1958.

Lambert, Gilles. Operation Hazalah: Budpaest 1944: les jeunes sionistes face aux nazis et aux juifs de Hongrie. Paris: Hachette, 1972. Biblio.: p. 191. Eng. trans. pub. by Bobbs-Merrill, 1974. 235 p. under the title

458

Operation Hazalah.   trans. by Robert Bullen and Rosette
Letellier.

Laquer, Walter, Z.   "The Kastner Case." _Commentary_
(December 1955): 500-511.

Nagy-Talavera, Nicholas M.   _The Green Shirts and the
Others. A History of Fascism in Hungary and Rumania._
Stanford, Calif.: Hoover Institution Press, 1970.

Macartney, Carlile A.   _October 15: A History of Modern
Hungary, 1929-1945_. 2 vols. Edinburgh: Edinburgh
University Press, 1957. 494 p. 519 p.; N.Y.: Praeger,
1957, under the title: _History of Hungary, 1929-1945_. 2
vols. 493 p. 519 p. Bibliography. Index.

Rotkirchen, Livia.   "Hungary: An Asylum for the refugees
of Europe." _Yad Vashem Studies_, 7 (1968): 127-142.

Vago, Bela.   "The Intelligence Aspects of the Joel Brand
Mission." _Yad Vashem Studies_, 10 (1941): 11-128.   The
best analysis is by Y. Bauer. "The Mission of Joel
Brand." (1978, cited above, c,2) Brand did fail.   The
West failed. For Himmler the Brand mission was a smoke-
screen; what Himmler principally wanted was to move
toward "a separate peace with the West and an alliance
against Russia." (Bauer, p. 147).

Vago, Bela.   "The British Government and the Fate of
Hungarian Jewry in 1944." In _Rescue Attempts_...(1977,
cited above).

Weissberg, Alex.   _Desperate Mission: Joel Brand's Story_.
trans. from the German by Constantine FitzGibbon and

Drew Foster-Melliar. N.Y.: Criterion Books, 1958. 310
p. Also pub. under the title: Advocate for the Dead;
the story of (Joel Brand) by Alex Weissberg. London:
Deutsch, 1958; Toronto, Collins, 1958. See Y. Bauer
(1978).

ITALY (see Part 3, section b and section c).

Battaglia, R. Storia della resistenza italiana. rev.
ed. Turin: Giulio Einaudi editore, 1964. Includes
discussion of the fate of the Jews of Rome.

Carpi, Daniel. "The Catholic Church and Italian Jewry
under the Fascists." Yad Vashem Studies, Vol. 4 (1960):
43-54.

Kessel, Albrecht von. "The Pope and the Jews." In The
Storm over the Deputy. ed. by Eric R. Bentley. N.Y.:
Grove Press, 1964.

Ledeen, Michael A. "Italian Jews and Fascism."
Judaism, 18:3 (Summer 1969): 277-298.
Michaelis, M. German-Italian Relations...(1978, cited
in Part 3, section b, section c).

Parri, F. and F. Venturi. "The Italian Resistance and
the Allies." In European Resistance Movements...(1964,
cited above).

Poliakov, L. and J. Sabille. Jews under the Italian
Occupation. (1955, cited above).

Rosengarten, Frank. The Italian anti-Fascist Press (1919-1945) from the Legal Opposition Press to the Underground Newspapers of World War II. Cleveland: Case Western Reserve University Press, 1968. XX, 263 p.

Vaccarino, M.G. "La résistance au fascisme en Italie de 1923 à 1945." In European Resistance Movements...(1964, cited above).

Vitale, Massimo Adolfo. "The Destruction and Resistance of the Jews in Italy." In They Fought Back. (1967, cited above. section a).

Waagenaar, Sam. The Pope's Jews. La Salle, Ill.: Library Press, Bk. Open Court, 1974. 487 p. illus.

LATVIA

Bilmanis, Alfred. A History of Latvia. Westport, Conn.: Greenwood Press, 1957.

Katz, Josef. One Who Came Back: The Diary of a Jewish Survivor. trans. from the German by Hilda Reach. N.Y.: Herzl Press and Bergen-Belsen Memorial Press, 1973. 277 p. The recollections of a German Jew who was transported to Nazi camps in Latvia. Uses the diary form but written after his liberation.

LITHUANIA

Bar-On, Zvi and Dov Levin. The Story of an Underground: The Resistance of the Jews of Kovna (Lithuania) in the

Second World War. In Hebrew with Eng. summary. Jerusalem: Yad Vashem, 1962.

Bauer, Yehuda. "Rescue Operations through Vilna." Yad Vashem Studies, 9 (1973): 215-224.

Eckman, Lester and Chaim Lazar. The Jewish Resistance: The History of the Jewish Partisans in Lithuania and White Russia during the Occupation, 1940-1945. N.Y.: Shengold, 1977. 282 p.

Gringauz, Samuel. "The Ghetto as an Experiment of Jewish Social Organization (Three Years of Kovno Ghetto)." JSS, XI:I (January 1949): 3-20.

Neshamit, Sarah. "Rescue in Lithuania during the Nazi Occupation." In Rescue Attempts...(1977, cited above. section b).

THE NETHERLANDS

Avni, Haim. "The Zionist Underground in Holland and France and the Escape to Spain." In Rescue Attempts...(1977, cited above, section b).

Beem, Hartog. "The Jewish Council (Judenrat) of the Province of Vriesland (Holland)." Yad Vashem Bulletin, 17 (December 1965): 21-23.

Frank, Anne. The Diary of a Young Girl. trans. from the Dutch by B.M. Mooyaart-Doubleday. Introd. by Eleanor Roosevelt, N.Y.: Doubleday, 1952. 7-285 p. 2nd ed. Foreword by Storm Jameson. London: Vallentine, 1954. 224 p. plates.

462

Jong, Louis de. "Anti-Nazi Resistance in the Netherlands." In European Resistance Movements...(1964, cited
above, section b.).

Jong, Louis de. "The Dutch Resistance Movements and
the Allies, 1940-1945." In European Resistance Movements. (cited above).

Michman, Joseph. "The Controversial Stand of the Joodse
Raad in the Netherlands, Lodewijk E. Visser's Struggle."
Yad Vashem Studies, X (1974): 9-68. On the conflict
between the collaborationist Jewish Council and L.
Visser and the Coordination Committee that refused to
compromise with the Germans.

Presser, Jacob. The Destruction of the Dutch Jews.
trans. from the Dutch by Arnold Pomerans. N.Y.: Dutton,
1969. 556 p. illus.: pub. in England under the title:
Ashes in the Wind; The Destruction of Dutch Jewry.
London: Souvenir, 1969. 556 p. illus.

Taubes, Israel. "The Jewish Council of Amsterdam." Yad
Vashem Bulletin, 17 (December 1965): 25-30.
Warmbrunn, Werner. The Dutch under German Occupation,
1940-1945. N.Y.: Oxford University Press, 1963.

NORWAY (also see Sweden)

Kjelstadli, Sverre. "The Resistance Movement in Norway
and the Allies, 1940-1945." In European Resistance
Movements...(1964, cited above, section b).

Rost, Nella. "Les juifs sous l' occupation allemande dans les pays scandinaves." In Les Juifs en Europe, 1939-1945. Paris: Editions du Centre. 1947.

POLAND   (see section a and b, above; and Original Testimony, Part 5).

Ainsztein, Reuben. "New Light on Szmuel Zygelbojm's Suicide." Yad Vashem Bulletin, 15 (August 1964): 8-12. On the Polish Jewish leader who killed himself in London to call attention to the plight of the Jews.

Bartoszewski, Wladyslaw and Sofia Lewin. eds. Righteous among the Nations: How Poles Helped the Jews, 1939-1945. London: Earlscourt Publishers Ltd., 1969. American ed., The Samaritans; Heroes of the Holocaust ed. by Alexander T. Jordan. N.Y.: Twayne, 1970. 442.

Bartoszewski, W. The Blood Shed Unites Us...Warsaw: Interpress, 1970.

Bauminger, A. "The Rising in the Cracow Ghetto." Yad Vashem Bulletin, 8-9 (1961): 22-25.

Berenstein, Tatana and Adam Rutkowski. Assistance to the Jews in Poland. trans. from the Polish by E. Rothert. Warsaw: Polonia, 1963.

Blumenthal, Nachman. Conduct and Actions of a Judenrat: Documents from the Bialystok Ghetto. Jerusalem: Yad Vashem, 1962.

Blumenthal, Nachman. "German Documents on the Bialystok Ghetto Revolt." Yad Vashem Bulletin, 14 (1964): 19-25.

Blumenthal, Nachman. "A Martyr or a Hero? Reflections on the Diary of Czerniakov." Yad Vashem Studies, 7 (1968): 165-172.

Cholawski, Shalom. Soldiers from the Ghetto. San Diego, CA.: A.S. Barnes, 1980. On the anti-Nazi activities of the Jews of Nesvich.

Gutman, Yisrael. The Jews of Warsaw. Bloomington, Ind.: Indiana University Press, 1982. (cited above, 1).

Kermish, Joseph. "New Jewish Sources for the History of the Warsaw Ghetto Uprising." Yad Vashem Bulletin, 15 (August 1964): 27-33.

Kermish, Joseph. "The Activities of the Council for Aid to Jews ("Zegota") in Occupied Poland." In Rescue Attempts...(1977, cited above, section b).

Kermish, Joseph. "Emmanuel Ringelblum's Notes Hitherto Unpublished." Yad Vashem Studies, 7 (1968): 173-183.

Klibanski, Bronia. "The Underground Archives of the Bialystok Ghetto (Founded by Mersik and Tenebaum)." Yad Vashem Studies, 2 (1958): 295-329.

Korman, Gerd. "Warsaw Plus Thirty: some Perceptions in the Sources and Written History of the Ghetto Uprising." In VIVO Annual of Jewish Social Science, 15 (1974): 367-372.

Lazar, Chaim. _Muranowsky 7: The Warsaw Ghetto Rising_. Tel Aviv: Massada Press, 1966.

Meed, Vladka. (pseud. Feigele (Peltel) Miedzyrzechi). _On Both Sides of the Wall: Memoirs from the Warsaw Ghetto_. Israel: Beit Lohamei Hagettaot, 1972.

Ringelblum, Emmanuel. _Polish-Jewish Relations During the Second World War_. ed. with Introd. by J. Kermish and with annotations by J. Kermish and S. Krakowsky. trans. from the Polish. N.Y.: Howard Fertig, Jerusalem: Yad Vashem, 1976. Argues that Poles did very little to help Jews; cf. W. Bartoszewski (1969, 1970, cited above).

Rowe, Leonard. "Jewish Self-Defense: A Response to Violence." In _Studies on Polish Jewry, 1919-1939: The Interplay of Social, Economic and Political Factors in the Struggle of a Minority for Its Existence_. ed. by Joshua A. Fishman. N.Y.: YIVO, 1974. pp. 105-149.

RUMANIA

Artzi, A. "The Underground Activities of the Pioneer Movements in Rumania during World War II." _Yad Vashem Bulletin_, 12 (1962): 34-41.
Kluger, Ruth and Peggy Mann. _The Last Escape_. Garden City, N.Y.: Doubleday, 1973.

Lavi, Theodor. "Documents on the Struggle of Rumanian Jewry for its rights during the Second World War." _Yad Vashem Studies_, 4 (1960): 261-316.

8

um 。

Lavi, Theodor. "The Vatican's Endeavors on Behalf of Rumanian Jewry during the Second World War." Yad Vashem Studies, 5 (1963): 405-419.

Lavi, Theodor. "The Background to the Rescue of Rumanian Jewry during the Period of the Holocaust." In Jews and non-Jews in Eastern Europe, 1918-1945. ed. by Bela Vago and George L. Mosse. N.Y.: Wiley, 1974.

SLOVAKIA

Knieva, Emil F. "The Resistance of the Slovak Jews." In They Fought Back... (1967, cited above. section a).

Rotkirchen, Livia. "Activities of the Jewish Underground in Slovakia." Yad Vashem Bulletin, 8-9 (1965): 25-31.

SOVIET UNION

Ainsztein, Reuben. Jewish Resistance in Nazi Occupied Eastern Europe. (1974, cited above, sect. a).

Arad, Yitzhak. "Jewish Family Camps in the Forest: An Original Means of Rescue." In Rescue Attempts... (1977, cited above, section b).

Bar-On, Ziv. "The Jews in the Soviet Partisan Movement." Yad Vashem Studies, 4 (1960): 167-190.

Levin, Dov. "The Attitude of the Soviet Union to the Rescue of Jews." In Rescue Attempts (1977, cited above).

Schwarz, Solomon M.   The Jews in the Soviet Union.
Syracuse: Syracuse University Press, 1951.

ADDENDUM

On Finland, see Felix Kersten.   The Kersten Memoirs,
1940-45.   London: 1956.   Finland, a German ally, with-
stood the pressure of Himmler and the Finnish Jews were
not deported.

4. The Refugee: (for thousands of people a stamped piece of paper meant the difference between life and death).

> The last chapter in the Nazi persecution of the Jews was written in the displaced-person camps and in the emigration of survivors during the years after the war in Europe. *Robert W. Ross.* So It Was True: The American Protestant Press and the Nazi Persecution of the Jews (1980).

Major studies on the U.S. and the refugee include Arthur Morse, *While Six Million Died* (1968), Wyman, *The Abandonment of the Jews* (1984), David S. Wyman, *Paper Walls* (1968), Henry L. Feingold, *The Politics of Rescue* (1970), Saul S. Friedman, *No Haven for the Oppressed* (1973), Barbara McDonald Stewart, *United States Government Policy on Refugees, 1933-1940* (1982), Leonard Dinnerstein, *America and the Survivors of the Holocaust* (1982). For Canada and Great Britain, see Abella and Troper (1979, 1983), Wasserstein (1979).

Abella, Irving and Harold Troper. "'The Line must be drawn somewhere': Canada and Jewish Refugees, 1933-9." Canadian Historical Review, 60:21 (1979): 178-209. The grim story of the Canadian government's refusal to admit Jewish refugees. "Of the more than 800,000 Jews seeking refuge from the Third Reich in the years from 1933 to 1939, Canada found room within her borders for approximately 4000." (p. 81).

Abella, Irving and Harold Troper. None is too many; Canada and the Jews of Europe, 1933-1948. N.Y.: Random House, 1983. 336 p. Thorough research. Won the 1983 National Jewish Book Award (Holocaust).

Adler-Rudel, S. "The Evian Conference on the Refugee Question." LBIY, 13 (1968): 235-73. At this major international conference in Evian, France (1938), no nation offered the Jews safe haven. See D. Wyman (1984, cited below). Described as the "Jewish Munich."

Agar, Herbert. The Saving Remnant: An Account of Jewish Survival. 269 p. maps. N.Y.: The Viking Press, 1960.

Arendt, Hannah. "We Refugees" (Jan. 1943). Rpt. in The Jew as Pariah. ed. by Ron Feldman. Grove, 1978.

Bauer, Yehuda. From Diplomacy to Resistance: A History of Jewish Palestine, 1939-1945. trans. from the Hebrew by Alton M. Winters. Phila.: JPS, 1970. 432 p.

Bauer, Yehuda. Flight and Rescue: BRICHAH. N.Y.: Random House, 1970. 369 p. maps.

Bentwich, Norman D.M. They Found Refuge, An Account of British Jewry's Work for Victims of Nazi Oppression. Introd. by Viscount Samuel. London: Cresset Press, 1956. 227 p.

Rescue and Achievement of Refugee Scholars; The Story of Displaced Scholars and Scientists, 1933-1952. Introd. by Lord Beveridge. (Studies in social life, I). London: Heineman, 1955. 107 p.

Cohen, Naomi W. Not Free to Desist: American Jewish Committee, 1906-1966. Phila.: JPS, 1972. See on rescue efforts in the 1940's.

Dekal, Ephraim. B'RIHA: Flight To The Homeland. N.Y.: Herzl Press, 1972.

Dinnerstein, Leonard. America and Survivors of the Holocaust. N.Y.: Columbia University Press, 1982. Biblio.: pp. 373-396. The first comprehensive and systematic study of U.S. treatment of Jewish refugee survivors. Dinnerstein uses documents and manuscript evidence that previous scholars (e.g., Robert Divine, American Immigration Policy, 1924-1952, Yale, 1957) did not have access to. Immigration policy "failed to meet the needs of the majority of the Jewish D.P.'s" (p. 271). Reviewed by J. Brandes, AHR, 88:1 (Feb. 83): 215-16.

Dobkowsky, Michael N. ed. Politics of Indifference: Documentary History of Holocaust Victims in America. Washington, D.C., University Press, 1982. Part I is on diplomatic actions relating to refugees, Part 2 is on the reception of refugees in America.

Eck, Nathan. "The Rescue of Jews with the Aid of Passports and Citizenship Papers of Latin American States." In On the European Jewish Catastrophe and Resistance:

Yad Vashem Studies. Vol. I. Jerusalem: Yad Vashem, 1975.

Feingold, Henry L. The Politics of Rescue: The Roosevelt Administration and the Holocaust, 1938-1945. New Brunswick: Rutgers University Press, 1970. Rpt. with new material, N.Y.: 1980. (cited above, a:3).

Friedman, Saul S. No Haven for the Oppressed: United States policy toward Jewish Refugees, 1938-1945. Detroit: Wayne State University Press, 1973. Includes bibliographical references. A major critical study.

Habe, Hans. The Mission. N.Y.: Coward-McCann, 1966. An historical novel based on the unsuccessful efforts to save Austrian Jews at the Evian Conference on Political Refugees (July 1938). "All evil takes place with the tacit connivance of the good..."

Haesler, Alfred A. The Lifeboat is Full: Switzerland and the Refugees, 1933-1945. trans. by C.L. Markman. N.Y.: Funk & Wagnalls, 1969. Switzerland had the best geographical position for refugees but it was the most hostile nation among the neutrals. They insisted on the "J" stamp in 1938 and thus stigmatized German Jews. In 1939 illegal refugees were expelled. In September 1942 the Swiss government upheld the police orders that refused refugees at the border. But the number of Jews (ca. 28,000) who found refuge in Switzerland was the largest number for any single state in Europe.

Halibut, Anthony. Exiled in Paradise: German Refugee Artists and Intellectuals in America from the 1930's to the Present. N.Y.: Viking Press, 1983. Vivid interesting life stories.

Hirschmann, Ira A. The Embers Still Burn. N.Y.: Simon & Schuster, 1949.

Krantzler, David. Japanese, Nazis and Jews. The Jewish Refugee Community of Shanghai, 1938-1945. Foreword by Abraham G. Duker, N.Y.: Yeshiva University Press, 1976. A study of Japanese attitude and policies toward Jews and the refuge of Shanghai in which ca. 18,000 Jews survived the war. vide also: Felix Gruenberger, "The Jewish Refugees in Shanghai." JJS, 12 (1950): 329-348. On Japanese policies and plans relating to the Jews, see Marvin Tokayer and Mary Swartz, The Fugu Plan, The Untold Story of the Japanese and the Jews during World War II. (N.Y.: Paddington Press Ltd., 1979). The Japanese "Jewish experts" believed the anti-Semitic nonsense in The Protocols of the Elders of Zion but they wanted to use the alleged Jewish power, money, and influence to assist Japan. In return they were willing to offer Jews a safe haven from anti-Semitism (Shinto Japan had no anti-Semitic tradition).

Marrus, Michael R. and Robert O. Paxton. Vichy France and the Jews. N.Y.: Schocken Books, 1983. 432 p. Documents a connection between hostility toward refuges in the late 1930's and Vichy's anti-Semitism and xenophobia. Orig. pub. as Vichy et les juifs. Calmann-Levy, 1981.

Mashberg, Michael. "American Diplomacy and the Jewish Refugee, 1938-1939." In VIVO Annual of Jewish Social Science. 15 (1974): 339-365.

Meyer, Michael A. "The Refugee Scholars Project of the Hebrew Union College." In A Bicentennial Festschrift for Jacob Rader Marcus. HUC Press, 1976. pp. 359-375. In the period, 1935-1942, HUC brought eleven scholars to America: "the episode reflects favorably on HUC, while providing additional evidence of the State Department's callous indifference to the plight of refugees."

Morse, Arthur D. While Six Million Died; A Chronicle of American Apathy. N.Y.: Random House, 1968. 420 p. Morse, a professional journalist, uses evidence from the State Department archives to fault U.S. policy as morally callous, lethargic and ineffective. (cited above, a:3).

Nadich, Judah. Eisenhower and the Jews. N.Y.: Twayne, 1953. By Eisenhower's first advisor on Jewish affairs.

Nawyn, William E. American Protestanism's Response to Germany's Jews and Refugees, 1933-1941. (Cited above, Part 3, c). Reviewed by Henry Feingold, AHR, 89:3 (June 1984): 872-3.

Neuringer, Sheldon Morris. American Jewry and United States Immigration Policy, 1881-1953. Ph.D. Dissert. (Department of History) University of Wisconsin, 1969.

Proudfoot, Malcolm J. European Refugees, 1939-52: A Study in Forced Population Movement. Evanston, Ill.: Northwestern University Press, 1956. A basic work, and see the earlier study by Joseph B. Schechtman, European Population Transfers, 1939-1945. N.Y.: Oxford University Press, 1946.

Rabinowitz, Dorothy. New Lives: Survivors of the Holocaust Living in America. (Borzoi Book). N.Y.: Knopf,
1976. 242 p. Personal narratives of refugees and survivors in America.

Schaber, Will   ed. Aufbau (Reconstruction): dokumente
einer Kultur im exile. N.Y.: Overlook Press, 1972. 416
p. A documented study of post-Hitler emigration.

Sherman, A.J. Island Refuge, Britain and Refugees from
the Third Reich, 1933-39. 1973. (cited above, a:3)

Stewart, Barbara McDonald. United States Government
Policy on Refugees, 1933-1940. (Makers of Modern
America series, ed. Frank Freidel). N.Y.: Garland Pub.
1982.

Stoessinger, John George. The Refugee and the World
Community. Minneapolis: University of Minnesota Press,
1956.

Szajkowski, Zosa. "The Consul and the Immigrant." JSS,
36, (1974): A study of visa policies on Jewish refugees.

Tartakower, Ariel and K.R. Grossman. The Jewish
Refugee. N.Y.: Institute of Jewish Affairs, 1944. XIII,
676 p.

Thomas, Gordon and Max Morgan Witts. The Voyage of the
Damned. N.Y.: Stein & Day, 1974. Fawcett, 1975. 317 p.
A grim and terrible story. Biblio.: p. 315-320.

Wasserstein, Bernard. Britain and the Jews of Europe,
1939-1945. N.Y.: Oxford University Press, 1979. (cited
above, c:3).

Wischnitzer, Mark. To Dwell in Safety: The Story of Jewish Migration Since 1880. Phila.: JPS, 1948. XXX, 368 p. maps. Still important.

Wyman, David S. Paper Walls: America and the Refugee Crisis, 1938-1941. Amherst, Mass.: University of Mass. Press, 1961. 306 p. An important study of U.S. unresponsiveness: after the war started U.S. restrictions on immigration laws reduced the number of German Jews who could qualify for visa to ten percent.

Wyman, David S. The Abandonment of the Jews: America and the Holocaust 1941-1945. N.Y.: Pantheon Books. 1984. (cited above, c:3).

E. Original Testimony and Survivor Literature. Memoirs, Journals, Diaries. (See also Part IV, Part VI) The cri de coeur of the memorialists of the tremendum is the silence of God. (A.A. Cohen, 1981, p. 95).

Survivors of the Holocaust have left accounts in more than twenty languages. For an intorduction to testimony in English, see Janet Ziegler, World War II: Books in English, 1945-1965 *(Stanford, CA: Hoover Institute, 1971), Section VI: "Social Import of the War." Also see Jacob Robinson and Philip Friedman,* Guide to Jewish History under Nazi Impact *(NY: YIVO Institute for Jewish Research, 1960), Chapter 16: "Collections of Personal Narratives and Anthologies." Important other works are: S. Ezrahi,* By Words Alone *(Chicago, 1980), Chapter 4: "Literature of Survival"; A.H. Rosenfeld,* A Double Dying *(NY: 1980), Chapter 2: "Holocaust and History"; T. Des Pres,* The Survivor *(NY: 1977); J. Glatstein, et al.,* Anthology of Holocause Literature *(Philadelphia: 1969), and the comprehensive collections ed. by Azriel Eisenberg,* Witness to the Holocaust, *(NY: 1981),* The Lost Generation *(NY: 1982). From a Ruined Garden... ed. by J. Kugelmass and J. Boyarin (NY: 1983) is valuable.*

The most important Diary/Chronicle sources are The Warsaw Diary of Adam Czerniakow *(1979),* THe Chronicle of the Todz Ghetto 1941-1944 *(1984), C. Kaplan,* Scroll of Agony *(1965), E. Ringelblum,* Notes from the Warsaw Ghetto *(1958), Z. Kalmonovitsch (1953). And see* Shielding the Flame: An Intimate Conversation with Dr. Marek Edelman, the Last Surviving Leader of the Warsaw Ghetto Uprising, *by Hanna Krall, trans. by J. Stasinka and L. Weschler. Intro. by Timothy Garton Ash (NY: Holt, 1986). Survival literature, by displaced individuals often working in a second or third language, struggles with the difficulty of communicating the experienced Horrors. "When the great terror came, / I fell dumb." (Nelly Sachs). But also it is filled with the need to* tell the story, pay the debt to the dead, *and to* bear witness." *And now see the articulate and profound work by David G. Roskies,* Against the Apocalypse. Responses to Catastrophe in Modern Jewish Culture *(Harvard, 1984), ch. 8-10.*

On the question of Resistance (See Part IV) and Survival, note the words of Jacob Katz:

Moral judgment can only be pronounced on individuals when we have fully imagined the plight they were in, and that is why any such moral judgment has to be preceded by a reconstruction of the situation as exact as historical sources will permit. (*Commentary*, May 1975)

Amery, Jean. <u>At the Mind's Limits</u>: <u>Contemplations by a Survivor on Auschwitz and its Realities</u>. trans. from the German by Sidney Rosenfeld. Bloomington, Indiana

University Press, 1980. XIV, 111 p. Five autobiographical essays that describe victimization and the struggle for understanding. "At the Mind's Limit" (on the intellectual in Auschwitz), "Torture ("Whoever was Tortured, Stays Tortured"), "How much home does a person need." "Resentments," "On the necessity and impossibility of being a Jew." In his Preface to the 1977 reissue, Ameny--who defines himself as a "Catastrophe Jew," a Jew "without positive determinants -- worries and warns about new forms of anti-Semitism and insists that "there is really nothing that provides enlightenment on the eruption of radical Evil in Germany... this Evil really is singular and irreducible in its total inner logic and its accursed rationality." (VIII).

Berg, Mary. Warsaw Ghetto: A Diary. trans. from the Polish by Norbert and Sylvia Glass. N.Y.: L. B. Fisher, 1945. One of the first substantial accounts of the Warsaw Ghetto; from October 1939 (Berg was then sixteen) to July 1942 when she was released thanks to the pressures of her American father.

Berkowitz, Sarah B. Where are My Brothers? Foreword by Solomon Z. Ferziger. N.Y.: Helios, 1965. 127 p. On the endless scream that was Auschwitz.

Bettelheim, Bruno. The Informed Heart, Autonomy in a Mass Age. Glencoe, Ill.: The Free Press, 1960. (cited in c:4, above). Highly influential but replete with abstractions.

Bezwinska, Jadwiga. ed. Amidst a Nightmare of Crime: Manuscripts of Members of Sondercommando. trans. by

Krystyna Michalik. Oswiecim, Poland, 1973. Includes the diary of Salmen Lewenthal; his buried manuscript was unearthed in 1962.

Birenbau, Halina. Hope Is the Last to Die: A Personal Documentary of Nazi Terror. trans. from the Polish by David Walsh. N.Y.: Twayne, 1972. 246 p. "While still in camp I decided that if I lived to see liberation, I would write down everything I saw, heard and experienced." (p. 244). An unembellished memoir by a Jewish-Polish teenager. (1939-45).

Boehim, Eric. ed. We Survived. The Stories of Fourteen of the Hidden and Hunted of Nazi Germany. New Haven: Yale University Press, 1949. Now see Rothchild (1981), Eisenberg (1981).

Bor, Josef. The Terezin Requiem. (cited in Part f, below).

Borwicz, Michel. Ecrits des condamnes à mort sous l'occupation nazie, 1939-1945. (1954) 2nd ed., rev., Paris: Gallimard, 1973. A study of Holocaust literature by a survivor and a historian. Cited in Roskies (1984, pp. 199-200) and discussed in C. Haft (1973, cited below, f).

Borzkowski, T. Between Falling Walls. Israel: Ghetto Fighters House, 1972. trans. from the Yiddish by M. Kohansky. 229 p. On the Warsaw Ghetto Revolt.

Buber-Neumann, Margarete. Under Two Dictators. trans. by Edward Fitzgerald. N.Y.: Dodd, Mead; London: Victor

480

Gollancz, 1949. A survival memoir: Ravensbruck and a Stalinist camp.

The Chronicle of the Todz Ghetto 1941-1944. ed and abr. with Introd. and footnotes by Lucjan Dobroszychi. Polish text trans. by Richard Lourie; German text trans. by Joachim Neugroschel, Jean Steinberg and Howard Stern. New Haven and London: Yale University Press, 1984. LXVIII, 551 p. photos, maps. Appendix. Polish and German Street Names. Index. Annotations for both the specialist and general reader. An immensely significant chronicle, a collective work, kept from Jan. 12, 1941 until July 31, 1944. Stark and moving in its under-statement and simplicity. Feb. 8, 1944: "...The situation in the ghetto is well-typified by the price that potato peels now bring--60 marks a kilogram. Rutabaga scraps: 20-25 marks."

Cohen. The Abyss: A Confession. trans. by James Brockway. N.Y.: Norton, 1973. Cohen was a prison doctor at Westerbork and later at Auschwitz.

Delbo, Charlotte. None of Us Will Return. trans. from the French by John Githens. N.Y.: Grove Press, 1969. A sensitive memoir (Auschwitz). In contrast to other survival memoirs, Delbo's style is impressionistic prose poetry. This is Vol. I of Auschwitz et après, Vol. 2, "Une Connaissance inutile (1970), Vol. 3, Mesure de nos jours (1971).

Donat, Alexander. ed. The Death Camp Treblinka: A Documentary. N.Y.: The Holocaust Library, 1979. Includes once unavailable survivor accounts and biblio-graphical information.

Donat, Alexander. The Holocaust Kingdom: A Memoir. N.Y.: Holt, Rinehart & Winston, 1965. An invaluable source for the Warsaw Ghetto, including the Revolt, the camp of Maydanek, etc. On the conditions of survival: "This is a jungle and hence the only law is the law of the strongest...Everyone here is shit." (Contrast this perspective with that of Bettleheim and Frankl). Donant quotes a Kapo (Jewish guard): "I...if only one of us is to survive, I want to be that one. No matter what the cost." (pp. 168-169).

Dorian, Marguerite. ed. The Quality of Witness: A Rumanian Diary 1937-44. Phila.: JPS, 1983. Won the 1984 National Jewish Book Award (Holocaust).

Ekart, Antoni. Vanished Without Trace. trans. by Egerton Sykes and E.S. Virpsha. London: Max Parrish, 1954.

Fackenheim, Emile. "Sachsenhausen 1938: Groundwork for Auschwitz." Midstream, 21 (April 1975): 27-31. While he had firsthand knowledge of this camp, Fackenheim suggests that eyewitness accounts ("deception of the victims" was basic to the camp system) may be less reliable than studies done after the events.

Ferderber-Salz, Bertha. And the Sun Kept Shining...N.Y.: Holocaust Library, 1980. 233 p.

Finker, Moshe. The Diary of Young Moshe: The Spiritual Torment of a Jewish Boy in Nazi Europe. Jerusalem: Yad Vashem, 1971. Narrative of the personal and religious despair of a young Jew in Belgium: "What can God mean by all that is befalling us and by not preventing it from happening." (p. 26). He perished in Auschwitz at the age of 16.

Frank, Anne. The Diary of a Young Girl. trans. by B.M. Mooyaart-Doubleday. N.Y.: Modern Library, 1952. (also discussed in f:2). Anne's optimism defines this moving document as pre-Holocaust. It is also true that the full tragedy of the events is not immanent in the narrative itself. According to Bettleheim: "...Anne Frank died because her parents could not get themselves to believe in Auschwitz. And her story found wide acclaim because for us too, it denies implicitly that Auschwitz ever existed. If all men are good, there was never an Auschwitz." B. Bettleheim, The Informed Heart (cited above, p. 254). There is a measure of truth in this but he blames the victims and misreads Anne's statement.

Frankl, Victor E. From Death Camp to Existentialism. trans. from the German by Ilse Lasch. Boston: Beacon Press, 1959. rev. and enl. version under the title: Man's Search for Meaning: An Introduction to Logotherapy. Beacon, 1963. Frankl argues that one should will to be "worthy of" one's sufferings. "His (man's) unique opportunity lies in the way in which he bears his burden." (p. 78). It is doubtful if these worthy maxims apply to the "concentrationary universe" except through retrospective philosophical in-reading. See the discussion in L. Langer (1982, cited below).

Friedlander, Saul. When Memory Comes. trans. from the French (1978) by Helen R. Lane. N.Y.: Farrar, Straus & Giroux, 1979. Friedlander ("I was born in Prague at the worst possible moment, four months before Hitler came to power.") survived the Holocaust by being placed in a French Catholic school. His powerful memoir tells of the attitudes and fate of the assimilated Jewish bourgeoisie of Central Europe.

Friedman, Philip. Martyrs and Fighters. London, 1954. (cited above, Part 4).

Gluck, Gemma (La Guardia). ed. by S.L. Shneiderman. My Story. N.Y.: McKay, 1961. 116 p.

Goldstein, Bernard. The Stars Bear Witness. trans. from the Yiddish by Leonard Shatzkin. N.Y.: Viking Press, 1949. Dolphin paperback ed. under the title: Five Years in the Warsaw Ghetto. (1961). Goldstein, a man of high principle and immense courage, was the leader of the Socialist Bund in the Ghetto. He survived the destruction of the Ghetto. The journal covers events from October 1939 to June 1945.

Grynberg, Henryk. Child of the Shadows. trans. from the Polish by Celina Wieniewskaj. Hartford, Conn.: Hartmore House, 1969. 127 p. A personal memoir with a fictional story, "The Grave."

Hardman, Leslie H. The Survivors: The Story of the Belsen Remnant, told by [the Author] and written by Cecily Goodman. Foreword by Lord Russell of Liverpool. London: Vallentine, Mitchell, 1958. 113 p.

Hart, Kitty. I Am Alive. London and N.Y.: Abelard-Schuman, 1962. Imprisoned in an Auschwitz work camp, Hart describes the attempts at disassociation from the environment of horror.

Heimler, Eugene. Night of the Mist. trans. from the German by Andre Ungar. N.Y.: Vanguard, 1959; Pyramid Books under the title: Concentration Camp (1961). Valuable as personal memoir and as historical source. Argues that despite brutalization it was possible to remain human: "Buchenwald taught me to be tolerant of myself, and by that means tolerant to others." (p. 189). Buchenwald was not Auschwitz but nevertheless contrast this statement with P. Levi (If This is a Man) and with the image in E. Wiesel's Night.

Heyman, Eva. The Diary of Eva Heyman. trans. by Moshe M. Kohn. Jerusalem: Yad Vashem, 1974. Set in Hungary early in 1944. Heyman died in Auschwitz at the age of 13.

Hillesum, Ettey. An Interrupted Life: the Diaries of Ettey Hillesum, 1941-1943. Introd. by J.G. Gaarlanet. trans. from the Dutch by Arno Pomerans. N.Y.: Pantheon Books, 1983. 226 p. Notes, p. 224-226. There has been tremendous European response to these diaries. Hillesum was part of an assimilated, privileged family of Dutch Jews; she began her writing at about the same time as Anne Frank, who was in hiding a short way away. Hillesum perished in Auschwitz at the age of 29. Her writings reveal an independent mind and original religious sensibility.

Kalmonovitsch, Zelig. "A Diary of the Nazi Ghetto In Vilna." VIVO Annual of Jewish Social Science, 8 (1953): 9-81. The impressions (June 22, 1941-June 1943) of an erudite Yiddish philologist and one of the founders of YIVO.

Kalmonovitsch, Zelig. "Pondering Jewish Fate: From Zelig Kalmanovitsch's Diary." In Lucy Dawidowicz, ed. A Holocaust Reader. N.Y.: Behrman House, 1976. pp. 225-233.

Kalmonovitsch, Zelig. Yoman begeto Vilna ukhtavim miha'izavon shenimtsa' baharisot. (A Diary of the Vilna Ghetto and Posthumous Writings Discovered in the Ruins). ed. and with an Introd. by Shalom Luria. Israel: Moreshet and Sifriat Poalim, 1977. Kalmanovitsch (1885-1944) became known as "The Prophet" of the ghetto. His journal written in Hebrew was "a cross between a diary and a philosophical notebook." He had a "global vision of Jewish sanctity." (D. Roskies, 1984, cited above, p. 199, 271).

Kantor, Alfred. The Book of Alfred Kantor. N.Y.: McGraw-Hill, 1971.

Kaplan, Chaim Aron. Scroll of Agony: The Warsaw Diary of Chaim A. Kaplan. ed. and trans. by Abraham I. Katsch. N.Y.: Macmillan, 1965; Collier, 1973. Kaplan was a Russian-born educator, writer and Hebrew scholar; he and his wife were killed in Treblinka. His Diary was discovered by Katsch some twenty years after the destruction of the Ghetto. The Diary is informative and elegiac and also "the despondent chronicle of Polish Jewry in its death throes." "Blessed is the eye that has not beheld all this!" (p. 36) A. Rosenfeld (cited above, 1981, p. 44). The title derives from the following incident: some Rabbis, forced to leave their homes, appeared in Warsaw carrying a Torah scroll, their "most sacred possession." "The scroll of agony which the Rabbis of Praga unrolled before us touched our souls."

(August 27, 1940). "There is no end to our scroll of agony. I am afraid that the impressions of this terrible era will be lost because they have not been adequately recorded. I risk my life with my writing, but my abilities are limited..and I can guarantee the factualness of these manifestations ("the fruits of a great many facts") because I dwell among my people and behold their misery and their souls' torment." (p. 189).

Katz, Josef. One Who Came Back: The Diary of a Jewish Survivor. trans. from the German by Hilda Reach. N.Y.: Herzl Press, 1972.

Kessel, Sim. Hanged at Auschwitz. trans. by M. and D. Wallace. N.Y.: Stein & Day, 1972.

Kielar, Wieslaw. Anus mundi: 1500 days in Auschwitz/ Birkenau. trans. from the German by Susanne Flatauer. N.Y.: Times Books, 1980. 312 p. Memoirs.

Klein, Gerda W. All But My Life. N.Y.: Hill & Wang, 1957. 246 p. Autobiography.

Knapp, Stefan. The Square Sun. London: Museum Press, 1957. 172 p. illus. Autobiography.

Kogan, Eugen. The Theory and Practice of Hell. trans. by Heinz Norden. N.Y.: Farrah, Straus, 1953; London: Secker & Warburg, 1950. Kogan was a leader in the political underground in Buchenwald for nine years. Prisoners adopted "a whole system of mimicry toward the SS" that served to "camouflage" their real intentions. (p. 282). Cf. Bettleheim.

Korczak, Janusz. Ghetto Diary. N.Y.: The Holocaust Library, 1978. The very allusive and personal diary of the martyred director of an orphan home for Jewish children. Full title: The Warsaw Ghetto Memoirs of Janusz Korczak. trans. from the Polish with an Introd. by E.P. Kulawiec. Washington, D.C.: University Press of America, 1978.

Kraus, Ota and Erich Kulka. The Death Factory: Document on Auschwitz. trans. by Stephen Jolly. Oxford: Pergamon Press, 1966.

Krehbiel-Darmstadter. Briefe aus Gurs und Limonest, 1940-1943. Heidelberg, 1970. "...among the most important eyewitness accounts of the protracted French phase of the final solution." (Frederic V. Grunfeld, 1979, p. 254-255). Krehbiel was a Protestant convert and social worker, she was sent from Drancy to Auschwitz in Feb. 1943.

Kruk, Herman. Togbukh fun vilner geto. ed. by Mordecai W. Bernstein. Yiddish (Diary of the Vilna Ghetto). N.Y.: YIVO, 1961. Kruk, a secular intellectual and Bundist, recorded the plight of Vilna Jews from June 1941 to the middle of 1943.

Kugelmass, Jack and Jonathan Boyarin. ed. and trans. with an Introd. From a Ruined Garden: The Memorial Books of Polish Jewry. N.Y.: Schocken Books, 1983. 275 p. Includes a Geographical Index and a Bibliography by Zachary M. Baker. A very significant contribution. These selections drawn from sixty memorial books, reflecting what surviving townspeople considered most important about their shtetlekh, introduce the memorial-book genre (yizker-bikher) to the English reader. Recent studies of the Holocaust have overlooked "the single most important act of commemorating the dead on the part of Jewish survivors." (p.1).

Langbein, Hermann. Menschen im Auschwitz. Wien: Europauerlag, 1972. By a communist leader in the camp underground.

Langer, Lawrence L. Versions of Survival. The Holocaust and the Human Spirit. Albany: State University of N.Y. Press, 1982. (SUNY series in modern Jewish literature and culture). In this intelligent and articulate study, Langer argues that the survivor vocabulary is inadequate to the experience. Survivor literature reflects the tension between memory and retrospective consciousness, being influenced by a sense of what should have been done. Moreover, the telling modifies what is being told.

Leitner, Isabella. Fragments of Isabella: A Memoir of Auschwitz. ed. and with an epilogue by Irving A. Leitner. N.Y.: Thomas Y. Crowell, 1976.

Lengyel, Olga. Five Chimneys: The Story of Auschwitz. trans. by Clifford Coch and Paul Weiss. Chicago: Ziff-Davis, 1947; London: Mayflower Press, 1972. Lengyel, a Jewish doctor forced to work in the Auschwitz infirmary, had to kill babies to save their mothers: "And so the Germans succeeded in making murderers of even us. To this day the picture of these murdered babies haunts me." (p. 100-101).

Levi, Primo. If This is a Man. trans. from the Italian (1958) by Stuart Woolf. N.Y.: Orion Press, 1959; Collier paperback. ed. under the title: Survival in Auschwitz: The Nazi Assault on Humanity (1961). The account of imprisonment in Auschwitz (Dec. 1943-Jan. 1945) by an Italian-Jewish chemist of deep sensibility and intelligence. "We are slaves...condemned to certain death, but we still possess one power...the power to refuse consent." (p. 39). Bettleheim, Frankl, Heimler would apparently agree with this image of the "power to refuse consent." But the bulk of Levi's material itself belies that image. "Their life is short, but their number is endless; they, the Muselmanner, the drowned, form the backbone of the camp, an anonymous mass...of non-men who march and labour in silence, the divine spark dead within them, already too empty to really suffer." (p. 103). "To destroy a man is difficult, almost as difficult as to create one...but you Germans have succeeded. Here we are, docile under your gaze; from our side you have nothing more to fear..." (p. 177). And Levi speaks with despair of "the paralysing sensation of being totally helpless in the hands of fate." (p. 184). And pertinent to the various theologi-cal attempts to make sense of Auschwitz: "Today I think that if for no other reason than an Auschwitz existed, no one in our age should speak of Providence." (p. 187). Levi concludes his narrative with the bitter question: "Are these the survivors of Auschwitz, actually men?"

Levi, Primo. The Awakening. trans. from the Italian (1963) by Stuart Woolf. Boston: Little, Brown & Co. 1965; pub. in England under the title: The Truce (1965). An account of the liberation of Buna (attached to Auschwitz) and the ordeal of Levi in returning home.

"...I felt the tattooed number of my arm burning like a sore." (p. 218).

Levin, Meyer. In Search; An Autobiography. N.Y.: Horizon Press, 1950. 524 p. Levin thought that the role of the American writer toward the Holocaust should be "midwife to the authentic recitations of the victims themselves." (S. Ezrai, cited above, 1980, p. 200). Levin states that he collected information from "every survivor I could unearth" but "this tragic epic cannot be written by a stranger to the experience, for the survivors have an augmented view which we cannot attain...they are like people who have acquired the hearing of a whole range of tones outside normal human hearing." (p. 173).

Lwinska, Pelagia. Twenty Months at Auschwitz. trans. by Albert Teichner. N.Y.: Lyle Stuart, 1968.

Lingens-Reiner, Ella. Prisoners of Fear. London: Victor Gollancz, 1948. A non-Jewish surviver's account of imprisonment in Auschwitz and Dachau. "We camp prisoners had only one yardstick: Whatever helped our survival was good, whatever threatened our survival was bad and to be avoided." (p. 142).

Mapaparte, Curzio. Kaputt. trans. from the Italian by C. Foligno. N.Y.: Dutton, 1946. By an Italian journalist.

Maurel, Micheline. An Ordinary Camp. trans. from the French by Margaret S. Summers. Preface by François Mauriac. N.Y.: Simon & Schuster, 1958. 141 p. Pub. in London under the title Ravensbruck (1958). Contains the

bitter exhortation to "Be happy, you who torture your-
self over metaphysical problems...oh, how happy, you who
die a death as normal as life, in hospital beds or in
your homes." (p. 140).

Meed, Vladka. On Both sides of the Wall: Memoirs from
the Warsaw Ghetto. Israel: Ghetto Fighters House, 1972;
N.Y.: Jewish Labor Committee, 1972.

Michel, Jean. Dora. trans. from the French (1975) by
Jennifer Kidd. N.Y.: Harper Row and Winston, 1979. By a
French resistance member who survived the little-known
(but considered by some as the worse) camp of Dora, near
Nordhausen, where rocket technology was developed.
Michel contends that the secrecy attending the camp is
related to the use made of its rocket facilities and
technology by the U.S. in its postwar rocket space
programs. Cf. the vivid images in the 1973 novel by
Thomas Pynchon, Gravity's Rainbow.

Minco, Marga. Bitter Herbs. trans. from the Dutch by
Roy Edwards. London: Oxford University Press, 1960. By
a schoolchild who survived the occupation in Holland.

Muller, Filip. Auschwitz Inferno. The Testimony of a
Sonderkommando. Literary collaboration by Helmut
Freitag. ed. and trans. by Susanne Flatauer. London:
Routledge and Kegan Paul, 1979. XII, 180 p. illus.

Newman, Judith Sternberg. In the Hell of Auschwitz.
N.Y.: Exposition, 1964.

Nyiszli, Miklos. Auschwitz: A Doctor's Eyewitness
Account. trans. from the Hungarian by T. Kremer and R.

Seaver, with Foreword by Bruno Bettleheim. N.Y.: Frederich Fell; Greenwich, Conn.: Fawcett Crest, 1960. The memoir of a Hungarian Jewish physician who was the chief "research physician" of the crematoria. According to A. Rosenfeld the account adopts a "clinical perspective" as a defensive strategy, "that is "tempered by feelings of guilt..." (cited above, 1980, p. 55).

Pawelczyska, Anna. Values and Violence in Auschwitz: A Sociological Analysis. Berkeley, Ca.: University of California Press, 1979. Pawelczyska was imprisoned in Auschwitz, see, esp., "A Place in the Structure of Terror," p. 68-82. Her analysis ignores the profound difference between the situation of Jewish and non-Jewish prisoners.

Pawlowicz, Sala. (Kaminska) with Kevin Klose. I Will Survive. N.Y.: W.W. Norton: 1962. 286 p. By a survivor of Bergen-Belsen and other camps.

Perl, Gisella. I Was a Doctor in Auschwitz. N.Y.: International Universities Press, 1948. 189 p.

Pisar, Samuel. Of Blood and Hope. N.Y.: Little, Brown, 1980. A reflective autobiography that includes his vivid account of Auschwitz imprisonment.

Poller, Walter. Medical Block, Buchenwald; the personal testimony of inmate 996, block 36. London: Souvenir, 1961. 277 p.

Ringelblum, Emmanuel. Notes from the Warsaw Ghetto: The Journal of Emmanuel Ringelblum. ed. and trans. by Jacob Sloan. N.Y.: McGraw-Hill, 1958; Schocken Books, 1974.

The extremely significant Yiddish diary, objective, terse and understated, of a Jewish historian, teacher, and archivist of the Warsaw ghetto. The Sloan edition is a translation of selections--he did not have access to the original 2-vol. Warsaw edition or its copy in Israel. The journal covers day-to-day events from Jan. 1940 to Dec. 1942. Ringelblum founded the Oneg Shabbat (Sabbath celebrants), the secret archives of the ghetto. His archivist commitment led him to refuse a rescue offer made by the Polish underground. He and his family were murdered by the Nazi in 1944. A collection from his archive has been translated from Yiddish into Hebrew and published in Tel Aviv: Zakhor, 1969: Kiddush Hashem: ktavim miymey hasho'ah (Kiddush Hashem: Writings from the Holocaust), ed. by N. Blumental and J. Kermish.

Rosen, Donia. The Forest, My Friend. trans. by Mordecai S. Chertoff. N.Y.: Bergen-Belsen Memorial Press, 1971. 117 p.

Rothchild, Sylvia. ed. Voices from the Holocaust. N.Y.: New American Library, 1981. The taped memories of 250 people now living in America.

Rousset, David. The Other Kingdom. trans. from the French, L'univers concentrationnaire and with an Introd. by Raman Guthrie. N.Y.: Reynal and Hitchcock, 1947. 173 p. In "the other kingdom," a "universe apart, totally cut off, the weird kingdom of an unlikely fatality," the "classic forms of statement and metaphor" are unyielding clay: "Normal men do not know that everything is possible... The concentrationees do know... They are set apart from the rest of the world by an experience impossible to communicate." "The concentrationary universe...lives on in the world like a dead planet laden with corpses." (pp. 10-11, 168).

Rubinstein, Erna F. The Survivor in Us All; A Memoir of the Holocaust. Hamden, Conn.: Archon Books, 1983. 185 p. Epilogue, p. 185. The narrative of a Polish Jewish family, and the story of the four sisters who survived. "The moments of despair were so overwhelming that one had to reach with all her might for something to hold on to, for hope, for strength, for sanity...The line between life and death was extremely thin, and one could only cross it with a determination to live, to survive, with the inner power drawn by some from love or the tremendous power of faith and infinite prayer." (p. 101).

Rubinowicz, David. The Diary by David Rubinowicz. trans. by Derek Bowman. Edmonds, Wash.: Creative Options Pub., 1982. 81 p. A Warsaw Ghetto diary (1940-1942) by a boy of 12.

Rudashevski, Yitzhok. The Diary of the Vilna Ghetto: June 1941-April 1943. trans. and ed. by Percy Matenko. Israel: Beit Lohamei Hagettaot and Hakibbutz Hameuchad Pub. House, 1973.

Salomon, Charlotte. Charlotte: A Diary in Pictures. trans. by Ralph Manheim. Comment by Paul Tillich. Biographical notes by Emil Straus. N.Y.: Harcourt, Brace, 1963. A young German Jewish girl's surviving record of colored drawings. Drawn in southern France before she was deported to Auschwitz, her drawings form a visual counterpart to the more hopeful diary of the younger Anne Frank.

Salomon, Charlotte. Charlotte: Life or Theatre, an autobiographical play. trans. by Leila Vennewitz. N.Y.: Viking Press, 1981. 784 p. The story of her life in paintings, dialogue and musical tones. She perished in Auschwitz in 1943, age 26.

Schnabel, Ernst. Anne Frank: A Portrait in Courage. trans. by Richard and Clara Winston. N.Y.: Harcourt, Brace, Harbrace paperback Library, 1958.

Sereny, Gitta. Into That Darkness. N.Y.: McGraw-Hill, 1974. On Franz Stangel, whom she interviewed.

Shalit, Levi. This is How We Died. trans. from the Yiddish by Adah Fogel. Munich, 1949. A writer's account of a ghetto in Lithuania. "During times of starvation the ghetto depended upon the smugglers-- defiant dealers and life givers who moved about the ghetto in tight-lipped silence..."

Shifman, Nusja and Inja Shifman. My Whole Life is Still Before Me. trans. from the Yiddish by Max Rosenfeld. Jerusalem: Yad Vashem, 1962. Letters from the ghetto by two sisters.

Siegal, Aranka. Upon the Head of a Goat: A Childhood in Hungary, 1939-1944. N.Y.: Farrar, Straus & Giroux, 1981.

Solomon, Michael. Magadan. Foreword by Irving Layton. N.Y.: Auerbach, 1971; Phila.: Vertex Books, 1971. 243 p.

Stiffel, Frank. The Tale of the Ring: A Kaddish. Wain- scott, N.Y.: Pushcart Press, 1984. 348 p. illus. Winner of the Second Annual Editors' Book Award. A memoir written shortly after the war. Detailed information on survival strategies and types of social/ethnic differentiation within the Warsaw Ghetto, Treblinka, Kobier and Auschwitz. Stiffel's personal code was "...man is born with dignity; he dies when his dignity is gone; therefore, if he wants to stick to life, he must strive to keep his dignity intact, regardless of circumstances." (p. 212).

Szmaglewska, Seweryna. Smoke Over Birkenau. trans. by Jadwiga Rynas. N.Y.: Henry Holt, 1947.

Szalet, Leon. Experiment "E"; A Report from an Extermination Laboratory. trans. by Catherine B. Williams. N.Y.: Didier, 1946. 284 p.

Teg, Nechama. Dry Tears: The Story of a Lost Childhood. Westport, Conn.: Wildcat Pub. 1982.

Tillion, Germaine. Ravensbruck. trans. from the French by Gerald Satterwhite. N.Y.: Doubleday, Anchor Books, 1975. XXIII, 256 p. A survivor's account of the camp for women.

Trepman, Paul. Among Men and Beasts. trans. from the Yiddish by Soshana Perla and Gertrude Hirschler. N.Y.: As. Barnes & Co., and World Fed. of Bergen-Belsen Assocs, Inc., 1978. 229 p.

Unsdorfer, S.B. The Yellow Star. N.Y.: Thomas Yose-loff, 1961. 205 p.

Vrb, Rudolf and Alan Bestic. I Cannot Forgive. N.Y.: Grove Press, 1964. 281 p. "Those who were different died in Auschwitz, while the anonymous, the face-less ones, survived." (p. 145). rev. ed.: Factory of Death. London: Corgi Books, 1964.

Wdowinski, David. And We are Not Saved. N.Y.: The Philosophical Library, 1963. 123 p.

Wechsberg, Joseph. ed. and with an Introductory pro-file. The Murderers Among Us: The Wiesenthal Memoirs. N.Y.: McGraw-Hill, 1967. 340 p. illus.; London: Heine-mann, 1967. 321 p. plates, maps. The memoirs of a survivor who devoted his life to finding Nazis and was successful in locating Eichmann and Franz Stangel.

Wein, Abraham. "Memorial Books as a source for Research into the History of Jewish Communities in Europe." Yad Vashem Studies, 9 (1973).

Weiss, Reska. Journey Through Hell; A Woman's Account of her Experiences at the hands of the Nazis. London: Vallentine, Mitchell, 1961. 255 p.

Wells, Leon Weliczker. The Janowska Road. N.Y.: Macmillan, 1963. Rpt. under the title: The Death Brigade, N.Y.: The Holocaust Library, 1978. Harrowing and numbing account of the fate of Jews in eastern Galicia. Forced to work on the "death brigade," Wells describes prisoners who "...go to the fire without pro-test...They have had enough...everyone feels that the

498

world is his enemy; even the children in diapers feel
this." (p. 207). Autobiographical, age 16 to 20.

Wiechert, Ernst. Forest of the Dead. trans. from the
German by Ursula Stechow. N.Y.: Greenberg, 1947. An
autobiographical novel by a German writer interned in
Buchenwald. "He felt a crack run through God's image, a
crack that would not ever heal."

Wiernik, Yankel. A Year in Treblinka; an inmate who
escaped tells the day-to-day facts of one year of his
torturous experience. trans. from the Yiddish by Moshe
Speigel. N.Y.: Undser Tsait, 1944. O. 5-46 p. (pa.)
Wiernik, born in Poland in 1889, helped organize the
August 1942 revolt in Treblinka. He escaped. E. Wiesel
descriped Wiernik as a "carpenter by profession and hero
by choice." One can compare Wiernik's account with J.
Steiner's (1967, cited in section following). Wiernik
is more concrete, less ideological.

Ziemian, Joseph. The Cigarette Sellers of Three Crosses
Square. trans. from the Polish by Janina David. Minn.:
Lerner Publications Co., 1975. An account of a group of
young Warsaw Ghetto escapees who survived by peddling
cigarettes.

Zylberberg, Michael. A Warsaw Diary, 1939-1945.
London: Vallentine, Mitchell, 1969. 220 p. illus.

Zywulska, Krystana. I Came Back. trans. from the
Polish by Krystyna Cenkalska. London: Dennis Dobson;
Roy, 1951. 246 p. A survivor's account of imprisonment
in Poland during the Occupation and of the hell of
Auschwitz in the fall of 1944.

F. Language and Atrocity. Literature and the Holocaust.

The central critical issue in this section is on the relation between language, and specifically imaginative literature, and the Holocaust. The following are arguable options.

A) Silence is alone appropriate to Holocaust horror.

B) Language can confront the event but only in radically altered form, e.g., dissonance, surrealism.

C) The 'Holocaust' has no sui generis meaning, its interpretation is relative to the tradition of a community. The archetypes of the Jewish pre-Holocaust literature of catastrophe provides an interpretational framework.

1. Literary Critical Studies. Anthologies. Collections of Critical Essays.

Alexander, Edward. The Resonance of Dust: Essays on Holocaust Literature and Jewish Fate. Columbus, Ohio: Ohio State University Press, 1979. XX, 256 p. Bibliography. Index. A contribution to critical theory and a valuable discussion of I.B. Singer, Nelly Sachs, Jacob Glastein, Chaim Grade, and of Saul Bellow's Mr. Sammler's Planet. Alexander confronts the question of

the "incredibility of the Holocaust" but he seems not to
have advanced much beyond Hilberg in his assertion "that
the inability of the victims themselves to credit the
threat and then the actuality of destruction was a
function not only of human psychology and the mad
inventiveness of the Germans but of Jewish history and
Jewish sensibility." (Chap. 1).

Alter, Robert. "Confronting the Holocaust." In After
the Tradition. N.Y.: E.P. Dutton and Co., 1969. pp.
163-80.

Alter, Robert. Defenses of the Imagination: Jewish
Writers and Modern Historical Crisis. Phila.: JPS,
1978. 262 p. See, esp., "Uri Zvi Greenberg: A Poet of
the Holocaust." pp. 103-118. Also on Greenberg, see D.
Roskies (cited below), A. Mintz (cited below).

Alvarez, A. "The Literature of the Holocaust." Commentary (Nov. 1964). Rpt. in Beyond All This Fiddle. N.Y.:
Random House, 1968. pp. 22-33. Includes bibliographical
footnotes. Makes the highly abstract statement that
Holocaust literature is "our own under-literature," a
"paranoid vision" of the annihilation of lives and identities in mass culture.

Bentley, Eric. ed. The Storm over the Deputy. N.Y.:
Grove Press, 1965.

Best, Otto F. Peter Weiss. trans. from the German by
Ursule Molinaro. N.Y.: Frederick Ungar Pub. Co., 1976.

Betsky, Sarah Zweig. ed. and trans. Onions and Cucumbers and Plums: 46 Yiddish Poems in English. Detroit:

Wayne State University Press, 1958. 2nd printing with Preface and Introd. Detroit: Wayne State University Press, 1981. 259 p. Biographical Notes. An excellent valuable work that includes the poems in script, transliteration, and translation.

Bosmajian, Hamida. <u>Metaphors</u> <u>of</u> <u>Evil</u>: <u>Contemporary</u> <u>German</u> <u>Literature</u> <u>and</u> <u>the</u> <u>Shadow</u> <u>of</u> <u>Nazism</u>. Iowa City, Iowa: University of Iowa Press, 1979. 247 p. Contains an analysis of Hochhuth's "The Deputy," poems by P. Celan, N. Sachs; and autobiographical fiction by G. Grass, U. Johnson, etc.

Burnshaw, Stanley, Ted Carml, and Ezra Spicehandler. eds. <u>The</u> <u>Modern</u> <u>Hebrew</u> <u>Poem</u> <u>Itself</u>. N.Y.: Holt, Rinehart and Winston, 1965. See Parts 2 and 3. Discussed more fully in Part 5, chap. 3,e.

Cargas, Harry James. <u>Harry</u> <u>James</u> <u>Cargas</u> <u>in</u> <u>Conversation</u> <u>with</u> <u>Elie</u> <u>Wiesel</u>. N.Y.: Paulist/Newman Press, 1976. 126 p. The dialogue begins with Cargas' question: "Why are you not mad?" Wide range of topics touched upon. The conversation demonstrates that Wiesel's central conviction is that the Holocaust is the defining event of the epoch.

Cargas, Harry James. ed. <u>Responses</u> <u>to</u> <u>Elie</u> <u>Wiesel</u>: <u>Critical</u> <u>Essays</u> <u>by</u> <u>Major</u> <u>Jewish</u> <u>and</u> <u>Christian</u> <u>Scholars</u>. N.Y.: Persea books, 1978. In these dozen or so essays, Wiesel's work is examined from psychological, literary, and theological perspectives. Much repetition. Two of the best essays are: Byron L. Sherwin (Wiesel and the Kabbalah) and the analysis of style by Robert Alter.

Cargas, Harry James.   ed. When God and Man Failed: non-Jewish views of the Holocaust. N.Y.: Macmillan, 1981. 238 p. Poems, sermons, prayers and essays (uneven in quality) by members of the U.S. Holocaust Memorial Council. Recommended essays: John Pawlikowski, Robert Drinan, Bernard Lee.

Cernyak, Susan E. German Holocaust Literature. Ph.D. Dissert. 1973, University of Kansas. See: Language and Literature, Modern. P. 4248 in Vol. 34/07-A, Dissert. Abstracts International.

Des Pres, Terrence. The Survivor...(1976, cited above, part 5).

Eliach, Yaffa. ed. Hasidic Tales of Holocaust (1982, cited below, 3).

Ezradi, Sidra DeKoven. "Holocaust Literature in European Languages." In EJ Yearbook 1973. Jerusalem: Keter Pub.. House, 1973. pp. 104-119. An excellent overview. Biblio.: p. 119.

Ezradi, Sidra DeKoven.   By Words Alone: The Holocaust in Literature. Foreword by Alfred Kazan. Chicago: University of Chicago Press, 1980. 262 p. A major work; subtle and profound. Comprehensive in range, from the "documentary" to the "mythical." In agreement with A. Rosenfeld on basic points. Argues that even the most "palpable reconstruction of Holocaust reality is blunted by the fact that there is no analogue in human experience." (p. 3). But see the challenge to this position raised by D. Roskies (1984, cited below).

Friedlander, Albert H. ed. with Introd. Out of the
Whirlwind: A Reader of Holocaust Literature. Prologue
by Elie Wiesel. Cincinnati: HUC Press, N.Y.: Doubleday,
1968. 536 p. illus. Bibliographical references. 34
sections with Introductory notes; the carefully selected
materials include autobiography, biography, fiction,
history.

Glatstein, Jacob. comp. Anthology of Holocaust Literature. ed. by J. Glatstein, I. Knox, S. Margoshes;
associate eds. M. Bernstein, A.B. Fogel. Phila.: JPS,
1968. Includes Biblio.: p. 409-412, Glossary, Biographical notes. Much of the material is translated from
Yiddish. Avrom Zak has edited a Yiddish anthology of
Holocaust literature: Khurbm: antologye (Buenos Aires:
Musterverk fun der yidisher literatur, 1970).

Gros, Nathan, Itamar Yaoz-Kest, Rina Klinov. eds. and
Hasho'ah bashirah ha'ivrit. (The Holocaust in Hebrew
Poetry: An Anthology) Israel: Yad Vashem and Hakibbutz
Hameuchad, 1974.

Grunfeld, Grederick V. Prophets Without Honour...
(1979, cited in Part 5, chap. 3:e).

Haft, Cynthia. The Theme of Nazi Concentration Camps in
French Literature. (New Babylon: studies in the behav-
ioral sciences, 12). The Hague: Mouton, 1973. 227 p.
Discussed in Part 5, chap. 3:d.

Halperin, Irving. Messengers from the Dead: Literature
of the Holocaust. Phila.: Westminster Press, 1970. 144
p. A critical discussion of novels, diaries, and
eyewitness accounts. Halperin's title is taken from E.

Wiesel. Should be read with the works of E. Alexander, L. Langer, A. Rosenfeld, D. Roskies, A. Mintz.

Hamburger, Michael. From Prophecy to Exorcism; The Premises of Modern German Literature. London: Longmans, Green and Co., 1965. (Cited in Part 5, chap. 3,e).

Hoffman, Frederick. The Mortal No: Death and the Modern Imagination. Princeton, N.J.: Princeton University Press, 1964. 507 p. The second part of this complicated, abstract and voluminous study discusses 20th-century technological violence and impersonal annihilation.

Howe, Irving, and Eliezer Greenberg. eds. A Treasury of Yiddish Poetry. N.Y.: Holt, Rinehart and Winston, 1970. 378 p. Glossary. Index of poets. Index of titles. Unfortunately the originals are not included. (Cf. S. Betsky, above). Trans. of A. Reisen, M. Leib, M.L. Halpern, H. Levick, C. Grade, J. Glatstein, in chronological order.

Kohn, Murray J. The Voice Of My Blood Cries Out: The Holocaust as Reflected in Hebrew Poetry. N.Y.: Shengold, 1979. 224 p. Biblio: p. 219-224. No index. Includes valuable quotations but conceptually unrigorous and sometimes confused. "...the horrors of the Holocaust defy human ability to convey the tragic truth. It is beyond expression." (p. 206). But on p. 207 we read: "Since the poetry was highly individualistic and emotional, it spoke the truth in simple terms..."

Langer, Lawrence L. The Age of Atrocity: Death in Modern Literature. Boston: Beacon Press, 1978. 256 p.

Discusses Mann, Camus, Solzhenitsyn, but see especially
the original chapter on Charlotte Delbo.

Langer, Lawrence L.   The Holocaust and the Literary
Imagination. New Haven, CT.: Yale University Press,
1975. 300 p. Of major importance: raises the central
question of how literature can confront the Holocaust
without deadening its horror through the imposition of
esthetic form. Langer's level of comparative literary
analysis is high (although sometimes too abstract). Cf.
D. Roskies (1984, cited below) on the question of Holocaust as unique within Jewish experience. Langer's
study is reviewed by Arthur A. Cohen, N.Y. Times Bk.
Review (Jan. 18, 1976): 19.

Langer, Lawrence L. Versions of Survival... (1983, cited
above. Sec. E).

Leftwich, Joseph. ed. The Golden Peacock: A Worldwide
Treasury of Yiddish Poetry. 1939. updated Rpt. N.Y.:
Thomas Yoseloff, 1962. A valuable anthology, organized
by historical period.

Leftwich, Joseph.   comp. and trans. The Way We Think: A
Collection of Essays from the Yiddish. 2 vols. N.Y.:
Thomas Yoseloff, 1969. 841 p.

Mintz, Alan.   Hurban. Responses to Catastrophe in Hebrew
Literature. N.Y.: Columbia University Press, 1984. XIV,
283 pp. Very valuable, cf. D. Roskies (1984, cited
below). In Part 3, "Survivors and Bystanders," Mintz
analyzes the place of the Holocaust in Israeli literature and gives penetrating interpretations of Uri Z.
Greenberg and Aharon Appelfeld. Mintz argues against

isolating the Holocaust from Jewish historical memory. The Zionist rejection of the shtetl undercut the classical Jewish traditions of response to catastrophe. The spiritual and artistic resources of these traditions have not yet been explored. Mintz's analysis of Hebrew texts complements the study of Yiddish texts in Roskies (1984).

Mintz, Ruth Finer. ed. and trans. with an Introd. Modern Hebrew Poetry. Berkeley, Ca.: University of California Press, 1966. 371 p. Notes on the Poems, Notes on the Poets. Includes 115 poems. See Part lll, "The Modernists," and Part IV, "The Younger Poets."

Murdock, Brian. "Transformation of the Holocaust: Auschwitz in Modern Lyric Poetry." Comparative Literature Studies, II:6 (1974): 123-50.

Pawel, Ernst. "Fiction of the Holocaust." Midstream, 16:6 (June-July 1970): 14-26. A survey of novels and memoirs that uses the notion of the Holocaust as a prototypical event in Jewish history. (Cf. D. Roskies, 1984, cited below).

Rosenfeld, Alvin H., and Irving Greenberg. eds. Confronting the Holocaust: The Impact of Elie Wiesel. Bloomington,IN.: Indiana University Press, 1979. 239 p. Bibliography. The proceedings of a 1976 conference on "The Work of Elie Wiesel and the Holocaust Universe." 12 essays and an Introduction. Essays by J. Roth, B. Sherwin; R. Lamont discuss influences upon and aspects of Wiesel's works, and M. Berenbaum analyzes Wiesel's notion of the convenant between Israel and its memories of death and pain.

Rosenfeld, Alvin H.   A Double Dying; Reflections on
Holocaust Literature. Bloomington and London: Indiana
University Press, 1980. 210 p. Biblio.: p. 200-10.   A
sensitive, informed, honest and eloquent study.   The
title is taken from E. Wiesel's statement: "at
Auschwitz, not only man died but also the idea of man."
Rosenfeld attempts to grasp the problematics of Holocaust literature in theoretical terms, then he moves to
discussion of the literature within the major genres.
He attempts to "see Holocaust literature against the
history that has produced it" and tries to define the
kind of knowledge we acquire from Holocaust literature.
He insists that Auschwitz is not a metaphor for anything
and there are no metaphors for it.   Holocaust literature
involves a new order of consciousness, a shift in
imagination and in being.   Compare and contrast with D.
Roskies (1984, cited below).

Roskies, David G.   Against the Apocalypse. Responses to
Catastrophe in Modern Jewish Culture.   Cambridge:
Harvard University Press, 1984. 374 p.   Includes Notes,
Primary Sources Cited, Illus. Index.   A learned,
eloquent and subtle study; the argument locates the
Holocaust experience within the history of Jewish
suffering. Postwar Jewish writers used pre-Holocaust
archetypes, the destruction of the Temple, Martyrdom,
the pogrom.   "The Jewish people are at the point
of...allowing the Holocaust to become the crucible of
their culture.   I have set out to challenge this
apocalyptic tendency by arguing for the vitality of
traditions of Jewish response to catastrophe..."(p.9).

Steiner, George.   Language and Silence: Essays on
Language, Literature and the Inhuman.   N.Y.: Atheneum,

1967. 426 p. Argues that "the world of Auschwitz lies outside speech as it lies outside reason." (p. 123). This statement is true in the sense that the "well-tempered clavichords" of conventional language became mute in confronting the reality of l'univers concentrationnaire. However, many sensitive writers have expressed something of the universe through new idioms, imagery and style, e.g., use of dissonance and innuendo. Also some writers (e.g., A. Schwartz-Bart) have confronted the Holocaust by invoking the tradition of Jewish suffering and Martyrdom. (see, A. Mintz, above; and D. Roskies, above).

Szeintuch, Yechiel. Yiddish and Hebrew Literature under the Nazi Rule in Eastern Europe: Yitzhak Katzenelson's Last Bilingual Writings and the Ghetto Writings of A. Sutzkever and I. Spiegel. Hebrew. 2 vols. Dissert.: Hebrew University, 1978. Meticulous Research, cited by D. Roskies.

Wiesel, Elie. "The Holocaust as Literary Inspiration." In Dimensions of the Holocaust. Evanston, IL.: Northwestern University Press, 1977. Notes the emergence of a new genre--the literature of testimony--and argues that "Anyone who does not actively, constantly engage in remembering and in making others remember is an accomplice of the enemy."

Yuter, Alan J. The Holocaust in Hebrew Literature. From Genocide to Rebirth. N.Y.: Associated Faculty Press, 1983. 137 p. Notes. Selected Bibliography, no index. Short introductory-level summaries of works by modern Israeli writers; lacks critical thrust and density of scholarship.

2. Poetry and Plays

**Coal black milk of morning/we
drink it at noon and at daybreak/we
drink it at night.** *Todesfuge*, Paul
Celan.

The problem facing Holocaust writers, one-eyed seers, is
whether any artistic representation of Holocaust horror
will detract from that horror and contain the potential
"no matter how remote--to squeeze out pleasure."
(Adorno). Writers confronting the Holocaust experience
a double-bind: expression is necessary but expression
is impossible. They would agree with Nelly Sachs that
"This can be put on paper only/with one eye ripped out."
The objectives of the playwrights are to give homage to
the victims, to educate the audience, raise basic moral
questions, and to draw lessons from the horror. (R.
Skloot, 1982, 14 ff.) On the poetry of A. Kovner and D.
Pagis, see A. Mintz (1984, p. 259).

Poetry.

Borenstein, Emily. <u>Night of the Broken Glass</u>.
Mason, Texas: Timberland Press, 1981. Vivid and startling Holocaust poetry.

Celan, Paul. <u>Speech-Grille</u> <u>and</u> <u>Selected</u> <u>Poems</u>. trans.
by Joachim Neugroschel. N.Y.: E.P. Dutton & Co., 1971.
255 p. Celan, an anagram for Paul Ancel, was born in
legendary Czernowitz (Romania) in 1920; he survived the
ghetto, death camp, labor camp. But his body was found
in the Seine in 1970, an apparent suicide.

Celan, Paul. <u>Selected</u> <u>Poems</u>. trans. by Michael
Hamburger and Christopher Middleton, with an Introd. by
Michael Hamburger. Middlesex, England: Penguin Books,
1972. On Celan, see Jerry Glenn, <u>Paul</u> <u>Celan</u> (N.Y.:
Twayne, 1973); includes a selected bibliography. "The
essential element of his poems is this grappling with
the horrors of our age." (p. 155). <u>Todesfugue</u>, "Fuge of
Death," is "perhaps the most celebrated poem on the
subject of the Holocaust in Western Europe" (L. Langer,
1975, cited above, p. 9).

> "Black milk of daybreak we drink it
>   at nightfall...
> he whistles his Jews out and orders
>   a grave to be dug in the earth
> he writes when the night falls to
>   Germany
> your golden hair Margarete
> your ashen hair Shulamith we are
>   digging a grave in the sky
> it is ample to lie there
> he plays with the serpents and
>   dreams death comes as a master from
>   Germany...

Celan, Paul. <u>Poems,</u> <u>A</u> <u>Bilingual</u> <u>Edition</u>. sel. trans.
and Introduced by Michael Hamburger. N.Y.: Persea

Books, 1980. 307 p. Celan saw his poems as "a sort of homecoming." They were "messages in a bottle" and a "desperate dialogue," or "ways of a voice to a receptive you," and attempts to "keep yes and no unsplit." Written in a German that "could not and would not be the German of the destroyers," Celan's poetry expresses "the experience of being God-forsaken." Confronting the "dialectic of light and darkness," Celan's poetry, unlike that of Nelly Sachs, offered no final consolation or acceptance.

Feldman, Irving. The Pripet Marshes and Other Poems. N.Y.: Viking Press, 1965. 55 p. Feldman, an American poet, imagines himself and his family transplanted into the ghetto in the Pripet Marshes (Ukraine) the moment before the Germans arrive: "But there isn't a second to lose, I snatch them all back, for, when I want to, I can be a God. No, the Germans won't have one of them! This is my people, they are mine."

Gershon, Karen (Kate). Selected Poems. N.Y.: Harcourt, Brace and World, 1966. 64 p. Confessional poety of directness and simplicity by a German-born poet who was in the Children's Transport of 1938 that brought 10,000 Jewish children to England. (See (ed.) We Came As Children; A Collective Autobiography. N.Y.: Harcourt, 1966). Gershon attempts a poetic reconstruction of the last days of her parents, lives, when "I was not there to comfort them."

Glatstein, Jacob. Poems. trans. from the Yiddish by Etta Blum. Tel Aviv: I.L. Peretz Pub. House, 1970. Glatstein was born in Lubin in 1896, and came to America in 1914. He was "a master of the Yiddish language and

one of the most challenging poets of Jewish experience
in this century." (A. Rosenfeld, 1980, cited above. p.
119).

Glatstein, Jacob. The Selected Poems of Jacob Glatstein. trans. from the Yiddish with an Introd. by Ruth
Whitman. N.Y.: October House, 1972. 185 p. "We received the Torah on Sinai/and in Lublin we gave it back.
Dead men don't praise God, the Torah was given to the
living. And just as we all stood together/at the giving
of the Torah, so did we all die together at Lubin." The
image of God in this and other poems suggests that
Glatstein sees a radical displacement and diminishment
of Deity as a result of the Holocaust. "I love my sad
god, my brother refugee..." And in another moving poem
he writes: "Without Jews there is no Jewish God. If we
leave this world, The light will go out in your tent."

Greenberg, Uri Zvi. "To God in Europe, II," trans. from
the Hebrew by Robert Friend, in S.Y. Penueli and A.
Ukhamani, eds. Anthology of Modern Hebrew Poetry. Vol. 2
(Jerusalem: Institute for the Translation of Hebrew
literature and Israel Universities Press, 1966). Greenberg (b. 1896) was a Dionysian poet of revolt and "the
preeminent apocalyptist of his age." (Roskies, 1984,
cited above, p. 266 and see pp. 266-274). The Holocaust
experience made him a neoclassical poet of national
lament and consolation. "Go wander about Europe, God of
Israel, and count Your sheep: how many lie in ditches,
their 'Alas' grown dumb: how many in the cross's shadow,
in the streets of weeping, as if in the middle of the
sea." idem., "To God in Europe, III: No Other Instan-
ces," idem., Vol. 2. Greenberg's Rehovet hanahar
(Streets of the River), "a massive work of national

lament," was published in 1951 (D. roskies) 2nd ed. Jerusalem & Tel Aviv: Schocken. 1954. For analysis of "Streets of the River," see Robert Alter, "Uri Zvi Greenberg: A Poet of the Holocaust," in Defenses of the Imagination: Jewish Writers and Modern Historical Crisis. (Phila.: JPS, 1977), pp. 103-118.

Hecht, Anthony. The Hard Hours; Poems. N.Y.: Atheneum, 1967. 103 p. In "'More Light More Light'" (for Heinrich Blucher and Hannah Arendt) Hecht compares a burning at the stake, a horrible death but within a framework of meaning, to the murder of 2 Jews and a Pole by a Nazi "outside a German wood." And "Not light from the Shrine at Weimar beyond the hill/Nor light from Heaven appeared." (pp. 64-65).

Heyen, William. The Swastika Poems. N.Y.: Vanguard Press, 1977. 82 p.

Hill, Geoffrey. Somewhere Is Such a Kingdom; Poems 1952-1971. Introd. by Harold Bloom. Boston: Houghton Mifflin Co., 1975. XXV, 130 p.

Katzenelson, Yitzhak. The Song of the Murdered Jewish People. trans. from the Yiddish and annot. by Noah H. Rosenbloom, with an essay, "The Threnodist and the Threnody of the Holocaust." pp. 119-133. Bilingual facsimile ed., rev. by Y. Tobin. Hakibutz Hameuchad, Ghetto Fighters House, 1980. 133 p. A searing lament: "False and cheating heavens...You cheated us--eternally." Written in Vittel, an Auschwitz transit camp.

Klein, A.M. Collected Poems. comp. by Miriam Waddington. Toronto: McGraw Hill, Ryerson Press: N..Y.:

McGraw Hill, 1974. 373 p. The poetry of a gifted Montreal Jewish poet who used neoclassical forms; see "The Hitleriad" (1944), and "The Psalter of Avram Haktani." (1944), pp. 186-234.

Kolmar, Gertrud. Dark Soliloquy: The Selected Poems of Gertrud Kolmar. trans. from the German by Henry A. Smith. N.Y.: Seabury Press, 1975. Foreword by Cynthia Ozick. Also, Das Lyrische Werk (München, 1960), Briefe an die Schwester Hilde: 1938-1943 (München, 1970). Kolmar was deported to Auschwitz from Berlin in Feb. 1943 and never heard from again. According to Langer (1982, cited above) she had little premonition of her own fate and had built inner defenses against outer reality.

Kovner, Abba. Selected Poems of Abba Kovner and Nelly Sachs. trans. from the Hebrew and from the German by Shirley Kaufman and Nurit Orchan. Middlesex, Eng.: Penquin Books, 1971. For an analysis of his major epic poem "Hamafte'ah tsalal" (The Key Sank, 1950, 1965) see A. Mintz (1984, cited above, pp. 260-263. "..the complete Zionist poem on the Holocaust..." (p. 262).

Kovner, Abba. A Canopy in the Desert. trans. from the Hebrew by Shirley Kaufman, with Ruth Adler and Nurit Orchan. Pittsburgh: University of Pittsburg Press, 1973. Kovner, born in the Crimea in 1918, organized the revolt in the Vilna ghetto and issued the first call for resistance (Jan. 1, 1942), escaping the city he fought as a partisan in the forests.

Kovner, Abba. ed. Scrolls of Fire: A Nation Fighting for its Life. trans. by Shirley Kaufman, with Dan Laor.

Paintings by Dan Reisinger. Bilingual ed. Jerusalem: Keter, 1981. A richly illustrated book with a liturgical framework, "a rallying cry for collective survival in the name of past martyrdoms." (Roskies, 1984, cited above, p. 14). He has special authority within Hebrew letters as being "both a survivor and a Palmah [Israeli War of Independence] fighter, all the more so because his identity as a survivor was that of a fighter as well." A. Mintz (1984, cited above, p. 260).

Levi, Primo. Shema: Collected Poems of Primo Levi. trans. from the Italian by Ruth Feldman and Brian Swann. London: Menard Press, 1976. By an Italian Jewish chemist who survived Auschwitz (see Part 5, above).

Meyers, Bert. The Dark Birds. N.Y.: Doubleday & Co., 1968. 68 p. Lucid, vivid and sparse poetry that juxtaposes realism and fantasy. Images of death, displacement and helplessness permeate the poems and shape the images of the "ordinary." The children "smile/Their teeth are the stones in the graveyard at noon." "'They who Waste Me': When I ask for a hand, they give me a shovel...I sigh, whoever breathes has inhaled a neighbour."

Milosz, Czeslaw. Selected Poems. N.Y.: Seabury Press, 1973. By a Polish intellectual and powerful poet.

Pagis, Dan. Selected Poems. trans. from the Hebrew by Stephen Mitchell. Oxford: Carcanet Press, 1972. Pagis was born in Bukovina in 1930; he escaped from a Ukrainian concentration camp in 1944 and made his way to Jerusalem where he is now a professor.

Pagis, Dan. Points of Departure. trans. from the Hebrew by Stephen Mitchell. Introd. by Robert Alter. Bilingual ed. Phila.: JPS, 1981. Ponder the intense: "Written in Pencil in the Sealed Railway Car," (Katuv be'iparon bakaron hehatum). "here in this carload/i am eve/ with abel my son/ if you see my other son/ cain son of man/ tell him that i." And ponder "Testimony," and "Instructions For Crossing The Border." "Pagis' image of the survivor as an invented man, torn between contradictory instructions to forget and to remember, is one of the strongest moments in Hebrew literature." A. Mintz (1984, cited above, p. 268. see p. 263ff.)

Pilinszky, Janos. Selected Poems. trans. by Ted Hughes and Janos Csokits. N.Y.: Persea Books, 1976. 67 p. Pilinszky was born in Budapest in 1921; see the short, vivid "Passion of Ravensbruck."

Plath, Sylvia. Ariel. N.Y.: Harper & Row, 1965. 86 p. Vivid and powerfully painful poems that often draw on Holocaust materials, e.g., in "Daddy." A. Rosenfeld (1980, cited above, p. 181) finds Plath guilty of "imaginative misappropriation of atrocity." Her famous novel is The Bell Jar (London, Faber: 1965, 258 p.)

Radnoti, Miklos. Clouded Sky. trans. from the Hungarian by Steven Polgar, Stephen Berg, and S.J. Marks. N.Y.: Harper & Row, 1972. 113 p.

Rezinkoff, Charles. Holocaust. By the Well of Living and Seeing; New and Selected Poems. ed. with an Introd. by Seamus Cooney. L.A.: Black Sparrow Press, 1974. 173 p. A documentary poem, based on the Nuremberg trials and the Eichmann trial.

Rozewicz, Tadeusz. <u>Selected</u> <u>Poems</u>. trans. from the
Polish with an Introd. by Adam Czerniawski. London:
Penguin Books, 1976. 140 p. Born in 1921, Rozewicz's
earlier verse is dominated by the horror of the Nazi
period.

Rozewicz, Tadeusz. <u>The</u> <u>Survivor,</u> <u>and</u> <u>Other</u> <u>Poems</u>.
trans. with an Introd. by Magnus J. Krynski and Robert
A. Maguire. (Lockert lib. of poetry in Tr.) Princeton,
N.J.: Princeton University Press, 1977. 160 p.

> "I am twenty-four
> led to slaughter
> I survived.
> These labels are empty and synonymous:
> man and beast
> love and hate
> friend and foe
> light and dark."

Sachs, Nelly. <u>O</u> <u>the</u> <u>Chimneys;</u> <u>Selected</u> <u>Poems,</u> <u>incl.</u> <u>the</u>
<u>verse</u> <u>play,</u> <u>Eli</u>. trans. from the German by Michael
Hamburger, Christopher Home, Ruth and Matthew Mead, and
Michael Roloff. N.Y.: Farrar, Straus and Giroux, 1967.
XXI, 387 p.

> "Arms up and down,
> Legs up and down
> And on the ash-gray receding horizon of
>   fear
> Gigantic the constellation of death
> That loomed like the clock face of ages."
> ("What Secret Cravings of the Blood")

See Stephen Spender, "Catastrophe and Redemption: 'O the
Chimney.' by Nelly Sachs," New York Times <u>Sunday</u> <u>Book</u>
<u>Review</u> <u>Section</u>, 8 (October, 1967): 5, 34. "One terrible

aspect of our century is that fantasies horrible as the worst nightmares of writers like Baudelaire and Dostoevsky in the previous century have become literally true...to experience in its intensity the horrors of our time almost inevitably means being maimed or destroyed by it."

Sachs, Nelly. The Seeker, and Other Poems. trans. from the German by Ruth and Matthew Mead and Michael Hamburger. N.Y.: Farrar, Straus and Giroux, 1970. 398 p. Sachs (1891-1970) won the Nobel Prize in 1966. She was influenced by medieval mysticism and German Romanticism, but her postwar poetry is centered on the Holocaust and she speaks "for the consumed world of the victim: she mourns the loss, less in judgment than commemoration." (Langer, 1982, cited above, p. 219, passim). Ultimately, but in no easy way, she thinks Jewish suffering is absorbed into the Divine Unity: their "dying discourse/is woe-filled winds

> and
>
> like a glassblower, fashion
> a vanished form of love
> for the moth of God."

Sklarew, Myra. From the Backyard of the Diaspora. Washington, D.C.: Dryad Press, 1976.

Snodgrass, William DeWitt. The Fuhrer Bunker. Brockport, N.Y.: BOA Editions, 1977.

Sutzkever, Abraham. Burnt Pearls: Ghetto Poems. trans. from the Yiddish by Seymour Mayne. Introd. by Ruth R. Wisse. Oakville, Ontario: Mosaic Press--Valley Editions, 1981.

"And no one--even I--scraped dead by days
Can still recognize the woman washed in
    flame
For whom, of all her joys
Burnt pearls in ashes is the sum of what
    remains."

Sutzkever (b. 1913) survived the destruction of Vilna
Jewry in 1941 and his poetry "captured the collective
tragedy in epic form." He sought "continuities and
correspondences that would bridge the living and the
dead." (D. Roskies, 1984, cited above, p. 227, 250).
Sutzkever's retrospective collection of Holocaust poetry
is entitled Lider fun yam-hamoves (Poems of the Dead
Sea: From the Vilna Ghetto, Forests, and Wanderings).
N.Y. and Tel Aviv: Bergen-Belsen Memorial Press, 1968.

Sutzkever, Abraham. "Green Aquarium" (1953-1954),
trans. from the Yiddish with an Introd. by Ruth R.
Wisse. Prooftexts, 2:1 (1982): 95-121.

Taube, Herman. A Chain of Images; Poetic Notes. N.Y.:
Shulsinger Brothers, 1979. 180 p. illus.

Wiesel, Elie. Ani Maamin: A Song Lost and Found Again;
Music for the Cantata Composed by Darius Milhaud.
trans. from the French by Marion Wiesel. N.Y.: Random
House, 1973. 107 p. The music was first performed at
Carnegie Hall in Nov. 1973. This is a poetic retelling
of a Talmudic story about the silence of God. Ani
maamin beviat ha-Mashiah (I believe in the coming of the
Messiah) is one of the Thirteen Articles of Faith of
Maimonides.

Yevtushenko, Yevgeni. "Babiy Yar," In Selected Poems. trans. with an Introd. by Robin Milner-Gullard and Peter Levi, S.J. N.Y.: E.P Dutton, 1962. 92 p. pp. 82-84. "Over Babiy Yar/there are no memorials."

Zeitlin, Aaron. "I Believe." In A Treasury of Yiddish Poetry. ed. by Irving Howe and E. Greenberg (cited above, f). "Who is so volcanic as my God?/If he is Sinai to me,/He is Maidanek as well." (pp. 321-323.) On Zeitlin and on his poem "Monologue in Plain Yiddish" see D. Roskies, 1984, cited above, pp. 190-191. "For Zeitlin, traumatized by his losses, America is the last burial ground for Yiddish and speech is an act of grotesque memorial." p. 191. "Monolog in pleynem yiddish" (Monologue in Plain Yiddish), 1945, in Lider fun khurbm un lider fun gloybn (Poems of the Holocaust and Poems of Faith), Vol. I (of II) N.Y.: Bergen Belsen Memorial Press, 1967. pp. 98-104.

Plays

Abramson, Glenda. Modern Hebrew Drama. N.Y.: St. Martin's Press, 1979. See Part III, chap. 2: "The Plays of the Holocaust." Discusses Leah Goldberg, Ben-Zion Tomer, Moshe Shamir and others.

Amichai, Yehuda. Bells and Trains. In Midstream (October 1966): 55-66.

Amir, Anda. This Kind Too. trans. by Shoshanna Perla. N.Y.: World Zionist Organization, 1972.

Bentley, Eric R. ed. The Storm Over The Deputy. N.Y.: Grove Press, 1964. 254 p. Includes Bibliography. Bentley writes that the Deputy created "the largest storm ever...in the whole history of the drama." This useful collection of essays contains an interview with R. Hochhuth.

Borchert, Wolfgang. The Outsider. In Postwar German Theatre; An Anthology of Plays. trans. and ed. by Michael Benedikt and George E. Wellwarth. N.Y.: E.P. Dutton, 1967. XXVI, 348 p. pp. 52-113.

Delbo, Charlotte. Who Will Carry the Word? trans. from the French (1974) by Cynthia Haft. In The Theatre of the Holocaust. ed. and with an Introd. by Robert Skloot. Madison: The University of Wisconsin Press, 1982. pp. 273-325. Delbo (b. 1913) was arrested because of her participation in the French resistance. Her play reflects her experience in Auschwitz and "offers one of the most lucid images we have of what it means to be a "survivor" in an age of atrocity." (Langer, 1978, p. 207).

Eliach, Yaffe and Uri Assaf. The Last Jew. trans. from the Hebrew by Yaffe Eliach. Israel: Alef-Alef Theatre Publications, 1977.

Frisch, Max. Andorra; a play in 12 scenes. trans. from the German by Michael Bullock. N.Y.: Hill and Wang, 1964. 88 p. (pa.).

Goldberg, Leah. The Lady of the Castle. trans. from the Hebrew by Ted Carmi. Tel Aviv: Institute for the trans. of Hebrew Literature, 1974. Also discussed in

522

Modern Hebrew Drama by Glenda Abramson (1979, Part III, chap. 2. cited above).

Goodrich, Frances and Albert Hackett. *The Diary of Anne Frank*. N.Y.: Random House, 1956. 174 p. (Based upon the book, *Anne Frank: The Diary of a Young Girl*, 1956). First performed in 1955, the play, in a concession to the amnesia *Zeitgeist* of the 1950's, weakens the particularity of Jewish history and Jewish suffering as manifest in the *Diary*.

Hochhuth, Rolf. *The Deputy*. trans. from the German by Richard and Clara Winston. Preface by Albert Schweitzer. N.Y.: Grove Press, 1964, 352 p. Hochhuth, born in 1931, is a German Protestant who published *Der Stellvert Reten* in 1963. It is a tract--in dramatic form and resting upon solid historical study--whose purpose was to involve people in the dreadful fate of the Jews. It contains learned, eloquent and anguished reflections upon the silence of Pius XII during the Holocaust, and on the fact and the implications of the radical evil manifest in the Holocaust (e.g., the Doctor, modeled in part on the infamous Dr. Mengele). The two other central characters are Kurt Gerstein and the idealist-martyr Riccardo Fontana, based in part upon Provost Bernhard Lichtenberg of Berlin's St. Hedwig's Cathedral, who publicly sided with the Jews. Pub. in England under the title: *The Representative* (London: Methuen, 1963). The acting edition of *The Deputy* was produced by Jerome Rothenberg.

Kaiser, George. *The Raft of the Medusa*. In *Post War German Drama* (cited above). This allegory about Nazi-

Jewish relationships develops the image of corrupted childhood. (Cf. J. Kosinski).

Lampell, Millard. The Wall; A Play in 2 Acts; based on the Novel by John Hersey. 1961. 159 p.

Megged, Aharon. The Burning Bush. trans. by Shoshana Perla. N.Y.: World Zionist Organization, 1972.

Miller, Arthur. Incident at Vichy; A Play. N.Y.: Viking Press, 1965. 70 p.

Sachs, Nelly. Eli: A Mystery Play of the Sufferings of Israel. trans. by Christopher Holme. In O the Chimneys. N.Y.: Farrar, Straus and Giroux, 1967. pp. 309-85. "The new Pentateuch, I tell you, the new Pentateuch, is written with the mildew of fear/on the walls of the deathcellars!"

Sartre, Jean Paul. The Flies, A Play in 3 Acts. trans. from the French (Les mouches, 1944) by Stuart Gilbert. Printed with No Exit. A Play in One Act (Huis clos), 166 p. The Flies, the first work in which Sartre expounds his ethics of freedom, was also a powerful condemnation of the Vichy regime and a celebration of the Resistance. In murdering Aegisthus (the German invader) and overthrowing Jupiter, Orestes dramatizes the power of freedom against tyranny.

3. Novels and Stories. (For Hebrew works by Amichai, Bartov, Gouri, Kanink, see Part III of A. Mintz's Hurban (1984, cited above)).

> Most people in our time have the
> face of Lot's wife, turned toward
> the Holocaust and yet always
> escaping. *Y. Amichai*

Aichinger, Ilse. Herod's Children. a trans. of Die
Grossere Hoffnung (1948) by Cornelia Schaeffer. N.Y.:
Atheneum, 1963. 238 p. On the innocence of children
entering alone into Terror. The novel begins with a
dream. Ellen, a little girl with an 'Aryan' father and
a Jewish mother, dreams of a ship carrying children
"with the wrong grandparents, children without a pass-
port or visa, children for whom nobody could vouch,
now." Aichinger collapses the distinction between the
living and the dead. Children play "hide-and-seek"
among the gravestones: "The dead will play with us,
testify for us...vouch for us. Swear that we're alive
and that we are like all the others." (p. 45).

Amichai, Yehuda. Not of This Time, Not of This Place
trans. from the Hebrew (Lo' me 'Akhshav, lo' mika'n,
1963) by Shlomo Katz. N.Y.: Harper & Row, 1968. 344 p.
The first major Israeli novel directly to confront the
Holocaust. Amichai's confessional and poetic novel
depicts physical and spiritual escape from and encounter
with the horror of the Holocaust. The protagonist is
torn between love (Jerusalem) and death (Weinberg,
Germany). His attempts to find vindication and redress
and to absorb the Holocaust experience are futile.

Appelfeld, Aharon. Badenhaim 1939 (Boston: Godine,
1980). And The Age of Wonders (Boston: Godine, 1981).
Two novellas. On Appelfeld, see chap. 6 of Hurban by
Alan Mintz (cited above, pp. 203-238). Influenced by

Kafka's modernism, Appelfeld's stories create "the aura of a credible fictional world." (p. 205). Born in 1932 in Chernowitz, Appelfeld was an orphan survivor and "For Appelfeld as Survivor, the Holocaust was the founding event of the self." (p. 204). But his Hebrew lacks "Judaic allusion," is detraditionalized and this "greatest writer of the Holocaust in Hebrew... stands apart from Hebrew literary history." (p. 238).

Bassani, Giorgio. The Garden of the Finzi-Continis. trans. from the Italian by Isabel Quigly. N.Y.: Atheneum, 1965. 293 p. A sensitive novel on the fate of assimilated Italian Jews. An excellent film has been made from this novel.

Bassani, Giorgio. The Smell of Hay. trans. by William Weaver. (Helen and Kurt Wolff bk.). N.Y.: Harcourt Brace Jovanovitch, 1975. 193 p. Ten stories and a novella concerning Jewish lives in Ferrara under the Fascist regime.

Bassani, Giorgio. "A Plague on Via Mazzinio." In Five Stories of Ferrara. trans. by William Weaver. N.Y.: Harcourt Brace Jovanovich, 1971.

Becker, Jurek. Jacob the Liar. trans. from the German and with a Preface by Melvin Kornfeld. (Helen and Kurt Wolff bk.). N.Y.: Harcourt Brace Jovanovich, 1975. Becker, an East-German novelist, "blurs the distinction between truth and implausibility by depicting a world of the Big Lie intent on murder, a world in which lying can also become the supreme act of resistance." (D. Roskies, 1984, cited above, p. 191).

Bellow, Saul. Mr. Sammler's Planet. N.Y.: Viking Press, 1970. With few exceptions, American fiction confronted the Holocaust directly only in the 1960's. Bellow's first novel, The Dangling Man (1944) was largely insulated from the atrocity happening in Europe. It is not until Mr. Sammler's Planet "that there appears in Bellow's fiction a Jew who has lived through and absorbed the major cataclysms of Jewish history in the twentieth century." (Ezrahi, 1980, cited above, p. 177; see also E. Alexander, "Imagining the Holocaust..." Judaism (Summer 1973): 288-300). Bellow intends Sammler as a prototype of the Holocaust writer: maimed by the experience but also made wise, a one-eyed seer. Mr. Sammler, "sorry for all, and sore at heart," was a survivor (pp. 126-130, 150) who sees that the modern "liberation into individuality has not been a great success." (p. 208) It is a failure because its forms repudiate models. "But individualism is of no interest whatever if it does not extend truth." The human spirit "knows what it knows, and the knowledge cannot be gotten rid of. The spirit knows that its growth is the real aim of existence." (pp. 214, 215, citations from the Fawcett pb. ed. 1971, 286 p.).

Ben-Amos, Dan. To Remember, To Forget. trans. from the Hebrew by Eva Shapiro. Phila.: JPS, 1968.

Berger, Zdena. Tell Me Another Morning. N.Y.: Harper & Row, 1961. 242 p. A first person narrative of the Holocaust and return, told with tenderness and tolerance toward the self. "The only thing that remains is the I in me...Hang on to it as the last wall." (p. 78).

Boll, Heinrich. Billiards at Half Past Nine. trans. from the German (Billard um Halbzehn; roman. DTV, 1959, 1970) by Patrick Bowles. N.Y.: McGraw Hill, 1962. 280 p. See also: Adam; and The Train. trans. by Leila Vennewitz. N.Y.: McGraw Hill, 1970. 268 p. Full titles: And where were you, Adam?; The train was on time. Also read: The Clown (1963) and Group Picture with Lady. trans. by Leila Vennewitz. N.Y.: McGraw Hill, 1973. Boll's (1911-1985) fiction depicts the absurdity and horror of war and fascism. He received the Nobel Prize for Literature in 1972. "The Nazi period could have happened only in Germany," he said, "because the German education of obedience to any law and order was the main problem" (N.Y. Times, July 17, 1985, p. 13). A collection of his short stories (generally not his best writing) has now been published: The Stories of Heinrich Boll, trans. by L. Vennewitz (Knopf, 1986, 688 p.) Includes five novellas. The images are predominately negative, sorrowful, bleak: "All streets lead to stations, and from stations you go off to war."

Bor, Josef. The Terezin Requiem. trans. from the Czech by Edith Pargeter. London: Heineman, N.Y.: Knopf 1963. 112 p. Bor, a lawyer in prewar Czechoslovakia, was sent to Terezin in 1942. This work is a chilling and vivid account of the performance of Verdi's "Requiem" (a "documentary" novel) by a company of prisoners who used the music as a cry of protest. "Libera me! slashed Maruska's passionate cry. Libera nos! thundered the gigantic choir for the last time." (These last bars were changed to a fortissimo).

Borchert, Wolfgang. "In May, in May cried the Cuckoo." In The Man Outside. trans. from the German by David

Porter. London: Calder and Boyars, 1966. "Let the cuckoo cry of your lonely hearts be silent... and no dictionary and no press has syllables or signs for your wordless world-rage, for your exquisite pain, for the agony of your love...Since for the grandiose roar of this world and for its hellish stillness the paltriest words are lacking. All we can do is: to add up, collect the sum, count it, note it down."

Borges, Jorge Luis. "Deutsches Requiem" and "The Secret Miracle." In Labyrinths, Selected Stories and Other Writings. ed. by Donald A. Yates and James E. Irby. N.Y.: New Directions, 1964. By the master and dean of imaginative Latin American literature.

Borowski, Tadeusz. This Way for the Gas, Ladies and Gentleman, and Other Stories. select. and trans. from the Polish by Barbara Vedder. N.Y.: Viking Press, 1967. 159 p. (1948). Borowski was imprisoned in Auschwitz and Dachau from 1943 to 1945. He committed suicide in 1951. His stories are realistic, non-moralistic; stark in simplicity and terrible in nihilistic black humour which is fully effective in displaying the "concentration-camp mentality." "So, you're still alive, Abbie? And what's new with you?" 'Not much. Just gassed up a Czech transport.'" That I know. I mean personally?" "Auschwitz," Our Home (A Letter). Borowski refuses to alter brutal reality by appeal to moralism or aesthetic form.

Bryks, Rachmil. A Cat in the Ghetto; 4 Novelettes. trans. from the Yiddish by S. Morris Engel. Introd. by Sol. Liptzin; Preface by Irving Howe. N.Y.: Bloch, 1959. 160 p. Depicts the life and death struggle in the Todz ghetto. Note the defiance: "No, he (the Nazis) will not turn us into mad dogs! On the outside we look like corpses, but inside we have preserved the image of God."

Bryks, Rachmil. Kiddush Hashem. trans. from the Yiddish by S. Morris Engel. (Jewish legacy bk.) N.Y.: Behrman House, 1977. 113 p. (pa.)

Buczkowski, Leopold. Black Torrent. trans. by David Welsh. Cambridge, Mass.: MIT Press, 1969. 200 p.

Camus, Albert. The Plague. trans. by Stuart Gilbert. N.Y.: Random House, 1948. On one level, Camus is inter- preting survival under the German occupation and making the recommendation that "The only means of fighting a plague is-- common decency."

Cohen, Arthur A. In the Days of Simon Stern. N.Y.: Random House, 1973. 464 p. This "philosophically provo- cative novel by a contemporary American-Jewish thinker, is an apocalyptic legend of the founding of a secret "Society for the Rescue and Resurrection of Jews." (Ezrahi, 1980, cited above, p. 212). An ambitious theological novel: "The Messiah is at last uptown." Also read Cohen's An Admirable Woman (Boston: David R. Godine, 1983, 228 p.), a tight and impressive novel in memoir form but the excursus on Hannah Arendt (pp. 195- 199) is obtrusive and incorrect, i.e., she did not regard "Eichmann's evil as banal." (p. 199). However, in a general sense Arendt is the basis or source for the "admirable woman" image. Cited also in chap. 3, e.

Del Castillo, Michel. Child of our Time. trans. from the French by Peter Green. N.Y.: Knopf, 1958, 281 p.

The Holocaust seen through the perception of the child: a vivid example of "the literature of the displaced."

Eliach, Yaffe. ed. with Foreword. Hasidic Tales of the Holocaust. Hovering Above the Pit. N.Y.: Oxford University Press, 1982. 266 p. Notes. Glossary. Index. 89 stories told to Eliach, or to her students, by "ultra-Orthodox" Hasidic Jews who confronted death with rare courage, hope and even degrees of humour. Yaffa regards the Hasidic tale as a literary form that could confront the Holocaust horror. The tale itself was a form of resistance, a tool for survival. Some of the tales can be cited, e.g., "Good Morning, Herr Muller" (Part 3), as supporting the argument that Jewish suffering and response during the Holocaust had pre-Holocaust historical and literary links (e.g., A. Swartz-Bart, D. Roskies) and post-Holocaust hopes (e.g., V. Frankl, B. Bettelheim). But the connecting threads seem very thin in the face of the sheer magnitude and depths of the terror and sadism (e.g., see the notes on the Janowska camp, etc.).

Epstein, Leslie. King of the Jews. N.Y.: Coward, McCann & Geoghegan, 1979. 350 p. Modeled on Rumkowski, the leader of the Todz Ghetto Judenrat; exhibits "The tendency to treat the Holocaust as entertainment..." (A. Rosenfeld (1980, cited above, p. 170ff)).

Fuks, Ladislav. Mr. Theodore Mundstock. trans. from the Czech by Iris Urwin. N.Y.: Orion Press, 1968. 214 p. This Czech survivor novel is an "exercise in the imagination of survival." "There are thoughts that crush. There is desperation heavy as the blocks piled up into the pyramids of Egypt." (p. 17).

Gary, Romain. The Dance of Genghis Cohn. trans. from the French (1968) by the author with the assistance of Camilla Sykes. N.Y.: World Pub. Co., 1968. 244 p. Gary, like Jakov Lind, rejects the paradigms of tragedy and black humour for that of madness. "Culture is when mothers who are holding their babies in their arms are excused from digging their own graves before being shot." The Dance of Genghis Cohn is about a Jewish Berlin night club comic who, murdered by a Nazi, becomes a dybbuk.

Gascar, Pierre. (pseud. Pierre Fournier). "The Season of the Dead." In Beasts and Men; and The Seed. trans. from the French by Jean Steward and Merloyd Lawrence. N.Y.: Meridian Books, 1960. 374 p. Gascar's images evoke death as disfigurement--"every death invents death anew" and the "anarchy of death" that usurps the natural cycle.

Goes, Albrecht. Unquiet Night (1950), The Burnt Offering (1954), The Boychik (1965). In Men of Dialogue: Martin Buber and Albrecht Goes. ed. by E. William Rollins and Harry Zohn. Preface by Maurice Friedman. N.Y.: Funk & Wagnalls, 1969. See discussion of Goes and of these three novellas in Preface and Introd. by Rollins and Zohn. Goes: "The destruction of our language was being successfully carried out according to plan. Such a plan did exist. Men deprived of their language become as corpses, and corpses never disobey." (Unquiet Night). Goes, a chaplain in the German Army, was deeply influenced by Buber.

Gouri, Haim. The Chocolate Deal. trans. from the Hebrew by Seymour Simckes. N.Y.: Holt, Rinehart and

Winston, 1968. 141 p. According to A. Mintz (1984, cited above, p. 277, n.8) this is the best example of "Holocaust fiction as a displaced literary idiom, separate from previous national literary histories." This first novel by an Israeli poet and journalist (he covered the Eichmann trial) is a parable on the moral ambiguities of survival.

Gouri, Haim. The Seven Little Lanes. trans. from the Yiddish by Curt Leviant. N.Y.: Bergen-Belsen Memorial Press, 1972. 111 p.

Grade, Chaim. "My Quarrel with Hersh Rasseyner." (from the collection Mother's Sabbath). In A Treasury of Yiddish Stories. ed. by Irving Howe and Eliezer Greenberg. N.Y.: Viking Press, 1954. Two former Yeshiva classmates meet as refugees in Paris after the war. Their impassioned discussion is not on their own loss and pain but on questions of theodicy and human conduct.

Grass, Gunter. Dog Years. trans. from the German by Ralph Manheim. N.Y.: Harcourt, Brace & World, 1965. 570 p. Grass's line, "I've been unable to capture the this-is-how-it-was, the substantial reality that throws a shadow," is an effective expression of the incommunicability of the Holocaust. Skillful in anti-Nazi satire, Grass's surrealistic style depicts the Holocaust more adequately than realistic fiction.

Grass, Gunter. The Tin Drum. Baltimore: Penguin Books, N.Y. and Toronto: Random House, London: Secker & Warburg. 1963. 591 p. A trans. of Die Blechtrommel (1959) by Ralph Manheim, it is a brilliant allegorical interpretation of World War II Germany. (Made into a

powerful film). Also read "What Shall We Tell Our
Children?" (1979), in On Writing and Politics 1969-1983,
by G. Grass, trans. by Ralph Manheim, Introd. by Salmon
Rushdie. (N.Y.: Harcourt Brace Jovanovich, 1985), pp.
75-90. "Basically, Auschwitz was not a manifestation of
common human bestiality; it was a repeatable consequence
of a network of responsibilities so organized and so
sub-divided that the individual was conscious of no
responsibility at all." "Since Auschwitz, Christian
institutions (in Germany, at least) have forfeited their
claim to ethical leadership." "What shall we tell our
children? Take a good look at the hypocrites. Distrust
their gentle smiles. Fear their blessing." (pp. 88-90).

Green, Gerald. Holocaust. N.Y.: Bantam Books, 1978.
408 p.

Grynberg, Henryk. Child of the Shadows; incl. The
Grave. trans. by Celina Wieniewska. London: Vallentine,
Mitchell, 1969. 127 p.

Hersey, John. The Wall. N.Y.: Alfred A. Knopf, 1950.
O. 632 p. On the Warsaw ghetto uprising. This fiction
that pretends to be based on fact, an eyewitness account
of the events as recorded in the "Levinson Archive," is
misleading in its basic image. Ringelbaum, the model
for Hersey's protagonist, was not a recluse, outsider,
and loner.

Hilsenrath, Edgar. Night. trans. from the German by
Michael Roloff. London: W.H. Allen, 1967. 515 p.
Hilsenrath, a German-Jewish novelist, "explores the
stark, pitiless landscape of death, and eliminates
access to the outside world and hope for the future

534

through a constriction in the language and frame of reference." (Ezrahi, 1980, cited above, p. 60). Cf. Borowski.

Hilsenrath, Edgar. The Nazi and the Barber. trans. from the German by Andrew White. N.Y.: Doubleday & Co., 1971. 383 p. Rpt. under the title: The Nazi and the Jew. N.Y.: Manor Books, 1977.

Jabes, Edmond. The Book of Questions. trans. from the French by Rosmarie Waldrop. Middletown, Conn.: Wesleyan University Press, 1976. 175 p.

Jabes, Edmond. The Book of Yuke (and) Return to the Book. (This is The Book of Questions, 2 & 3), trans. from the French by Rosmarie Waldrop. Middletown, Conn.: Wesleyan University Press, 1977. 236 p.

Kanfer, Stefan. The Eighth Sin. N.Y.: Random House, 1978. 88 p.

Kaniuk, Yoram. Adam Resurrected. trans. from the Hebrew by Seymour Simckes. N.Y.: Atheneum, 1971. 370 p. A comic novel (humor as a technique for dealing with shock and horror) of patients in an Israeli mental hospital for Holocaust survivors.

Karmel, Ilona. An Estate of Memory. Boston: Houghton Mifflin, 1969. 444 p. A novel of survival, narrated from the perspectives of four women, focussed on the care for a child born in the camp. It "is perhaps the most moving account of the temptations, the devotions, the sacrifices, and the breakdowns in the fragile network of group survival in concentration camp literature." (Ezradi, 1980, cited above, p. 70).

Ka-tzetnik 135633 (Yehiel De Nur). <u>Atrocity</u>. N.T.: Lyle Stuart, 1963. And other works (1969, 1971, 1977).

Klein, A. (Abraham) M (Moses). <u>The Second Scroll</u>. Toronto: McClelland and Stewart, 1966 (1951). A novel using symbolic technique on the creation of the Israeli state. For more on A.M. Klein (1909-1972) see above, and Part 3, chap. 3, sec. e. Consult <u>A.M. Klein</u>, ed. by T.A. Marshall (Toronto: Ryerson Press, 1970, XXV, 165 p.).

Kosinski, Jerzy. <u>The Painted Bird</u>. 1965. 2nd ed. with an Introd. by the author. Boston: Houghton Mifflin Co., 1976. In this harrowing fairy tale of a nameless boy struggling for survival in occupied eastern Europe metaphor powerfully conveys the reality of dehumanization. Called "the most relentless example of the imaginative representation of the Holocaust, because it universalizes the demonic values of the concentrationary universe and traces the inception and growth of evil in the soul of a young child-a slow but sure catechism that ensures the propagation of evil as the legacy of concentrationary civilization." (Ezrahi, 1980, cited above, p. 153). Also read: <u>Steps</u>.

Kuznetsov, Anatoli V. (A. Anatoli, pseud.). <u>Babi Yar. A Document in the Form of a Novel</u>. trans. from the Russian by David Floyd. N.Y.: Farrar, Straus & Giroux, 1970. 477 p. A documentary "Novel" (how is this form possible for an event like this?) of the murder of 33,000 Jews at Babi Yar, outside of Kiev in Sept. 1941.

The gifted British poet and novelist D.M. Thomas in his surrealistic novel, The White Hotel (Viking, 1981), uses Kuznetsov as a source.

Langfus, Anna. The Whole Land Brimstone. trans. from the French by Peter Wiles. N.Y.: Pantheon, 1962. 318 p. Also: Saute, Barbara (1965), The Lost Shore (1962). Powerful authentic fictional explorations of the emotional states and "thanatopsis" of the survivor. The Whole Land Brimstone is a sensitive Polish Jewish girl's narrative of the Nazi invasion of Poland.

Levi, Carol. The Watch. trans. from the Italian by John Farrar. N.Y.: Farrar, Straus and Yoring, 1951. 442 p.

Lind, Jakov. Soul of Wood and other stories. trans. from the German (1962) by Ralph Manheim. N.Y.: Grove Press, 1964. 190 p. Using irony and "gallows humour" Lind responds to the horror of the mad-sane, abnormal-normal universe of the Holocaust with its inversion and perversion of meaning: "Those who had no papers entitling them to live lined up to die." (Soul of Wood, p. 7). Born in Vienna in 1927, Lind survived the war as a laborer in Germany using a forged identity. See his Counting My Steps: An Autobiography. N.Y.: Macmillan, 1969.

Lind, Jakov. Landscape in Concrete. trans. from the German by Ralph Manheim. N.Y.: Grove Press, 1966. 190 p. Lind's first novel "is an apocalyptic vision of postwar man transmuted into a heartless, violent creature." (Ezrahi, 1980, cited above, p. 159).

Lustig, Arnost. Night and Hope. (Children of the Holocaust). trans. from the Czech by George Theiner. N.Y.:
E.P. Dutton, 1962. 206 p. A collection of stories set
in the Terezin ghetto. Born in Prague in 1926, Lustig
survived Buchenwald and Auschwitz. Now a professor in
America, he is the author of ten Holocaust novels and
five screenplays, including the acclaimed "Shop on Main
Street."

Lustig, Arnost. A Prayer for Katerina Horovitzova.
trans. from the Czech by Jeanne Nemcova. N.Y.: Harper &
Row, 1978. The very moving and tragically lyrical story
of the life and death of a nineteen-year-old Jewish
dancer who killed an Auschwitz lieutenant who had
attempted to shame her.

Lustig, Arnost. Diamonds of the Night. trans. by
Jeanne Nemcova. Washington, D.C.: Inscape Publishers,
1978. Vol. 3 of Children of the Holocaust.

Lustig, Arnost. Darkness Casts No Shadow. trans. by
Jeanne Nemcova. Washington, D.C.: Inscape Publishers,
1978. 173 p. (vol. 2 of Children of the Holocaust).
The terribly sad account of the escape of two Jewish
boys from a train, their capture and execution.

Malaparte, Curzio. Kaputt. trans. from the Italian by
Cesare Foligno. N.Y.: E.P. Dutton & Co., 1946. O. 5-407
p.

Morante, Elsa. History, A Novel. trans. from the
Italian by William Weaver. N.Y.: Knopf, 1977. 561 p.

Munk, Georg (Paula Buber). Muckensturn. Ein Jahr im Leben einer kleinen Stadt. ("Storm of Gnats..."). Heidelberg: Verlag Lambert Schneider, 1953. This novel (by Martin Buber's wife) describes the Nazi takeover of Heppenheim, a village near Berlin, where the Bubers were living in 1933. "In this swarm of gnats the great community with its pathology is mirrored."

Prager, (Marl) Moshe. Sparks of Glory. trans. by Mordecai Schreiber. N.Y.: Shengold Publishers, 1974. 154 p. illus.

Presser, Jacob. Breaking Point. trans. from the Dutch by Barrows Mussey. Cleveland: World Pub. Co., 1958. 92 p. By the Dutch historian (1899-1970) who wrote The Destruction of the Dutch Jews (1969). This is a first-person narrative of an individual awaiting deportation in the Dutch camp at Westerbork.

Rawicz, Piotr. Blood from the Sky. trans. from the French (1961) by Peter Wiles. N.Y.: Harcourt, Brace & World, 1964. 316 p. With deep theological bitterness, Rawicz writes: "word became flesh, and flesh smoke." Blood from the Sky is described by A. Alvarez as "an imaginative projection of the dead-end moral nihilism embodied in the camps."

Rosen, Norma S. Touching Evil. N.Y.: Harcourt, Brace and World, 1969. 269 p. A novel that uses a "witness-through-the-imagination" technique to portray "the intrusion of monstrous evil into the domestic realm" and the contradiction between the concentrationary universe revealed at the Eichmann trial and the "affluent society." (Ezrahi, 1980, cited above, pp. 208ff).

Rosenfeld, Isaac. __Alpha__ __and__ __Omega;__ __Stories__. N.Y.: Viking Press, 1966. 279 p. A posthumous collection of stories, "allegories of terror" written out of deep moral commitment. Kafka was his mentor. See S. Ezrahi (1980, cited above), p. 197.

Rudnicki, Adolf. __Ascent__ __to__ __Heaven__. trans. from the Polish by H.C. Stevens. N.Y.: Roy Publishers, 1951. O. 11-204 p. In this collection of stories about Polish-Jewish suffering, "The Crystal Stream" pictures the destruction of the Warsaw Ghetto. "Over an area which the eye could encompass only with difficulty, where formerly the greatest concentration of Jews in Europe had been housed, there was nothing but rubble and broken brick." This brief story "is a legend or myth of the 'immanence' of the apocalypse and its victory over the memory and the promise--of Paradise." (Ezrahi, 1980, cited above, p. 163).

Samuels, Gertrude. __Mottele;__ __a__ __Partisan__ __Odyssey__. (Joan Kahn bk.). N.Y.: Harper & Row, 1976. 179 p.

Schaeffer, Susan Fromberg. __Anya__. N.Y.: Macmillan, 1974. 489 p. An example of American "realistic" fiction that attempts to express the Holocaust experience.

Schwartz-Bart, Andre. __The__ __Last__ __of__ __the__ __Just__. trans. from the French by Stephen Becker. N.Y.: Atheneum, 1960. 374 p. An eloquent, deeply moving, and widely-read novel about Ernie Levy, one of the six million, and the last of the Levy line of the __Lamed-Vov__ __Zaddikim__, the 36 Just Men upon whom the existence of the world depends. The author integrates the Holocaust into the

540

history of Jewish suffering but not in a simplistic way.

Segal, Lore Groszmann. Other People's Houses. (Plume bk.) N.Y.: New American Library, 1973. 312 p.

Semprun, Jorge. The Long Voyage. trans. from the French by Richard Seaver. N.Y.: Grove Press, 1964. 236 p. An intensely personal and reflective "disaster novel" based on Semprun's experience of Buchenwald. The camp is not the locale for the novel, but the train experience. The continuous use of the present tense serves to establish "the concentrationary universe sub specie aeternitatis... (Ezradi, 1980, cited above, p. 74).

Shapiro, Lamed. Discussed in chap. 3,e.

Shaw, Robert. The Man in the Glass Booth. N.Y.: Harcourt, Brace and World, 1967. 180 p. A not very impressive and somewhat sensationalized fictional response to the Eichmann trial. That trial was a "watershed" (Ezrahi) for both American and Israeli fiction that sought to confront the Holocaust.

Singer, Isaac Bashevis. The Slave. trans. from the Yiddish by Cecil Hemley and the Author. N.Y.: Farrar, Straus and Cuddahy, 1962. 311 p. An historical romance set in Poland in the 17th century, after the Chmielnicki massacres.

Singer, Isaac Bashevis. "The Slaughterer." In The Seance. N.Y.: Farrar, Straus and Giroux, 1968. Describes the growing abhorrence of Yoineh Meir, the town _shohet_, to his job as ritual slaughterer. "Thou art a slaughterer!...The whole world is a slaughter-house!" (p. 291).

Singer, Isaac Bashevis. _Enemies, A Love Story_. trans. from the Yiddish by Aliza Shevrin and Elizabeth Shub. N.Y.: Farrar, Straus and Giroux, 1972. 280 p.

Sperber, Manes... _than a tear in the sea_. trans. by Constantine FitzGibbon. N.Y.: Bergen-Belsen Memorial Press, 1967.

Spiraux, Alain. _Time Out_. trans. by Frances Keene. N.Y.: Times Books, 1978.

Steiner, George. "The Portage to San Cristobal of A.H." _The Kenyon Review_, n.s. I:2 (Spring 1979): 1-120.

Steiner, Jean-Francois. _Treblinka_. trans. from the French by Helen Weaver. Introd. by Simone de Beauvoir. N.Y.: Simon and Schuster, 1967. 415 p. A widely-read but unsuccessful attempt at documentary fiction on the death factory in Poland. Part of the problem with the work is that Steiner projects ideological notions upon his characters. Steiner's book contributed to the debate about the "passivity" of the Jews. (In eighteen months, 700,000 people, including the Warsaw ghetto, were murdered at Treblinka; but there was an uprising and escape in the summer of 1944).

Stern, Daniel. _Who Shall Live, Who Shall Die?_ N.Y.: Lancer Books, N.Y.: Crown 1963. 319 p.

Styron, William. Sophie's Choice. N.Y.: Random House, 1979. 515 p. Sophie, the "poor straw-haired Polish darling," endures ultimate evil in Auschwitz, survives; falls in love with Nathan, a brilliant, unbalanced New York Jew, and they end their sufferings together in suicide. (The plot is well-known now due to the movie). Styron's intent is noble and profound but his writing is often wooden or derivative (e.g., Thomas Wolfe). There is also the question of Styron using the Holocaust to illustrate the category of extreme experience. More serious is the question of the erotic exploitation of Auschwitz. (see A. Rosenfeld, 1980, cited above, chap. 8). His central male characters seem based on the sterotypes of the young experienced Southerner and brillant neurotic NYC Jew.

Tomkiewicz, Mina. Of Bombs and Mice; A Novel of War-Time Warsaw. trans. from the Polish by Stefan F. Grazel. N.Y.: Thomas Yoseloff, 1970. 336 p.

Uhlman, Fred. Reunion. London: Adam Books, 1971. 74 p. N.Y.: Penguin Books, 1978. The tension in this sensitive gem builds tremendously. The story begins in Stuttgart in 1932 and concerns the deep friendship between two sixteen-year-old school-mates, one an assimilated Jew and the other a von Hofenfel aristocrat.

Uris, Leon. Mila 18. N.Y.: Doubleday & Co., 1961. 539 p. An attempt at documentary fiction relating to the Warsaw ghetto and uprising.

Wallant, Edward Lewis. The Pawnbroker. N.Y.: Harcourt, Brace and World, London: Gollancz, 1962. 279 p. In this American novel, clearly influenced by survivor literature, Sol Nazerman, a refugee, is emotionally and morally anaesthetized. In the end he experiences a rather "sacramental" redemption. (The famous movie version featured Rod Steiger).

Wiesenthal, Simon. The Sunflower; With a Symposium. trans. from the German by H.A. Piehler. N.Y.: Schocken Books, 1976. 216 p.

Wiesel, Elie. Wiesel, often hailed as the literary spokesman for the Holocaust, has said that he writes "To wrench those victims from oblivion. To help the dead vanquish death." He has also said that it is impossible to write a novel about Auschwitz. His autobiographical Night (ET. 1960) is set in Auschwitz and through "statement by understatement" details the death of his father, his survival, and his loss of religious faith. "Not to transmit an experience is to betray it: this is what Jewish tradition teaches us."

Dawn. trans. from the French by Frances Frenaye. N.Y.: Hill and Wang, 1961. 89 p.

The Accident. trans. from the French by Anne Borchardt. N.Y.: Hill and Wang, 1962. 20 f. N.Y.: Avon Books, 1970. "My legends can only be told at dark. Whoever listens questions his life...The heroes of my legends are cruel and without pity. They are capable of strangling you."

The Gates of the Forest. trans. from the French by Frances Frenaye. N.Y.: Holt, Rinehart and Winston, 1966. 226 p. On the themes of faith and friendship.

The Town Beyond the Wall. trans. from the French by
Stephen Becker. New ed. N.Y.: Holt, Rinehart and
Winston, 1967. 179 p. N.Y.: Avon Books, 1969. The
epigraph is from Dostoevsky: "I have a plan to go mad."
Asserts that "Down deep man is not only an executioner,
not only a victim, not only a spectator: he is all three
at once." The image of the "simple spectator" (p. 150)
is a symbolic embodiment of the average person during
the Holocaust, passive and indifferent. But beyond
silence there is the moral demand to respond to the
suffering of others. "Blessed is he capable of surpris-
ing and being surprised." (p. 124).

A Beggar in Jerusalem. trans. from the French by Lily
Edelman and the author. N.Y.: Random House, 1970. 211
p. N.Y.: Avon Books, 1971. Explores the themes of
history and the Return. And see The Oath (Random
House, 1973). On silence as a better response to evil
than speech. See also: Harry James Cargas in Conversation with Elie Wiesel. N.Y.: Paulist Press, 1976.
Wiesel says: "Night was the foundation; all the rest is
commentary. In each book, I take one character out of
Night and give him a refuge, a book, a tale, a name, a
destiny of his own." (p. 3). "The story that I try to
tell is, first of all, a story of night which the
Kaballah calls Shvirat hakelim--the breaking of the
vessels--that something happened at the origin of creation, a cosmic cataclysm." (p. 85). A sympathetic and
documented study of Wiesel is Robert McAfee Brown's,
Elie Wiesel. Messenger to all Humanity. See The Vision
of the Void: Theological Reflections on the Works of
Elie Wiesel. Middletown, Conn.: Wesleyan University
Press, 1979. Biblio.: p. 203-212. For a new biography
of Wiesel see Ellen Norman Stern, Elie Wiesel: Witness

for Life (N.Y.: Ktav, 1982), and for a recent literary analysis see Ellen S. Fine, "Elie Wiesel's Literary Legacy." JBA, 41 (1983-1984): 57-69. Night is a condensation and translation into French of Wiesel's Yiddish account of the camp nightmare (Un di Velt Hot Geshvign-- And the World Has Remained Silent) written in 1956 in Argentina (Buenos Aires: Tsentral farband fun poylishe yidn in Argentine) after Wiesel had been urged by the French Catholic novelist Francois Mauriac to break his vow of silence. According to Roskies the Yiddish original is much longer than the French and English versions and has a different message. "Themes of Madness and existential despair are not as highlighted in the Yiddish narrative, which ends with the engage writer's appeal to fight the Germans and anti-Semites who would consign the Holocaust to oblivion." (Roskies, 1984, cited above, p. 301). Roskies charges that both Wiesel and I.B. Singer (in The Family Moskat, trans. from the Yiddish by A.H. Gross, N.Y.: Farrar, Straus & Giroux, 1950) have attempted "to curry favor with the non-Jewish and noncommitted world..." and "...facing a potentially infinite audience were willing to use catastrophe for cultural rapprochement." (ibidem, p. 302).

CHAPTER 2:

STUDIES OF ZIONIST THOUGHT AND HISTORY

Introductory Comments

Around 1900, the only literature in English on the history of Zionism was a pamphlet by Max Nordau, translated by Israel Cohen. Nordau's Zionistische Schriften appeared in 1909 but it was another decade before a general history of Zionism in English was published. Nahum Sokolow's two-volume History of Zionism (1919) is still valuable although largely uncritical and mainly focused on Britain. In the mid-30's, the two-volume study Die Zionistische Bewegung by Adolf Boehm appeared. In 1932 the second edition of Leonard Stein's Zionism was published, and in 1941 Lotta Levensohn's general account Outline of Zionist History was published in New York. These two works are valuable but small in compass. Israel Cohen, who lived through much of what he wrote about, published a fuller synthesis in 1945, The Zionist Movement. The work was revised in 1946 with an added chapter, "Zionism in the United States" by B.G. Richards. In the 1950's and 1960's several general, but partisan, histories were published, Rufus Learsi, Fulfillment: The Epic Story of Zionism (1951), H. Parzen, A Short History of Zionism (1965). B. Litvinoff, who uses new sources, has most recently produced two works on Chaim Weizmann (1976, 1982, cited below). In 1975, David Vital's The Origins of Zionism was published; Vital argues that the "Zionist revolution" recreated a normal Jewish existence. The sequel

to this work, Zionism, The Formative Years, was published in 1982. In 1972, Walter Laqueur's A History of
Zionism appeared and while not a definitive study it is
the most substantial of the histories to date.

The theme of Zionism as revolutionary is central
to the 1981 study, The Making of Modern Zionism, The
Intellectual Origins of the Jewish State by Shlomo
Avineri. Avineri, a close student of Marxist thought,[1]
was Director-General of Israel's Ministry for Foreign
Affairs until resigning after the elections of 1977.
One of the central assumptions in this thoughtful and
gracefully written work is that true internationalism
leads through the path of nationalism. Avineri inter-
prets Zionism not simply or solely as a response to
anti-Semitism but as a revolution against both Jewish
history and Gentile history. Avineri seeks to "delin-
eate a number of aspects of Zionist thought" in order to
clarify aspects of the problems of modern Jewish identity. But he is only partially successful in this; he
has too many chapters, covers too many individuals, and
in a snap-shot fashion, and ignores major Jewish
thinkers, e.g., Buber, Magnes, Zangwill. He completely
neglects the binational movement in Palestine, Brit
Shalom and Ichud. He does not draw on archival
materials, has no bibliography and relies for entire
chapters, e.g., 4 and 5, upon selections in A.
Hertzberg's anthology (rev. ed., 1969). Chapter 8 on
Ben Yehuda is very thin, the discussion of Krochmal and
Graetz is intelligent and interesting but here the range

[1]See The social and Political Thought of Karl Marx
(Cambridge: Cambridge University Press, 1968).

and depth is restricted by not consulting pertinent studies, e.g., Abraham I. Katsch, "Krochmal and Zionist Thinkers" (JQR, Oct.-Dec. 1946), L. Simon's biography of Ahad Ha-am (1960), and the recent studies of A.D. Gordon by H. Rose (1964), A. Perlmutter (1971) and E. Shavid (1970). Bernard Avisdai in his brilliant, scholarly, and personal The Tragedy of Zionism (1985) views Zionism as revolutionary but contends that the movement has run its course and current attempts to invigorate Zionism impede the realization of democratic goals. Zionism is "tragically obsolete" and Zionist ideas "an invitation to authoritarian forces to set the terms of national debate." (p. 322).

The justification of Zionism on the grounds that Emancipation was a failure is carried to an extreme by Hillel Halkin in his Letters to an American Jewish Friend. A Zionist's Polemic (1977). Halkin thinks that diaspora Judaism is doomed. A penetrating rebuttal to this virtual equation of Judaism and Zionism (defined in very narrow terms) is present in Martin Buber's On Zion. The History of an Idea (1973, originally published as Israel and Palestine, The History of an Idea. (1952)). Only the power of "authentic faith" makes Zionism meaningful, not machines or guns or land per se. "It goes without saying that Palestine did not make itself the Holy Land, but what made it Holy Land was its election by the living God." (p. 125). Without the presence of the "hidden Zion," the Jewish state will become power unblessed by grace.

This brief discussion of Avineri, Avisdai, Halkin, and Buber manifests how messy, emotional and controversial Zionist historiography is. As the

American Jewish philosopher Morris R. Cohen wrote in
1946: "But the discussion of Zionism is beset with the
additional difficulty that clear and honest thinking is
subtly hindered by the fact that really plain speaking
is almost unattainable." This observation is correct;
the terms "Zionist" and Zionism" are often used in
imprecise ways, frequently as slogans, either positive
or negative. The highest form of understanding may be
self-evidence but this type of certitude is not manifest
in the intensely passionate field that we are here
reviewing. Hence the need for exact definitions and
exacting standards of evidence is urgent. There are
several varieties of Zionist thought, "mystical,"
rabbinic-legal, secular nationalist, secular humanist,
socialist/Marxist. The standards of evidence range from
the treatment of questions of causality to the use of
footnotes and bibliographical structure. Here the
question of "should" arises: good critical bibliography
"should" be an effective tool and map to chart the field
of knowledge and to advance perspective. The cognitive
map as perspective device is valuable to the extent that
it advances knowledge, deepens perspective and helps
clear the fogs of error and prejudice.

A. Archives and Papers, Bibliographic and Reference Works, Periodicals and Year Books. The Papers of Zionist Leaders.

Archives and Papers (see el-Khalidi and Khadduri (1974, cited below)) and Philip Jones, comp. Britain and Palestine, 1914-1948 (Oxford University Press, 1978).

Archives of the central offices of the World Zionist Organization and the Jewish Agency. Central Zionist Archives, Jerusalem. Includes the archives of the Vienna, Cologne and Berlin offices, Vienna, 1897-1905; Cologne, 1905-1911; Berlin, 1911-1920.

Archives of the Copenhagen Office of the Zionist Organization, 1915-1920. Central Zionist Archives, Jerusalem.

Archives of the Geneva Office of the Zionist Organization and of the Jewish Agency for Palestine (Representative at the League of Nations), 1925-1948. Central Zionist Archives, Jerusalem.

Archives of Hoveve Zion Organizations. Central Zionist Archives, Jerusalem.

Archives of the Jewish Territorial Organization, London, 1905-1926. Central Zionist Archives, Jerusalem. This organization, associated most often with I. Zangwill, favoured the settlement of Jews on an autonomous territory, not necessarily Palestine.

Files of Territorial Zionist Organizations and collections of documents concerning Zionist parties and the
history of Zionism in various countries. Central
Zionist Archives, Jerusalem.

Hadassah, Women's Zionist Organization. New York.
Established in 1912, the world's largest Zionist organization.

Hoveve Zion was a pre-Herzlian movement to encourage
Jewish settlement and national revival in Palestine.
This collection includes the archives of the Central
Committee in Odessa (1882-1917) and of societies and
associations in Vilna, Kovno, Rumania and England in the
last two decades of the nineteenth century.

Jewish Agency. Documents Relating to the Palestine
Problem. London, 1945. 96 p. A collection of excerpts
from documents and speeches, designed to contest the
1939 White Paper and the 1940 Land Regulations.

Jewish Agency. The Jewish Case Against the Palestine
White Paper. Documents Submitted to the Permanent Man-
dates Commission of the League of Nations. London,
1939. 35 p. Includes a letter by Weizmann protesting
the White Paper of May 1939 and memorandum on the legal
aspects of the White Paper.

Jewish Agency. The Jewish Case before the Anglo-
American Committee of Inquiry on Palestine as Presented
by the Jewish Agency for Palestine: Statements and
Memoranda. Jerusalem, 1947. 686 p.

Zionist Archives and Library, New York. Founded in 1939, the library contains thousands of published volumes, unpublished material, photographs, recordings and maps.

Zionist Organization. Zionist Congresses. <u>Minutes of the...Zionist Congress, 1897-</u>. Places of publication, usually in the same year as the congress, include Vienna, Berlin, London, and, in recent years, Jerusalem.

Bibliographic and Reference Works (See Part I, also).

American Zionist Council. <u>Selected</u> <u>and</u> <u>Annotated Bibliography</u> <u>on the State of Israel and the Zionist Movement</u>. N.Y.: American Zionist Council, 1957.

<u>Encyclopedia of Zionism and Israel</u>. ed. by Raphael Patai. N.Y.: Herzl Press, 1971.

<u>Encyclopedia Judaica</u>. 16 vols. and Yearbooks. Jerusalem: Keter, 1971.

el-Khalidi, Walid and J. Khadduri. eds, <u>Palestine and the Arab Israeli Conflict, An Annotated bibliography</u>. Beirut: Institute for Palestine Studies, 1974.

<u>Guide to American Holy-Land Studies.</u> <u>Vol. I: American Presence</u>. ed. by Nathan M. Kaganoff. N.Y.: Arno Press, 1980.

<u>Palestine and Zionism; An Author and Subject Index to Books, Pamphlets and Periodicals</u>. 1st-11th, Jan. 1946/Dec. 1948-1956. N.Y.: Zionist Archives and Library of Palestine Foundation Fund. 11 vols. in 3. From bimonthly and annual numbers.

Periodicals and Year Books.

Commentary (N.Y.: American Jewish Committee). Monthly since 1946. Contains articles on and discussion of Zionism.

Dispersion and Unity. Vol I--1959--Jerusalem: World Zionist Organization. Title varies.

Herzl Year Book: Essays in Zionist History and Thought. ed. by Raphael Patai. 6 vols. N.Y.: Herzl Press, 1959-1965. Contains essays and research papers, Rpt. ed. by R. Patai. Freeport, N.Y.: Books for Libraries Press, 1970.

Kirjath Sepher. Israeli bibliographic journal.

Midstream. (N.Y.: Theodor Herzl Foundation). Monthly since 1955. Contains articles on Zionism. Vol. 1 (Autumn, 1955) is devoted to Zionism.

Heymann, Michael. ed. The Minutes of the Zionist General Council: The Uganda Controversy: Vol. I. Jerusalem: Israel Universities Press, 1971. Minutes of the meetings, Basle, August 1903. Includes an essay on the state of the Zionist movement.

Udin, Sophie A. The Palestine Year Books. 2 vols. N.Y.: Parish Press, for the Z.O.A. 1945/1946. On Jewish activities in Palestine and the contributions of American Zionism.

Wolf, Lucien. Notes on the Diplomatic History of the Jewish Question, with Texts of Treaty Stipulations and Other Official Documents. London: Jewish Historical Society of England, 1919. 133 p. Resolutions of congresses and conferences, etc; submitted as a background paper to the 1919 Peace Conference.

World Jewish Congress. Unity in Dispersion: A History of the World Jewish Congress. N.Y.: 1948. 381 p. An official history of the first twelve years of the W.J.C. (1936-1949).

Zion (Jerusalem, Historical Society of Israel). A quarterly for research in Jewish history. Title varies.

The Zionist Year Book. 1951/52-London: Zionist Federation of Great Britain and Ireland.

The Papers of Zionist Activists and Leaders

Borochov, Ber. Correspondence and writings, primarily concerning the Poale Zion movement, 1907-1917. American Jewish Archives, Cincinnati, Ohio. Borochov attempted a synthesis of Zionism and Marxism. See Part 3, Sec. 3.

Carpi, Leone. Papers. Central Zionist Archives, Jerusalem. Carpi (1887-1964) was an Italian Zionist leader (a Revisionist), active in the organization of illegal immigration to Palestine.

De Hass, Jacob. Papers. Central Zionist Archives, Jerusalem. Zionist Archives and Library, New York City. De Haas (1872-1937) was secretary of the Federation of American Zionists, and editor of the Maccabean.

Frankfurter, Felix. Papers. Central Zionist Archives, Jerusalem. ca. 17 items (1914-1919, and 1930-1932). Frankfurter (1822-1965) was a U.S. Supreme Court justice (1939-1962), associated with the Brandeis group, and member of the delegation to the Paris Peace Conference in 1919.

Friedenwald, Harry. Papers. Central Zionist Archives. ca. 1,000 items, 1911-1941. Friedenwald (1864-1950) was president and honorary president of the Federation of American Zionists, 1904-1918.

Herzl, Theodor. Papers. Central Zionist Archives, Jerusalem. Includes his hand-written diaries, the files of the editorial office of his weekly, Die Welt, and about 4,500 letters. On Herzl, see Part 3, sec. 2 (below).

Hess, Moses. Papers. Central Zionist Archives, Jerusalem. See Part 3, Sec. 3 (below).

Jabotinsky, Zev (Vladimir). Papers. Jabotinsky Institute in Israel, Tel Aviv. ca. 10 items (1919). On Jabotinsky, see Part 3, Sec. 3 (below).

Jacobson, Victor (Avigdor). Papers. Central Zionist Archives. Jerusalem. Jacobson (1869-1934) was a Zionist leader before World War I and was involved in "diplomacy" with leaders within the Ottoman Empire.

Kalischer, Zvi Hirsch. Papers. Central Zionist Archives. Jerusalem. On Kalischer, see Part 3, sec. 2, below.

Kallen, Horace. Papers. ca. 20 folders, 1920-1939. Kallen archives, YIVO Institute for Jewish Research, New York City. Kallen (1882-1974) was a prominent philosopher, a pluralistic secular humanist influenced by James and Dewey; and an educator at the New School for Social Research.

Klatzkin, Jakob. Papers. Central Zionist Archives, Jerusalem. On Klatzkin, see Part 3, Sec. 2 below.

Lilienblum, Moshe Leib. Papers. Central Zionist Archives, Jerusalem. See the discussion of Lilienblum in S. Avineri, The Making of Modern Zionism. (1981).

Mack, Julian William. Papers. Zionist Archives and Library, New York City. Collection covers: 1910-1934. Mack (1866-1943) was a U.S. judge, a founder and president of the American Jewish Congress (1918) and president of the Z.O.A. (1918).

Nordau, Max. Papers. Central Zionist Archives, Jerusalem. See Part 3, Sec. 2, below.

Pines, Yehiel Michael. Papers. Central Zionist Archives, Jerusalem. Pines (1843-1913) was an early leader of "Religious" Zionism.

Schapira, Ziv Hermann. Papers. Central Zionist Archives, Jerusalem. Schapira (1840-1893) argued that land in Palestine should be subject to Jewish nationalization.

Sokolow, Nahum. Papers. Central Zionist Archives, Jerusalem. On Sokolow, see Part 2 (below).

Stein, Leonard. Papers. Central Zionist Archives, Jerusalem. Stein, an Anglo-Zionist author, was political secretary of the World Zionist Organization, 1920-1929, and legal adviser to the Jewish Agency, 1930-1939.

Szold, Henrietta. Papers. Central Zionist Archives, Jerusalem. ca. 6 linear feet, 1920-1945. Szold (1860-1945) was a founding leader of Hadassah; she devoted 25 years to public and social welfare causes in Palestine. Other Szold papers are in the Schlesinger Library, Radcliffe College, Cambridge, Mass.

Tolkowski, Samuel. Papers. Central Zionist Archives, Jerusalem. Includes diaries from the period 1916-1919, when Tolkowski was an active Zionist in England (and present at the 1919 Peace Conference), and from the period after 1919 when he lived in Palestine.

Tschlenow, Yechiel. Papers. Central Zionist Archives, Jerusalem. Tschlenow (1863-1918), a Russian Zionist leader, was Vice-President of the Zionist Executive after 1911.

Ussishkin, Menachem. Papers. Central Zionist Archives, Jerusalem. Ussishkin was a Russian born Zionist leader (1863-1941) active in Hoveve Zion and the W.Z.O.

Warburg, Otto. Papers. Central Zionist Archives, Jerusalem. Warburg (1859-1938) was President of the W.Z.O. from 1905 to 1911.

Weizmann, Chaim. Papers. Rehovoth, Israel. Includes his correspondence, political memoranda and scientific papers. Weizmann (b. 1874, Russian Poland, d. 1952) was a gifted research chemist, first President of Israel, and leading figure in the W.Z.O. for about a quarter of a century. His technical help to the British during World War I strengthened Zionist political negotiations with the British government in 1917. His papers and letters are being edited by Meyer Weisgal and others; see M. Weisgal, ed. The Letters and Papers of Chaim Weizmann: Vol I. (Oxford: Oxford University Press, 1968). 447 p. Covers the period 1885-1902.

Zangwill, Israel. Papers. Central Zionist Archives, Jerusalem. Zangwill (1864-1926) was an Anglo-Jewish novelist, poet and playwright who broke with the Zionist Organization on the question of whether Palestine was the only possible site for a Jewish state. He formed the Jewish Territorial Organization.

B. History and Theory. General Works.

Arendt, Hannah. The Jew as Pariah: Jewish Identity and Politics in the Modern Age. ed. with an Introduction by Ron H. Feldman. N.Y.: Grove Press, 1978. See Part II: "Zionism and the Jewish state."

Avisdai, Bernard. The Tragedy of Zionism. Revolution and Democracy in the Land of Israel. N.Y.: Farrar Giroux, 1985. 389 p. As the Zionist once wrote elegies to Orthodoxy so this work is Avisdai's elegy to Zionism: "My point is that it may finally be time to retire everybody's Zionism, time for more democracy, for what some Zionists used to call "normalcy." (p. 12).

Ben-Ezer, Ehud. ed. Unease in Zion. Foreword by Robert Alter. N.Y.: Quadrangle/New York Times Book Co., 1974, Jerusalem: Jerusalem Acad. Press, 1974. 352 p. Includes bibliographical references. Good biographical notes. Leading Israeli intellectuals were asked: "What has the real price of Zionism been?" See, esp., the interviews with G. Scholem, M. Buber, and E. Simon's "The Arab Question as a Jewish Question."

Berlin, Isaiah Sir. "The Origins of Israel." In The Middle East in Transition, ed. by W.Z. Laqueur. N.Y. 1958. First given as a lecture in 1953. Reflections on Israel's social image as derived from East-European Jewish culture.

Boehm, Adolf. <u>Die</u> <u>Zionistische</u> <u>Bewegung</u>. 2nd ed., 2 vols. Berlin: Juedischer Verlag, 1935-1937. Vol. I was first published in 1923.

Brichner, Balfour. <u>Zionism,</u> <u>Judaism,</u> <u>and</u> <u>Racism</u>. N.Y.: National Conference of Christians and Jews, 1975. A Study Guide. 16 p. Biblio.: p. 16.

Buber, Martin. <u>On</u> <u>Zion</u>: <u>The</u> <u>History</u> <u>of</u> <u>an</u> <u>Idea</u>. trans. from the German by Stanley Goodman. New Foreword by Nahum N. Glatzer. London: East and West Library; N.Y.: Schocken Books, 1973. Originally pub. as <u>Israel</u> <u>and</u> <u>Palestine,</u> <u>The</u> <u>History</u> <u>of</u> <u>an</u> <u>Idea</u>. (East and West Library, 1952). Contains Biographical Appendix, Intro- duction. Part I: "The Testimony of the Bible," Part II: "Interpretation and Transfiguration," Part III: "The Voice of the Exile," Part IV: "The Zionist Idea." Buber argues that without the dimension/reality of the "hidden Zion" the Jewish state becomes power without grace. Buber maintained this approach to Zionism into his old age. In his 1957 address on "Israel's Mission and Zion" he critizes D. Ben-Gurion for overstressing the politi- cal factor and thus producing a secularization that politicizes life. "Israel's Mission and Zion." <u>Forum</u>, IV (1957). Rpt. in <u>Israel</u> <u>and</u> <u>the</u> <u>World</u>. N.Y.: Schocken Books, 1963.

Buber, Martin. <u>A</u> <u>Land</u> <u>of</u> <u>Two</u> <u>Peoples</u>: <u>Martin</u> <u>Buber</u> <u>on</u> <u>Jews</u> <u>and</u> <u>Arabs</u>. ed. with commentary by Paul R. Mendes- Flohr. N.Y.: Oxford University Press, 1983. XIII, 319 p. Writings by Buber (1918-1965), much of it unknown in English. Buber remained firm in his commitment to binationalism and in his critique of <u>Realpolitik</u>.

Carpi, Daniel and Gedalia Yoger. eds. Zionism: studies in the history of the Zionist movement and of the Jewish community in Palestine. English ed. Tel Aviv: Tel Aviv University 1975. Specialized Hebrew monographs in translation; see, e.g., Menachem Friedmann, "The First Confrontation Between the Zionist movement and Jerusalem Orthodoxy after the British Occupation (1918)." pp. 103-126.

Chertoff, Mordecai S. ed. Zionism: A Basic Reader. N.Y.: Herzl Press, 1975. II, 92 p. illus., maps.

Cohen, Israel. A Short History of Zionism. London: Muller, S.J.R. Saunders & Co., Toronto: 1951. 280 p.

Cohen, Israel. The Zionist Movement. ed. and rev. with supplementary chapters on "Zionism in the United States" by Bernard G. Richards. N.Y.: Z.O.A. 1946. 400 p. Biblio.: pp. 378-386. In this valuable synthesis, Cohen attempts to fit the many aspects of Zionism into logical and chronological order.

Cohen, Israel. ed. The Rebirth of Israel: A Memorial Tribute to Paul Goodman. Foreword by Israel Brodie, Chief Rabbi, and Introduction by Selig Brodetsky. Leon E. Goldston. 1952. XIV, 338 p. Rpt. Westport, Conn: Hyperion Press, 1976. Biblio.: p. 52-58.

Cohen, Michael J. Palestine and the Great Powers, 1945-1948. Princeton, N.J.: Princeton University Press, 1982. 417 p.

Cohen, Stuart A. English Zionists and British Jews: The Communal Politics of Anglo-Jewry, 1895-1920. Princeton, N.J.: Princeton University Press, 1982. 349 p.

Davis, Moshe. ed. Zionism in Transition. N.Y.: Arno Press, Herzl Press, 1980. Includes essays by Urbach, Rotenstreich, et al. The volume documents or manifests current confusions about Zionism, its ideologies (?) and its direction or focus (?).

Deshen, Shlomo and Moshe Shokeid. The Predicament of Homecoming: Cultural and Social Life of North African Immigrants in Israel. Ithaca, N.Y.: Cornell University Press, 1974. Biblio.: p. 237-245. An institutional and phenomenological study of the conflict between the "messianic vision" of North African Jews (c. 400,00 in a population of 2.7 million) and Israeli realities.

Einstein, Albert. About Zionism: Speeches and Letters. trans. and ed. with an Introd. by Leon Simon. London: Soncino Press, 1930. N.Y.: MacMillan, 1931. 9-94 pp. These speeches and letters were composed during the 1920's and deal with Jewish assimilation and nationalism, the Jews and Palestine, and the Jews and the Arabs.

el-Khalidi, Walid and J. Khadduri. eds. Palestine and the Arab-Israeli Conflict. Beirut, Institute for Palestine Studies, 1974. See the detailed and comprehensive section on Zionism.

el-Khalidi, Walid and J. Khadduri. eds. From Heaven to Conquest: Readings in Zionism and the Palestine Problem until 1948. Beirut, IPS, 1971.

Fein, Leonard J. "Israel and Zion." Judaism, 21:1 (1973): 7-17. Fein argues that the concepts of Zion and Exile are correlative in a way that the terms Israel and Diaspora are not, i.e., one can choose between Israel and the Diaspora but the knowledge of Exile prevents any confusion of Zion with a particular place or people.

Fisch, Harold. The Zionist Revolution, A New Perspective. N.Y.: St. Martin's Press, 1978. Includes bibliographical references and index. Fisch argues that Zionism derives more from the Biblical myth of the covenant than from the Enlightenment.

Flapan, Simha. Zionism and the Palestinians. Harper & Row, 1979; London: Croom Helm, 1979. 361 p. By an Israeli intellectual who has promoted dialogue with Palestinians. See S. Flapan ed. When Enemies Dare to Talk; An Israeli-Palestinian debate. London: Croom Helm, 1979. 129 p.

Frankel, Josef. Dubnow, Herzl and Ahad Ha-Am. London: Ararat Pub. Co., 1963. Frankel discusses similarities as well as the profound differences.

Giniewski, Paul. Dans les oubliettes de l'histoire. pref. de Robert Aron. Bruxelles: Vander, 1975. Includes bibliographical references and index. Presents a current French view of Zionism.

Givet, Jacques. The anti-Zionist Complex. a trans. of Israel et le génocide inachève by Evelyn Abel. rev. and updated by the author. Englewood, N.J.: SBS Pub. 1981. XVII, 166 p.

Goldberg, Israel (Rufus Learsi). Fulfillment: the Epic Story of Zionism. Cleveland World Pub. Co., 1951. Bibliographical note: p. 411. A well-written general history: Zionism is the sum total of the thoughts, emotions and deeds "stirred by the land called Holy."

Gonen, Jay Y. A Psychohistory of Zionism. N.Y.: Mason/ Charter, 1975. Biblio.: p. 347-363. An imaginative but often logically questionable application of psychoanaly- tical models to Jewish history. Note, e.g., "Most of all, the Zionist movement was characterized by its focus on a rapid transition from inferiority to overcompensa- tion."

Goodman, Paul and Arthur D. Lewis. eds. Zionism: Problems and Views. Introd. by Max Nordau. London: T.F. Unwin, 1916. N.Y.: Bloch. 286 p.

Goren, Arthur A. ed. Dissenter in Zion; From the Writings of Judah L. Magnes. Cambridge, Mass.: Harvard University Press, 1982. 554 p. illus.

Gottheil, Richard J.H. Zionism. (Movements in Judaism) Phila.: JPS, 1914. 258 p. The focus is on Zionist ideas. Gottheil (1862-1936) was an early leader of American Zionism.

Halkin, Abraham S. ed. Zionism in Jewish Literature. N.Y.: Herzl, 1961. 135 p.

Halkin, Hillel. "Zionism Revisited: The Historic Enterprise." Commentary, 55:5 (May 1973): 74-78.

Halkin, Hillel. Letters to an American Friend: A
Zionist's Polemic. Phila.: JPS, 1977. A passionate,
provocative but extreme and untenable treatise.
Halkin's reduction of Judaism to secular Jewishness
involves a complete rejection of post-exilic Jewish
history, a negation of the Diaspora and an exaltation of
Power. Halkin is like Berdichevski (1865-1921) who "saw
only tension and affirmed only revolt." Halkin
dismisses Jewish ethics ("claptrap") and thinks Judaism
is "anti-intellectual." For a penetrating opposite
argument and perspective, vide B. Avisdai (1985 above).

Halpern, Ben. The Idea of the Jewish State. (Harvard
University Middle Eastern Studies, 6) Cambridge, MA.:
Harvard University Press, 1961, 2nd ed. 1969. 638 p.
Bibliography. Index. A probing, systematic (sometimes
sociological), and analytical study of the development
of the idea of a Jewish state from the level of ideology
to institutionalization. Covers the many strands in
Zionism and its relationship to world Jewry. Not for
beginning students.

Halpern, Ben. "Zionism and Israel." The Jewish
Journal of Sociology, 3 (December 1961): 155-173.

Hattis, Susan Lee. The Bi-National Idea in Palestine
during Mandatory Times. (Thésis Université de Genève)
Haifa: Shikoma Pub. Co., 1970. 355 p. Biblio.: p. 325-
336. Writing about Brit Shalom (Covenant of Peace,
founded in 1925 under the initiative of Arthur Ruppin,
and dedicated to Jewish-Arab understanding and a
binational state with population parity) she said: "They
were not defeatist who were willing to make any concession for the achievement of peace, they simply realized

that the Arabs were justified in fearing a Zionism which
spoke in terms of a Jewish majority and a Jewish state.
Their belief was that one need not be a maximalist,
i.e., demand mass immigration and a state to be a faithful Zionist...What was vital was a recognition that both
nations were in Palestine as of right."

Hertzberg, Arthur. ed. with Introd. and biographical
notes. The Zionist Idea; A Historical Analysis and
Reader. Foreword by Emanuel Neumann. Phila.: JPS &
Meridian Books, 1960. 638 p. Bibliography. The basic
standard anthology, of use for both beginning and
advanced study. The brief biographical profiles are
useful but the emphasis is on major works and ideas.

Hertzberg, Arthur. "Judaism and the Land of Israel."
Judaism, 19:4 (1970): 423-434. Argues that Exile did
not break the covenant between the people and the land.
Israel is distinctive among the nations because it is
both secular and has a "religious mystique." (cf.
Halkin, 1967, cited above).

Kaplan, Jacob. Judaisme francais et sionisme. Paris:
A. Michel, 1975.

Kedourie, Elie. Arabic Political Memoirs and Other
Studies. London: Frank Cass, 1974. 327 p. Bibliography. Index. Specialist level essays, most of them
previously published, on the failure of constitutionalism in the Middle East. Lucid style and based on deep
study of source materials. Advanced students should
note the original essay: "The Impact of the Young Turk
Revolution on the Arab Provinces of the Ottoman Empire."

Kedourie, Elie. In the Anglo-Arab Labyrinth: The McMahon-Husayn Correspondence and its Interpretations, 1914-1939. (Cambridge Studies in the hist. & theory of politics). Cambridge: Cambridge University Press, 1976. 330 p.

Kedourie, Elie. ed. Zionism and Arabism in Palestine and Israel. London: Frank Cass, 1982. 255 p.

Kedourie, Elie and Sylvia G. Haim. eds. Palestine and Israel in the 19th and 20th Centuries. London, Frank Cass, 1982.

Kohn, Hans. Reflections on Modern History: The Historian and Human Responsibility. Princeton: Van Nostrand, 1963. See the essays, "Judaism and Nationalism," and "Zion and the Jewish National Idea," pp. 179-211. In the latter essay (orig. pub. in The Menorah Journal, 1958), Kohn posits a conflict between "love of Zion" as intrinsic to Judaism and 19th-century nationalism. Unfortunately, the latter force won out in the Zionist movement.

Kolatt, Israel. "Reflections on the Historiography of Zionism and the Yishuv." The Jewish Cathedra, I (Jerusalem 1981): 314-327.

Laqueur, Walter Z. "The Jewish Question: Zionism and New Anti-Semitism." Encounter, 37:2 (August 1971): 43-52.

Laqueur, Walter Z. "Zionism: The Marxist Critique and the Left." Dissent, 18:6 (December, 1971): 560-74.

Laqueur, Walter Z.   A History of Zionism. N.Y.: Holt, Rinehart & Winston, 1972. 639 p. illus. chapter biblio-graphies, Glossary.   Index. Biblio.: p. 599-615.   A competent, reasonably objective study, sympathetic but not uncritical. Now supercedes Sokolow (1917) and more recent works. The standard study and the best work for the general reader. Laqueur concentrates on the "main lines of development" and may not adequately cover all areas of importance, e.g., "religious" Zionism and Sephardic Zionism. He is good on Labor Zionism and the chapter on Zionism and the Arabs, "The Unseen Question," is particularly valuable.

Litvinoff, Barnett.   Road to Jerusalem: Zionism's Imprint on History. London: Weidenfeld & Nicolson, 1966. (First pub. under the title: To the House of their Fathers, 1965). Biblio.: p. 301-303. Chronology. Pre-sents a summary of the ideas of leading Zionists.

Litvinoff, Barnett.   Weizmann. Last of the Patriarchs. N.Y.: G.P. Putnam's Sons, 1976. 288 p. A biography.

Litvinoff, Barnett.   The Essential Chaim Weizmann, The Man, The Statesman, The Scientist. N.Y.: Holmes & Meir, 1982.

Lucas, Noah. The Modern History of Israel. London: Weidenfeld and Nicolson; N.Y.: Praeger, 1975. 500 p. Includes maps, notes, annotated Bibliography of works in English.   Indices. In chap. 2, "Zionist Doctrines and Nineteenth-Century Palestine," Lucas argues that Zionism was a radical break from messianism, "transmuting it from an essentially religious insight to a doctrine of secular politics." (p. 21). Other scholars, e. g., J.

Katz, posit continuity between messianism and Zionism. This first-rate critical book is in 3 parts: origins, the state in the making, the nation in the making. Lucas is critical of the pre-state Zionist movement vis a vis the indigenous Arabs and in his epilogue he is critical and pessimistic about post-1967 Israeli policies.

Mandel, Neville J. The Arabs and Zionism before World War I. Berkeley, Ca.: University of California Press, 1976. XXIV, 258 p. On Arab anti-Zionism before the Balfour Declaration of 1917.

Namier, Louis B. Conflicts; Studies in Contemporary History. London: MacMillan, 1942. 232 p. Essays by the distinguished historian and Zionist. See Norman Rose, Lewis Namier and Zionism. (Oxford: Clarendon Press, 1980).

O'Brien, Conor Cruise. The Siege. The Saga of Israel and Zionism. N.Y.: Simon & Schuster, 1986. 298 p.

Rabinowicz, Oscar K. Fifty Years of Zionism; a historical analysis of Dr. Weizmann's "Trial and Error." London: R. Anscombe, 1950. (An expansion of three lectures delivered...on June 5, 12, and 19, 1949 before the Zionist Study Group in London). Bibliographical footnotes. Rabinowicz notes the errors and omissions in Weizmann's Trial and Error, presents an analysis of the historical parts of the work and of Weizmann's views on Zionist policy.

Rabinowicz, Oscar K. Arnold Toynbee on Judaism and Zionism, A Critique. London: W.N. Allen, 1974.

Bibliographical references and index. Argues that Toynbee's critique of Zionism fails to consider the deeper philosophical, religious, and national aspects of the problem and situation.

Ra'i, Yaacov. "The Zionist Attitude to the Arabs, 1908-1914." Middle Eastern Studies, 4 (April 1968): 198-242.

Reinharz, Jehuda. Chaim Weizmann. The Making of a Zionist Leader. New York: Oxford University Press, 1985. 566 p. Biblio.: p. 529-556. Index. photos. A major scholarly work that covers Weizmann--with focus on his Zionism and his work in chemistry--up to World War I. The first of two volumes. See, esp., chapter 12, "The Theory and Practice of Synthetic Zionism" and chapter 16, "A Hebrew University in Jerusalem." Reinharz makes clear that Weizmann, despite his own claim, did not invent the term "synthetic Zionism"; also, on the personal level Weizmann was an "elitist" with expensive tastes and often poor practical judgment, guilty of "greed and vanity" in the Perkin affair (1913) and not above an infatuation with a Gentile woman and her daughter at the same time. (chap. 15). The author credits Weizmann with awareness of the need for a peaceful understanding with the Arabs of Palestine, although there is too little discussion of this; and praises him for arguing that Zionist policies should not be evaluated solely on a financial basis. (pp. 384-86).

Rotenstreich. Nathan. Essays on Zionism and the Contemporary Jewish Condition. N.Y.: Herzl Press, 1980. Using a challenge-response model, Rotenstreich projects Zionism as an alternative to the rejection of history and to assimilation.

Sachar, Howard M. A History of Israel: From the Rise of
Zionism to our Time. N.Y.: Knopf, 1976. Biblio.: p.
839-883. A comprehensive and solid work, see chap. I,
III.

Sacher, Harry. ed. Zionism and the Jewish Future.
London: John Murray, 1916. An important collection of
essays. They have intrinsic merit and also have
historical value as attempted counters to Anglo-Jewish
assimilationism of the time. Includes a study of Jewish
history by Sacher, an essay on anti-Semitism by Albert
M. Hyamson, essays by Leon Simon, Richard Gottheil,
Norman Bentwich, N. Sokolow. C. Weizmann, in his
"Zionism and the Jewish Problem," argued that East
European Jewry was the spiritual center of Jewish life.
Moses Gaster in "Judaism as a National Religion" argued
that "the Jewish faith is a profession of national and
religious unity..."

Sanders, Ronald. The High Walls of Jerusalem. A History
of the Balfour Declaration and the Birth of the British
Mandate for Palestine. N.Y.: Holt, Rinehart & Winston,
1984. 747 p. maps, Notes and Bibliography, Index. A
major new synthesis.

Scholem, Gershom. "Israel and the Diaspora." In On
Jews and Judaism in Crisis. N.Y.: Schocken Books, 1976.
pp. 244-260. This was a lecture given in 1969 and pub.
in Judaica, 2 (Frankfurt am Main, 1970).

Shavit, Yaakov. "Zionist Historiography: Trends and
Tendencies." Jewish Book Annual, 42 (1984-85): 17-30.
Notes the contrast between those who view Zionism as

"revolutionary" and those who stress its continuity with Jewish history.

Sokolow, Nahum. History of Zionism, 1600-1918. Introd. by A.J. Balfour. 1919. Rpt. with new Introduction by Arthur Hertzberg. N.Y.: Ktav, 1969, 2 vols. Biblio.: pp. 449-460, Vol. 2. Sokolow (1861-1936) was President of the W.Z.O. from 1931 to 1935. His work, the first general history in English, concentrates on developments in England. Vol. 2 includes documents. Sokolow also wrote Hibbath Zion (The Love for Zion) (Jerusalem, 1935), in Hebrew.

St. John, Robert. Tongue of the Prophets: The Life Story of Eliezer ben Yehuda. Rpt. N.Y.: Doubleday, 1961. 349 p. Yehudah is credited with a major role in the Hebrew language revival in Palestine.

Stein, Leonard. Zionism. London: E. Benn, 1925, N.Y.: Greenberg, 1925. VII, 11-218 p.

Stein, Leonard. The Balfour Declaration. London: Vallentine, Mitchell, N.Y.: S&S, 1961. 681 p. Bibliography, Appendix, Index. trans. into Hebrew in 1962. A detailed account of the Zionist diplomacy in Britain and elsewhere during World War I. Stein was a participant in the negotiations both before and after the issuance of the Declaration.

Stein, Leonard, Dvorah Barzilay, and A. Chalon. eds. The Letters and Papers of Chaim Weizmann: Vol. 7: series A: August 1914-November 1917. London, O.U.P. 1975.

Studies in Zionism: an International Journal of Social, Political and Intellectual History. Tel Aviv: Institute for Zionist Research. 1980-, biyearly.

Tal, Uriel. "Jewish Self-Understanding and the Land and the State of Israel." Union Seminary Quarterly Review, 26 (1971): 351-381. There are three approaches to Zionism: legal-halakic neo-mystical (Buber), "non-observant" (Hebrew humanism). All three give meaning to the Land and see in Israel a hope that points to redemption.

Talmond, J.L. "Types of Jewish Self-Awareness: Herzl's "Jewish State" After Seventy Years (1896-1966). In Israel Among the Nations. London: Weidenfeld and Nicolson, 1970. pp. 88-129. Talmond reflects on the successes and failures of Zionism and makes perceptive comments on Herzl's ideas and personality.

Teveth, Shabtai. Ben-Gurion and the Palestinian Arabs. From Peace to War. New York: Oxford University Press, 1985. 234 p. Notes. Index. By the biographer of Ben-Gurion. Argues on the basis of letters, notes from closed meetings, and diaries that Ben-Gurion was alert to Arab hostility toward Zionism as early as 1910. His public plea for reconciliation from 1919 to 1929 was only a delaying tactic until the Yishuv had gained greater strength, and his advocacy of a compromise solution between 1929 and 1936 was a tactic designed to win more British support for the Zionist cause. Ben-Gurion's thought changed from the vision of Zionism as founded on "peace, justice, and progress" to Zionism as "a movement for relative justice with the Jews its sole concern, a movement prepared to wage war and to take the country, by force, if necessary." (viii).

Trevor-Roper, Hugh R. Jewish and Other Nationalism. London: Weidenfeld and Nicolson, 1962. (Based on the 5th Herbert Samuel lecture, Oct. 2, 1961, under the auspices of the British Friends of the Hebrew University of Jerusalem). 24 p. Asserts that nationalism is dead in Europe but not in Israel, the last product of European nationalism.

Tsur, Jacob. La révolte juive. Paris: Plon, 1970. An account of the rise of Zionism until 1948.

Tsur, Jacob. Zionism. The Saga of a National Liberation Movement. a trans. of L'Epopée du sionisme (1976). New Brunswick, N.J.: Transaction Books, 1977. 112 p. Includes: Note on the Author. An introductory and partisan overview by a former Israeli ambassador to France. Tsur defines Zionism as "the Jewish people's movement of national liberation."

Vital, David. The Origins of Zionism. Oxford, Eng.: Clarendon Press, 1975. Biblio.: pp. 377-385. Vital discusses the history of Zionism, the Zionist context, the Hibbat Zion movement, political Zionism. He argues that "Zionism re-created the Jews as a political nation."

Vital, David. Zionism, The Formative Years. N.Y.: Clarendon Press, 1982. 514 p. The sequel to The Origins of Zionism.

C. Varieties of Thought

1. Political, Territorial, Revisionist Zionists (For Weizmann, See Part II)

Herzl, Theodor. (1860-1904). Herzl brought political Zionism into the arena of world opinion; he convened the first Zionist Congress in Basel, 1897, founded the World Zionist Organization, wrote The Jewish State (1896) and Alteneuland (1902).

Ellern, Hermann. ed. Herzl, Hechler, The Great Duke of Baden and the German Emperor, 1896-1904. Tel Avi: Ellern's Bank, 1961. The facsimile of documents found by H. and B. Ellern.

Herzl, Theodor. Gesammelte Zionistische Schriften. ("Collected Zionist Writings"). 5 vols. Berlin: Judischer Verlag, 1934-35. Vol. I contains Speeches and Essays and Der Judenstaat; Vols. II-IV, Herzl's diaries; and Vol. V includes a play, "The New Ghetto," letters and Alteneuland. On "The New Ghetto" see Theodore Herzl: A Portrait for His Age. ed. by Ludwig Lewison. (N.Y.: 1955). In his plays, Herzl depicted the frustrations of the middle-class, emancipated Jews imprisoned in a "new," "invisible," "moral ghetto." Herzl's novel, Alteneuland, was indebted to T. Hertzka's utopian socialist novel Freiland (1890). The title is a variation on the name of the famous Prague synagogue

Altneuschul (Old-New Synagogue). Written in 1902, the novel pictures Palestine in 1923 as a cooperative commonwealth with universal suffrage, free universal schooling, and the full equality of women.

Herzl, Theodor. <u>Kitvei Herzl</u>. ("Herzl's Writings") 10 vols. Hebrew. Jerusalem: Zionist Library, 1960/61. This collection includes <u>Der Judenstadt, Alteneuland</u>, diaries, plays, essays and articles. The last volume contains a biography of Herzl by A. Bein, based on Bein's 1934 biography in German.

Herzl, Theodor. <u>Zionistische Schriften</u>. ed. by Leon Kellner. Berlin: Judischer Verlag, 1920. A collection of letters, essays, speeches before the Zionist Congresses, an autobiography, and <u>Der Judenstaat</u>.

Herzl, Theodor. <u>Der Judenstaat: Eine moderne Lösung der Judenfrage</u>. ("The Jewish State: A Modern Solution to the Jewish Question"). Leipzig and Vienna: Breitenbach, 1896. 86 p. Herzl argues that anti-Semitism cannot be eliminated. Therefore a Jewish state is necessary. Emancipation did not solve the Jewish problem, in fact it contributed to the problem: "In the principal countries where anti-Semitism prevails, it does so as a result of the Emancipation of the Jews." (5th ed. pp. 25-26).

Herzl, Theodor. <u>The Jewish State; an attempt at a modern solution of the Jewish question</u>. trans. by Sylvia D'Avigdor, as rev. by Israel Cohen. Foreword by Chaim Weizmann. N.Y.: Scopus, 1943. III p. Herzl believed that: "If you will, it is no fairytale."

Herzl, Theodor.   The Jewish State.... trans. by Sylvia
D'Avigdor, rev. by Israel Cohen, further rev. by Jacob
M. Alkow.   Includes a biography based on the work of
Alex Bein.   Special anniv.   ed. N.Y.:   American Zionist
Emergency Council, 1946. 11-160 pp. 4th ed. trans. by S.
D'Avigdor (rev.).   Foreword by Israel Cohen.   London: R.
Searl, 1946. 79 p.

Herzl, Theodor.   Tagebucher.   ("Diaries").   3 vols.
Berlin: Judischer Verlag, 1922-1923.   The first edition
of Herzl's diaries (1895-1904) was prepared by an
editorial board that included Hans Herzl, Leon Kellner,
Sigmund Katznelson, and Martin Buber.

Herzl, Theodor.   The Complete Diaries of Theodor Herzl.
ed. by R. Patai.   trans. by Harry Zohn.   5 vols.   N.Y.
and London: Herzl Press and T. Yoseloff, 1960.   After
the First Zionist congress, Herzl wrote in his Diary:
"In Basle I laid the foundation for the Jewish State.
Perhaps in five years, and certainly in fifty, everyone
will know it."

Herzl, Theodor.   The Diaries of Theodor Herzl.   ed. and
trans. by M. Lowenthal.   N.Y.: Dial Press, 1956.   Cover
the period from June 2, 1895 to May 16, 1904, and repre-
sent about 1/3 of the German original.   Herzl's entries
are characterized by spontaneity.

Herzl, Theodor.   Old-New Land.   trans. from the German
Alteneuland (1902) with rev. footnotes by Lotta Levensohn.   2nd ed. N.Y.: Block Pub. Co., 1960. XXI, 295 p.
New Preface by E. Neumann.   This utopian novel
envisioned a tolerant "state" with no enemies.   For an
analysis of Alteneuland in comparison with Der Juden-

<u>staat</u>, see Lewis Mumford, "Herzl's Utopia," <u>Menorah</u> <u>Journal</u>, 9:3 (August 1923).

Herzl, Theodor. <u>Im</u> <u>Anfang</u> <u>der</u> <u>Zionistischen</u> <u>Bewegung.</u> <u>Eine</u> <u>Dokumentation</u> <u>auf</u> <u>der</u> <u>Grundlage</u> <u>des</u> <u>Briefwechsels</u> <u>zwischen</u> <u>Theodor</u> <u>Herzl</u> <u>und</u> <u>Max</u> <u>Bodenheimer</u> <u>von</u> <u>1896</u> <u>bis</u> <u>1905</u>. Frankfurt A. M. Europaische Verlagsanstadt, 1965.

Literature on Herzl

The recent literature is extensive, especially in biographies. Among these the work by Amos Elon, <u>Herzl</u> (N.Y: Holt, Rinehart & Winston, 1975) is recommended. Writing about 40 years after Bein's biography, Elon makes a new and updated appraisal of Herzl's career. He uses Herzl's records, diaries and letters, and Israeli, German, French and British archival material, together with Jewish and non-Jewish memoirs by contemporaries of Herzl. Among other things, Elon throws important new light on early Zionist contacts with Arabs. In his <u>Alteneuland</u>, Herzl envisioned a new society, tolerant and peaceful. The motto: "Man, thou art my brother." History is not randomness but also it is no simple working-out of human intention. Modern Israel is not an Alteneuland, and one notes the irony of Herzl's Zionism in its role as midwife of Palestinian-Arab nationalism.

Another very different recent study is Desmond S. Steward's <u>Theodor</u> <u>Herzl</u> (N.Y.: Doubleday, 1974, 395 p.) Steward's focus is on Herzl, the individual; and he attempts "to discover the human being who lived from 1860 to 1904 and who combined the qualities of dreamer and man of action to a unique degree." Herzl's dream was that of an entrepreneur: "I have decided to place myself at the head of an effort for the Jews." (1895).

Also valuable is André Chouraqui's A Man Alone. Jerusalem: Israel Universities Press, 1968. This is a trans. of Theodor Herzl (Paris: Seuil, 1960). Chouraqui is an Algerian-born Israeli writer and politician.

Among older studies, vide Jacob De Haas, Theodore Herzl: A Biographical Study. 2 vols. (Chicago: Leonard, N.Y.: Brentano's, 1927) 371, 376 p. illus. De Haas (1872-1937), was an active Zionist. Also see Israel Cohen, Theodor Herzl: Founder of Political Zionism. (N.Y.: Yoseloff, 1959, 399 p.); and Jozsef Patai, Star over Jordan: the life of Theodor Herzl, trans. from the Hungarian by Frances Magyar (N.Y.: Philosophical Library, 1946, VIII, 356 p.) The best of the older studies is Alex Bein, Theodor Herzl, A Biography, trans. from the German (1934) by Maurice Samuel. (Phila.: JPS, 1940, 545 p; latest ed. with full bibliography, 1970). Bein has also edited a collection of Hebrew articles and essays on Herzl and some of his colleagues (Following Herzl, Tel Avi: Massada, 1954). For the memoirs of Saul R. Landau, one of Herzl's advisors, see Sturm und Drang in Zionismus (Vienna, 1937), includes letters and documents.

On Herzl's political thought, see Joseph Adler, The Herzl Paradox; Political, Social and Economic Theories of a Realist. (N.Y.: Hadrian Press, 1962). See also: Herzl Year Book: Essays in Zionist History and Thought. ed. by Raphael Patai. 6 vols. (N.Y.: Herzl Press, 1958-1965). These are essays and research papers on various aspects of Zionist history and on Herzl.

Moses Hess (1812-1875)

Hess, Moses (Moshe). Ketavim. ("Writings"). 2 vols.
ed. by Martin Buber. Jerusalem: Zionist Library, 1954-
1956. Vol. I contains Hess's Zionist writings. Hess's
thought was influenced by Z. Kalischer (see below) and
by Hegel. See Ronald Sanders, "Moses Hess: the Hegelian
Zionist." Midstream, 8:1 (1962): 57-69. During his
life, Hess was known as a Socialist and little attention
was paid to his Jewish nationalism (which anticipates
Herzl, in some respects, by about 25 years). Judaism
for Hess was a national religion; social justice was its
aim, not individual salvation.

Hess, Moses (Moshe). Rome and Jerusalem; A Study in
Jewish Nationalism. trans. of Röm und Jerusalem
(Leipzig: 1862) by Meyer Waxman. ed. N.Y.: Bloch, 1943;
265 p. Philosophical Library, 1958. Hess, a friend of
Marx (who called him "our communist Rabbi") is often
considered the first modern Zionist thinker. His bold
and daring vision was formed before the Socialist movement and the revolutionary movement in Russia had
ripened. He was the first Jewish socialist to define
Jewish nationalism as revolutionary.

Hess, Moses (Moshe). The Works of Moses Hess. An
Inventory of his Signed and Anonymous Publication, MSS.
and Correspondence. ed. by Edmund Silberner. Leiden:
1958. Quarto, 1250 p. And vide Ausgewahlte Schriften.

Ausgewahlt und eingeleitet von H. Lademacher. (Koln,
J. Melzer, 1962). Biblio.: p. 439-461.

Hess, Moses (Moshe). Moses Hess Briefwechsel. ("Moses Hess Correspondence"). ed. by Edmund Silberner. The Hague: 1959. On Hess see the following, Theodor Zlocistic, Hess: Eine Biographische Studie (Berlin: 1921), Auguste Cornu, Moses Hess et la gauche Hegelienne (Paris, 1934), Edmund Silberner, Moses Hess: Geschichte seines Lebens (Leiden: Brill 1966), Isaiah Berlin, Life and Opinions of Moses Hess (Cambridge, Eng.: 1959). An interesting account, but less commanding than the study by that I. Berlin, is Mary Schulman's Moses Hess: Prophet of Zionism (N.Y. T. Yoseloff, 1963) 128 p. See also John Weiss, Moses Hess, Utopian Socialist. (Studies: [social science, 8] Detroit: Wayne State University Press, 1960, 77 p.) On Hess' involvement with Palestinian colonization schemes, see E. Silberner, Moses Hess Briefwechsel (cited above, 530-3, 538-40). Also see the discussion of Hess in S. Avineri, The Making of Modern Zionism. (1981, cited above); now vide Avineri's Moses Hess: Prophet of Communism and Zionism (N.Y.: N.Y. University Press, 1985. XII, 266 p.).

Vladimir Jabotinsky (Zhabotinskii) (1880-1940)

Jabotinsky, Vladimir. The Jewish War Front. London: Allen and Unwin, 1940. 255 p. Pub. under the title: War and the Jews. Foreword by Pierre van Passem and a conclusion by John H. Patterson. N.Y.: Dial Press, 1943, Toronto: Longmans, 1943. 5-252 pp. This work contains an attack on the Palestine White Paper of 1939 and demands that a Jewish state be made a war aim of the Allies.

Jabotinsky, Vladimir. The Story of the Jewish Legion. trans. by Samuel Katz. N.Y.: Beechhurst, 1946. Foreword by J.H. Patterson.

Jabotinsky, Vladimir. Ketavim ("Writings"). 18 vols. Tel Aviv: Ari Jabotinsky, 1947-1959. A classified and annotated collection of essays, articles, plays and speeches, translated from Russian or Yiddish. Jabotinsky's autobiography is in Hebrew only (Jerusalem, 1947). On his thought and action, see chap. 7 of W. Laqueur's History of Zionism (cited above) and the bibliography therein, pp. 608-610. See also the discussion in S. Avineri, The Making of Modern Zionism (cited above). The standard study in English is by Joseph B. Schechtman, The Jabotinsky Story, Vol. I: Rebel and Statesman: the early years (N.Y.: Yoseloff, 1956); vol. 2: Fighter and Prophet: the last years (Yoseloff, 1961) 643 p. In Hebrew see J. Schechtman and Y. Benari, History of the Revisionist Movement, vol. I (Tel Aviv, 1970). Oscar K. Rabinowicz's Vladimir Jabotinsky's Conception of a Nation (N.Y.: Beechhurst Press, 1946), 5-31 p. is an admiring tract. It is interesting to note that Arthur Koestler's novel Thieves in the Night; Chronicle of an Experiment. (London, N.Y., Toronto: Macmillan, 1946) is dedicated to Jabotinsky. On Revisionism in Poland in the inter-war period, see chap. 7 of Zionism in Poland (1981) by E. Mendelsohn (cited below).

Jakob Klatzkin (1882-1948)

Klatzkin, Jakob. Krisis und Entscheidung im Judentum. ("Crisis and Decision in Jewry"). Berlin: Judischer Verlag, 1921.

Klatzkin, Jacob. "Boundaries." trans. by A. Hertzberg. In The Zionist Idea, ed. by A. Hertzberg (cited above). pp. 316-327. Klatzkin's Zionism rejects the possibility of creative Jewish life in the Diaspora. Judaism is nationalistic, with land and language defining "nation."

Klatzkin, Jacob. In Praise of Wisdom. trans. by A. Ragelson. N.Y.: Fischer, Toronto: McClelland, 1943. O. 7-312 pp. A collection of philosophical aphorisms.

Max Simon Nordau (Max Simon [Simhah Meir] Sudfeld) (1849-1923)

Max Nordau To His People. ed. with an Introd. by B. Netanyahu. N.Y.: Scopus, 1941. 218 p. A collection of essays and speeches by this early political Zionist. Nordau was a physician, prolific writer, journalist, and author of Die Conventionellen Lugen der Kulturmenschheit (1884), trans. into English, The Conventional Lies of our Civilization (Chicago: Schick, 1884) and Degeneration. trans. from the 2nd German ed., Introd. by George L. Mosse (N.Y.: Fertig, 1968), XXXIV, 566 p. Nordau met Herzl in Paris in 1892 and served as vice president of the Zionist congresses. After Herzl's death in 1904, Nordau fought with the "practical Zionists" who advocated colonization of Palestine without insisting on some form of political sovereignty. For a discussion of Nordau, see chap. 10 of S. Avineri's The Making of Modern Zionism (cited above).

Like his friend Herzl, Nordau blamed modern Jewish misery on the Enlightenment: "Such is the existing liberation of the emancipated Jew in Western Europe. He has given up his specifically Jewish character, but the peoples let him feel that he has not acquired their special characteristics." To His People, pp. 70-71. His argument for Zionism, then, was that it would re-create communal Jewish identity.

Max Simon Nordau. Zionistische Schriften. ("Zionist Writings"). ed. by the Zionistisches Aktions-Komitee. Cologne and Leipzig: Judischer Verlag, 1909; Berlin, 1923. Includes speeches, and Nordau's addresses to the Zionist congresses, 1897-1907, lectures, articles, letters and poems.

Max Simon Nordau. Ktavim Zioniyim. ("Zionist Writings"). ed. by B. Netanyahu. 4 vols. Jerusalem: Zionist Library, 1960-1962. A collection of articles and essays, including Nordau's speeches at the Zionist Congresses. The fourth volume contains a detailed bibliography.

On Nordau, see Anna and Max Nordau, Max Nordau; A Biography. trans. from the French. N.Y.: Nordau Committee, 1943. O. VI, 440 p. illus. This biography by his wife and his daughter includes a list of Nordau's works, pp. 439-440. For an analysis of Nordau's social theory see Meir Ben-Horin, Max Nordau: Philosopher of Human Solidarity. N.Y.: Herzl Press, 1965. A bibliography of Nordau's writings is included. For a study of some of Nordau's correspondence with I. Goldziher, see A. Scheiber, "Max Nordau's Letters to Ignace Goldziher." JSS, 18 (July 1956): 199-207, includes bibliography, Appendix: 7 letters in German.

Leo Pinsker (Lev Semenovich) (1821-1891)

Pinsker, Leo. Autoemancipation: a call to his people by a Russian Jew. Based on the 2nd ed. of the trans. of Autoemanzipation...(Berlin, 1882) by D.S. Blondheim. rev. and ed. by Arthur S. Suger. N.Y.: Z.O.A. (Pamphlet series, 3), 1947; London: R. Searl, 1947. O. 36 p. An incisive and embittered pamphlet occasioned by the pogroms of 1871 and most decisively by the government-encouraged horrors of 1881. Pinsker argued the necessity of a Jewish state (but not necessarily in Palestine) in order to escape anti-Semitism, "an inherited aberration of the human mind." (p. 8). The Jews, he wrote, "are not a living nation; they are everywhere aliens; therefore they are despised..." The only solution is "the auto-emancipation of the Jews; their return to the ranks of the nations by the acquisition of a Jewish homeland." (p. 35). Pinsker's anonymous pamphlet provoked strong reactions in the pre-Herzl generation, preparing some minds for the concept of a Jewish state. Pinsker became a leader in the Love of Zion movement which did some small-scale colonization in Palestine.

Pinsker, Leo. Road to Freedom; Writings and Addresses. ed. trans. from the German and with an Introd. by B. Netanyahu. N.Y.: Scopus, 1944. 142 p.

Pinsker, Leo. Y.L. Pinkster: Mevaser Ha-Thiyah Ha-Leu'mit. ("Y.L. Pinsker: Founder of National Renaissance"). Tel Aviv: Massada, 1960. Contains Pinsker's Autoemancipation and essays about it, speeches, announcements, and letters to and from Pinsker. Pinsker wrote: "The great ideas of the eighteenth and nineteenth centuries have not passed by our people without leaving a trace. We feel not only as Jews; we feel as men. As men, we, too would fain live and be a nation like the others."

Israel Zangwill (1864-1926)

Israel Zangwill. Speeches, Articles, and Letters. select. and ed. by Maurice Simon. Foreword by Edith Ayrton Zangwill. London: Soncino Press, 1937. O. XII, 357 p. Zangwill disagreed with other Zionists on the question of Palestine as the site for a Jewish state and he founded and was president (1905-1925) of the Territorial Organization. See his: The East African Question: Zionism and England's Offer (N.Y.: Maccabean Pub. Co., 1904). On the East African question see Oscar K. Rabinowicz, "New Light on the East Africa Scheme." In The Rebirth of Israel. ed. by Israel Cohen (1952, cited above), pp. 77-79; and see the major work by Robert G. Weisbord, African Zion; the Attempt to Establish a Jewish Colony in the East Africa Protectorate, 1903-1905. N.Y.: JPSA, 1968, 347 p.

Israel Zangwill. "Be Fruitful and Multiply." London: Jewish Territorial Organization, Pamphets Series No. 3, 1909. This contains proposals for the colonization of Mesopotamia (Iraq). There is a recent study in Hebrew of the Territorialist ideas about Iraq by Michael Heymann, The Zionist Movement and the Schemes for Settlement in Iraq after Herzl. (Tel Aviv: Tel Aviv University, 1965). Expressive of an anti-Zionist point of view is H.A. Farisi, "Israel Zangwill's Challenge to Zionism," Journal of Palestine Studies, 15 (Spring 1975): 74-90. On Zangwill's life and thought, see

Joseph Leftwich, _Israel Zangwill_ (London: James Clarke, 1957; N.Y.: Yoseloff, 1957) 306 p. On intellectual and political topics, see Maurice Wohlgelernter, _Israel Zangwill: a study_. (N.Y.: Columbia University Press, 1964, XVI, 344 p. Biblio.: p.. 321-334). Zangwill was a versatile writer--among his works are _Children of the Ghetto: a study of a peculiar people_ (1892), _The King of Schnorrers: grotesques and fantasies_ (1894), a picaresque novel about an 18th-century rogue, and _Dreamers of the Ghetto_ (1898), a book of essays on famous Jews. The title and theme of his play, _The Melting Pot; a drama in four acts_ (1909), has become fixed in American awareness.

2. Religious, Cultural, Mystic Zionists, Zionism.

Alkalai, Jehudah. Kitve Jehudah Alkalai. ("Writings of
Jehudah Alkalai"). Jerusalem: 1945. Alkalai (1798-
1878), a precursor of modern Zionist thought, called for
an organized establishment of Jewish colonies in
Palestine.

Avisdai, Bernard. The Tragedy of Zionism (1985). cited
above). See chap. 2: "Cultural Zionism."

Bentwich, Norman. For Zion's Sake; A Biography of Judah
L. Magnes, First Chancellor and First President of the
Hebrew University of Jerusalem. (Jacob H. Schiff
library). Phila.: JPS, 1954. 329 p. Bentwich served as
an attorney general of Palestine and was a professor of
international law at the Hebrew University. See his
autobiography, My Seventy-Seven Years (Phila.: JPS,
1961)

Buber, Martin. On Zion (cited in part 2, above), and
Israel and the World: Essays in a Time of Crisis. N.Y.:
Schocken Books, 1963.

Buber, Martin. J.L. Magnes, and E. Simon. Towards
Union in Palestine. 1947. N.Y.: Greenwood, 1972.

Kalischer, Zvi Hirsch. Derishat Zion (Ziyyon) v'Hevrat
Eretz Noshevet. ("Seeking Zion and the Settlement of an
Awakening Land"). 2nd ed. Thorn: 1886. First pub. in
1862 by the Kilonisations-Verein fuer Palestine, the

first society for the settlement of Palestine, and the precursor of the Hibbat Zion in the West. Kalischer (1795-1874) thought that redemption of Israel required human effort. On his initiative the Mikveh Israel agricultural school was established in 1870 under the auspices of the Alliance Israelite Universelle. His ideas, ahead of their time, influenced Moses Hess and others. See Hertzberg (1960, cited above), pp. 108-14, "Kalischer," EJ, Vol. 10, 708-709 (with bibliography), Avineri (1981, cited above, pp. 48-55). An Orthodox Jew, Kalischer reveals how deep the impact of modernization was upon Jewry; like Alkalai he demystified the redemptive process, bringing out "the dialectical relationship between human praxis and providential design." Avineri (1981), p. 54.

Lilienblum, Moshe Leib. Kol Kitve M.L. Lilienblum. ("All the Writings of Moshe Leib Lilienblum"). Odessa: 1910-1913. Born in Lithuania, Lilienblum moved to "enlightened" Odessa in 1869. He was a first-generation Maskil (enlightened one) and he initially thought that Russian Jews could adjust to modernity through education and religious reforms. The pogroms of 1881 (as was also true for Pinsker) radically altered his views. See chap. 6 in Avineri (1981). (cited above).

Ahad Ha'am (Asher Ginzberg) (1856-1927)

Ahad Ha'am. Nationalism and the Jewish Ethic: Basic Writings of Ahad Ha'am. ed. with an Introd. by Hans Kohn. N.Y.: Schocken Books, 1962. Born in the Russian Ukraine, Ha'am went to Odessa at the age of 22, where he joined the central committee of Hoveve Zion (Lovers of

Zion). His famous essay of 1889, "This is Not the Way," argued the need for a spiritual basis for Zionism. He was a strong supporter of a Jewish nationalist home, which would be a model for the diaspora. He was a sharp critic of the political Zionism of Herzl, thinking that a Jewish state should be the end product of a spiritual renaissance.

Ahad Ha'am. Selected Essays by Ahad Ha'am. ed. trans. from the Hebrew and with an Introd. by Sir Leon Simon. Phila.: JPS, 1912. 347 p. N.Y.: Meridian Books, 1948. Ha'am was a gifted prose stylist, finely tuned, precise and clear. The essay was his primary form.

Ahad Ha'am. Essays, Letters, Memoirs by Ahad Ha'am. trans. from the Hebrew and ed. by Sir Leon Simon. (Philosophica Judaica) Oxford, East and West Library, 1948. 354 p. Ha'am interpreted Jewish teachings as the expression of the moral and rational character of Judaism. Ha'am lived in Palestine from 1921 until his death in 1927. A six-vol. collection of his letters (Iggerot Ahad Ha'am) was published in 1923-25, and his last letters and memoirs were published in 1931 (Ahad Ha'am: Pirge zikhronot we-iggerot).

On Ahad Ha-am, see the discussion in Avineri (1981, cited above), and the biography by Sir Leon Simon. Ahad Ha'am (Asher Ginzberg): A Biography. (Phila.: JPS, 1960, 348 p.). This is a detailed study, particularly in regard to the early years; and it has a substantial bibliography, pp. 321-332.

Smolenskin, Perez. Kol Silfrei Perez Smolenskin. ("All the Writings of Perez Smolenskin"). 6 vols. Jerusalem:

1905-1910. Smolenskin (1841-1885) was an archetypical member of the generation of Russian Jews who experienced the beginnings of Emancipation in Russia but then saw their hopes crushed by the pogroms of 1881. That atrocity initiated massive emigration from Russia. Emigration, Smolenskin argued, should assert collective identity. Thus: "If the wave of emigration is to direct itself to one place, surely no other country in the world is conceivable except Eretz Israel." A. Hertzberg, The Zionist Idea. (cited above), p. 157.

Smolenskin, Perez. Ma'marin. ("Essays"). 4 vols. Jerusalem: 1925-1926. For a selection from his writings in English, vide A. Hertzberg, The Zionist Idea. pp. 145-157. "...we intend neither to attempt to force the arrival of the Messiah, nor to establish our Kingdom now. We seek only to provide bread, in a land in which there is hope that those who labor on it will find rest." (1881). Also on Smolenskin, see chap. 6 in Avineri (1981, cited above), pp. 54-64. And see Charles H. Freundlich, Peretz Smolenskin: His Life and Thought; A Study of the Renascence of Jewish Nationalism. (N.Y.: Bloch, 1966), 278 p.

3. Socialist Zionism, Labor Zionism.

> The guidelines of the new Jewish
> state must be justice, rational
> planning, and social solidarity...
> The hope for a Messiah, always
> the basic sentiment of the *Galut*
> Jew, will be converted into political
> fact.

Introduction

Introductory readings for this section include
chapter 6 of W. Laqueur's Zionism (cited above), pp.
270-337; A. Hertzberg, ed. The Zionist Idea (cited
above), Part 6, pp. 329-395. N. Levin, While Messiah
Tarried, Part IV. Entries in the "Zionism in Russia"
and "Zionism in the U.S." are pertinent here. Moses
Hess (cited in Section I) could also be discussed here.
In N. Syrkin's Introduction to his Yiddish translation
of Rome and Jerusalem, he wrote: "Moses Hess is not the
founder of Zionism...but he is the founder of Socialist
Judaism..." The focus in this section is on N. Syrkin,
B. Borochov and A. D. Gordon (not a "Socialist-Zionist".
The thought of Martin Buber is also highly significant,
see Paths in Utopia, trans. by R.F.C. Hull with an
Introduction by Ephraim Fischoff (Boston: Beacon Paper-
backs, 1958). See chapters on Proudhon, Kropotkin, and
Landauer. And see chapters 11 and 12 in M. Friedman's
Martin Buber's Life and Work. The Early Years, 1878-
1923 (N.Y.: E.P. Dutton, 1981) and vide chap. 3, "The
Conquest of Labor," in B. Avishai's The Tragedy of

Zionism (cited above, 1985). On Moses Hess, _vide_ section 3, above.

Borochov and Syrkin agreed with the Jewish Social- ist Bund on the predominant importance of the Jewish proletariat. They disagreed with the Bund and agreed with the Zionists on the endemic character of anti- Semitism in the Diaspora. The Bund, like the Marxist leadership generally, thought that anti-Semitism would be abolished when class oppression was abolished. The Marxist-Zionists could not accept this notion. Their problem, then, was to combine revolutionary activisim-- through the Jewish proletariat--with Zionist territor- ialism.

General histories of Socialism have paid little attention to Jewish Socialism and virtually no attention to Zionist-Socialism. This situation has been remedied, in part, by recent studies, e.g., see the well- researched (but contains no bibliography) _While Messiah Tarried, Jewish Socialist Movements, 1871-1917_ by Nora Levin (N.Y.: Schocken Books, 1977). See also Ezra Mendelsohn, "The Jewish Socialist Movement and the Second International, 1889-1914." _JJS_, 26 (1964): 131- 46, E. Mendelsohn, _Class Struggle in the Pale_ (Cambridge, 1970), and Mendelsohn, _Zionism in Poland: the formative years, 1915-1926_ (Yale University Press, 1981), Biblio.: pp.359-364; chap. 3 is on Poale Zion. Earlier research has been done by R. Abramovitch, "The Jewish Socialist Movement in Russia and Poland (1897- 1919)," in _The Jewish People: Past and Present_, 4 Vols. (N.Y.: 1949), Vol. 2, pp. 369-98; and see Mark Jarblum, _The Socialist International and Zionism_. trans. by M. Hurwitz (N.Y.: 1933). The Jewish Bund was founded in

Vilna in 1897, its history in Poland is covered by B.K. Johnpoll in his The Politics of Futility: The General Jewish Workers Bund of Poland, 1917-1943 (Cornell University Press, 1967. 298 p.). Also see Henry J. Tobias, The Jewish Bund in Russia; from its Origins to 1905 (Stanford University Press, 1972), 409 p. Also Koppell Pinson, "Arkady Kremer, Vladimir Medem, and the Ideology of the Jewish "Bund"; JSS, 7 (July 1945); Jacob S. Hertz, "The Bund's Nationality Program and its Critics in the Russian, Polish and Austrian Socialist Movements." YIVO Annual (1969); Charles E. Woodhouse and Henry J. Tobias, "Primordial Ties and Political Process in Pre-Revolutionary Russia: The Case of the Jewish Bund." Comparative Studies in Society and History, no. 3 (April 1966). And on the emergence of the Jewish labour movement in Russia, see M. Mishkinsky in Zion, 31:1-2 (1966), Eng. Abstract, VIII, IX. For a useful general survey, see "Socialism and the Jews." EJ, Vol. 15, 34-38, and "Socialism, Jewish." EJ, Vol. 15, 38-52.

Nachman Syrkin (1864-1924). This visionary prophet of Socialist-Zionism gave a penetrating analysis of anti-semitism and made a realistic assessment of the Jewish situation in modern class society.

Syrkin, Nachman. Essays on Socialist Zionism. N.Y.: Young Poale Zion Alliance, 1935. O. 5-64 p. Also, for an early exposition of the concepts of Labour Zionism, see Syrkin, Die Judenfrage und der sozialistische Juden-staat (Bern, 1898).

Syrkin, Marie. Nachman Syrkin: Socialist Zionist. N.Y.: Herzl and Sharon, 1961. Biographical memoirs by Syrkin's daughter that include essays by N. Syrkin in translation. In his "A Call to Jewish Youth" (1901) Syrkin argued that the Jewish problem can only be solved through Jewish national emancipation and the emergence of a classless society. Anti-Semitism is a result of the unequal distribution of power in society. "As long as society is based on might, and as long as the Jew is weak, anti-Semitism will exist." "The Jewish Problem and the Jewish State." In The Zionist Idea, ed. by A. Hertzberg (cited above), p. 340.

Further related reading: A.L. Patkin, The Origins of the Russian-Jewish Labour Movement (Melbourne, 1947; N.Y.: Bloch, 1947, 275 p.), Jonathan Frankel, Prophecy and Politics; Socialism, Nationalism, and the Russian Jews, 1862-1917. (Cambridge: Cambridge University Press, 1981), XXII, 686 p., a major scholarly study. See also chapter 23 of Nora Levin, While Messiah Tarried...(1977, cited above), Ben Halpern, "Nachman Syrkin." Jewish Frontier, 41, no. 8 (October 1974); and "Labor Zionism in Russian." In Russian Jewry, 1960-1917, ed. by J. Frunkin, et al. (N.Y.: Yoseloff, 1966).

A.D. Gordon (1856-1922). This mystical Zionist inspired and was the ideologist of the first Palestinian Jewish labor part, *Hapoel Hatzair*. Gordon was known as the apostle of the Religion of Labor.

Gordon, Aaron David. Selected Essays. trans. from the Hebrew by F. Burnce. ed. by N. Teradyon and A. Shohat. Biographical sketch by E. Silberschlag. N.Y.: League

for Labor Palestine, Bloch, 1938. XV, 303 p.   Gordon
emigrated to Palestine in 1904. He refused a position
as a librarian to do manual farm labor. He believed
that alienation could be ended only when Jews returned
to Palestine and developed the "soil." "We who belong
to a people that in our striving for complete regeneration, we have no choice but to base the life we seek
wholly upon its natural foundation. We must return
fully to nature, to work, to creativity, and to a sense
of order and spirituality characteristic of family-
nationhood." (Fundamentals).

Gordon, Aaron David.   Kitve ("Writings"). 5 vols. Tel
Aviv, 1925-28. Gordon was influenced by early Russian
socialism, populism, and by Tolstoy. He advocated a
Zionist "socialism" that would replace the class
struggle by a gospel of mutual love and a religion of
individual labor within a community "for the renewal of
life of a renewed people." Gordon's influence inspired
the founding of the first Kibbutz in Palestine, Deganya
(1909). His ideas and impact "reflected the transition
of Zionism from its character as an aspect of European
life to that of a thrusting force in the Middle East."
(Lucas, 1974, cited above, p. 38.). For the early days
of the collective settlements (kvutza), see Harry
Viteles, A History of the Co-Operative Movement in
Israel: a source book. 4 books. (London, Vallentine,
1967-68); and Alex Bein, The Return to the Soil, a
history of Jewish settlement in Israel. trans. from the
Hebrew by I. Schen (Jerusalem and N.Y.: Z.O., 1953, 576
p. illus.). The standard works in Hebrew are by Berl
Katznelson (Tel Aviv, 1940, 1958). And now see: Berl:
The Biography of a Socialist Zionist 1887-1944 by Anita
Shapira. trans. from the Hebrew (1980) by Haya Galai

(Cambridge: Cambridge University Press, 1984), IX, 400 p. Index.

For works on Gordon, see the essay in Great Jewish Thinkers of the Twentieth Century, ed. by S. Noveck (Washington D.C.: B'nai B'rith, 1963), and the discussion in Avineri (1981, cited above, pp. 151-158). Avineri calls Gordon "the first significant Zionist thinker whose ideas emerged through the confrontation with reality in Palestine itself." p. 151. See also Herbert H. Rose, The Life and Thought of A.D. Gordon: Pioneer Philosopher and Prophet of Modern Israel. (N.Y.: Bloch, 1964); and Amos Perlmutter. "A.D. Gordon: A Transcendental Zionist." Middle Eastern Studies, 7 (1971): 81-87. Perlmutter documents Russian populist influence on Gordon's thought. In Hebrew there is a recent study by Shavid Eliezer, The Individual: The World of A.D. Gordon (Tel Aviv: Am Oved, 1970). This contains excerpts from Gordon's writings, and reviews his activities and points of view.

Some of the philosophical challenges of Gordon's thought are discussed by Nathan Rotenstreich in his Jewish Philosophy in Modern Times; from Mendelssohn to Rosenzweig. (N.Y.: Holt, 1968), pp. 239-52. S. Avineri defines Gordon's Zionism as "an actual praxis, to be carried out by those who want to participate in this momentous revolt of the Jewish people against its own history." And this revolt is "also close to the basic tenets of Jewish religion as a practical way of life..." (1981, cited above, p. 158).

Ber (Baer) Borochov (1881-1917). Borochov sought to integrate Jewish nationalism with orthodox Marxism and founded Poale Zion (Workers of Zion). It requires great conceptual ingenuity to make Marxism and Jewish nationalism compatible. For Marx and the other early founders, Jewish nationality was a fictional image.

Borochov, Ber. Nationalism and the Class Struggle: A Marxian Approach to the Jewish Problem. selected writings. ed. by Moshe Cohen. trans. from the Yiddish with an Essay by Abraham G. Duker. N.Y.: Young Poale Zion Alliance, 1937. 5-205 p. Borochov postulated an inevitable dynamic force ("stychischer prozess") that produced spontaneous concentrated emigration to Palestine. Then the forces of production within the Jewish economy would create a class struggle leading ultimately to a socialist society, in which "Jewish misery" (Judennot) ceased to exist.

Borochov, Ber. The National Question and the Class Struggle. trans. by L. Jessel. Chicago, 1935. This was his first major study. See also: Sozialismus und Zionismus (Vienna, 1932), and Die Grundlagen des Poalezionismus ("The Foundations of Poale Zion") (Frankfurt/M, 1969). Zionism involves the reconstruction of the Jewish economy.

Borochov, Ber. Ketavim ("Writings"). 3 vols. ed. by L. Levita and D. Ben-Nahum. Tel Aviv: Sifriat Poalim and Hakibbutz Hameuchad, 1956, 1968.

On Borochov, see Amos Perlmutter, "Dov Ber-Borochov: A Marxist-Zionist Ideologist." Middle Eastern Studies, 5 (January 1969): 32-43. For a recent study of Socialist-Zionism by a "disciple" of Borochov, see Allon Gal, Socialist-Zionism, Theory and Issues in Contemporary

Jewish Nationalism. (Cambridge, Mass.: Schenkman, 1973. 223 p.). A survey of Zionist Marxism is given by I. Kolatt in "Zionist Marism." In Varieties of Marxism. ed. by Shlomo Avineri (The Hague: M. Nijhoff, 1977, pp. 227-270).

D. Zionism in Germany. German-speaking Zionists.

Scholars assert that the majority of German Jews were indifferent or hostile to Zionism before World War I. How does one explain this? One could say that the degree of anti-Semitism in the Wilhelmian Rechtstaat was relatively mild (no Dreyfus case, or Odessa-type pogroms) but more basic was the desire of German Jewry to integrate with German culture. This integration was not perceived as abandonment of one's religion as an individual Jew, but the existence of a specific Jewish problem was denied. Hence the Zionist avowal of nationality was viewed by the assimilated Jew as irrelevant or as a threat to their individual rights. One may note the famous Rabbinic proclamation: "Judaism enjoins its adherents to serve the fatherland to which they belong with utmost devotion and to promote its national interests with all their heart and all their might."

Leading German Zionists included Wolffsohm, Blumenfeld, Bodenheimer. The early cultural Zionists included H. Kohn, B. Freiwel, E.M. Lilein and Martin Buber. Buber saw cultural Zionism as a world-view, an "inner agitation" that would nourish Jewish culture and create whole human beings. See M. Friedman, Martin Buber's Life and Work. The Early Years, 1878-1923. (N.Y.: E.P. Dutton, 1981), chap. 3-4.

The studies of the early period are in German or Hebrew--E. Auerbach, (1969), R. Lichtheim (1970)--but there are two good recent studies in English, Poppel

(1977, cited below) and J. Reinharz (1975, cited below).
The excellent works on diplomatic history by I. Friedman
(1973, 1977) have made new advances in perspective.

Aschheim, Steven E. The Eastern European Jew in German
and Brothers and Strangers; Jewish Consciousness, 1800-
1923. Madison, WI.: the University of Wisconsin
Press, 1982. See chap. 3, "Zionism and the Ostjuden.
The Ambiguity of Nationalization," pp. 80-99, passim.
On Nathan Birnbaum (1864-1937) who is said to have
coined the term "Zionism" and "discovered"/affirmed the
Ostjuden for Western Jewry, see pp. 114-116, and notes.

Biale, David. Gershom Scholem...(Cambridge, Mass.:
Harvard University Press. 1979. (cited above). See chap.
3: "From Berlin to Jerusalem." pp. 52-78.

Blumenfeld, Kurt. Erlebte Judenfrage: Ein Viertel-
jahrhundert deutscher Zionismus. ("The Jewish Question
as it was Experienced: A Quarter Century of German Zionism") Stuttgart: Deutsche Verlagsanstalt, 1962. The
memoirs of the President of the German Zionist Federation from 1923 to 1933. Of "Jewish family of German
culture," Blumenfeld (1884-1963) thought that Zionism,
which was however not a matter of doctrine but of revelation (Offenbarung), was the only answer to "The Jewish
Question." Blumenfeld called his version of Zionism
"post-assimilatory," meaning it was for assimilated Jews
who had no secure base to oppose anti-Semitism and it
was for Jews who lacked contact with Jewish culture.
Blumenfeld was a close friend, mentor and "spiritual
godfather" to Hannah Arendt. See Elisabeth Young-
Bruehl, Hannah Arendt: For Love of the World (Yale
University Press, 1982).

Blumenfeld, Kurt. Im Kampf um den Zionismus, Briefe aus fünf Jahrzehnten. (Veroffentlichung des Leo Baeck Instituts) Deutsche Verlags-Anstalt, 1976. Letters to fellow Zionists. Includes an essay on Blumenfeld and German Zionism.

Bodenheimer, Max Isidor. Prelude to Israel; The Memoirs of M.I. Bodenheimer. ed. by Henrietta Hannah Bodenheimer. trans. from the Hebrew by I. Cohen. N.Y.: T. Yoseloff, 1963. 417 p. illus. The memoirs of an important German political Zionist (1865-1940).

Brenner, Lenni. Zionism in the Age of the Dictators. London: Croom Helm, 1983.

Buber, Martin. Israel and Palestine. N.Y.: Schocken Books, 1963. a trans. of Israel und Palastina: zur Geschichte einer Idee. (Zürich, 1950). Also on Buber see preceding section. Contains Buber's profound analysis of the growth of the Zionist movement and of personalities within the movement. In 1901 Buber became editor of Die Welt, the official Zionist organ. But at the Fifth Zionist Congress in 1901 he opposed Herzl in terms of a cultural Zionism focussed on spiritual rebirth. Buber and his friends made the first proposal for a University in Palestine. He opposed Herzl's identification of the movement with himself, Herzl's external, diplomatic, political approach and also his "Uganda" proposal. Buber was deeply moved and influenced by both Herzl and Ahad Ha'am. He contrasted them in terms of a leader (Herzl), teacher (Ha'am) polarity. "Leading without a teaching attains success: Only what one attains is at times a downright caricature of what ...one wanted to obtain..."

Cohn, E.B. David Wolffsohn. Amsterdam, 1939. Wolffsohn was Herzl's successor as President of the W.Z.O.

Esh, Shaul. "Kurt Blumenfeld on the Modern Jew and Zionism." JJS, (Dec. 1964): 232-42.

Friedman, Isaiah. The Question of Palestine, 1914-1918: British-Jewish-Arab Relations. London: Routledge & Kegan Paul, 1973, N.Y.: Schocken Books, 1973. 433 p. An important study of the role of Palestine in W.W.I. diplomacy. Friedman uses materials (Foreign Office documents) not available to Stein (The Balfour Declaration 1961) and reaches some different conclusions. He rejects the notion of Palestine as the "twice-promised land," arguing that Britain secured the mandate because of strategic interests. Essentially it was the War Cabinet and not Weizmann and the Zionists that brought about the Balfour Declaration. The French statement of June 1917 supporting the "Renaissance of Jewish Nationality" was also a spur to the British. It helped Zionist respectability and edged the British toward support of Zionist goals to forestall the French.

Friedman, Isaiah. Germany, Turkey, and Zionism, 1897-1918. Oxford, Eng.: Clarendon Press, 1977. 461 p. This essential work, an expansion of his doctoral dissertation, includes appendices and full bibliography. Friedman collates and tests the documents and claims that "facts alone determined my conclusion." He argues that "It was the competition of the belligerent powers to win the goodwill of World Jewry that put Zionism on the map." The Germans were the "chief protectors" of the Zionists because the German government saw in

Zionism an instrument to advance their own interests in the middle Orient and to solve the Jewish problem in Eastern Europe in the aftermath of the war.

Gross, Walter. "Zionist Students, Movement." LBIY, 4 (1959): 143-165.

Grossman, Kurt R. "Zionists and non-Zionists under Nazi rule in the 1930's." Herzl Year Book, LV (1961-1962): 329-344. Includes 10 documents. And see chap. 3 & 4 in M. Friedman, Martin Buber's Life and Work, The Middle Years, 1924-1945. (N.Y.: E.P. Dutton, 1983, pp. 34-73).

Grunwald, Kurt. Turkenhirsch; A Study of Baron Maurice de Hirsch, Entrepeneur and Philanthropist. Jerusalem: Israel Program for Scientific Translation, Hartford, Conn.: Davey & Co., 1966. 139 p. A monograph on the Bavarian Jewish entrepreneur (1831-1896) who proposed the establishment of a Jewish settlement in Argentina. Grunwald describes his contacts with Zionist leaders and his disputes with Herzl.

Lichtheim, Richard. Ruckketir; Lebens-Erinnerungen aus der Frühzeit des deutschen Zionismus. Stuttgart: Deutsche Verlags-Anstalt, 1970. Memoirs of the early period by a Zionist leader and authority on this period.

Mosse, George L. "The Influence of the Volkish Idea on German Jewry." In Germans and Jews. N.Y.: Howard Fertig, 1970. By a major scholar.

Poppel, Stephen M. Zionism in Germany, 1897-1933; the Shaping of a Jewish Identity. Phila.: JPS, 1976. 234 p. Biblio.: 217-229. The thesis of this detailed study, in

part a corrective to the tendency to treat the world
movement as a whole, is that the German Zionists were
correct in their rejection of liberal assimilationist
ideology. They were optimistic about national restoration, pessimistic about Jewish life in Germany. This
correct comprehension of the German Jewish situation was
their real function.

Reinharz, Jehuda. Fatherland or Promised Land: The
Dilemma of the German Jew, 1893-1914. Includes full
bibliography. A scholarly study of the Centralverein
Deutscher Stattsburger Judischen Glaubens and the Zionistische Vereinigung fur Deutschland, two competing
organizations representing Deutschtum on one hand and
Judentum on the other. The tension was complicated by
German anti-Semitism. Except for a truce period during
the First World War, the "question of the primacy of
Deutschtum or Judentum dominated the intellectual milieu
of the German Jews until the Nazis decided the issue in
1933." (p. 234).

Reinharz, Jehuda. Dokumente zur Geschichte des
deutschen Zionismus, 1882-1933. Tübingen: Mohr, 1981.

Weltsch, Robert. "Deutscher Zionismus in der Ruckshau."
In Zwei Welten. Tel Aviv, 1962. Weltsch (b. 1891 in
Prague) was a close friend of Kafka's and a noted
Zionist editor and journalist. He was famous for his
1933 editorial, "Wear the Yellow Badge with Pride." Rpt.
in Out of the Whirlwind...ed. by Albert H. Friedlander,
pp. 119-123. (cited above, c:1).

Wistrich, Robert S. Socialism and the Jews; The
Dilemmas of Assimilation in Germany and Austria-Hungary.

(Littman Library of Jewish Civilization). Rutherford,
N.J.: Fairleigh Dickinson University Press, 1982. 435
p.

E. Zionism in the United States. (completed Spring, 1981; revisions, Fall 1984).

The Zionist question is central to modern U.S. Jewish historiography. The historical canvas is broad and many monographic studies remain to be done. There is a wealth of personal literature, biographies and memoirs but much of this is uncritical. There is no fully adequate comprehensive study. However we now have two solid narrative histories by M. Urofsky (1975, 1978) which supplement the valuable study by S. Halperin (1961). The intelligent sociological study by Y. Shapiro (1971) makes real advances, although it needs more historical focus.

E. Livneh, a contemporary Israeli writer, has insisted that there "never existed in America a Zionist Movement in the accepted (European) sense of the term. Zionist organizations in America always have a purely pro-Israel character and no more." It is correct that Zionism in the U.S. had a completely different milieu than that of Eastern and Central Europe. It was shaped by different motifs and traditions, namely the Progressive movement with its emphasis on practicality, efficiency and humanitarianism. M. Kaplan's fervent writings on Zionism (see Part 5, chap. 3:c) typify a purely American Zionist stance: rejection of the necessity of immigration ('aliyah), rejection of kibbutz galuyot (ingathering of the Exiles) and rejection of the notion of shelilat ha-golah (rejection of the diaspora).

Blau, Joseph L. Judaism in America; From Curiosity to Third Faith. Chicago: University of Chicago Press, 1976. 156 p. Includes bibliographical references and Index. Contains a section on Zionism in the U.S.

Brandeis, Louis Dembitz and Josephine C. Goldmark. The Jewish Problem, How to Solve It. 1912. 5th ed. N.Y.: Z.O.A. 1919. 24 p. One of the most significant statements on Zionism made by Brandeis. See E. Rabinowitz, Louis D. Brandeis: the Zionist chapter of his life. (N. Y.: Philosophical Library, 1968).

Brandeis, Louis Dembitz. On Zionism; a collection of addresses and statements. comp. and ed. by Solomon Goldmann. Foreword by Felix Frankfurther. N.Y.: Z.O.A. VIII, 156 p.

Brandeis, Louis Dembitz. Zionist Speeches of Louis Dembitz Brandeis. A critical ed. by Barbara Ann Harris. Ann Arbor, Mich.: Xerox University Microfilms, 1974. An "Authorized facsimile" of the editor's Dissert., University of California, 1967. The standard biography of Brandeis is by Alpheus T. Mason, Brandeis: A Free Man's Life (N.Y.: Viking, Toronto, MacMillan, 1946), XIII, 713 p. See also Melvin Urofsky, A Mind of One Piece: Brandeis and American Reform (N.Y.: Scribner, 1971, 210 p. And see Letters: Vol. 3 (1913-1915): Progressive and Zionist. ed. by Melvin I. Urofsky and David W. Levy. (Albany, N.Y.: State University of N.Y.: 1973), 705 p. See also, A. Gal, Brandeis of Boston (Harvard, 1980). Zionism in the U.S. before Brandeis became its leader "was a ragtag movement, without organization, funds, or political knowhow." (Leonard Baker, Brandeis and Frank-

furter. A Dual Biography, N.Y.: Harper, 1984, p. 74).
Brandeis was drawn toward Zionism out of concern for the
plight of Eastern European Jewry. He also saw Zionism
as a counter to the growing anti-Semitism in America and
as a challenge to the American myth of the melting pot.
"My approach to Zionism was through Americanism. The
Jewish renaissance in Palestine will enable us to perform our plain duty to America." (quoted in Baker,
ibidem, p. 79). Also see: Brandeis Avukah annual of
1932; a collection of essays on contemporary Zionist
thought; dedicated to Louis D. Brandeis. ed. by Joseph
S. Shubow, et al. N.Y.: American Student Zionist Organization, 1932. XXV, 808 p.

Cohen, Naomi Wiener. American Jews and the Zionist
Idea. N.Y.: Ktav, 1975. 172 p. Includes "Note on
sources" and Index. Cohen's work is largely based on
secondary sources but it is informative and intelligent
in its overview of American Zionist history from 1917 to
1967. She demonstrates that the American response to
the Zionist idea took its cue from the American scene
and was linked with Progressivism. She argued that
support for Israel is "the lowest common denominator for
American Jewish group identity."

Cohen, Naomi Wiener. "The Reaction of Reform Judaism
in America to Political Zionism." In The Jewish Experience in America. V: At Home in America. Waltham,
Mass.: AJHS, and Ktav, 1969. pp. 149-182. Originally
published in AJHSP, 40 (1950/51): 361-94. A survey of
the opposition to Zionism within the Reform movement.
The Reform critique rested on the assumptions that
Dispersion was a given and that Judaism was a universal
prophetic religion.

Duker, Abraham G. "The Impact of Zionism on American Jewish Life." In Jewish Life in America. ed. by T. Friedman and R. Gordis. N.Y.: Horizon Press, 1955.

Feinstein, Marvin. American Zionism, 1884-1904. N.Y.: Herzl Press, 1965. 320 p. See for information on the Love of Zion movement.

Feldblum, Ester Yolles. The American Catholic Press and the Jewish State, 1917-1959. N.Y.: Ktav, 1977. Includes a substantial bibliography. Feldblum argues that many Catholics were shocked by the establishment of Israel and the Papacy was non-committal. These attitudes, she claims, reflected the ancient Christian image of dispersion as a form of divine punishment.

Fink, Reuben. ed. America and Palestine; The Attitude of Official America and of the American People Toward the Rebuilding of Palestine as a Free and Democratic Jewish Commonwealth. 2nd ed. N.Y.: Herald Square Press, 1945. O. 538 p. A collection of speeches in favour of Zionism by American congressmen and officials.

Fineman, Irving. Woman of Valor, the Life of Henrietta Szold, 1860-1945 N.Y.: Simon and Schuster, 1961. 448 p. illus. Szold, a founder of the Woman's Zionist Organization of America, is sometimes called American Jewry's most distinguised contribution to Israel. Like Buber and Magnes she was a supporter of the binational idea. For earlier studies, see Rose Zeitlin, Henrietta Szold; Record of a Life. (N.Y.: Dial, 1952), XVI, 263 p., and

the full and sympathetic account by Marvin H. Lowenthal,
Henrietta _Szold_: _Life_ _and_ _Letters_ (N.Y.: Viking Press,
1942) IX, 350 p.

Fishman, Hertzel. _American_ _Protestantism_ _and_ _a_ _Jewish_
State. Detroit: Wayne University, 1973. 249 p. Cf.
Feldblum (above). Fishman argues that American Protestantism was "liberal" in its attitude toward Jews as
individuals but maintained a "persistently hostile attitude toward Jewish peoplehood." Reinhold Niebuhr was
the only major exception. See the distressing information in D. Wyman, _The_ _Abandonment_ _of_ _the_ _Jews_ (1984,
cited above. Part 5, chap. 1, sec. C:3)

Friesel, Avyatar. _The_ _Zionist_ _Movement_ _in_ _the_ _United_
States, _1897-1914_. Tel Aviv: Hakibbutz Hameuchad, 1970.
319 p. In Hebrew except for title and table of
contents.

Gittelson, R. and J. Eisenberg. "American Jews and
Israel: Two Views." _Midstream_, 18:2 (Feb. 1972): 58-67.

Goldmann, Nahum. _Memories_: _The_ _Autobiography_ _of_ _Nahum_
Goldmann: _The_ _Story_ _of_ _a_ _Lifelong_ _Battle_ _by_ _World_
Jewry's _Ambassador_ _at_ _Large_. trans. by Helen Sebba.
London: Weidenfeld and Nicolson, 1970. first pub. under
the title: _The_ _Autobiography_ _of_ _Nahum_ _Goldmann_: _Sixty_
Years _of_ _Jewish_ _life_. London: Holt (1969). Born in
Eastern Europe and educated in Germany, Goldmann became
a Zionist leader (and _enfant_ _terrible_) in the 1930's.
He headed the W.Z.O., the World Jewish Congress, and in
the 1940's was a leader of the U.S. Jewish Agency. He
pressed for an understanding with the Arabs and advocated a Middle East Federation. (p. 285, _passim_).

Gottheil, Richard. "Zionism." In Jewish Encyclopedia. 12 (1906): 672. By an American (1862-1936) Orientalist, educator, and Zionist. Author of Zionism (1914, cited above) and Brandeis on Zionism (Washington, D.C., 1942).

Grinstein, H.B. "Orthodox Judaism and Early Zionism in America." In Early History of Zionism in America. (papers presented at the Conference convened by the AJHS and the T. Herzl foundation, in NYC on Dec. 26-27, 1955). ed. by Isidore S. Meyer. N.Y.: Herzl and AJHS, 1958. pp. 219-27. The author argues that, with the exception of the "ultra religious" fringe, Orthodox Jews in America supported Zionism (contrast the "neo-Orthodox" in Germany).

Halkin, Hillel. Letters to an American Jewish Friend; A Zionist's Polemic. Phila.: JPS, 1977. 246 p. (cited above, Part 2) Halkin contends that Diaspora Jewry is doomed and Jewish life is possible only within the national home. He creates an image of "two planets, one teeming with new if embattled life, the other atmospherically exhausted, on its way to being dead as the moon."

Halpern, Ben. "Brandeis' Way to Zionism." Midstream, 17 (October 1971). Argues that Brandeis, late in life, embraced Zionism because he needed a community that he could identity with. An alternative interpretation is that of Y. Shapiro (AJHQ, Dec. 1965), who contends that Brandeis accepted Zionism to advance his political career. Neither view as it stands is fully convincing. See also Ben Halpern, The American Jew (N.Y.: Herzl Foundation, 1956).

Halperin, Samuel. The Political World of American Zionism. Detroit: Wayne State University Press, 1961. 431 p. This scholarly work includes a 20-page bibliography. Halperin concentrates on the 1928-1949 period and poses one central question: "how does an interest group grow in influence?" Of significance is his claim that by 1946 it was virtually impossible to distinguish between Zionists and non-Zionists.

Kallen, Horace M. Zionism and World Politics; A Study in History and Social Psychology. N.Y.: Doubleday & Co., 1921. XXI, 345 p. Kallen (b. 1882) was a pluralistic, philosophical naturalist and pragmatist, in the tradition of William James. He argued that Zionism was an anti-assimilative, democratic movement that extended the assumptions of "liberalism" from the individual to the group. See also Judaism at Bay (N.Y.: 1932) and The Struggle for Jewish Unity (pamphlet, Washington, D.C.: 1933). Selections from these two works are in A. Hertzberg, ed. The Zionist Idea (cited above). pp. 526-533.

Kaplan, Mordechai M. The Future of the American Jew. N.Y.: MacMillan, 948. XX, 571 p. By a gifted and original "Reconstructionist" philosopher of Judaism (see entries in Modern Thought section of Bibliography). "The role of American Jewry in relation to Eretz Israel is similar to the role of the American home front in relation to the battle front during the recent World War."

Kaplan, Mordechai M. A New Zionism. 2nd ed. N.Y.: Herzl Foundation, 1954. 172 p. Kaplan argues that

Zionism should/must strengthen Jewish consciousness in the Diaspora.

Katzman, Jacob. Commitment: The Labor Zionist Life-Style in America. N.Y.: Labor Zionist Letters, 1975. Memoirs; on labor Zionism. See Part 3: Section 3 (above).

Knee, Stuart E. The Concept of Zionist Dissent in the American Mind, 1917-1941. N.Y.: Robert Speller & Sons, 1980. 268 p.

Lewisohn, Ludwig. Israel. N.Y.: Bobi and Liverwright, 1925. XV, 19-280 p. Lewisohn (1882-1955) was a writer and literary critic; his espousal of Zionism can be seen in the anthology he edited, Rebirth; a book of modern Jewish thought (N.Y.: Harper, 1935), 341 p.

Lipsky, Louis. A Gallery of Zionist Profiles. N.Y.: Farrar, Straus and Cudahy, 1956. 226 p. Foreword by Maurice Samuel. Profiles, sketches and impressions of personalities in the Zionist movement. Lipsky's acerbic style is refreshing as a contrast to uncritical and worshipful Zionist biography.

Lipsky, Louis. Thirty Years of American Zionism. 2 vols. N.Y.: Nesher, 1927. Lipsky, "the faithful work-horse of American Zionism" (Urofsky), provides information on the American Federation of Zionists.

Mack, Julian W. Americanism and Zionism. 2nd ed. N.Y.: Z.O.A. 1918. 15 p. Mack (1866-1943) was a judge and active leader in Zionist organizations. See Harry Barnard, The Forging of an American Jew: The Life and

Times of Judge Julian Mack (N.Y.: Herzl, 1974). In the
early 1920's, Mack was second to Brandeis as Zionist
leader. The Brandeis-Mack faction was defeated
(resigned) during the 1921 Cleveland Convention but they
were back in power in 1930.

Mayer, Isidore S. ed. Early History of Zionism in
America (cited above). N.Y.: Herzl foundation, 1958.
340 p. This collection of essays includes biblio-
graphies.

Neumann, Emanuel. In the Arena: An Autobiographical
Memoir. N.Y.: Herzl, 1976. Includes bibliographical
references and Index. Foreword by Arthur Hertzberg.
Neumann was a president of the Z.O.A. and considered the
"field general" for the Jewish state from 1939 to 1948.

Parzan, Herbert L. "Conservative Judaism and Zionism,
1896-1922." JSS, 25 (October 1961): 235-264. Conservative Judaism, under the influence of Solomon Schechter,
defended Zionism. Parzan's article complements that of
Cohen on Reform Judaism (see above) and Grinstein's
essay on Orthodoxy (above).

Parzan, Herbert L. "American Zionism and the Quest for
a Jewish State, 1939-43." Herzl Yearbook, 4 (1962).

Patai, Raphael. ed. Herzl Year Book: Essays in Zionist
History and Thought: Vol. 4-5. N.Y.: Herzl Press, 1963-
64. On Zionism in America, 1894-1919.

Polish, David. Renew our Days; The Zionist Issue in
Reform Judaism. Foreword by Richard G. Hirsch,

Jerusalem: World Zionist Organization/World Union for Progressive Judaism, 1976. 276 p.

Reznikoff, Charles. ed. Louis Marshall, Champion of Liberty. Introd. by Oscar Handlin. 2 vols. (Jacob R. Schliff lib. of Jewish contributions to Am. democracy). Phila.: JPS, 1957. XIIII, 500, 501 p. Marshall was not a "political Zionist" but he helped form the tradition of American support for Jewish presence in Palestine. His efforts helped reunite American Jewry. See Urofsky (1975, cited below).

Rischin, Moses. "American-Jewish Committee and Zionism, 1906-1922." AJHSP, 49 (1959/60): 188-201. See also, Ben Halperin, "The American Jewish Committee." The Jewish Frontier, 10 (December 1943): 13-16.

Rosenblatt, Bernard A. Two Generations of Zionism: Historical Recollections of an American Zionist. Introd. in italicized insertions by Gaalyahu Cornfeld. N.Y.: Shengold, 1967. 286 p. Rosenblatt was an American jurist who founded the American Zion Commonwealth.

Rubin, Jacob A. Partners in State Building; American Jewry and Israel. N.Y.: Diplomatic Press, Inc. 1969. 283 p. A popular, anecdotal work.

Samuel, Maurice. The Worlds of Maurice Samuel. Selected Writings. ed. with an Introd. by Milton Hindus. Foreword by Cynthia Ozick. Phila.: JPS, 1977. XXXII, 445 p. These writings of Samuel (1895-1972) include material on Zionism in America.

618

Samuel, Maurice. Harvest in the Desert. Phila.: JPS,
N.Y.: Knopf, Toronto: Ryerson, 1944. 316 p. A sympathetic "personal" story (a "fusion of research and
record and impression") of the growth of the "Jewish
Homeland." No bibliography, no index.

Schechtman, Joseph B. The United States and the Jewish
State Movement; The Crucial Decade, 1939-1949. N.Y.:
Herzl Press, T. Yoseloff, 1969. Biblio.: p. 453-459.

Schechter, Solomon. "Zionism: A Statement." In
Seminary Addresses, And Other Papers. Cincinnati: Ark
pub. Co., 1915. Rpt. in A. Hertzberg, ed. The Zionist
Idea (cited above). pp. 504-513. This outstanding
Rabbinics scholar and gifted educator gave a Zionist
temper to the U.S. Conservative movement.

Shankman, Samuel. Mortimer May: Foot Soldier in Zion.
N.Y.: Bloch, 1963. 224 p. illus. (pub. for Southeastern
Region, Z.O.A.). A biography of a President of the
Z.O.A.

Shapiro, Yonathan. Leadership of the American Zionist
Organization, 1897-1930. Urbana, IL.: University of
Illinois Press, 1971. 295 p. Biblio.: p. 277-289. This
important study (his Ph.D. dissert.) parallels Poppel's
work (1976, cited above) on German Zionism. Shapiro
defines Zionism as an "ideology of survival for the
Jewish community of the United States." Shapiro argues
that around 1930 Zionist ideology in America was transformed from a social movement focused on fundamental
change to an organization with the limited aim of helping upbuild Palestine as a national home. This shift

correlates with the   acculturation process of the
American Jewish community.

Urofsky, Melvin I. American Zionism from Herzl to the
Holocaust. Garden City, N.Y.: Doubleday & Co., 1975.
538 p.

Urofsky, Melvin I.   We Are One! American Jewry and
Israel. Garden City, N.Y.: Anchor Press/Doubleday,
1978. 536 p.

Urofsky, Melvin I.   A Voice that Spoke for Justice; The
Life and Times of Stephen S. Wise. (SUNY Series in
Modern Jewish History). Albany, N.Y.: State University
of New York Press, 1982. 439 p.

F. Studies of Zionism in England, France, Russia, Hungary, Poland, Italy, South Africa and Czechoslovakia.

Background reading. Cecil Roth, A History of the Jews in England. 3rd ed. (Oxford University Press, 1964). 311 p.

Bentwich, Norman D. M. Early English Zionists, 1890-1920. Tel Aviv, 194 ?

Brodetsky, Selig. Memoirs: From Ghetto to Israel. London: Weidenfeld and Nicolson; Toronto: McClellan, 1960. 323 p. A British Zionist leader, Brodetsky (188 - 1954) was President of the Hebrew University from 1949 to 1951.

Eliot, George. Daniel Deronda. N.Y.: Harper, 1876. (cited below, Part 2, chap. 3:f). In this work (her last), Eliot, one of the great novelists of the Victorian Age (b. 1819 d. 1880) projects a pre-Herzl Zionist vision. Daniel (not one of her most realized characters), after discovering that he is Jewish, marries Mirah Cohen. She is a poor Jewish girl and foil to the upper-class snob, Gwendolen Harleth. Daniel leaves for Palestine to establish a new home for his family. Eliot sought "the illumination of great facts that widen feeling" (DD).

Goodman, Paul. Zionism in England, 1899-1949: A Jubilee Record. 2nd ed. London: Zionist Federation of Great

Britain and Ireland, 1949. O. 86 p. Goodman's (b. 1875 d. 1949) brief history concentrates on the period 1899-1929.

Levenberg, S. "Zionism in British Politics." In The Jewish National Home 1917-1942. ed. by Paul Goodman. London, 1943.

Rose, Nicholas A. The Gentile Zionists; A Study in Anglo-Zionist diplomacy, 1929-1939. London: Cass, 1973. 242 p. Biblio.: p. 228-232. An account of the political (and personal, to some extent) activities of Gentile Zionists in the 1930's.

Sokolow, Nahum. History of Zionism, 1600-1918. 2 vols. Introd. by A.J. Balfour. London: Longmans 1919. Iiii, 313; Iiii, 480 p. 89 portraits and illus. select. and arranged by Israel Solomons. Rpt. 2 vols. in I. with Introd. by Arthur Hertzberg. N.Y.: Ktav, 1969. Basing himself mainly on published materials in Yiddish, Hebrew and English, Sokolow concentrates on the development of the Zionist idea in England, including its reflection in non-Jewish literature and popular culture, and its relationship to British politics in the Near East. Vol. 2 contains documents. For Sokolow's life, see Hertzberg's "Introduction" and Simcha Kling, Nachum Sokolow: Servant of his People (N.Y.: Herzl, 1960), 205 p.

Stein, Leonard. The Balfour Declaration. London: Vallentine, Mitchell, 1961. (Cited in Part 2, above). According to D.Z. Gillon, in "The Antecedents of the Balfour Declaration," Middle Eastern Studies, 5 (Jan. 1969): 131-150, Balfour had almost nothing to do with the Declaration, Zionism was a sub-issue. The British were primarily concerned with their role in Palestine.

Stein, Leonard. Promises and Afterthoughts: Notes on Certain White Papers Relating to the Palestine Conferences. London: Jewish Agency, 1939. A 34 p. critique of the Arab and British interpretations of the Husayn-McMahon correspondence. Now see E. Kedourie (1976, cited above, Part 2).

Stein, Leonard. Memorandum on the "Report of the Commission on the Palestine Disturbances of August 1929." London: Jewish Agency, 1930. A critique of the Shaw Commission Report.

Stein, Leonard. The Palestine White Paper of October, 1930: Memorandum. London: Jewish Agency, 1930. The 89-page official Zionist critique of the Passfield White paper.

Weisgal, Meyer W. and Joel Carmichael. eds. Chaim Weizmann: A Biography by Several Hands. Preface by David Ben-Gurion. London: Weidenfeld; N.Y.: Atheneum, 1963. 364 p. plates. Trans. into Hebrew (Jerusalem, 1964). Thirteen authors, often using materials in the Weizmann archives, cover different aspects and periods of Weizmann's career.

Weizmann, Chaim. The Letters and Papers of Chaim Weizmann. gen. ed. Meyer W. Weisgal. London: Oxford University Press, 1968. A series intended to include 25 vols. 3 vols. of Series A, Letters, were published in 1972, covering the period from Summer 1885 to December 1904. Hebrew ed. Ketavim (Jerusalem: Bialik Institute,

1969). Vol. I, Summer 1885-29 October 1902; ed. by Leonard Stein in collaboration with Gedalia Yogev. Oxford: Oxford University Press, 1968. Q. 492 p.

Weizmann, Chaim. Trial and Error: The Autobiography of Chaim Weizmann. 2 vol. limited autog. ed. N.Y.: Harper, 1949. O. VIII, 498 p. Rpt. N.Y.: Schocken Books, 1966.

FRANCE

Hyman, Paula. From Dreyfus to Vichy. The Remaking of French Jewry, 1906-1939. N.Y.: Columbia University Press, 1979. 338 p. See chap. 6, "The Infiltration of Zionism." pp. 153-178, and chap 7. The native French leadership rejected Zionism, whose support came from immigrant Jews. But despite organizational weakness, Zionism helped transform French Jewry through cultural renaissance and by providing an alternative to assimilation.

Lazare, Bernard. Antisemitism; its history and causes. trans. from the French (1894). London: Britons Pub. Co., 1967. 208 p. This early work contained the "seeds" of Lazare's later rejection of assimilation and espousal of Jewish nationalism. Lazare (1865-1903), "one of Zionism's great originals" was deeply influenced by the Dreyfus affair. See Hannah Arendt, "Herzl and Lazare" (1942), in The Jew as Pariah (N.Y.: Grove Press, 1978), pp. 125-130. And see: "Jewish Nationalism and Emancipation" (a partial trans. of Lazare's Le fumier de Job) in The Zionist Idea, ed. by A. Hertzberg (cited above), pp. 471-476.

Marrus, M.R. The Politics of Assimilation: A Study of the French Jewish Community at the time of the Dreyfus Affair. Oxford: The Clarendon Press, 1971. See chap. 7, "Bernard Lazare and the Origins of Jewish Nationalism in France," and chap. 9, "The Zionist Revolution."

Spire, André. "Herzl's Influence in France: the Growth of the Zionist Idea and its Effect on Judaism." In Theodor Herzl...ed. by M. Weisgal (cited above).

Sullivan, A. "The Dynamics of French Resistance to Zionism in the 19th and Early 20th Centuries." Middle East Forum, 44:4 (1968): 45-64.

Tsur, Jacob. La révolte Juive. Paris: Plon, 1970.

Tsur, Jacob. Zionism: The Saga of a National Liberation Movement (cited above, Part 2).

Weill, Julien. Zadoc Kahn, 1839-1905. Paris: Alcan, 1912. The life of the Grand Rabbi of France. He took a cautious and neutral position on Zionism. Kahn blunted the attack upon Zionism that arose within the "assimilated" Jewish community but also proposed the slogan: "Neither to Jerusalem nor to Basel." He thought that anti-Semitism was merely momentary and could "not stop the continuous progress which France is making in the direction of right and reason." See Marrus (cited above), p. 278 ff.

Weinberg, David H. A Community on Trial; The Jews of Paris in the 1930's. Chicago: University of Chicago Press, 1977. 239 p. Biblio.: pp. 223-232. Weinberg states that "natives by and large rejected the notion of a Jewish peoplehood."

TSARIST RUSSIA AND THE SOVIET UNION (See Bibliography in H.M. Sachar (1985, cited above), pp. 505-508.

Baron, Salo W. The Russian Jew under Tsars and Soviets. N.Y.: MacMillan, 1964. 427 p. 2nd ed. 1976.

Brym, Robert J. The Jewish Intelligentsia and Russian Marxism; A Sociological Study of Intellectual Radicalism and Ideological Divergence. London: MacMillan, 1978; N.Y.: Schocken Books, 1978. 157 p. Biblio.: p. 135-155. Contains rich notes. Brym argues (gegen J. Katz and others) that Zionism had class roots.

Cannon, E. The Political Culture of Russian Jewry During the Second Half of the 19th Century. Ph.D. Dissert., University of Massachusetts, 1974.

Dubnow, Simon. History of the Jews in Russia and Poland; from the earliest times until the present day. 3 vols. trans. from the Russian by I. Friedlaender. Phila.: JPS, 1916-20. vol. I. From the beginning until the death of Alexander I (1825); From the death of Alexander I to the death of Alexander III (1825-1894); From the accession of Nicholas II until the present day. 413, 429, 411 p. By a very learned and outstanding historian; Dubnow's focus was on social and economic events and structures.

Frankel, J. Prophecy and Politics (1981, cited above).

Frumkin, Jacob et al. eds. <u>Russian Jewry, 1860-1917</u>. trans. by Mirra Ginsburg. (Sponsored by the Union of Russian Jews, Inc., ed. board, Gregor Aronson, et. al.) N.Y.: Yoseloff, 1966. 492 p.

Gitelman, Zvi Y. <u>Jewish Nationality and Soviet Politics; The Jewish Sections of the CPSU, 1917-1930</u>. Princeton, N.J.: Princeton University Press, 1972. 573 p. Biblio.: pp. 527-557. A high-level work of scholarship, written under the auspices of the Columbia University Research Instit. on communist affairs.

Goldman, Guido G. <u>Zionism Under Soviet Rule, 1917-1928</u>. N.Y.: Herzl, 1960. 136 p. An account of the abolition of organized Zionism by the Soviet government during the first decade after the 1917 Bolshevik takeover.

Kochan, Lionel. ed. <u>The Jews in Soviet Russia since 1917</u>. London: Oxford University Press (for the Inst. of Jewish Affairs), 1970. 357 p. Includes important essays.

Kohn, Hans. <u>Nationalism in the Soviet Union</u>. trans. from the German (1932) by E.W. Dickes. N.Y.: Columbia University Press, 1933. XI, 164 p.

Sachar, Howard M. <u>Diaspora</u> (185, cited above), chap. 14-16, and bibliography, pp. 505-508.

Schechtman, J.B. "The U.S.S.R., Zionism, and Israel." in Kochan (cited above), pp. 99-124.

Schechtman, J.B. <u>Star in Eclipse: Russian Jewry</u>

Revisited. N.Y.: Yoseloff, 1961. 255 p. plates. A history of Russian Jewry since 1959.

HUNGARY For Eastern Europe, see the work by Paul Lendvai, Antisemitism without Jews (Garden City, N.Y. 1971) and chapters XII-XIII in H.M. Sachar, Diaspora (cited above).

Braham, Rudolph L. The Politics of Genocide: The Holocaust in Hungary (cited above, Part 5, chap.1, c, and note other entries). See the discussion and bibliography in H.M. Sachar (1985) pp. 338-373, 504-505, includes analysis of Romania.

Britton, Livia Elvira. A Decade of Zionism in Hungary; The Formative Years--The Post-World War I Period, 1918-1928. Ann Arbor, Mich.: Xerox University Microfilms, 1974. An authorized facsimile of the author's dissertation, New York University, 1968. Biblio.: pp. 233-255. Covers historical background (the period of assimilation, 1867-1918), Jewish nationalism, the effects of the Treaty of Trianon, inner conflicts in the Zionist movement.

POLAND

Heller, Celia S. On the Edge of Destruction, Jews of Poland Between the Two World Wars. N.Y.: Columbia University Press, 1977. A major study.

Mendelsohn, Ezra. Zionism in Poland; The Formative Years, 1915-1926. New Haven, CT.: Yale University

Press, 1982. 373 p. Biblio.: pp. 359-364. Appendix 1,2, Glossary. Index. The outstanding, definitive work; solid and detailed. For recent information and bibliography, see H.M. Sachar, Diaspora (N.Y.: Harper & Row, 1985), pp. 323-337, 503-504.

ITALY

Bondy, Ruth. The Emissary: A Life of Enzo Sereni. trans. from the Hebrew by Shlomo Katz. Afterword by Golda Meir. 1st American ed. Boston: Little, Brown, 1977. 265 p. illus. Includes bibliographical references and Index. A moving biography of an Italian philosopher, Zionist leader and parachutist who was killed in Dachau, 18 November 1944.

Lattes, Dante. Letture del risorgimento ebraico. Firenze, 1948.

Lattes, Dante. In Scritti in memoria di Leone Carpi. ed. by D. Carpi et al. (1967).

SOUTH AFRICA

Shimoni, Gideon. "Jan Christian Smuts and Zionism." JSS, (Fall 1977): 269-298. Discusses the motives for Smuts' Gentile pro-Zionism.

Shimoni, Gideon. Jews and Zionism: The South African Experience (1910-1967). Cape Town: Oxford University Press, 1980. 428 p. Zionism in South Africa was the mode of Jewish identification before the religious traditions were well established. The Zionist mode of identity has largely been a function of the "inter-colour pluralism" and "intra-white dualism" that characterizes South Africa. This extremely interesting and intelligent study includes bibliographical notes. For recent discussion, see H.M. Sachar, Diaspora (cited above, 1985) pp. 186-197, and bibliography (up to 1980 only), pp. 497-499.

CZECHOSLOVAKIA

The Jews of Czechoslovakia, Vol. II. NYC. (The Society for the History of Czechoslovak Jews). Phila.: JPS, 1971. See Oskar K. Rabinowicz, "Czechoslovak Zionism: Analecta to a History," p. 19-123. And now read pp. 316-323 in H.M. Sachar, Disapora (above, 1985) and for bibliography, p. 504.

G. Jewish Critiques of Political Zionism.

...Of a Jewish state with cannons, flags and metals I know nothing, not even in the shape of a dream... *Martin Buber to Stefan Zweig (1919)*

He who seeks the perfection of the soul... should not seek it along the avenue of politics... *Max Weber*

I have often wondered how different Zionism might have been had Herzl not been a Viennese journalist but a shopkeeper in a Damascus bazaar. Would Zionism have realized that Palestine was a part of a big area inhabited by Arabs? *Uri Avinery*

It is not fitting for Jacob (i.e., people of Israel) to engage in political life at a time when statehood requires bloody ruthlessness and demands a talent for evil. *Rav Kook (quoted in S. Avineri,* The Making of Modern Zionism, *p. 197)*

Arendt, Hannah. "Zionism Reconsidered." In The Jew as Pariah (cited above, Part 2), pp. 131-163. Originally pub. in the Menorah Journal (October 1944): 162-196. "Zionism was and is supported by the Great Powers like a rope supports for hanging: only folly could dictate a

policy which trusts a distant imperial power for protec-
tion, while alienating the good will of neighbors."
"The real goal of the Jews in Palestine is the building
up of a Jewish homeland. This goal must never be sacrificed to the pseudo-sovereignty of a Jewish state." "To
Save the Jewish Homeland." (1948). Rpt. in The Jew as
Pariah (cited above, Part 2), p. 192.

Avinery, Uri. Israel Without Zionists; A Plea for Peace
in the Middle East. N.Y.: MacMillan, 1968. 215 p. Born
in Germany in 1923, Avinery was an Irgun commando,
founder of the Semitic Action Movement, non-Zionist
member of the Knesset, and editor of the popular former
weekly, Ha'olam Hazeh ("This World"). He was an initia-
tor of the New Force party (it won 1.2% of the vote in
the 1965 elections) that "advocates that Israel should
cease to declare itself a Jewish state, but rather
become a pluralist one. It believes in full equality of
the Israeli Arabs, in a complete separation of synagogue
and state, and for promulgation of a written constitution..." Avinery wants to make common cause with Arab
nationalists in a Semitic confederacy whose goal would
be gradual disarmament and the pooling of political
power.

Avishai, Bernard. The Tragedy of Zionism Revolution and
Democracy in the Land of Israel (1985, cited above).
See, esp., chap. 10, "Democracy or Zionism?" The Zionist Revolution ran its course, "stopped short of its
liberal-democratic goals..." and efforts to reinvigorate
Zionism in Israel will bring "more misfortune." Avishai
argues that "some of the reasons for Israel's failure as
a democracy are internal to the logic of the Zionist
Achievements." (pp. 9-10).

Ben-Ezer, Ehud. ed. Unease in Zion (cited above, Part 2).

Berger, Elmer. The Jewish Dilemma: The Case Against Jewish Nationalism. N.Y.: Davin-Adair, Co., 1945. 257 p. Born in 1908, Berger is a U.S. Rabbi, publicist and President of the American Jewish Alternatives to Zionism. As far as we know, this organization has very little influence.

Berger, Elmer. A Partisan History of Judaism. N.Y.: Praeger, Devin-Adair. 1951. XVI, 142 p.

Berger, Elmer. Judaism or Jewish Nationalism; The Alternative to Zionism. N.Y.: Bookman, 1957. 207 p.

Berger, Elmer. Letters and Non-Letters: The White House, Zionism and Israel. (Monograph Series no. 3) Beirut: Institute for Palestine Studies, 1972. 55 p.

Berger, Elmer. Who Knows Better Must Say So! Beirut: Institute for Palestine Studies, 1970. Berger argues that Zionist policy is based upon "superior force" and "fait accompli diplomacy." The Israeli concern for security should not be at the expense of the Palestinians and the U.S. must influence Israel, its "client state," to make genuine peace offers.

Bober, Arie. ed. The Other Israel; the Radical Case Against Zionism. N.Y.: Garden City, Doubleday (Anchor Books), 1972. 264 p. Includes bibliographical references. Consists of articles and statements by members of the Israeli Socialist Organization that advocate an all-Middle-East proletarian party to fight "imperialism, Zionism and Arab reaction for the socialist revolution."

Buber, Martin. Israel and the World. N.Y.: Schocken Books, 1963. (See on Buber, above, Part 2). Buber draws the distinction between legitimate and arbitrary nationalism, i.e., "all sovereignty becomes false and vain when in the struggle for power it fails to remain subject to the Soverign of the world. See chap. 14, "Buber versus Ben-Gurion," of Maurice Friedman's Martin Buber's Life and Work, The Later Years, 1945-1965. (N.Y.: E.P. Dutton, 1983), pp. 332-371. "Buber regarded the existence of Israel as dependent upon its integration into a federation of the Near East." pp. 332-333. Also, M. Buber, A Land of Two Peoples.

Chomsky, Noam. "Nationalism and conflict in Palestine." In Reflections on the Middle East Crisis, ed. by Herbert Mason. The Hague: Mouton, 1969.

Chomsky, Noam. Peace in the Middle East? Reflections on Justice and Nationhood. Foreword by Irene L. Gendzier. N.Y.: Pantheon Books, 1974. XVIII, 198 p.

Davis, Uri. "Journey Out of Zionism: The Radicalization of an Israeli Pacifist." Journal of Palestine Studies, 1:4 (1972): 59-72.

Davis, Uri and N. Mezvinsky. eds. Documents from Israel, 1967-1973: Readings for a Critique of Zionism. London: Ithaca Press, 1975. Includes material from the Hebrew press and periodicals on discrimination against Arabs.

Deutscher, Isaac. The Non-Jewish Jew and Other Essays. London: Oxford University Press, 1968. Deutscher (b. near Cracow, 1907, d. 1967) was a historian of Soviet affairs and the biographer of Trotsky. Like Trotsky, he was an anti-Zionist in the 1920's but later regretted that position, viewing Israel as a "Raft State" and "historic necessity" given the reality of anti-Semitism. But he was sympathetic to the Arab position in the 1967 war and regarded Israel as a "reactionary outpost of American neo-colonialism."

Domb, Y. ed. Transformation: The Case of the "Neturei Karta." London, 1958. On Torah Judaism vs. "Gentile" Nationalism.

Dubnow, Simon M. Nationalism and History; Essays on Old and New Judaism. ed. with an Introd. by Koppel S. Pinson. Phila.: JPS, 1958. 385 p. Dubnow (1860-1941) thought that the "abnormal" existence of diaspora Jewry might be a higher form of historical development than territorial nationalism.

Friedman, Maurice. Martin Buber's Life and Work. The Middle Years, 1923-1945. N.Y.: E.P. Dutton, Inc., 1983. See chap. 1. "Zionism in the Twenties." pp. 3-20. Buber believed that a genuine national pride "would bring the Jews nearer to the Arabs so that together they might build up the land. The only truly Palestinian forms are those of the Arabs. 'We have not lived with the Arabs in Palestine but next to them,' Buber said, and added that if this continued to be the case, the situation in Palestine would inevitably deteriorate to the place where the Jews would find themselves living against the Arabs. It is characteristic of Zion that it cannot be built with every possible means but only <u>bemishpat</u> (Isaiah I:27), only "with justice," Buber said in Antwerp in 1932. p. 18.

Jastrow, Morris, Jr. <u>Zionism</u> <u>and</u> <u>the</u> <u>Future</u> <u>of</u> <u>Pales-</u> <u>tine</u>: <u>The</u> <u>Fallacies</u> <u>and</u> <u>Dangers</u> <u>of</u> <u>Political</u> <u>Zionism</u>. N.Y.: MacMillan, 1919. XIX, 159 p.

Kohn, Hans. "Ahad Ha'am: Nationalist with a Difference." In <u>Zionism</u>: <u>The</u> <u>Dream</u> <u>and</u> <u>the</u> <u>Reality,</u> <u>A</u> <u>Jewish</u> <u>Critique</u>. ed. by Gary V. Smith (cited below) pp. 21-37. Originally published in <u>Commentary</u> (1958). (See entries on Ahad Ha'am in Part 3, Section 2). Ahad Ha'am believed in the permanence of the Diaspora and in the necessity for a spiritual-national center in Palestine. How this center was achieved was essential: "The main point, upon which everything depends, is not how much we do but how we do it." Ethical and spiritual values must determine the national <u>Geist</u>. In his "Zion and the Jewish National Idea" (cited above, Part 2) Kohn reflected upon the tensions within Zionism between Jewish tradition, modern humanism, and the militaristic <u>Zeitgeist</u> of this century, arguing that the "humanist Zionism" of Weismann was replaced by the program of Jabotinsky with the result that "militarization of life and mind" prevailed over the Jewish tradition.

Leon, Abraham. <u>The</u> <u>Jewish</u> <u>Question</u>: <u>A</u> <u>Marxist</u> <u>Interpre-</u> <u>tation</u>. trans from the French (1946). N.Y.: Pathfinder, 1970. 270 p. A Trotsky-based perspective that rejects Zionism and calls for an international Jewish proletariat.

Magnes, Judah L.   See selections in Dissenter in Zion; from the writings of Judah L. Magnes.   ed. by Arthur A. Goren.   Harvard University Press, 1982. 554 p.

Magnes, Judah L.   "Like All the Nations" (1929). Jerusalem, 1930.   See the biography of Magnes by Bentwich (cited above).   In this pamphlet Magnes (1877-1948) declared that the Jewish people did not need a Jewish state to "perform its great ethical mission as a national-international entity."   As M. Friedman states, the binational idea was very widespread in Palestine from 1925 to 1933 and was not some form of "treasonous anti-Zionism." Among its supporters were Buber, Kohn, Weltsch, Bergmann; and Chaim Weizmann, first President of Israel, was a strong supporter of "parity."

Petuchowski, Jakob J.   Zion Reconsidered.   N.Y.: Twayne Pub., 1967. 143 p.   Petuchowski argues that the Zionist concerns of American Jewry are basically philanthropic and thus conflict with the political objectives of Zionism.   Selections from this book are included in the Smith reader (cited below).

Selzer, Michael.   ed. and with an Introd.   Zionism Reconsidered; The Rejection of Jewish Normalcy.   N.Y.: MacMillan, 1970. XXII, 259 p.   An uneven collection (e.g., why include P. Roth? and the essay by Y. Kaufmann is not critical of political Zionism per se but only of the alleged anti-Semitism of some of its exponents) that can be compared with the collections of Stevens (1962), Avinery (1968), Khalid (1971), Smith (1974), U. Davis and N. Mezvinsky (1974). No bibliography. In his "Introduction," Selzer argues that the Jew is alien to the political world; classical Judaism repudiated power ("The very essence of the revolution (Jewish) was to radicalize the world through Jewish powerlessness and suffering." XVII). Thus political Zionism is counter-revolutionary. It goes against Jewish history by making power a value. Selzer's analysis is extreme, although valuable as a counter to the militaristic ("Revisionist") Zionism that exalts "normalcy" even in the form of cluster bombs. But Jewish "powerlessness" was in part forced upon the Jewish people; and it is insensitive to praise "Jewish powerlessness and suffering" after the Catastrophe of this century. Moreover, even a superficial view of Judaism makes manifest the real attachment to the Land of Israel. However, the question of power itself is not the crucial question; it is a question of power in what context and for what ends, power with Grace or power that knows no leaven of the Spirit.

Selzer, Michael. The Aryanization of the Jewish State. N.Y.: (Black Star Bk.) White, 1967. 126 p. Selzer accuses the Ashkenazi establishment of cultural genocide against Oriental/Sephardic/North African Jews. "Culturally, if not politically, the Ashkenazi has done everything possible to confirm the Arab allegation that Israel is 'an outpost of Western imperialism.'" (p. 92).

Selzer, Michael. The Wineskin and the Wizard. N.Y.: MacMillan, 1970. 241 p. Argues that the glitter of "normalcy" and power ("Judaism rejects power") has corrupted Jewish existence. Judaism is an "ideal" rather than a "circumstance."

Smith, Gary V. ed. <u>Zionism, The Dream and the Reality,
a Jewish Critique</u>. N.Y.: (Barnes & Noble bk.) Harper,
1974. 325 p. A "critical reader" on the "myths" of
Jewish secular nationalism. Includes bibliographical
references, glossary of names, glossary of terms, notes
on the authors.

Stone, I.F. <u>Underground to Palestine, and Reflections
Thirty Years Later</u>. N.Y.: Pantheon Books, 1978. See,
esp., "Confessions of a Jewish Dissident."

Timerman, Jacobo. <u>The Longest War; Israel in Lebanon</u>.
trans. from the Spanish by Miquel Acoca. London: Chatto
& Windus, N.Y.: Vintage Books, 1983. 167 p. By the
Argentine journalist (now living in Israel), author of
<u>Prisoner without a name, cell without a number</u>. trans.
from the Spanish by Toby Talbot. (London: Weindenfeld
& Nicolson, 1981). This is a sharp critique of the
Israeli operation in Lebanon.

H. Anti-Zionist Opinion and Perspective (particularly recommended is E. Said (1980), and E. Zureik (1979)).

Abu-Lughod, Ibrahim, Bala Abu-Laban. eds. Settler Regimes in Africa and the Arab World; The Illusion of Endurance. (AAUG Monograph series, 4) Wilmette, Ill.: Medina University Press International, 1974. A collection of articles including the famous "Responses to Settler Regimes" by D. Berrigan.

Abu-Lughod, Ibrahim. ed. The Transformation of Palestine. Evanston, Ill.: Northwestern University Press, 1971. On the question of the Palestinian exodus in 1948, see the essay by E. Childers, pp. 165-202; his study of Arab newspapers and broadcasts revealed no "orders to leave."

Aruri, Naseer and Edmund Ghareeb. Enemy of the Sun: Poetry of Palestinian Resistance. Washington, D.C.: Drum and Spear Press, 1970.

Bagrash, G. "The United States and the Zionist Organization." Arab Journal, 5:1-2 (1968): 43-47.

Davis, Uri, Andrew Mack and Nira Yuval-Davis. eds. Israel and the Palestinians. London: Ithaca Press, 1975. 415 p. An anthology of critical papers. The volume had its genesis in a conference sponsored by the Richardson Institute in Dec. 1974.

el-Asmar, Fouzi. To Be an Arab in Israel. Foreword by
I.F. Stone. Introduction by Uri Davis. London:
Pinter, 1975. 215 p. An indictment of Israel by a
Palestinian Arab journalist. "It became apparent to me
that not only newspaper advertisements but also most
other things in this country, apart from laws and taxes,
were not for Arabs... it was as though we did not
exist." (p. 58).

Ghilan, Maxim. How Israel lost its Soul. Harmonds-
worth, Eng.: Penguin Books, 1974. 290 p. Includes
bibliographical references and index.

Hadawi, Sami. Bitter Harvest, Palestine 1914-67. N.Y.:
New World Press, 1967. Should be read with F. Turki
(below).

Jiryis, Sabri. The Arabs in Israel. trans. from the
Arabic by Inea Bushnaq. N.Y. & London: Monthly Review
Press, 1976. 314 p. On the rights of Arabs in Israel,
based largely on Israeli sources.

Khalidi, Walid. ed. From Haven to Conquest: Readings in
Zionism and the Palestine Problem until 1948. Beirut:
Institute of Palestine Studies, 1971.

Langer, Felicia. With My Own Eyes: Israel and the
Occupied Territories, 1967-1973. Foreword by Israel
Shakah. London: Ithaca, 1975. 170 p. By a lawyer who
defended Jewish deserters and Arab terrorists after the
1967 war. Shahak is a professor at The Hebrew University and chairman of the Israeli League of Human Rights.

Lilienthal, Alfred M. The Other Side of the Coin: An

American Perspective of the Arab-Israeli Conflict. N.Y.: Devin-Adair, 1965. 420 p. See also his massive The Zionist Connection: What Price Peace? (N.Y.: Dodd, Mead & Co., 1978).

Menuhin, Moshe. The Decadence of Judaism in our Time. 2nd impression with Postscript. Beirut: Institute of Palestine Studies, 1969.

Naufal, Sayyid. "A Short History of the Arab Opposition to Zionism and Israel." Islamic Review, 53:2 (Feb. 1965): 4-8 (March, 1965):11-14.

Rodinson, Maxime. Israel: A Colonial-Settler State? trans. from the French by David Thorstad. Introd. by Peter Buch. N.Y.: Monad Press, 1973. 120 p. First published in 1967 in Le conflit israelo-arab, a special issue of Les temps modernes. An influential work by a French Orientalist. In the earlier work, Israel and the Arabs (trans. from the French by M. Perl. N.Y.: Random House, 1969. 239 p.), Rodinson argues that the early phase of Zionist ideology was an integral part of the expansionist mentality of late 19th-century colonialism. Israel is a colonial settler state, "fait colonial." A less radical French view is presented by Amnon Kapeliouk in Israel. La Fin des mythes (Paris: Albin Michel, 1975).

Rokach, Livia. Israel's Sacred Terrorism--a study of Moshe Sharett. London: Ithaca Press, 1980. 68 p. 1962. Rpt. Beirut: Institute for Palestine Studies, 1970. Includes Appendix, Bibliography, Index. On links between Zionist activity and U.S. diplomacy, see Said, Edward W. The Question of Palestine. N.Y.: Times

Books, 1980. 265 p. Bibliographical Notes. Chapter Notes. Index. A "political Essay" that insists on "the richness of the question of Palestine..." Said's task "is to present the Palestinian story; the Zionist one is much better known and appreciated." (p. 118). "Rarely have the concepts of justice, realism and compassion played any role... in attempts to think about the Middle East, which has been commanded by outdated generalities like coarse nationalism and great-power interests..." (p. 235).

Smith, Pamela Ann. <u>Palestine</u> <u>and</u> <u>the</u> <u>Palestinians</u> <u>1876-1983</u>. N.Y.: St. Martin's Press, 1984. 279 p. maps, tables, Notes, Select Bibliography, Glossary of Arabic terms, Index. Based on "an extensive series of informal, unstructured interviews, interviews with Palestines from all walks of life..." (p. 2). The author tries to avoid "an abstract empiricism on the one hand and grand theorising on the other." (p. 3). Note the author's documentation for the claim that: "Zionist accounts of the flight and claims that the refugees left of their own accord or at the behest of the Arab governments are refuted in Erskine Childers, "The Other Exodus", <u>Spectator</u>, 12 May 1961, pp. 672-5, and in the <u>Progress</u> <u>Report</u> <u>of</u> <u>the</u> <u>United</u> <u>Nations</u> <u>Mediator</u> <u>on</u> <u>Palestine</u> (Count Bernadotte), Rhodes, September 1948 (Cmd. 7530, London, 1948)." (p. 239).

Stevens, Richard P. <u>American</u> <u>Zionism</u> <u>and</u> <u>U.S.</u> <u>Foreign</u> <u>Policy</u>, <u>1942-1947</u>. N.Y.: Pageant Press, 1962. Rpt. Beirut: Institute for Palestine Studies, 1970. Appendix, Bibliography, Index. On links between Zionist activity and U.S. diplomacy.

Stevens, Richard P. Zionism and Palestine Before the Mandate: A Phase of Western Imperialism. An Essay with a Selection of Readings. (Anthology series, no. 5) Beirut: Institute for Palestine Studies, 1972. 153 p. Includes bibliographical references.

Stevens, Richard P. and A.M. Elmessiri. (comp). Israel and South Africa: The Progression of a Relationship. N.Y.: New World Press, 1976. 214 p. Includes bibliographical references.

Taylor, Alan R. Prelude to Israel; An Analysis of Zionist Diplomacy, 1897-1947. N.Y.: Philosophical Library, 1959. Includes bibliography. On Zionist goals and diplomatic means.

Taylor, Alan R. and Richard N. Tetlie. Palestine: A Search for Truth. Washington D.C.: Public Affairs Press, 1970. Advocates a "humanist and moral approach" to the Israeli-Arab conflict.

Taylor, Alan R. The Zionist Mind; The Origins and Development of Zionist Thought. Beirut: IPS (Monograph series, 39) 1974. 218 p. Taylor argues that Zionism violates Judaism but concedes that "Few Arabs have taken the trouble to examine...the history and character of Zionism...they have remained unaware of the more moderate and less threatening facets and factions within Zionism, and have inadvertently helped to foster the ascendancy of those favoring a hard line Zionist policy premised on the existence of Arab intransigency." (p. 9).

Toynbee, Arnold. A Study of History. Vol. 12: Recon-
siderations. Oxford, Eng.: Oxford University Press,
1961. 740 p. For two critiques of Toynbee's views on
Jewish history see Maurice Samuel, The Professor and the
Fossil; some observations on Arnold J. Toynbee's 'A
Study of History.' (N.Y.: Knopf, 1956), 268 p. and O.K.
Rabinowicz, Arnold Toynbee on Judaism and Zionism
(London: W.H. Allen, 1974).

Turki, Fawaz. The Disinherited: Journal of a
Palestinian Exile. N.Y. & London: Monthly Review Press,
1972. 156 p. "So when Theodor Herzl, the European from
Vienna, spoke of creating "a rampart of Europe, an
outpost of civilization" against "Asian barbarism" in
Palestine, no one came forth to oppose the concept and
its execution. The event was applauded." (p. 12).
Turki faults the Israelis, the Arabs, and the Western
Powers for indifference, exploitation, and aggression
toward Palestinians.

Zionism, past and present. Moscow: "Social Sciences
today," Editorial Board, USSR Academy of Sciences, 1976.
Includes bibliographical footnotes. A collection of
Soviet Marxist articles on Zionism in Tzarist Russia,
the U.S. and in Israel. Contends that "Racism and
Zionism (are) two sides of the same coin." For essays
on Marxist/communist anti-Zionism, and anti-Israeli
propaganda, see Robert S. Wistrich. ed. The Left
Against Zion (N.Y.: Vallentine, Mitchell Biblio.
Distribution, 1980). Reviewed by Eric M. Breindel,
Commentary (July 1980): 72-74.

Zureik, Elia T. The Palestinians in Israel, A Study in
Internal Colonialism. (International Library of sociol-

ogy). London: Routledge & Kegan Paul, 1979. Includes bibliographical notes. Zureik, in a serious and major study, argues that the Israeli Arabs are a segregated industrial proletariat, casualties of Zionism's "internal colonialism." Reviewed by B. Avishai, New York *Review* *of* *Books* (Feb. 19, 1981): 18. A systematic analysis of Israeli control of Israel's Arabs is presented by Ian Lustick in his *Arabs* *in* *the* *Jewish* *State* (Austin: University of Texas Press, 1980). The Jewish population has, Lustik says, shown little sympathy for the dominated and isolated Arab minority. But, unlike Avishai, etc, he does not call for fundamental institutional change of the system of control, *vide* pp. 268-271.

CHAPTER 3:

MODERNITY AND MODERN THOUGHT.

A. Introductory Studies and Surveys. Collected Essays, Readers.
(And see Part I, Chapter 4).

Adler, Cyrus. ed. The Jewish Theological Seminary of
America: Semi-Centennial Volume. N.Y.: JTSA, 1939. O.
V, 194 p.

Alon, Gedalyahu. "The Lithuanian Yeshivas." In The
Jewish Expression. ed. by Judah Goldin. N.Y.: Bantam
Books, 1970.

Altmann, Alexander. Essays in Jewish Intellectual
History. Hanover, N.H.: pub. for Brandeis University
Press by the University Press of New England, 1981. X,
324 p. Bibliographical references and indices. (cited
below, rec.d).

Bamberger, Bernard J. "Beginnings of Modern Jewish
Scholarship." Yearbook of the Central Conference of
American Rabbis. 42 (1932):

Baron, Salo W. Modern Nationalism and Religion. (Col-
gate-Rochester Divinity School. Rausenbusch foundation
lectures, 1944). N.Y.: Harper & Row, 1947. 363 p.

Baron, Salo W. "The Modern Age." In Great Ages and
Ideas of the Jewish People. ed. by Leo W. Schwartz.
N.Y.: Random House, 1956. The five-page "Suggestions
for Further Reading" indicates some of the better literature.

Baron, Salo W.   History and Jewish Historians; Essays and Addresses. ed. with a Foreword by Arthur Hertzberg and Leon A. Feldman.   Phila.: JPS, 1964. 504 p. Includes extensive learned notes, Index. Part I contains five essays on history. Part III is on "Jewish Historians and their Viewpoints."

Ben-Horin, Meir and Abraham G. Duker.   eds. Emancipation and Counter-Emancipation. A Jewish Social Studies Reader. N.Y.: Ktav Books, 1975.   An "anthology of scholarly writing on aspects of modern Jewish life" that includes articles from Jewish Social Studies (1939- 1957). Contains Baron's essay "The Impact of the Revolution of 1848 on Jewish Emancipation," and H. Arendt's "Privileged Jews." Includes a valuable bibliography.

Ben-Sasson, H.H.   "Dynamic Trends in Modern Jewish Thought and Practice." In Jewish Society Through the Ages. ed. by H.H. Ben-Sasson and S. Ettinger. N.Y.: Schocken Books, 1971. pp. 329-344.

Cohen, Israel. Contemporary Jewry; A Survey of Social, Cultural, Economic, and Political Conditions. London: Methuen, 1950. O. XIV, 410 p. Includes a 6-page bibliography.

Dawidowicz, Lucy.   The Jewish Presence; Essays on Identity and History. N.Y.: Holt, Rinehart and Winston, 1977. 308 p. Lucid intelligent essays on Yiddish, the Holocaust, American Jewish history. Includes bibliographical footnotes.

Dawidowicz, Lucy.   ed. with Introd. The Golden Tradition; Jewish Life and Thought in Eastern Europe. N.Y.:

Holt, 1967; Boston: Beacon Press, 1967. 502 p. maps. 47
notes (largely in Yiddish) document the valuable Introduction on the contours of Eastern European Jewry. This
is a collection of primary materials on the response of
Eastern European Jewry to the challenges of modernity.

Dubnov, Simon M. History of the Jews; Vol. 5: From the
Congress of Vienna to the Emergence of Hitler. trans.
from the Russian 4th definitive rev. ed., Vol. 9 & 10 by
Moshe Spiegel. N.Y. and London: Yoseloff, 1973. 915 p.
And see Vol. 4 (1971) From Cromwell to the Napoleonic
era.

Elbogen, Ismar. A Century of Jewish Life, 1840-1940.
ed. by Solomon Grayzel. Phila.: JPS, 1944. XLIII, 814
p. A commanding overview, compare with H. Sachar (1975,
cited below).

Epstein, Isadore. Judaism: A Historical Presentation.
Baltimore: Penguin Books, 1959. Epstein, the general
editor of the Soncino Babylonian Talmud, is also author
of The Faith of Judaism; An Interpretation for our Times
(London: Soncino, 1954), 418 p.

Finkelstein, Louis. ed. The Jews: Their History,
Culture and Religion. 2 vols. Phila.: JPS, 1960. 4th
ed. N.Y.: Schocken Books, 1970. See the essays in Vol.
2 by Weinryb, Tartakower and others. Contains expert
discussion of aspects of modern Jewish history.

Flohr-Mendes, Paul R. and Jehuda Reinharz. eds. The Jew
in the Modern World. A Documentary History. N.Y.:
Oxford University Press, 1980. A valuable source reader
with more than 200 primary documents translated from

French, German, Hebrew, Portuguese, Russian and Yiddish sources. Includes an Appendix: "The Demography of Modern Jewish History," p. 525. Index, p. 543.

Fried, Jacob. ed. Jews in the Modern World. 2 vols. N.Y.: Twayne, 1962. A collection of essays on the Jewries of Israel, Europe and America.

Glatzer, Nahum N. Essays in Jewish Thought. University, Alabama: The University of Alabama Press, 1978. 295 of p. Index. One essay in Hebrew on the last year of Rosenzweig's life. See "The Beginnings of Modern Jewish Studies." (pp. 149-165). The formative period is 1818 to 1860 with the publication of L. Zunz's Etwas uber die rabbinische Literatur (1818), H. Graetz's Geschichte der Juden (1853--), A. Geiger's Urschrift und Ubersetzung der Bibel (1857), I.M. Jost's Geschichte des Judentums(1857), Z. Frankel's Einleitung in die Mischna (1859), L. Zunz's Die Ritus der synagogalen Poesie, (1859). For a bibliography of Glatzer's writings, see Texts and Responses (Glatzer Festschrift) ed. by M.A. Fishbane and P.R. Flohr (Leiden: E.J. Brill, 1975), pp. 307-323.

Goldin, Judah. ed. The Jewish Expression. N.Y.: Bantam Books, 1970. Contains 19 high-merit essays that span the Biblical period to modern Israel.

Grayzel, Solomon. A History of the Contemporary Jews from 1900 to the Present. Phila.: JPS, 1961; N.Y.: Meridian, 1961. 192 p.

651

Hertzberg, Arthur. ed. Judaism. (Great Religions of
Modern Man). N.Y.: Braziller, 1961. 256 p. An
anthology.

Jospe, Alfred. ed. with an Introd. Studies in Jewish
Thought: An Anthology of German Jewish Scholarship.
Detroit: Wayne State University, 1981. 434 p.

Litvinoff, Barnet. A Peculiar People: Inside World Jewry
Today. London: Weidenfeld and Nicolson, 1969. 308 p.

Mahler, Raphael. A History of Modern Jewry, 1790-1815.
ed. by Lionel Kochan. London: Vallentine, Mitchell,
1970; N.Y.: Schocken, 1971. XXIII, 742 p. An abridged
and edited version of the 4-vol. Hebrew study. Includes
an incisive analysis of antagonisms within Jewish social
structures.

Malino, Frances et al. eds. Essays in Modern Jewish
History: A Tribute to Ben Halpern. New Brunswick, N.J.:
Associated University Press, 1982. 343 p. Essays on
Zionism, French Judaism, "The Study of the Jewish Intel-
lectual," and an appreciation of Halpern and his
writings.

Maslin, Simeon J. Selected Documents of Napoleonic
Jewry. Cincinnati: HUAC, 1957.

Meyer, Michael A. "Where does the Modern Period of
Jewish History Begin?" Judaism, 24:3 (Summer 1975):
329-38. On trends in the historiography of modern
Jewish history.

Meyer, Michael A.   ed. with Introd. and notes.   Ideas of Jewish History. (Library of Jewish Studies)   N.Y.: Behrman House, 1974. 360 p.   A collection of readings. For advanced students.

Noveck, Simon.   ed. with introductory notes.   Contemporary Jewish Thought: A Reader.   Washington D.C.: B'nai B'rith Dept. of Adult Jewish Education, 1963. 378 p. For beginning level and advanced interests.

Noveck, Simon.   ed. with introductory notes.   Great Jewish Personalities in Modern Times.   Washington D.C.: B'nai B'rith Dept. of Adult Jewish Education, 1963. 366 p.   For beginning students.

Noveck, Simon.   ed. with introductory essays.   Great Jewish Thinkers of the Twentieth Century.   Washington D.C.: B'nai B'rith Dept. of Adult Jewish Education, 1963.   Q. 326 p.   Includes selections. For beginning-level students.

Roth, Leon.   Judaism: A Portrait.   N.Y.: Viking Press, 1961. 240 p.: Viking (Compass bk.), 1962.   A sensitive study by a philosopher alert to the dynamic of universalism and particularity within Judaism.   Roth wrote the major study, Spinoza (Boston, 1929), which gives some information on the religious background (there is some evidence that Spinoza did not want to be severed from the synagogue), and Roth wrote Spinoza, Descartes and Maimonides (Oxford, 1924, Rpt. N.Y.: 1963).

Ruppin, Arthur.   The Jews in the Modern World.   Introd. by L.B. Namier. (Studies in modern history)   London:

MacMillan, 1934. O. XXXI, 423 p. By an important
scholar.

Sachar, Howard M. The Course of Modern Jewish History.
1963; updated and expanded ed. N.Y.: Dell (a Delta bk.)
Pub. Co., 1977. 630 p. Includes a comprehensive bibliography. A standard work.

Sauna, Victor D. ed. Fields of Offerings; Studies in
Honor of Raphael Patai. Rutherfield N.J.: Fairleigh
Dickinson University Press, 1983. XX, 327 p. "Hebrew
section." Patai is a leading Jewish social anthropolo-
gist, author of The Hebrew Goddess, etc.

B. Jews and Jewries: Enlightenment, Emancipation, Anti-Semitism.
On contemporary Jewish life, see Barnet Litvinoff's A Peculiar
People, (London, 1969), and now see the comprehensive and
well-written study by Howard M. Sachar, Diaspora. An Inquiry
Into The Contemporary Jewish World. (NY: Harper & Row,
1985, 539 pp.; Bibliography, pp. 489-508).

Aschheim, Steven. Brothers and Strangers; the Eastern
European Jew in Germany and German Jewish Consciousness,
1800-1923. Madison, WI.: University of Wisconsin Press,
1982. XIV, 331 p. Biblio.: p. 307-323. Index. A highly
intelligent study, using literary and archival sources,
of the Ostjuden ("As a minority in Germany, Eastern Jews
felt doubly alien." p. 248; a Galut within Galut) in
the self-definition of German Jews. Eastern Jewish
culture was defined as "ghetto" culture but German Jews
also viewed Eastern Jews as the "real" or Ur Jew (see,
esp., chap. 8). The image of the Eastern Jew (who in
fact was legally and symbolically alien) "played a
central role in the genesis, mythology, and disposition
of pre-World War I German anti-Semitism." p. 62. But
this point as Aschheim goes on to argue in the excellent
chapter "Caftan and Cravat" must not blunt awareness of
the anti-Semite attack on the assimilated and assimilating ("new" Jew) Jew, despised because he sought to leave

the ghetto. In the minds of anti-Semitics the Ostjude was ultimately feared as a potential German Jew. It was the German-speaking Zionists who attempted to heal the East-West division in Jewry through the identity model of shared peoplehood: "we are a people, one people." (Herzl). "German Zionism had a real function for those Jews who were plagued with self-doubt and yet perceived that there was little hope for real integration within the German Volk." (p. 110).

Bach, H.I. The German Jew. A Synthesis of Judaism and Western Civilization 1730-1930 (Littman Library of Jewish Civilization). Oxford: Oxford University Press, 1984. 255 p.

Barnard, Frederick. M. "Herder and Israel." JSS, 28:1 (January, 1966): 25-33. Herder called for a two-fold solution to the Jewish problem: collective political rights and individual civil rights. Barnard notes similarities (but too quickly, and he is enthusiastically over-positive) between Herder and T. Herzl.

Barth, Karl. Protestant Thought: From Rousseau to Ritsch. N.Y.: Harper, 1959. 435 p. Published in London, S.C.M., 1959, under the title: From Rousseau to Ritsch. A trans. of 11 chapters of Die Protestantische Theologie im 19. Jahrhundert by Brian Cozens; trans. rev. by H.H. Hartwell. See, esp., "Man in the 18th Century," pp. 11-57 and "Lessing," pp. 118-149.

Barzilay, Isaac Eisenstein. "The Jew in the Literature of the Enlightenment." JSS, 17 (1956): 243-61. A comprehensive essay that sets forth 3 positions within Enlightenment thought: the liberals who supported Emancipation (Dohm, Mirabeau), those who opposed it, and those (e.g., Voltaire) who advocated "conditional" (i.e., contingent upon Jewish reforms) emancipation. See the bibliography in M. Meyer (1967, cited below) and J. Katz (1973, cited above).

Barzilay, Isaac Eisenstein. "The Background of the Berlin Haskalah." In Essays on Jewish Life and Thought Presented in Honor of Salo Wittmayer Baron. ed. by Joseph L. Blau, et al. N.Y.: Columbia University Press, 1959. Recommended; cf. J. Katz (1973, cited below). The major comprehensive study is in Hebrew: Azriel Shohet, Beginnings of the Haskalah among German Jewry in the First Half of the Eighteenth Century. (Jerusalem: Bialik Institute, 1960). Barzilay has two other pertinent studies, PAAJR, 29 (1960-61): 17-54; and JSS, 21 (1959): 165-92.

Barzilay, Isaac Eisenstein. "Moses Mendelssohn: A Study in Ideas and Activities." JQR, n.s. 52 (July 1961): 69-93; 52 (October 1961): 175-86.

Bein, Alex. "Modern Anti-Semitism and its Place in the History of the Jewish Question." In Between East and West, Essays Dedicated to the Memory of Bela Horovitz. ed. by A. Altmann. London: East and West Library, 1958.

Bernadete, M.J. Hispanic Culture and Character of the Sephardic Jews. 2nd corr. ed. N.Y.: Sepher-Hermon Press, 1982. Bernadete is the foremost scholar of Sephardic Jewry. And see: Marc C. Angel, The Jews of Rhodes: The History of a Sephardic Community. (N.Y.: Sepher-Hermon, 1978). 199 p.

Cassirer, Ernst. Philosophy of the Enlightenment. a
trans. of Die Philosophie der Aufklärung (1932) by
F.C.A. Koellen and J.P. Pettegrove. Princeton, N.J.:
Princeton University Press, 1951. 380 p. Cassirer
(1874-1945) was a student and friend of Herman Cohen and
author of the brilliant "neo-Kantian" Philosophy of
Symbolic Forms.

Edelstein, Alan. An Unacknowledged Harmony. Philo-
Semitism and the Survival of European Jewry. Westpoint,
Conn.: Greenwood Press, 1982. 235 p. Notes. Biblio.: p.
217-225. Index. Urges awareness of the role of philo-
semitism in Jewish history; that recommendation is sound
but the term 'harmony' is misleading and the label
'philo' needs critical analysis. For a study of the
17th century, see Hans J. Schoeps, Philosemitismus im
Barock. Religionsund geistesgeschichtliche Untersuchen
(Tübingen: Mohr, 1952, 216 p. Index); for England see D.
Katz (1982, cited below), for a brillant analysis of
Jewish self-hatred, see S. Gilman (1986, cited below).

Endelman, Todd M. The Jews of Georgian England, 1714-
1830; Tradition and Change in a Liberal Society.
Phila.: JPS, 1979. 370 p. Endelman's study advances
knowledge of the acculturation process within English
Jewry. He treats topics not fully explored before.

Ettinger, S. "The Beginnings of the Change in the
Attitude of European Society Towards the Jews." Scripta
Hierosolymita, Vol. 7 (Jerusalem 1961): 193-219. Very
important.

Feldman, Egal. The Dreyfus Affair and the American
Conscience, 1895-1906. Detroit, Michigan: Wayne State

University Press, 1981. IX, 187 p. Biblio.: p. 174-181.
Index. The affair caused many Americans to reexamine
their political and social values. The general Jewish
reaction was restrained and many Jews saw the affair as
a question of human justice and not as an anti-Semitic
issue. The Yiddish segment of American Jewry was an
outspoken exception to this and the small group of
American Zionists interpreted the event as proof that
assimilation was a failure (so T. Herzl, etc). The
central effect on Americans was in raising the question
of their own susceptibility to anti-Semitism.

Feuer, Lewis S. Spinoza and the Rise of Liberalism.
Boston: Beacon Press, 1965. 323 p.

Fishman, W.J. East End Jewish Radicals. London: Duck-
worth, 1976. A study of the rise of organized labour
among English immigrant Jews at the turn of the century.

Gay, Peter. The Enlightenment, An Interpretation; The
Rise of Modern Paganism. Vol. I of II Vols. N.Y.:
Knopf, 1966. 555 p. Powerful scholarship.

Graupe, Heinz Moshe. The Rise of Modern Judaism; An
Intellectual History of German Jewry 1650-1942. trans.
from the German by John Robinson. Huntington, N.Y.:
Robert E. Krieger Pub. Co., 1979. Biblio.: pp. 311-322.
A social and intellectual history of German Jewry during
the last three centuries.

Grose, Peter L. Israel in the Mind of America. N.Y.:
Knopf, 1983. 361 p. Notes on Sources. Index, photos.
Winner of the National Jewish Book Award (Israel), 1984.
A fluently written story of the theme of Jewish

restoration from the Puritans, who "found romance in linking Jewish and Anglo-Saxon destinies," through 1948.

Greenberg, Louis. Jews in Russia. ed. by Mark Wischnitzer. (Yale University historical pub. Miscellany, 45, 54). 2 vols. Yale University Press, 1944, 1951. Vol. I (210 p.) is on the struggle for emancipation to 1881. Vol. 2 (213 p.) is on the emancipation struggle, 1881-1917.

Hannover, Nathan Nata. The Abyss of Despair (Yeven Metzulah). trans. from the Hebrew by Abraham J. Mesch, with an Introd., biographical sketch of the author (d. 1683), and explanatory notes. Preface by Solomon Grayzel. N.Y.: Bloch, 1950. XV, 128 p. On the Chmielnick massacres of the late seventeenth century. The pogrom occurred during the Ukrainian uprising against the Polish nobility. This work "prefigures twentieth-century memorial books..." in its narrative descriptions of the pogroms and in its "section detailing the greatness of the Jewish life that was destroyed." J. Kugelmass and J. Boyarin, From a Ruined Garden. (N.Y.: Schocken Books, 1983, p. 7).

Hazard, Paul. European Thought in the Eighteenth Century, from Montesquieu to Lessing. trans. from the French by J. Lewis May. London: Hollis & Carter, 1954. See for Hazard's insights on the "climate of opinion" and his analysis of Lessing.

Hertzberg, Arthur. The French Enlightenment and the Jews. Phila.: JPS, 1968. 420 p. Argues that the mainstream Enlightenment thought of Voltaire and his followers found no appreciative room for Jews or

Judaism. Reviewed by H. Trevor-Roper, The New York Review of Books, 22 (August 1968): 11-14. For a different perspective, see Thomas J. Schlerteth in his The Cosmopolitan Ideal in Enlightenment Thought (University of Notre Dame Press, 1977); argues that Voltaire had his "tolerant" side and his attitudes were not always typical of the Enlightenment.

Holmes, Colin. Anti-Semitism in British Society 1876-1939. N.Y.: Holmes & Meier, 1979. 328 p. Indices. Notes. A balance, careful study. Racist anti-Semitism was not prevalent before 1914. Shows the role of the Protocols in Britain, points out the difference between Britain and other countries and makes the point that "...anti-Semitism was never a vehicle for political success in British society..." (pp. 233-34).

Hyamson, Albert M. "The Damascus Affair--1840." Transactions of the Jewish Historical Society of England. 16 (1945-51): 47-71. The standard detailed study of the infamous blood libel accusation.

Hyman, Paula. From Dreyfus to Vichy; The Remaking of French Jewry, 1906-1939. N.Y.: Columbia University Press, 1979. 338 p. Appendices. Notes. Bibliography. Index. illus. A historical study of changes in French Jewish identity under the impact of the immigrant community (chap. 3,5), Zionism (chap. 6) and the Jewish youth movements (chap. 7). "The ideology of emancipation had proved functional for French Jewry in the nineteenth century..." (p. 235) but the community's pursuit of new forms of expression was limited by the erosion of liberalism during the decline of the Third Republic.

Israel, Jonathan I. European Jews in the Age of Mercantilism 1550-1750. Oxford: Clarendon Press, 1985. 293 p. "Works Cited." Index. An engaging, intelligent, arguable study of the early modern period that claims the epoch of the 18th century was one of "decline." "Sephardim and Ashkenazim rose and fell together." (p. 257).

Kaplan, Mariona. The Jewish Feminist Movement in Germany, The Campaigns of the Judischer Frauenbund, 1904-1938. (Contributions in Women's Studies, 8). Westport, Conn.: Greenwood Press, 1979. A history of the JFB and its leader, Bertha Pappenheim. The JFB concentrated on the white slavery issue, using that problem to promote wider feminist goals. The work is significant in manifesting scholarly interest in the history of Jewish women.

Katz, David S. Philo-Semitism and the Readmission of the Jew to England 1603-1655. Oxford: Clarendon Press, 1982. 286 p. Biblio.: p. 245-271. Index. Demonstrates how the English interest in the Jews in the early 17th century was related to the glorification of Hebrew, the quest for a universal language, and the search for the lost 10 tribes.

Katz, Jacob. Judaism and Christianity against the Background of Modern Secularism." Judaism, 17 (1968): 299-315.

Katz, Jacob. Tradition and Crisis; Jewish Society at the End of the Middle Ages. N.Y.: Free Press of Glencoe, 1961. Jewish society at this time was "tradit-ional," i.e., Religious and cultural values derived from the past served as orientation in the present and gave continuity for the future.

Katz, Jacob. "The Jewish National Movement." In Jewish Society Through the Ages. (cited above, section a). pp. 267-283. Katz locates the distinctive feature of Jewish nationalism in its connection with traditional Messianism. (For a differing opinion, see N. Lucas, 1975, cited in Part 5, chap. 2). The national movement was one response to the social problem of the Jews, subject to discrimination and rejection. This essay is Rpt. in Emancipation and Assimilation (below), pp. 129-145.

Katz, Jacob. Emancipation and Assimilation: Studies in Modern Jewish History. Farnborough: Gregg Intern. Pub. 1972. 293 p. A collection of his essays, with an Introd. The emancipation did not solve the Jewish problem: "It merely transformed it into a social issue." (XI).

Katz, Jacob. "The Term 'Jewish Emancipation', its Origin and Historical Impact." In Studies in Nineteenth Century Jewish Intellectual History, ed. by A. Altmann. Cambridge, Mass.: Harvard University Press, 1964, pp. 1-25; and in Emancipation and Assimilation (above), pp. 21-45. The term began to be used for Jewish Affairs in 1828, and "Jewish Emancipation" became linked with the debate on "Catholic Emancipation." With Gabriel Riesser the term indicated the removal of shackles; it became a powerful motive term, carrying moral force and was "a promotive factor in shaping the course of events." (p. 23).

Katz, Jacob. "Kant and Judaism, the Historical Context." Tarbiz, 41 (1972): 219-237. Hebrew.

Katz, Jacob. Out of the Ghetto; The social background of Jewish Emancipation, 1770-1870. Cambridge, Mass.: Harvard University Press, 1973. 271 p. Notes. Index. A fine work, lucid and pleasant reading, balanced in judg- ment. Katz's work in historical sociology and the sociology of religion has made a lasting and valuable impact on Jewish studies. "Jews entered European society but did not merge with it. Rather, their community became a novel and singular social entity, and at the same time, a thoroughly changed but reorganized variation of the ancient Jewish community." (p. 216). "With the possible exception of France and Holland...the emancipation of the Jews was the result of a struggle that merged with the process of social and political changes leading these countries to a greater measure of modernization and constitutionalism. It was possible to link the case of the Jews with the general trend toward modernization only because in the preceding period--that of reform and civic betterment--the Jew was tacitly or explicitly acknowledged as a citizen of the state." (p. 198).

Katz, Jacob. Jews and Freemasons in Europe, 1723-1939. trans. from the Hebrew by Leonard Oschry. Cambridge, Mass.: Harvard University Press, 1970; Oxford, Eng.: Oxford University Press, 1970. 293 p. Katz uses the status of Jews within Freemansonry as an index of their general social status. The central contentions are summarized in Katz, "Freemasons and Jews," JJS, 9 (1967): 137-148, and Rpt. in Emancipation and Assimila- tion (1972, cited above). The Freemason lodges were founded in England in the 1720's. Their constitution called for absolute religious tolerance. But the lodges on the continent, and especially in Germany, restricted Jewish membership and eventually excluded Jews. At the end of the First World War the anti-Semitic right linked Freemasons and Jews in their conspiracy rhetoric, later used to full effect by the Nazis. There is bitter irony here.

Katz, Jacob. ed. The Role of Religion in Modern Jewish History. Proceedings of Regional Conferences of the Association for Jewish Studies held at the University of Pennsylvania and the University of Toronto in March-April, 1974. Cambridge, Mass.: Association for Jewish Studies, 1975. 171 p. Papers by J. Katz, M. Fox, M. Meyer, Z. Szajkowski, I. Friedman, M. Sklare, F. Talmage.

Katz, Jacob. From Prejudice to Destruction, Anti-Semitism, 1700-1933. Cambridge, Mass.: Harvard University Press, 1980. Notes, Index. This is now the leading general study. Katz focuses not simply on anti-Semitic ideologies but asks: "what were the social intentions and political goals that motivated the ideologues to use these ideas, and how did they adapt them to the needs of the situation at each particular time." (p. 9).

Kobler, Franz. Napoleon and the Jews. N.Y.: Schocken Books, 1976. 220 p. Notes. No index. On Bonaparte's Proclamation to the Jewish Nation (1799). "...Napoleon considered the Jewish people as a partner in his world-wide plans." (p. 213). And Kobler links Napoleon's

Jewish policy with the establishment of modern Israel. There seems to be some exaggeration here.

Lamberti, Marjorie. Jewish Activism in Imperial Germany: The Struggle for Civil Equality. New Haven, CT.: Yale University Press, 1978. XII, 235 p. "A substantial contribution to the controversy on the character of Jewish responses to anti-Semitism in Europe prior to the Holocaust. Lamberti argues that the left liberal lawyers who directed Jewish defense efforts in Germany from 1893 to 1914 were skillful political activists who courageously fought governmental discrimination." (T.Endelman). Cf. J. Wertheimer (1978, 1981, below).

Lamberti, Marjorie. Jewish Activism in Imperial Germany: the struggle for civil equality. (Yale University Historical Pubs, Miscellany) New Haven, CT.: Yale University Press 1978. xii, 235 p. Notes. Biblio.: pp. 221-230. Index. A careful study of the first German Jewish defense organization (Centralverein deutscher Staatsburger judischen Glaubens, 1893). Led by Maximilian Horwitz and Eugen Fuchs, the Centralverein "kept before the Germans the ideal of a pluralistic society... It cultivated civic courage among the Jews. It served notice to all Germans that any violation of the rights of Jewish citizens would be protested..." (p. 15). Lamberti's work is illuminating because it looks at Jewish defense efforts, 1893-1914, in their own time and setting and not from the hindsight of the Third Reich; and she connects Jewish defense with German party politics, especially the Progressive party and events in

Berlin. This work is correctly described by Todd Endelman as "a substantial contribution to the controversy on
the character of Jewish responses to anti-Semitism in
Europe prior to the Holocaust. Lamberti argues that the
left liberal lawyers who directed Jewish defense efforts
in Germany from 1893 to 1914 were skillful political
activists who courageously fought governmental discrimination."

Lea, Charlene A. Emancipation, Assimilation and Stereotype: The Image of the Jew in German and Austrian Drama
(1800-1850). (Modern German Studies, 2) Bonn.: Bouvier
Verlag Herbert Grundmann, 1978. 171 p. From Lea's Ph.D.
Dissert., University of Mass, 1978. Jewish writers in
this period were unable to halt the use of stereotypes
by gentile writers that exaggerated the Jewish role
in finance and business and ignored their movement out
of the ghetto.

Lebzelter, Giselag. Political anti-Semitism in England
1918-1939. N.Y.: MacMillan, 1978. 222 p. Notes.
Bibliography. Index. Fills a gap in the literature.
Contents: the manifestations of anti-Semitism, the myth
of the Jewish world conspiracy, studies of the political
anti-Semitic organizations, the Britons, the Imperial
Fascist League, and the British Union of Fascists
(Mosley). Part 3 is on reaction against anti-Semitism
from Jews and the leftwing.

Liebeschutz, Hans. "Jewish Thought and Its German Background." LBIY, I. London: East and West Library, 1956.
pp. 217-236.

Liebeschutz, Hans. "German Radicalism and the formation of Jewish political attitudes during the earlier part of the nineteenth century." In Studies in Nineteenth-Century Jewish Intellectual History, ed. by Alexander Altmann. Cambridge: Harvard University Press, 1964. Argues that Marx's "emphatic caricature of Judaism clearly shows that he was conscious of his own social connection with Jewry." (p. 158). But Marx was unaware of the Biblical origin of his view of history because he had adopted that view from the Hegelians.

Lipman, Sonia and V.D. eds. The Century of Moses Montefiore (Littman Lib. of Jewish Civilization) Oxford and N.Y.: Oxford University Press, 1985. 385 p. illus. Index. A collection of essays divided into 4 parts: The Man and His Circle, Foreign Affairs, The Holy Land, The Myth Emerges. Montefiore's life "touched modern Jewish history at perhaps more points than that of any other single figure..." (Preface, V.D. Lipman)

Magill, Stephen. Defense and Introspection: The First World War as a Pivotal Crisis in the German Jewish Experience. Ph.D. Dissert, 1977. University of California, L.A. History, Modern Page 5084 in Vol. 39/08-A, Dissertation Abstracts International. Magill studies the changes in the German Jewish situation from Aug. 1914 to Nov. 1918. In 1914 Jews were hopeful that through their participation in the war they would realize objective equality and social acceptance. This did not happen. Jews became identified with the defeat of the Empire and with the republic.

Marrus, Michael R. The Politics of Assimilation: A Study of the French Jewish Community at the Time of the

Dreyfus Affair. Oxford: Oxford University Press, 1971. In this excellent study, Marrus argues that by the time of the Dreyfus Affair, French Jewry had largely lost a sense of community and was thus unable to respond effectively to anti-Semitism.

Menes, Abraham. "The Jewish Socialist Movement in Russia and Poland (1870's-1897)." In The Jewish People Past and Present. Vol. II. N.Y.: Jewish Encyclopedic Handbooks, 1948.

Menes, Abraham. "Religious and Secular Trends in Jewish Socialism." Judaism, I:3 (July 1952): 218-226. Very general and non-analytical.

Meyer, Michael A. The Origins of the Modern Jew: Jewish Identity and European Culture in Germany 1749-1824. Detroit: Wayne State University Press, 1967. 249 p. Includes Notes, Bibliography, Index. An important historical analysis of Jewish identity as it manifested itself within German Jewry in the period from 1749 (Lessing's play, The Jews) to 1824 (the downfall of the Society for Culture and Science among the Jews). Modern Jewish intellectual history begins in this period. Chapters on Mendelssohn, Friedlander (his disciple who could not break from Judaism but could not find peace as a Jew), Zunz and the Wissenschaft ideal, etc. "Taken as a whole, the period testifies to the modern Jew's persistent desire to explain continued Jewish identification to himself and the world in terms of the cultural values dominant in his generation." (p. 9). The importance of the period is not in its "fragile answers but in its struggles with the question." (p. 182). The quest for Jewish self-definition has been a continuing challenge and problem.

Mosse, Werner E, Arnold Paucker and Reinhard Rurup. eds. Revolution and Evolution: 1848 in German-Jewish History. (Schriftenreihe wissenschaftlicher Abhandlungen des Leo Baeck Instituts, 39). Tübingen: J.C.B. Mohr, 1981. High-level work on German Jewry in the mid-19th century. Includes essays by J. Carlebach, A. Barkai, L. Schofer, I. Schorsch. Demonstrates that the 1848 revolution had little impact on German-Jewish history.

Oberman, Heiko A. The Roots of anti-Semitism in the Age of Renaissance and Reformation. trans. from the German (1981) by James Porter. Phila.: Fortress Press, 1983. XI, 163 p. Includes bibliographical reference. Notes. Appendix, Indices. Dramatis Personae, 1-12. A serious study of the anti-Judaism in Luther and its theological context of apocalyptic prophecy. Jews were a part of Luther's catalogue of the opponents of God - heretics, Turks, the Pope. Oberman refutes the common distinction between the early "Jew free" Luther and the latter anti-Semitic Luther. The anti-Judaism was not racial, "strictly speaking, 'anti-Semitism' did not exist prior to the race theory of the nineteenth century." Oberman's primary focus is on Luther but he discusses the mental climate of the times and other reformers, some of whom opposed Luther's statements on the Jews. Cf. H.H. Ben-Sasson, "The Reformation in contemporary Jewish Eyes," In Proceedings of the Israel Academy of Science and Humanities, 4 (1969-70): 239-329. For Jewish counters to the anti-Jewish sermons of Luther, see Selma Stern's study of Josel von Rosheim (Stuttgart, 1959: Et, JPS, 1965, cited in part 3, chap. 3,a).

Pelli, Moshe. <u>The</u> <u>Age</u> <u>of</u> <u>Haskalah.</u> <u>Studies</u> <u>in</u> <u>Hebrew</u> <u>Literature</u> <u>of</u> <u>the</u> <u>Enlightenment</u>. (Studies in Judaism in Modern Times, 5). Leiden: E.J. Brill, 1979. 255 p. Biblio.: p. 231-243. Contains very rich bibliographical comments and scholarly footnotes. A major contribution to the understanding of the age of Haskalah in Germany (the last quarter of the eighteenth century and the first two decades of the nineteenth century). This was an epoch of profound change, of the quest for modernization in religious education, practice and belief, and for the revival of Hebrew language and culture. Pelli discusses the impact of Deism (chap. one), argues (<u>gegen</u> Barzilay, <u>PAAJR</u>, 1955 and others) that the <u>maskilim</u> did not ignore the Talmud or "hate" it (chap. 3). In chap. 4 he discusses "The revival of Hebrew and revival of the people." Part 2 analyzes major <u>maskilim</u>, Wessely, Schnaper, Satanow, Berlin, Euchel.

Poliakov, Leon. <u>The</u> <u>History</u> <u>of</u> <u>Anti-Semitism</u>. cited in part 5, chap. 1,a.

Rozenblit, Marsha L. <u>The</u> <u>Jews</u> <u>of</u> <u>Vienna,</u> <u>1867-1914:</u> <u>Assimilation</u> <u>and</u> <u>Identity</u>. (SUNY series in Modern Jewish History, eds. Paula E. Hyman and Deborah Dash Moore) Albany, N.Y.: State University of New York Press, 1983. 284 p. Bibliography. Index. Uses quantitative sources to reveal "how assimilation affected all Viennese Jews..." (p. 11).

Ruether, Rosemary R. (1974, cited in Part 2, chap. 2).
Ruether argues that anti-Judaism is intrinsic to
Christian exegesis.

Salbstein, M.C.N. The Emancipation of the Jews in
Britain; The Question of the Admission of the Jews to
Parliament, 1828-1860. (Littman library of Jewish
civilization). Rutherford: Fairleigh Dickinson University Press, 1982. 266 p.

Sartre, Jean-Paul. Anti-Semite and Jew. trans.
(Réflexions sur la Question Juive, 1946) by George J.
Becker. N.Y.: Schocken Books, 1948. 153 p. A penetrating analysis of the "passion" of anti-Semitism as more
than opinion about Jews. It involves the whole personality: "The anti-Semite has chosen hate because hate is
a faith..." (p. 19). "The anti-Semite has cast his lot
for Evil so as not to cast his lot for Good." (p. 44).
But Sartre is mistaken and/or overstates some points;
e.g., "anti-Semitism would have no existence in a
society without classes and founded on collective owner-
ship..." (p. 150), and "for it (the Jewish community)
keeps a memory of nothing but a long martyrdom, that is,
of a long passivity." (pp. 66-67). It is unhistorical
to say that "...it is the anti-Semite who creates the
Jew." (p. 143). There is a sense in which this is true
(e.g., see discussion of the 'non-Jewish Jew' (sec.e.)
and note the experience of T. Herzl) but it ignores the
internal richness of Jewish tradition and the role of
choice in determining Jewish identity. A creative comparison could be developed between Sartre's analysis of
anti-Semitism and Jacques Maritain's, the greatest
French Catholic intellectual of this century (1882-
1973). The main influences on Maritain's attitude was

his wife, Raissa, of Russian Jewish background, Leon Bloy, and Charles Peguy. Anti-Semitism, in Maritain's view, was pathology and a "deformation of Christian conscience." One cannot understand "the history of Israel" except from a religious perspective (cf. See, "L'Impossible anti-semitisme," (1937, Eng. version in Ransoming the Times (N.Y.: Scribner, 1941)).

Schnapper, Dominique. Jewish Identities in France: An Analysis of Contemporary French Jewry. trans. by Arthur Goldhammer. Chicago: University of Chicago Press, 1983. LIII, 181 p. Contents: Practicing Jews, Militant Jews, Assimilated Jews. The Conclusion is rather vague. Appendix 1. List of Interviews. The most interesting aspect of this sociological study is on French Jews as a secularized nationality.

Schwartz, Leon. Diderot and the Jews. Rutherford, N.J.: Fairleigh Dickinson University Press, 1981. 206 p. illus. Notes. Selected Bibliography. Index. The first close monographic analysis of Diderot and the Jews and of Diderot's (1713-1784) views on human diversity ("there is no Jewish Nature..." p. 149). Counters the charge (in A. Hertzberg and others) that Diderot was anti-Semitic. Diderot and the philosophers were not racists and Diderot changed his earlier negative views (from his education, Grimm, Voltaire) on Jews in light of his experience of the "enlightened" Jews of Amsterdam (Voyage to Amsterdam). Schwartz states that "...Diderot's role in preparing the ideological climate for Jewish emancipation in France is unappreciated." (p. 160). (Cf. A. Hertzberg, cited above).

Schwarzfuchs, Simon. Napoleon, the Jews and the Sanhedrin. Foreword by Lionel Kochan. (Littman Library of Jewish Civilization). London: Routledge & Kegan Paul, 1979. XII, 218 p. Bibliographical Note. Notes. Index. Napoleon's reorganization of French Jewish life (the distinction between public role of citizen and private religious practice) was a major turning-point in the history of Judaism. Modern political Zionism rejected the results of emancipation but "it did not negate the new structure of Jewish society, and, although advocating a Jewish state, it rejected the old model of autonomous organization... it separated the leadership of the synagogue from... the state, thus remaining... faithful to the Napoleonic heritage in its attempt to find a balance between Judaism and the modern world." (p. 194). In French there is Robert Anchel's study, Napoleon et les Juifs (Paris, 1928) and in Hebrew see Barouh Mevorah, Napolen u-Tekufato (Napoleon and his Era), Jerusalem, The Bialik Institute, 1968), and cf. F. Kobler (1976, cited above).

Spiegel, Shalom. Hebrew Reborn. N.Y.: MacMillan, 1930; XIV, 479 p. Meridian paperback, 1962. 482 p. Notes. Index. An eloquent reflection on the "miracle" of the renascent Hebrew as a folk tongue and a discussion of writers in modern Hebrew from Moshe Chaim Luzatto (b. 1707, Padua) to the modern poet Saul Tchenichovski ("Baruch of Mayence," 1902, "This Be Our Revenge," 1920).

Stanislawski, Michael. Tsar Nicholas I and the Jews: The Transformation of Jewish Society in Russia 1825–1855. Phila.: JPS, 1983. 246 p. Tables, Notes, Biblio.: p. 219-27. Index. Winner of the National

Jewish Book Council Award (History). A well-written and
perspicacious analysis, grounded in knowledge of Russian
history and aware of the need for critical methodology.
Refutes some commonly held views, e.g., Jews and the
quotas (p. 18), why Lilienthal left Russia (pp. 85ff).
Stanislawski also presents new information on conver-
sions. Using a Lithuanian Russian Orthodox archive, he
divides voluntary converts into three types, the true
believers, the poor and the criminal, those seeking
professional and education advancement (the renegade was
later). The author reveals the depth of repressive
intervention into Jewish society by Nicholas and his
underlings and argues that this repression was "...not
motivated by raison d'état, compounded by the ineffici-
ency and essential conservatism of the imperial bureaucracy...It all started and ended with conscription." (p.
185ff.). Connected with the horrors of conscription was
the gruesome task that Jewish leaders faced of "select-
ing which Jews should be sacrificed for the benefit of
the community at large." (p. 186). Nicholas's policies
were also destablizing in the cultural and educational
realm (state-sponsored schools) and in the economic
order by hounding Jews out of their traditional jobs and
village homes without providing alternatives. "The
government claimed that it wanted to rationalize the
economic order and status of the Jews; all it accomp-
lished was to spawn more poverty..." (p. 186).

Sterling, Eleonore. "Jewish Reactions to Jew-hatred in
the first half of the nineteenth century." LBIY, 3
(1958): 103-121. Sterling claims that Marx used the
image of Judaism to illustrate self-alienation under
capitalism. See Marx (sec. e, below).

Szajkowski, Zosa. An Illustrated Sourcebook of Russian
Antisemitism, 1881-1978. 2 vols. N.Y.: Ktav, 1980.
Vol. 1, Nineteenth century, Vol. 2, Twentieth century.

Szajkowski, Zosa. Jews and the French Revolution of
1789, 1830 & 1848. N.Y.: Ktav, 1970. LV, 116 p. This
collection of specialized essays demonstrates the importance of local historical studies. Szajkowski
establishes that there was no single Jewish attitude
toward the French Revolutions.

Szajkowski, Zosa. Jewish Education in France, 1789-
1939. ed. by Tobey B. Gitelle. (Jewish Social Studies
monograph series, 2). N.Y.: Conference on Jewish Social
Studies, 1980. 166 p.

Wertheimer, Jack L. The Unwanted Element: Eastern
European Jews in Imperial Germany." LBIY, 26 (1981):
23-46. From his Ph.D. Dissert., Columbia, 1978. Sets
the encounter between Ostjude and German Jew within the
German milieu of anti-Semitism and xenophobia, and notes
how the German Jew aided and defended the immigrant,
despite private scorn and fear. Complements S. Aschheim
(1982).

William, Bill. The Making of Manchester Jewry 1740-
1875. Manchester: Manchester University Press, N.Y.:
Holmes & Meier, 1976. 454 p. Notes. Glossary. Biblio.:
p. 434-440. Appendices. Index. A detailed careful study
of the largest and possibly most influential Jewish
community in provincial England.

Wilson, Nelly. Bernard-Lazare, Antisemitism and the
Problem of Jewish Identity in Late Nineteenth-Century

France. Cambridge: Cambridge University Press, 1978.
Biblio.: 1. 326-340. An important study of an exemplary
figure (1865-1903) who played a leading role in the
Dreyfus Affair. Lazare (one of "les plus belles con-
sciences de notre temps") was a libertarian and
anarchist who believed "les Juifs ne seront libres que
lorsque les pays seront libres." Lazare saw Dreyfus as
a symbol of the persecuted Jew. But the Dreyfus family
was ungrateful and "In order to secure peace from anti-
Semitism and save the community at large, the silent
Jewish majority was ready to sacrifice Dreyfus and
ostracise Bernard-Lazare." (p. 279). But now see S.
Wilson (1982, cited below).

Wilson, Stephen. Ideology and Experience: Anti-Semitism
in France at the Time of the Dreyfus Affair. (Littman
Library of Jewish Civilization). London: Associated
University Presses, 1982. 812 p. Select Bibliography,
pp. 747-761. Tables, maps. A comprehensive and careful
study. The Jewish community during the Dreyfus Affair
was not as passive as generally believed.

Wistrich, Robert S. Socialism and the Jews: The Dilemmas of Assimilation in Germany and Austro-Hungary.
Rutherford, N.J.: Fairleigh Dickinson University Press,
1982. 435 p. Major scholarship.

C. Varieties of Modern Judaism. Historical and Sociological Studies. For a lucid introduction read D. Rudausky (1979, cited below), and see the outstanding short study by J. Blau (1966).

1. The United States. A note on Canada and Latin America.

Biale, Rachel. Women and Jewish Law. An Exploration of Women's Issues in Halakhic Sources. N.Y.: Schocken Books, 1984. 293 p. vide Epiloque. Urges more Talmud Torah for women and greater responsibility and leadership for women in Jewish life.

Blau, Joseph L. Modern Varieties of Judaism. N.Y.: Columbia University Press, 1966. 217 p. A basic study of Judaism in encounter with modernity. Blau's thesis is that the movements within Judaism (Reform, neo-Orthodox (E. Hirsch), Conservative, Zionism) are responses to modernity that effect substantial changes but without destroying continuity with tradition.

Brauner, Ronald A. ed. Shiv'im; Essays and Studies in Honor of Ira Eisenstein. (Publications of the Reconstructionist Rabbinical College,I). N.Y.: Ktav, 1977. 309 p. A Festschrift for the President of the Jewish Reconstructionist Foundation and editor of The Reconstructionist. Includes a variety of essays; S. Cahn, J. Gerber, A. Gottschalk, S. Poppel, etc.

Cohen, Hayyim J. The Jews of the Middle East 1860-1972. Jerusalem: Israel Universities Press, N.B.: New Jersey,

Transaction Books, 1973. 213 p. Notes. Biblio.: pp. 199-206. A sociological work, the first major monograph on the Jews of the Middle East in recent history; by a prof. at the Institute of Contemporary Jewry, Hebrew University.

Davis, Moshe. The Emergence of Conservative Judaism. The Historical School in 19th Century America. (The Jacob R. Schiff lib. of Jewish contributions to American democracy, 15). Phila.: JPS, 1963. 527 p. On the Conservative movement in America in relation to Z. Frankel's Historical School of Judaism in Germany.

Eisenstein, Ira and Eugene Kohn. eds. Mordecai M. Kaplan: An Evaluation. N.Y.: Reconstructionist Foundation, 1952. IX, 324 p. See also Eisenstein, "Mordecai M. Kaplan," In Great Jewish Thinkers of the Twentieth Century, ed. by Simon Noveck. (Washington D.C.: B'nai B'rith, 1963), pp. 253-278.

Freehof, Solomon B. Reform Responsa. Cincinnati: HUCP, 1960. 226 p. Freehof is the authority in this field.

Freehof, Solomon B. Recent Reform Responsa. Cincinnati: HUCP, 1963. 232 p.

Freehof, Solomon B. Reform Jewish Practice and its Rabbinic Background. 2 vols. in I. N.Y.: Union of American Hebrew Congregations, 1963. 196, 138 p.

Friedlander, Michael. The Jewish Religion. London. 1891. American ed. rev. and enlarged with a biography of the author. Foreword by T.H. Gaster. Preface by Joshua Bloch. N.Y.: Pardes Press, 1946. XXVI, 530 p.

Finkelstein, Louis. The Beliefs and Practices of Judaism. rev. ed. N.Y.: Devin-Adair, 1952. XV, 94 p.

Ginzberg, Louis. Students, Scholars and Saints. Phila.: JPS, 1928. XIII, 291 p. (pa.), ed. 1958. Strong essays by a great scholar, see, e.g., the study of Zacharias Frankel (1801-1875), one of the founders of the Historical School (Judaism must adopt a "positive historical approach," although what precisely this involved was not made clear) and its offshoot, the American Conservative movement. And see the essay on "Rabbi Israel Salanter," a leader in the musar (moralist) movement (vide Glenn, Goldberg, below).

Glenn, Menahem M. Gershon. Israel Salanter, Religious-Ethical Thinker; the story of a religious-ethical current in 19th century Judaism. N.Y.: Dropsie College Press, 1953. 219 p.

Goldberg, Hillel. Israel Salanter, Text, Structure, Idea; The Ethics and Theology of an Early Psychologist of the Unconscious. N.Y.: Ktav, 1982. 358 p. The first full systematic study of Salanter, the founder (1810-83) of the musar movement. cf. Glenn (1953, above); the major work is in Hebrew, The Musar Movement... (5 vols, Tel Aviv, 1953) by Dov Katz.

Goodman, Saul L. ed. The Faith of Secular Jews with an Introd. by Goodman. (Library of Judaic Learning) N.Y.: Ktav, 1976. The principle of inclusion is not very clear in this volume of wide-ranging essays.

Heller, James G. Isaac M. Wise: His Life, Work and Thought. N.Y.: HUCP, 1965. XXI, 819 p. A biography of

Wise, founder of the Hebrew Union College (1875) and the
Union of American Hebrew Congregations 1873, which
became the national organization for Reform congrega-
tions. On Wise, see the standard biography, Isaac
Mayer Wise by M.B. May (N.Y.: Putnam, 1916), and Israel
Knox, Rabbi in America: The Story of Isaac M. Wise
(Boston: Little, Brown, 1957); and see the discussion
in Philipson (cited below).

Helmreich, William B. The World of the Yeshiva. An
Intimate Portrait of Orthodox Jewry. N.Y.: The Free
Press, 1982. Biblio.: pp. 393-403. A richly dense and
detailed book, by a not uncritical "insider."

Kohler, Kaufmann. Jewish Theology... (1918, cited in
next section, c)

Kohler, Kaufmann. Studies, Addresses, and Personal
Papers. N.Y.: The Alumni Association of the Hebrew
Union College, Bloch, 1931. VIII, 600 p. And see Samuel
S. Cohon. ed. A Living Faith: Selected Sermons and
Addresses from the Literary Remains of Kaufmann Kohler.
(Cincinnati: HUC Press, 1948). Kohler (1843-1926) was
an intellectual giant in the American Reform movement.
"I do not believe that the Mosaic statues about
sacrifices, the incense, and the priestly apparel, or
the sanitary and criminal laws, are unchangeable ordin-
ances of God dictated from heaven. I distinguish in the
Bible the kernel from the husk, the grain from the
chaff, the spirit from the form."

Kraut, Ben. From Reform Judaism to Ethical Culture: The
Religious Evolution of Felix Adler. (Monographs of the
Hebrew Union College, 5; I. Edward Kiev Lib. Foundation

bk.) Cincinnati: HUC Press, 1979. 285 p. A scholarly study of one Jewish reaction to modernity that led to "apostasy."

Liebman, Charles S. "Reconstructionism in American Jewish Life" (AJYB, 71, 1970), in Aspects of the Religious Behavior of American Jews, N.Y.: Ktav, 1974, pp. 189-285. Very solid, argues that reconstructionism comes closer than Orthodoxy Reform or Conservationism to articulating a viable American Judaism but is largely a failure as an organized movement.

Neusner, Jacob. ed. Sectors of American Judaism: Reform, Orthodoxy, Conservatism, and Reconstructionism. (Understanding American Judaism, 2) N.Y.: Ktav, 1975.

Neusner, Jacob. ed. The Rabbi and the Synagogue. (Understanding American Judaism, 1) N.Y.: Ktav, 1975.

Parzen, Herbert. Architects of Conservative Judaism. N.Y.: Jonathan David, 1964. 240 p. Other important works are by Marshall Sklare, Conservative Judaism (Free Press, 1955), Moshe Davis (JPS, 1962), David Novack (Ktav, 1974).

Petuchowski, Jakob J. Prayerbook Reform in Europe: The Liturgy of European Liberal and Reform Judaism. N.Y.: World Union for Progressive Judaism, 1968.

Petuchowski, Jakob J. Ever since Sinai; A Modern view of Torah. 2d ed. rev. N.Y.: Scribe Pubs. 1968. 132 p.

Philipson, David. The Reform Movement in Judaism. N.Y.: MacMillan, 1907. new rev. ed. with an Introd. by

Solomon B. Freehof. N.Y.: Ktav, 1967. XXI, 503 p. A classical study.

Plaut, W. Gunther. The Rise of Reform Judaism. Vol I.: A Sourcebook of its European Origins. Preface by Solomon B. Freehof. N.Y.: World Union for Progressive Judaism, 1963. XXII, 288 p. Bibliographical Notes, Index. A well-organized anthology, with introductions; excerpts, essays, speeches, pronouncements by founders of Reform Judaism (1780-1870).

Plaut, W. Gunther. The Growth of Reform Judaism; American and European Sources until 1948. Foreword by Jacob K. Shankman. N.Y.: World Union for Progressive Judaism, 1966. XXII, 383 p.

Poll, Solomon. The Hasidic Community of Williamsburg: A Study in the Sociology of Religion. N.Y.: Free Press, 1962, 308 p. Schocken paperback ed. 1969. A well-respected work.

Radavsky, David. Emancipation and Adjustment; Contemporary Jewish Religious Movements, Their History and Thought. N.Y.: Diplomatic Press, 1967. 460 p. 3rd. Rev. ed.: Modern Jewish Religious Movements. A History of Emancipation and Adjustment. N.Y.: Behrman House, 1979. Foreword by Abraham I. Katsch. 460 p. (pa.). Notes, Biblio.: p. 435-450. Index. Clearly written, an excellent text for college courses. Covers "European Roots," American Shoots" (Reform, Conservative, Reconstructionism, Orthodoxy).

Rosen, Kopul. Rabbi Israel Salanter and the Musar Movement. London: Narod Press, 1945. 116 p. Cf. Goldberg (1982, cited above) and Glen (1953, cited above).

Rothkoff, Aaron. Bernard Revel; Builder of American Jewish Orthodoxy. Phila.: JPS, 1972. 378 p. Appendices, #IV, Bibliography of Revel's Writings. Notes, Biblio.: pp. 343-359. Index. illus. A well-researched biography of this Orthodox leader (d. 1940), scholar (Karaism was his primary interest) and founder of Yeshiva University (1928). Revel "pioneered a new system of Jewish education by combining talmudic and secular studies under the aegis of a single institution." (p. 223). Rev. corrected ed.: N.Y.: Jerusalem, Feldheim, 1981. 378 p.

Wiener, Max. comp. with a biographical Introd. Abraham Geiger and Liberal Judaism; The Challenge of the 19th century. Phila.: JPS, 1962. 305 p. And see Abraham Geiger, Judaism and Its History, in two parts. trans. from the German (Das Judentum und seine Geschichte, 3 vols, 1865-71) by Charles Newburgh. N.Y.: Bloch, 1911. O. 406 p.

The coverage below is very spotty and unsystematic. A comprehensive (50-60 p.) chapter in this work that surveyed scholarship on Judaism and Jewries in North America was lost in the Fall of 1983. As of that date there was no adequate comprehensive history of Jewries and Judaism in the U.S. The same was true of Canada. There are many local and state studies and recent solid material on the Jewish community in the South but many of the state studies are unrigorous, and much monographical work remains to be done. Students interested in this area should consult the AJYB (1899--see Index), AJHQ; the following lists some of the better scholarship in the last 15 years. Rudolph Glanz (1969, 1971 (immigration), 1976), Jacob R. Marcus (one of the deans in this field, 1969, 1970, 3 vols., 1971, 3 vols, 1971 (An Index...), 1972, 1975, 2 vols., Marcus and Abraham Peck (eds. 1984); S. W. Baron (1971); Leonard Dinnerstein (comp. 1971), Dinnerstein and M.D. Palsson (eds. 1973)-- Dinnerstein has studied anti-Semitism in the U.S. (1974) and wrote The Leo Frank Case (N.Y., 1968); Jacob Neusner (1971); Melvin I. Urofsky (1971, 1971, 1982)--Urofsky's specialities are Brandeis, and Zionism in America; Peter Wiernib (1973); David Sidorsky (ed. 1973, religious-cultural interest); Priscilla Fishman (ed. 1973); David Sidorsky (ed. 1973, sociological-social theory interests); Naomi W. Cohen (1975, cited in Part 5, chap. 1); David Meltzer (1976); Malcom H. Stern (1978, genealogy); Irvin Howe and Kenneth Libo (1979); N.N. Kaganoff and M.I. Urofsky (1979, southern Jewry--important research); Lucy S. Dawidowicz (1982, interpretative-cultural interests); Marc D. Angel (1982, on the Sephardim); Jeffrey Gurock (1983, bibliographical guide); Marc Lee Raphael (ed. 1983); Will Herberg (1955, rev. ed. 1983, classic in sociology). Other works are cited in Part 5, chap. 1, chap. 3. Among local, regional and state studies (and these vary greatly in merit) one should note the following: Ronald Sanders (1969, the lower East Side); B.G. Rudolph (1970, Syracuse); Vorspan and Gartner (1970, L.A.); B.W. Korn (1970, Mobile Alabama), and Korn has a number of important studies, both in intellectual and political Jewish American history; M. Silverman

(1970, Hartford, Conn.); J. Brandes (1971, N.J.); I.M.
Fein (1971, Baltimore); S. Cogan (1973, S.F.); Fred
Rosenbaum (1976, Oakland); Harold I. Shafran (1977, the
Western frontier); Steven Hertzberg (1978, Atlanta);
Robert E. Levinson (1978, Calif. Gold Rush); Myron
Berman (1979, Richmond VA) Lloyd P. Gartner (1978,
Cleveland); Irene Narell (1981, S.F.); Judith E. Endel-
man (1984, Indianapolis).

A note on Canada and Latin America.

In regard to Canada (Jewish population, 310,000 (1984))
much more careful, critical scholarship needs to be
done. There are no overall studies except the two-
volume work (1970, 1971) by Stuart E. Rosenberg; there
are a number of anecdotal studies and diaries/reminis-
cence-type works, but now see the valuable study of Jews
in Toronto by Stephen A. Speisman (1979), and Marion E.
Meyer's study of The Jews of Kingston (1983). Until
very recently Latin-American Jewry was neglected. The
work to start with is Martin H. Sable (Latin-American
Jewry: A Research Guide, 1978); and the impressive Jews
of the Latin-American Republics by Judith Laikin Elkin
(Chapel Hill: University of North Carolina Press, 1980,
298 p. Biblio.: p. 269-291). Elkin's goal was twofold,
to make the Latin-American Jewish diaspora visible to
Jewish scholars and to Latin Americanists. Using a wide
range of material she covers all the Latin-American
Republics over a two-century period. An excellent and
up-to-date bibliography is in Howard M. Sachar's Diaspora (N.Y.: Harper & Row, 1985), pp. 500-503. The
following entries are not found in Sachar. Martin A.
Cohen (1971, 2 vols.); Seymour B. Liebman (1974); I.T.
Lerner (1973); Robert Weisbrot (1979, Argentina), and

see the recent study on Argentinian Jewry, From Pale to Pampa... (N.Y.: Holmes & Meier, 1982) by E. Sofer. Note the bibliography of S. Liebman's writings, New World Jewry, 1493-1825 (Ktav, 1982), p. 251.

C:I)   UNITED STATES

Blau, Joseph L. Judaism in America; From Curiosity to Third Faith. Chicago: The University of Chicago Press, 1976. 156 p. Discussed above.

Cohen, Naomi. Encounter with Emancipation. The German Jews in the United States 1830-1914. Phila.: JPS, 1984. 407 p. Received the National Jewish Book Award (History) for 1985.

Glazer, Nathan. American Judaism. (The Chicago History of Amer. Civilization) Chicago: The University of Chicago Press, 1957. 175 p. By a major sociologist.

Goren, Arthur A. New York Jews and the Quest for Community; The Kehillah Experiment, 1908-1922. N.Y.: Columbia University Press, 1970. 361 p.

Grinstein, Hyman B. The Rise of the Jewish Community of New York 1654-1860. Phila.: JPS, 1945. XIII, 645 p.

Gurock, Jeffrey S. When Harlem Was Jewish, 1870-1930. N.Y.: Columbia University Press, 1979. 216 p. plates.

Herman, Simon N. Jewish Identity; A Social Psychological Perspective. Foreword by Herbert Kelman. N.Y.: Sage, 1978. 263 p. By the author of Israelis and Jews

(1965) and American Students in Israel (1970). States
that the "crucial variable" in Jewish identity is religious observance.

Himmelfarb, Milton. The Jews of Modernity. N.Y.: Basic
Books, 1973. 369 p. A significant interpretation.

Howe, Irving, with the assistance of Kenneth Libo.
World of our Fathers. N.Y.: Harcourt Brace Jovanovich,
1976. XX, 714 p. illus. A broadly conceived and magnif-
icently written study of the immigrant experience,
acculturation and the Jewish impact upon America (1880-
1920).

Janowsky, Oscar I. ed. The American Jew: A Reappraisal.
(The Jacob R. Schiff lib. of Jewish contributions to
American democracy, 22). Phila.: JPS, 1964. 468 p.
Historical and sociological studies of modern Jewish-
American life.

Jick, Leon A. The Americanization of the Synagogue,
1820-1870. Hanover, N.H.: Brandeis University, 1976.
247 p. A scholarly investigation of the efforts of
German Jews to reconstruct past communal patterns in the
New World.

Jung, Leo. "What is Orthodox Judaism?" In The Jewish
Library, ed. by Leo Jung, second series. N.Y.: Bloch,
1930. O. 308 p. "Even among Jews we find some who
consider orthodox Judaism as out of touch with modern
times. Never did they err more profoundly. Jewish law
develops through application of precedent to new
conditions, exactly as English or American law does."

Karp, Abraham J. _Haven and Home. A History of the Jews in America_ New York: Schocken Books, 1985. 401 p. Appendix 1-4, Notes, Index. Very readable and integrates primary source materials into the narrative. Karp argues that acculturation has worked but not as was predicted. It has spurred Jews to stress their religious heritage. American Jews have a "dual-image identity": before the world they are a religious community (one of the three great faiths (Herberg)), and internally they are a people with a unique civilization, a "peoplehood."

Liebman, Charles S. _The Ambivalent American Jew: Politics, Religion, and Family in American Jewish Life_. Phila.: JPS, 1973. 215 p.

Liebman, Charles S. _Aspects of the Religious Behavior of American Jews_. N.Y.: Ktav, 1974. 285 p. Contains three interesting, informative and thoughtful essays (orig. pub. in the _AJRY_, 1965, 1969, 1970) on "The Training of American Rabbis," "Orthodoxy in American Jewish Life," "Reconstructionism in American Jewish Life."

Moore, Deborah Dash. _At Home in America. Second Generation New York Jews_. (The Columbia History of Urban Life, Kenneth T. Jackson, General Editor). N.Y.: Columbia University Press, 1981. 303 p. Biblio.: pp. 265-287. Index. Tables. Appendix. The second generation "achieved a remarkable synthesis." They "devised a form of urban community imbued with American middle-class values, yet able to ensure the persistence of the Jewish group." p.16.

Neusner, Jacob. Stranger at Home: "The Holocaust," Zionism, and American Judaism. Chicago: University of Chicago Press, 1981.

Neusner, Jacob. Judaism in the American Humanities; Essays and Reflections. Chico, CA.: Scholars Press, 1981.

Rischin, Moses. The Promised City: New York's Jews, 1870-1914. Cambridge, Mass.: Harvard University Press, 1977.

Rivkin, Elias. Essays in American-Jewish History. Cincinnati: AJA, 1958. Rivkin states that "the position of the Jews in every society of the past has been as secure as the society itself. For every stress the Jews have been held essentially responsible; for every collapse they have been blamed."

Rose, Peter I. ed. with Introd. The Ghetto and Beyond: Essays on Jewish Life in America. N.Y.: Random House, 1969.

Rosen, Gladys ed. Jewish Life in America: Historical Perspectives. N.Y.: Ktav, 1978.

Sanders, Ronald. The Downtown Jews: Portraits of an Immigrant Generation. N.Y.: New American Library, 1976.

Schappes, Morris U. ed. A Documentary History of the Jews in the United States, 1654-1875. 3rd. ed. N.Y.: Schocken Books, 1976.

Silberman, Charles E. <u>A</u> <u>Certain</u> <u>People.</u> <u>American</u> <u>Jews</u>
<u>and</u> <u>Their</u> <u>Lives</u> <u>Today</u>. N.Y.: Summit Books, 1985. 458
p. Notes, Index. An informed and important study, but
basically too optimistic. Silberman argues that anti-
Semitism has declined and will never be a problem
because the American political consensus forbids
it...the exception here is the growth of anti-Semitism
among younger Blacks. He describes the transformation
by which American Jews have come "to live in a freer,
more open society than that of any Diaspora community in
which Jews have ever lived before."

Sklare, Marshall. ed. with Introd. and notes. <u>The</u> <u>Jews</u>
<u>in</u> <u>American</u> <u>Society</u>. (Library of Jewish studies).
N.Y.: Behrman House, 1974. 404 p. and see M. Sklare,
ed. with Introd. and Notes. <u>The</u> <u>Jewish</u> <u>Community</u> <u>in</u>
<u>America</u> (N.Y.: Behrman House, 1974, 383 p.). Skare is
a highly-regarded scholar in this field.

Stember, Charles Herbert et al. <u>Jews</u> <u>in</u> <u>the</u> <u>Mind</u> <u>of</u>
<u>America</u>. ed. by George Salomon. Preface by John
Slawson. Project director: Marshall Sklare. N.Y.:
Instit. of Human Relations Press and Basic Books, 1966.
413 p. Essays, reflecting different perspectives, on
Jewish-Christian relations, Jewish survival, anti-
Semitism.

Szajkowski, Zosa. <u>Jews,</u> <u>Wars,</u> <u>and</u> <u>Communism</u>. Vol. I.:
<u>The</u> <u>Attitude</u> <u>of</u> <u>American</u> <u>Jews</u> <u>to</u> <u>World</u> <u>War</u> <u>I,</u> <u>the</u>
<u>Russian</u> <u>Revolution</u> <u>of</u> <u>1917,</u> <u>and</u> <u>Communism,</u> <u>1914-1945</u>.
N.Y.: Ktav, 1972. XXVII, 714 p.

Waxman, Chaim I. America's Jews in Transition. Phila.: Temple University Press, 1983. 272 p. Tables and Maps, References, Index. An intelligent sociology of religion approach that challenges the theory that ethnic consciousness declines with each generation and questions the notion that modernity inevitably produces secularization. Waxman notes the increase in "intrinsic" Jewish cultural consciousness and argues that declining rates of formal religious affiliation does not indicate a decline of Judaism but may indicate "a search for alternative modes of Jewish expression." (p. 235).

Wischnitzer, Mark. To Dwell in Safety; The Study of Jewish Migration since 1800. Phila.: JPS, 1948. XXV, 368 p. maps. illus. Bibliographical references in the Notes, pp. 309-352. A still solid and valuable study of the migrations attendant upon modernity.

D. Philosophies and Philosophers of Judaism. Philosophical Theology, Apologetics, Interpretations of History. Beginning students should read J. Agus (1941), J. Blau (1962), S.H. Bergman (1963), S.T. Katz (1978). For more advanced levels, see J. Guttman (1964), A.A. Cohen (1963), N. Rotenstreich (1968), E. Fackenheim (1973).

Ahad Ha'am. See Part 5, chap. 2, c .

Agus, I.A. "Preconceptions and Stereotypes in Jewish Historiography." JQR, n.s. 51 (January 1961): 242-253. A conceptually sharp essay, largely a critique of S.W. Baron's treatment of aspects of medieval Jewish history, migration, use of the term 'serf.' Agus urges, correctly, the importance of comparative questions.

Agus, Jacob B. Modern Philosophies of Judaism; A Study of Recent Jewish Philosophies of Religion. N.Y.: Behrman House, 1941. XII, 388 p. Notes. supplementary Notes. No index. Includes studies of H. Cohen. F. Rosenzweig, Buber, and M. Kaplan. Argues that these thinkers agree in "basing religion upon the perception of ethical values." (p. 335). Clearly written, an excellent introduction.

Agus, Jacob B.   Banner of Jerusalem; The Life, Times and Thought of Abraham I. Kuk, The Late Chief Rabbi of Palestine. N.Y.: Bloch, 1946. 243 p. Rpt. under the title: High Priest of Rebirth: The Life, Times and Thought of Rabbi Abraham Isaac Kuk. N.Y.: Bloch, 1972.

Agus, Jacob B.   Guideposts in Modern Judaism; An Analysis of Current Trends in Jewish Thought. N.Y.: Bloch, 1954.

Agus, Jacob B.   The Evolution of Jewish Thought; From Biblical Times to the Opening of the Modern Era. (Ram's horn bks) N.Y.: Abelard-Schuman, 1960. 442 p.

Agus, Jacob B.   The Meaning of Jewish History. Foreword by Salo W. Baron. 2 vols. N.Y.: Abelard-Schuman, 1964. 231 p., 232 p.

Agus, Jacob B.   The Vision and the Way; An Interpretation of Jewish Ethics. N.Y.: Ungar, 1967. 365 p.

Agus, Jacob B.   Jewish Identity in an Age of Ideologies. N.Y.: Ungar, 1978. 463 p. Agus (U.S. rabbi, born 1911) is concerned with inter-faith dialogue and is critical of the "pseudo-messianic mystique in Zionism." He thinks that "the motive of nationalism is productive of good only when it is kept in the background as subordinate to the universal ideals of ethics and religion." (1941, p. 351).

Altmann, Alexander.   "Theology in Twentieth-Century German Jewry." LBIY, London: East and West Library,

1956. pp. 193-216. By an outstanding scholar of wide range.

Altmann, Alexander. "Franz Rosenzweig and Eugen Rosenstock-Huessy: An Introduction to Their Letters on Judaism and Christianity." JR, 24:4 (October 1944) Rpt. in Essays in Jewish Intellectual History (1981, cited above).

Altmann, Alexander. "Franz Rosenzweig on History." In Between East and West. ed. by Alexander Altmann. London: East and West Library, 1958. pp. 194-214.

Altmann, Alexander. "The New Style of Preaching in Nineteenth-Century German Jewry." In Studies in Nineteenth-Century Jewish Intellectual History. ed. by Alexander Altmann. Cambridge: Harvard University Press, 1964.

Altmann, Alexander. "Leo Baeck and the Jewish Mystical Tradition." Leo Baeck Memorial Lecture 17 (London, N.Y.: LBI, 1973). Rpt. in Essays in Jewish Intellectual History (1981), pp. 293-311.

Altmann, Alexander. Moses Mendelssohn; A Biographical Study. Universit of Alabama: The University of Alabama Press, 1973. 900 p. illus. full bibliography. The definitive, scholarly work; can be read together with M.A. Meyer's The Origins of the Modern Jew (1967, cited above), and see Altmann (1982, below).

Altmann, Alexander. Essays in Jewish Intellectual History. Hanover, N.H.: University Press of New England, 1981. 14 essays, one on Rabbinic Adam legends, four on medieval philosophy, a study of Ars Rhetorica among Jews in the Italian Renaissance, and four on pre-Zionist German thought.

Altmann, Alexander. Die trustvolle Aufklaerung: Studien zur Metaphysik und politischen Theorie Moses Mendelossohns. Stuttgart-Bad Cannstatt: Frommann-Holzborg, 1982.

Atlas, Samuel. From Critical to Speculative Idealism; The Philosophy of Solomon Maimon. The Hague: Martinus Nijhoff, 1964; N.Y.: Humanities Press, 1965. 335 p. See S. Maimon (cited below). Takes Maimon very seriously.

Baeck, Leo. "Harnacks Vorelesungen uber das Wesen des Christenthums." MGWJ, 45 (1901): 97-120. For discussion of Baeck's critique of Harnack's image of Judaism, see Walter Jacob (1965, cited below) and Albert H. Friedlander (chap. 3, 1968, cited below).

Baeck, Leo. The Essence of Judaism. rendition by Irving Howe based on the trans. by V. Grubenwieser and L. Pearl (1936), rev. ed. N.Y.: Schocken Books, paperback ed. 1961 (1948), 9-288 p. Das Wesen des Judenthums (1905) was a rebuttal of A. Harnack's What is Christianity? Baeck's work provided intellectual support for the German Jewish community. The "essence," Baeck wrote, "is characterized by what has been gained and preserved. And such constancy, such essence, Judaism possesses despite its many varieties and the shifting phases of its long career." The key terms are "mystery" and "commandment." Humility is the first paradox of religion, the second is "that man is completely dependent upon God and is yet free..." (1st ed., p. 75).

Baeck, Leo. "Why Jews in the World? A Reaffirmation of Faith in Israel's Destiny." Commentary, 3 (June 1947): 501-507.

Baeck, Leo. "Theology and History." Judaism, 13 (1964): 274-284. Pictures Jewish theology as the theologia viatorum, the theology of travelers exploring the paradox of mystery and commandment. Shows an appreciation of Protestant "dialectic theology."

Baeck, Leo. Judaism and Christianity; Essays. trans. with an Introd. by Walter Kaufmann. Phila.: JPS, 1964; N.Y.: Harper, 1966. 292 p. (pa.) For Baeck's view of Christianity see the essay "Romantic Religion." For close analysis of Baeck's writings see A.H. Friedlander, Leo Baeck. Teacher of Theresienstadt (N.Y.: Holt, Rinehart & Winston, 1968).

Baeck, Leo. This People Israel; The Meaning of Jewish Existence. trans. with an Introd. by Albert H. Friedlander. 2 vols. in I. N.Y.: Holt, Rinehart & Winston, 1965. XXII, 403 p. A beautifully written, poetical and learned essay (pub. in German in 1955: Dieses Volk: Judische Existenz) on Jewish experience, by a Progressive German rabbi and religious thinker (1873-1956). See Theodore Wiener, "The Writings of Leo Baeck: a bibliography." SBB, 1:3 (1954). Part of this work was written in Theresienstadt and it has been called "The Terezin Midrash" (E. Simon, cited in A.H. Friedlander, 1968, p. 213, n. 177).

Baer, Yitzhak K. Galut. trans. from the Hebrew by Robert Warshow. N.Y.: Schocken Books, 1947. 9-122 p.

This interpretative essay on the nature of diaspora Judaism can be compared with B. Dinur (cited below).

Bamberger, Fritz. "Zunz's Conception of History. A Study of the Philosophical Elements in Early Science of Judaism." PAAJR, 11 (1941): 1-25. Zunz considered the new Science of Judaism (founded in 1819 and focussed on understanding Judaism itself in terms of history) a means of regeneration for Judaism. "In working on ideas we produce always new ideas and new materials" (M. Meyer, 1967, cited above).

Belkin, Samuel. The Philosophy of Purpose. (Studies in Torah Judaism, series I) 3rd. ed. N.Y.: Yeshiva University, 1958. And see: Essays in Traditional Jewish Thought. N.Y.: Philosophical Library, 1957. 191 p.

Belkin, Samuel. In His Image; The Jewish Philosophy of Man as Expressed in the Rabbinic Tradition. (Ram's horn bks) N.Y.: Abelard-Schuman, 1961. 290 p. Belkin, a former President of Yeshiva University, argues that Judaism rests upon the two basic beliefs that creation belongs to the Creator and man is created "in His image."

Bergman, Samuel Hugo. Faith and Reason; An Introduction to Modern Jewish Thought. ed. and trans. by Alfred Jospe. N.Y.: Schocken Books, 1963. 158 p. (pa.) Consists of valuable short intellectual biographies of leading Jewish thinkers, including A.D. Gordon and Rav Kook. Includes a short "Suggestions for Further Reading."

Berkovits, Eliezer. God, Man, and History; A Jewish Interpretation. N.Y.: Jonathan David, 1959. 202 p. 2nd ed. Jonathan David, 1965. 192 p. (pa.).

Berkovits, Eliezer. Major Themes in Modern Philosophies of Judaism. N.Y.: Ktav, 1975. 248 p. Committed to Orthodox Judaism, Berkovits has written a critique of Buber (1962, cited above) and a critique of Reconstructionism, Reconstructionist Theology (N.Y.: Jonathan David, 1959). He has also authored a book on Prayer (Yeshiva, 1962).

Bird, Thomas E. ed. Modern Theologians: Christians and Jews. N.Y.: Association Press, 1967. 224 p.

Blau, Joseph L. The Story of Jewish Philosophy. N.Y.: Random House, 1962. Valuable. (Cf. S.T. Katz (1975, 1978).

Blau, Joseph L. Reform Judaism: A Historical Perspective. Essays from the Yearbook of the Central Conference of American Rabbis. N.Y.: Ktav, 1973. 529 p. Introd. by Blau. Biographical Notes. Covers a range of basic issues, Law and Authority, Ritual and Worship, etc.

Bokser, Ben Zion. "Jewish Universalism: An Aspect of the Thought of HaRav Kook." Judaism, 8 (1959): 214-219.

Bokser, Ben Zion. Judaism; Profile of a Faith. N.Y.: Knopf, Toronto, Random House, 1963. 293 p.

Borowitz, Eugene. "Hope Jewish and Hope Secular." Judaism, 17 (1968): 131-147. Borowitz is part of the

Reform tradition; he rejects both heteronomy (Orthodoxy) and autonomy in terms of a concept of God - Israel covenant.

Borowitz, Eugene.   A New Jewish Theology in the Making. Phila.: Westminster Press, 1968. 220 p.

Borowitz, Eugene.   How Can a Jew Speak of Faith Today? Phila.: Westminster Press, 1969. 221 p.

Borowitz, Eugene.   "The Problem of the Form of a Jewish Theology."   HUCA, 40/41 (1969-70): 391-408.   A valuable discussion of the thought of Heschel, Baeck, Kaplan, and Buber as alternative ways of imposing form on Jewish theology.   Describing the "God-Israel-Torah relationship" is the primary task of contemporary Jewish theology.

Borowitz, Eugene. Liberal Judaism. N.Y.: UAHC, 1984. 468 p. "Afterword." No bibliography. No index. A non-technical description of modern (contains a brief historical section) theories of Jewish belief.

Breslauer, S. Daniel. The Ecumenical Perspective and the Modernization of Jewish Religion. (Brown Judaica Studies, 5) Missoula, Montana: Scholars Press, 1978.

Brod, Max. Paganism, Christianity, Judaism. A Confession of Faith. trans. from the German (Heidentum, Christentum, Judentum: Ein Bekenntnisbuch (1921) by William Wolf. Preface by M. Brod. A collection of often insightful essays by Kafka's closest friend and editor. Brod argues that Judaism recognizes the truth in both paganism (affirmation of this world) and

Christianity (negation of this world). Moreover, Judaism comprehends both "noble" and "ignoble" misfortune.

Catchpole, David R. The Trial of Jesus: A Study in the gospels and Jewish Historiography from 1770 to the Present Day. (Studia post-biblica, 8) Leiden: E.J. Brill, 1971. 324 p. Discussed in Part 2, chap. 2, c. Argues that Jewish studies of the trial have been set in a context of debate, subject to apologetic motives.

Cohen, Arthur A. The Natural and the Supernatural Jew; An Historical and Theological Introduction. N.Y.: Pantheon Books, 1963. 326 p. Biblio.: pp. 315-321. Index. Cohen suggests that the Exile is a historical coefficient of being unredeemed. (see p. 6). "The adjustment of the Jew to the natural conditions of his environment divests him of the only weapon, his super-natural vocation, which allows him to survive what he must always survive--terrestrial history. ..The natural Jew as such has, we believe, no hope... It is precisely the genius of the Jew that he is unnatural...that he is unadjusted...that he is unreconstructed." (p. 217). This, in part, is a rebuttal to M. Kaplan.

Cohen, Arthur A. The Myth of the Judeo-Christian Tradi-tion. And Other Dissenting Essays. N.Y.: Schocken Books, 1971 (paperback ed. with new Preface). xxi, 223 p. Eloquent and sharply analytical essays. The central argument is that "theological enmity," not a shared tra-dition, exists between Jews and Christians. "The Jews do not need redemption in the same way as Christians for eternal life, as the Sabbath liturgy affirms, is already 'planted in our midst.'" (p. 211). The "myth" originated in the Enlightenment when both Christianity and Judaism were linked in respect to irrationality and intolerance. The heart of the Jewish-Christian contradiction is that one faith assumes fulfillment, the other faith denies it. "Judaism asserts that history is not redeemed. Christianity maintains that it is." (p. 159). Enmity on the level of belief should not bind Jews and Christians to the need for coming together "in the love and service of man" and developing the resources of "a Judeo-Christian humanism."

Cohen, Arthur A. The Myth of the Judeo-Christian Tradition. N.Y.: Harper & Row, 1970. XX, 223 p. Includes bibliographical footnotes. The eschatological issue of the Messiah is the decisive difference between the Jewish and the Christian theological tradition. However, the "resources of Judeo-Christian humanism" should be developed.

Cohen, Arthur A. and Mordecai M. Kaplan. If Not Now, When? Conversations Between Mordecai Kaplan and Arthur A. Cohen. N.Y.: Schocken Books, 1973. Intelligent and searching exchanges; Cohen is an acute critic of Kaplan, see Cohen (1963, pp.203-219).

Cohen, Arthur A. ed. The Jew; Essays from Martin Buber's Journal "Der Jude," 1916-1928. trans. by Joachim Neugroschel. University of Ala.: the University of Alabama Press; Phila.: JPS, 1980. 305 p. A very rich and exciting collection of essays. Cohen is to be praised for his selection and for his Introduction. One of the several interesting essays is "Dostoevski and the Jews" by A.S. Steinberg. "The Jewish question was one of the most insistent and burning issues for Dostoevski--his antisemitism derived basically from his one-sided messianism, the chosenness of the Russian people..."

Cohen, Arthur A. Tremendum (discussed in Part 5, chap 3, c:4)

Cohen, Jack. The Case for Religious Naturalism; Philosophy for the Modern Jew. N.Y.: Reconstructionist Press, 1958. 316 p. Naturalism is valuable as a critique of object-reification "supernaturalism," but naturalistic anecdotes cannot be relied upon as point de depart for full understanding of religious experience. Naturalistic philosophical theology is naive about human nature (the capacity for evil), insensitive to the mystery of the Numinous and slights the depth dimension of religious symbolism.

Cohen, Jack. Commentary. "Symposium on the State of Jewish Belief." (August 1966). N.Y.: American Jewish Congress. N.Y.: MacMillan, 1967. 280 p.

Dinur, Ben Zion. Israel and the Diaspora. trans. from the Hebrew by Merton B. Dugat. Phila.: JPS, 1969. 206 p. Introd. by Yitzhak Baer. In 3 parts, Israel in Diaspora, The Modern Period, The Rebirth of Israel (orig. pub. in The Jews...ed. by L. Finkelstein). Uses a model of Jewish nationalism in a rather circular (logically speaking) way.

Fackenheim, Emil L. "Samuel Hirsch and Hegel: A Study of Hirsch's Religions-Philosophie der Juden (1842)." In Studies in Nineteenth-Century Jewish Intellectual History. ed. by Alexander Altmann. Cambridge: Harvard

University Press, 1964. pp. 171-201. Hirsch accepted
Kant's philosophy of the autonomy of the moral will and
combined it with educative guidance from the Divine (via
Lessing). But this view of Revelation tends to dissolve
it into a finite-human category.

Fackenheim, Emil L.   Quest for Past and Future: Essays
in Jewish Theology.   Bloomington, Indiana: Indiana
University Press, 1968. 336 p.

Fackenheim, Emil L.   God's Presence in History: Jewish
Affirmations and Philosophical Reflections.   (Deems
Lectureship in Philosophy) N.Y.: N.Y. University Press,
1970. 104 p. A reflective examination of the Jewish
"root experiences" (Exodus, Sinai) in relationship to
the Holocaust and modern secularism.

Fackenheim, Emil L.   Encounters Between Judaism and
Modern Philosophy; A Preface to Future Jewish Thought.
N.Y.: Basic Books, 1973. 275 p. Notes. Index. In this
searching and passionate work, Fackenheim wrestles with
modern empiricism, Kantian moral philosophy, and Hegel-
ianism in its several configurations. The confrontation
with Hegel is decisive for the future of Jewish thought
but both Jewish affirmation and Hegelian optimism are
deeply challenged by the "Radical Anti-Spirit" manifest
in the Holocaust. This book is a critique of the
"Anti-Judaic bias that has vitiated modern philosophy
too deeply and too long." (p. 202). It is also a plea
for a Jewish existentialism posited on Jewish
uniqueness.

Fackenheim, Emil L.   To Mend the World. Foundations of
Future Jewish Thought. N.Y.: Schocken Books, 1982. A

highly intelligent and deeply-felt treatise. See, esp.,
Part 5: "Conclusion: _Teshuva_ Today: Concerning Judaism
After the Holocaust."

Fleischmann, Jacob. _The_ _Problem_ _of_ _Christianity_ _in_
Modern _Jewish_ _Thought_ (1770-1929). Jerusalem: The
Magnes Press, 1964. 190 p. In Hebrew. Title page in
English.

Fleischner, Eva. _Judaism_ _in_ _German_ _Christian_ _Theology_
since _1945;_ _Christianity_ _and_ _Israel_ _Considered_ _in_ _Terms_
_of_ _Mission_ (Atla Monograph Series, 8) The Scarecrow
Press and The American Theology Association, 1975. Foreword by Krister Stendal. 205 p. Selected Biblio.: p.
181-192. Index. On _Judenmission_ (the outgrowth of 18th-
century Pietism and carried out mainly by German
Lutherans) in the 19th and early 20th centuries. Part
22 discusses _Judenmission_ and Ecumenism, Mission vs.
Dialogue and the theological implications of The Church
and Israel. Her recommendations are sound: a) the
continuation of dialogue, b) an end to "the teaching of
contempt," c) an appreciation of post-biblical Judaism.
"We believe that Jewish experience and history are
paradigmatic, reflecting as in a microcosm human
experience...If Christians open themselves to this cry
of the Jew at Auschwitz, they may perhaps hope to attain
a deeper understanding of the word which the Jewish
scriptures have given to the world, the word 'redemption.'" (p. 154). This very positive affirmation does
not, of course, blunt objective theological differences
between the two traditions. It also must be noted that
on the emotional-psychological level recent Christian
openness appears to some Jews to be too little and too
late.

Friedman, Maurice. The Hidden Human Image. N.Y.: Delacorte Press, 1974. 402 p. These essays on current topics by America's leading Buber scholar apply some of the conclusions in Friedman's earlier works (1963, 1964, 1967).

Friedman, Maurice. ed. The Worlds of Existentialism, A Critical Reader; With Introductions and a Conclusion. N.Y.: Random House, 1964. XX, 562 p.

Friedman, Maurice. Problematic Rebel; An Image of Modern Man. N.Y.: Random House, 1963. 496 p. 2nd ed. 1970.

Friedman, Maurice. To Deny Our Nothingness; Contemporary Images of Man. N.Y.: Dial, 1967. 383 p. "The task of our age is to recover man's eclipsed humanity. To do this we must rediscover the hidden human image--an image of authentic human existence that may help us realize ourselves as unique persons, as partners in dialogue, and as genuinely human beings." (The Hidden Human Image. p. 268).

Friedman, Maurice. Martin Buber's Life and Works; The Early Years, 1878-1923. N.Y.: E. P. Dutton, 1982. XXIII, 455 p. plates. Notes. The definitive work. Basically uncritical; also Friedmann was sadly deprived of use of archival materal at the Hebrew University.

Friedman, Maurice. Martin Buber's Life and Works; The Middle Years, 1923-1945. N.Y.: E.P. Dutton, 1983. 398 p. plates. Notes.

Friedman, Maurice. Martin Buber's Life and Works; The Later Years, 1945-1965. N.Y.: E.P. Dutton, 1983. 493 p. plates. Notes. Index. Demonstrates how rich and varied Buber's intellectual and personal involvement was with the Jewish intelligentsia and Jewish causes.

Fromm, Erich. You Shall Be as Gods; a Radical Interpretation of the Old Testament and its Traditions. N.Y.: Holt, 1966; London: Jonathan Cape, 1967. 240 p. A sensitive and intelligent work but Fromm tends to read "humanism" into Biblical and Talmudic tests.

Glatzer, Nahum N. Essays in Jewish Thought. (Judaic studies, ser. 8) University of Ala.: University of Alabama Press, 1978. 295 p. See essays on Buber, Zunz, Rosenzweig, Kafka. (Cited above, sec. a).

Glatzer, Nahum N. ed. with an Introd. Leopold and Adelheid Zunz; An Account in Letters, 1815-1885. London: (East and West Library) Horovitz, 1958. XXVII, 427 p. In German; preface, introd. and notes are in English. Zunz has been described as "the foremost nineteenth-century protagonist of the Science of Judaism."

Gordis, Robert. A Faith for Moderns. N.Y.: Bloch, 1960. 316 p. Gordis (see Part 2, chap. 1) is both a biblical scholar and an interpreter and defender of Conservative Judaism. See also Judaism for the Modern Age (N.Y.: Farrar, Straus & Cudahy, 1955).

Gordis, Robert. Judaism in a Christian World. N.Y.: McGraw-Hill, 1966. 253 p.

Gordis, Robert.   The Root and the Branch; Judaism and the Free Society. Chicago: University of Chicago Press, 1962. 254 p.

Gordis, Robert and Ruth B. Waxman. eds. Faith and Reason; Essays in Judaism. N.Y.: Ktav, 1973. 388 p. Introd. by Robert Gordis. Note his comment: "the term 'Jewish theology' is itself alien to the Jewish tradition." (IX).   A collection of articles from the quarterly Judaism that cover a wide range of perspectives.

Greenstein, Howard R.   Judaism, An Eternal Covenant. Phila.: Fortress Press, 1983. 160 p. (pa.).

Guttmann, Julius. "The Principles of Judaism." Conservative Judaism, 14:1 (Fall 1959): 1-24. Distinguishes essence and accident in Judaism, defending the Mitzvah-form (whose purpose is active sanctification) over against the defunct notion of Divinely inspired Torah. "The Achievement of Judaism lies in the unity of faith and the unity of ethics." (p. 23). Comments by Harold M. Schulweis (pp. 24-28) and David Wolf Silverman (pp. 29-33).

Guttmann, Julius.   Philosophies of Judaism: The History of Jewish Philosophy from Biblical Times to Franz Rosenzweig. ed. and trans. from the German (1933) by David W. Silverman.   Introd. by R.J. Zwi Werblowsky. N.Y.: Holt, Rinehart & Winston, 1964; Doubleday Anchor Book, 1966. 546 p.   Includes bibliography.   This scholarly study presupposes knowledge of philosophy and is for advanced students. Guttmann is sometimes obscure and his classification scheme is simplistic.

Guttmann, Julius. On the Philosophy of Religion. ed. and Notes by Nathan Rotenstreich. trans. from the Hebrew by D.V. Herman. Jerusalem: The Magnes Press, Hebrew University, 1976. Glossary, indices, bibliographical footnotes. These are lecture notes. Guttmann was influenced by H. Cohen, E. Husserl, R. Otto. He argues for monotheism as the highest religosity, and criticizes the attempt to assimilate religion to any specific field, e.g., ethics.

Haberman, Joshua O. "Solomon Ludwig Steinheim's Doctrine of Revelation." Judaism, 17 (1968): 22-44.

Haberman, Joshua O. "Franz Rosenzweig's Doctrine of Revelation." Judaism, 18 (1969): 320-336.

Harris, Monford. "Theology and Jewish Scholarship." Judaism, 9 (1960): 331-338.

Hay, Eldon R. "Religion and the Death of God: Hsun Tzu and Rubenstein." South East Asia Journal of Theology, 11 (1970): 283-293.

Herberg, Will. "Rosenzweig's Judaism of Personal Existence." Commentary, 10:6 (December 1950): 541-550.

Herberg, Will. Judaism and Modern Man; An Interpretation of Jewish Religion. N.Y.: Farrar, Straus & Cuday, 1951. XI, 313 p. Paperback ed. N.Y.: Atheneum, 1970. Something of a classic in American Jewish theology. Herberg was influenced by Reinhold Niebubr and by Tillich's method of correlation; his image of theological truth is existential and biblical.

Herberg, Will.   Protestant, Catholic, Jew; An Essay in American Religious Sociology. 2nd ed. rev. Garden City, N.Y.: Doubleday Anchor Books, 1960. 309 p. An influential and path-breaking study. Recommended for college-level courses in U.S. history.

Herberg, Will.   "Judaism as Personal Decision." In Tradition and Contemporary Experience. ed. by Alfred Jospe. N.Y.: Schocken (Hillel) Books, 1970. pp. 77-90. Rpt. from Conservative Judaism, 22:4 (Summer 1968): 9-20. Conceives religion as "a quality of existence" that contains and demands decision and commitment.

Hertzberg, Arthur.   ed. Judaism. (Great Religions of modern man). N.Y.: Braziller, 1961. 256 p.

Hess, Moses.   See Zionist sec. of Bibliography.

Herzl, Theodor.   See Zionist sec. of Bibliography.

Himmelfarb, Milton.   ed. The Condition of Jewish Belief. N.Y.: MacMillan, 1966. Contains the ideas of 38 rabbis.

Hirsch, Samson Raphael.   Fundamentals of Judaism. Selections from the Works of S.R. Hirsch and Outstanding Torah-True Thinkers. ed. by Jacob Breuer. N.Y.: Feldheim, 1949. 282 p.

Hirsch, Samson Raphael.   Timeless Torah. An Anthology of the Writings of Samuel Raphael Hirsch. ed. by J. Breuer. N.Y.: Feldheim, 1957. 540 p. Hirsch (1808-1889) was the leading exponent of "Neo-Orthodoxy" in Germany in the late 19th century. He believed that spirit and freedom were a unity and that one identified with Deity by becoming an autonomous spiritual being.

Hirsch, Samson Raphael. Judaism Eternal; Selected Essays from the Writings of Samson Raphael Hirsch. ed. by Horeb Hirsch. trans. from the German, annot. with an Introd. and a short biography by Isidor Gruenfeld. 2 vols. London: Soncino Press, 1957. LXI, 270, 315 p. Contains essays on the calendar ("the catechism of the Jew is his calendar"), on Sabbath, and on the notion of freedom in Judaism.

Hirsch, Samson Raphael. The Nineteen Letters of Ben Uziel; Being a Spiritual Presentation of the Principles of Judaism. ed. and trans. from the German by Bernard Drachman with a pref. and biographical sketch of the author. N.Y.: Funk and Wagnalls, 1899. Rpt. N.Y.: Feldheim, 1969. An epistolary defense of Orthodox Judaism in the modern world.

Hoenig, Sidney B. ed. Jewish Identity, Modern Responsa and Opinions on the Registration of Children of Mixed Marriages. A documentary comp. by Baruch Litvin. N.Y.: Feldheim, 1965. 420 p. The responses of 43 scholars and leaders in world Jewry to Ben-Gurion's "What is a Jew?" query.

Horowitz, Irving Louis. Israeli Ecstasies/Jewish Agonies. N.Y.: Oxford University Press, 1974. 244 p. Essays written from the perspective of pluralistic liberalism on "the dialectic of Israeli achievements in contrast to Jewish agonies." Horowitz views Israel as the core of the Jewish identity crisis, and regards Jewish nationhood as the last gasp of a shattered

diaspora. Chapter 10, "The Jew as total Institution..."
is particularly interesting.

Jackson, Bernard S. ed. Modern Research in Jewish Law.
(Jewish Law Annual, Supplement, I) Leiden: E.J. Brill,
1980. 165 p. See the profound essay by I. Englard,
"Research in Jewish Law: Its Nature and Function."

Jacob, Walter. "Leo Baeck on Christianity. JQR, n.s.
56:3 (October 1965): 195-211. Baeck's interest in
Christianity was sparked by A. Harnack's The Essence of
Christianity. That work contained a picture of Judaism
that Baeck attacked as unhistorical, unscientific and
uninformed. See Baeck (above).

Jacob, Walter. Christianity Through Jewish Eyes; The
Quest for Common Ground. N.Y.: HUC Press, 1974. 284.
Compare with A.A. Cohen (The Myth... 1971, cited above).

Jacobs, Louis. Jewish Values. London; Vallentine,
Mitchell, 1960. 2nd ed. Hartford, Conn.: Hartmore House,
1969. 160 p.

Jacobs, Louis. Principles of the Jewish Faith; An
Analytical Study. N.Y.: Basic Books, 1964. 473 p.

Jacobs, Louis. We Have Reason to Believe; Some Aspects
of Jewish Theology Examined in the Light of Modern
Thought. 3rd ed. London: Vallentine, Mitchell, 1965.
157 p.

Jacobs, Louis. Faith. London: Vallentine, Mitchell,
1968. 231 p.

Jacobs, Louis. A Jewish Theology. London, Darton, 1973. 342 p. See also: Jewish Thought Today (The Chain of Tradition ser. 3). N.Y.: Behrman House, 1970; and Jewish Law (N.Y.: Behrman House, 1968).

Jacobs, Louis. Theology in the Responsa (Littman lib. of Jewish civilization). London: Vallentine, Mitchell; Routledge, 1975. 378 p.

Jacobs, Louis. A Tree of Life. Diversity, Flexibility, and Creativity in Jewish Law. (Littman lib. of Jewish Civilization) Oxford: Oxford University Press, 1984. 310 p.

Jospe, Alfred. ed. Tradition and Contemporary Experience: Essays on Jewish Thought and Life. N.Y.: Schocken Books, pub. for B'nai B'rith Hillel Foundations, 1970. 372 p.

Judaism, Vol. 3:4 (1954): 302-361. Articles on "Philosophies of Judaism in America," by E. Rachkman, Th. Friedman, H.M. Schulwies, S.S. Cohon, and C.B. Sherman.

Judaism, Vol. 16:3 (Summer 1967): 269-299. Articles on "Jewish Values in the Post-Holocaust future: A Symposium" by E. Fackenheim, R.H. Popkin, G. Steiner, Elie Wiesel, and discussion.

Kadushin, Max. Organic Thinking; A Study in Rabbinic Thought. N.Y.: JTSA, Behrman, 1938. XVI, 367 p. Also see Talmudic section of this Bibliography for comments on Kadushin.

Kadushin, Max. The Rabbinic Mind. N.Y.: JTSA, 1952. 3394 p. 2nd ed. with an appreciation by Simon Greenberg. N.Y.: Blaisdell, 1965. XXV, 414 p.

Kadushin, Max. Worship and Ethics; A Study in Rabbinic Judaism. Evanston, Ill.: Northwestern University Press, 1964. 329 p. In this powerful study Kadushin deepens and extends some of the arguments he developed in The Rabbinic Mind. He argues that rabbinic literature lacked all-inclusive and universal value criteria. What rabbinic literature did express were dynamic value concepts that motivate specific behaviour in specific contexts. Up to this point, Kadushin is convincing but one must ask about the relationship between general value concepts and concrete moral acts. Kadushin's position is that concrete moral acts specify and concretize value concepts. But then the question becomes: what is the agency or mechanism through which the value concept becomes concrete? One possibility is to invoke Deity as the "ground of limitation" (Whitehead) but this simply pushes the problem back a step. Another possibility is to attribute intensity or appetition to the value concept. This is what Kadushin does when he argues that a value concept has its own drive toward concretization. But the concept of "emotional drive" needs concrete elucidation before it can qualify as an explanation. Kadushin says that negative value concepts have "a drive away from concretization." (p. 25). But he gives no cogent argument as to why that should be the case. It seems that he defines "negative value concepts" in a circular way; they are simply unlawful/unhalakhic potentialities. The question of how the indeterminate becomes determinate cannot be resolved by this mixture of social psychology ("emotional drive") and naive

moralism ("negative value concepts"). Kadushin correctly rejects any dualistic distinction between the
individual and society, autonomous and heteronomous
acts. But he overstates things to the point of making
ethics a social product, "a pattern of concepts developed by society." (p. 83). This is to confuse morals
with mores. (Here Buber would be helpful to Kadushin's
thought).

Kaplan, Mordecai M. Judaism as a Civilization; Toward a
Reconstruction of American-Jewish Life. N.Y.: Behrman,
1934. enl. ed. N.Y.: Yoseloff, 1957. 601 p. N.Y.:
Schocken Books, 1967, 1981. 601 p. Notes. Index. Foreword by Kaplan, 1967; Preface by Kaplan, 1933. Introd.
by Arthur Hertzberg, 1981. Kaplan, the founder of the
Reconstructionist movement, was born in Lithuania in
1881. He was ordained at the JTSA in 1902 and was long
a dominant influence in that institution. A philosophical naturalist, Kaplan interpreted Judaism as an
evolving religious culture that must adapt to contemporary realities. See the discussion of Judaism as a "folk
religion." "Religion must continue to be the central
identifying characteristic of Jewish civilization...
Jewish Religion should ally itself with the modern
orientation toward religion as the spiritual reaction of
man to the vicissitudes of life, and as the expression
of the highest needs of his being." (p. 520). Some
aspects of this "classic" work are now dated (as Kaplan
himself stated, 1957 Foreword) but one can endorse
Kaplan's holistic approach to Judaism and the integrity
of his answers to the question of Jewish identity and
survival. But there are philosophical problems with
"naturalism" (although traditional types of supernatur-
alistic theism lack mental command) and any whole-

hearted or optimistic embrace of modernity is ruled out-
definitively by the perverse violence of the 1940's.

Kaplan, Mordecai M.   The Meaning of God in Modern
Jewish Religion. N.Y.: Behrman, 1937. 380 p.   Kaplan
insists that Judaism be brought "into harmony with the
best ethical and social thought of the modern world."
Kaplan, influenced by Dewey, defines concepts in terms
of their function. See critical comment to J. Cohen
(1958, above).

Kaplan, Mordecai M.   The Future of the American Jew.
N.Y.: MacMillan, 1948. O. XX, 571 p.

Kaplan, Mordecai M.   A New Zionism.   N.Y.: Theodor
Herzl foundation, 1955. 172 p.

Kaplan, Mordecai M.   Judaism Without Supernaturalism;
The Only Alternative to Orthodoxy and Secularism.   N.Y.:
Reconstruction Press, 1958. 254 p.   Kaplan's rejection
of biblical literalism led to his excommunication by the
Orthodox Union of Rabbis.

Kaplan, Mordecai M.   The Greater Judaism in the Making;
A Study of the Modern Evolution of Judaism.   N.Y.:
Reconstructionist Press, 1960. 565 p.

Kaplan, Mordecai M.   The Religion of Ethical Nationhood; Judaism's Contribution to World Peace.   N.Y.:
MacMillan, 1970. 205 p.

Katz, Steven T. ed. Jewish Philosophers. N.Y.: Bloch,
1975. XVI, 294 p. Includes the post-1945 period.

Katz, Steven T. Jewish Ideas and Concepts. N.Y.:
Schocken Books, 1978. 326 p. Organized by topic with a
good biographical index.

Katz, Steven T. Post-Holocaust Dialogues: Critical
Studies in Modern Jewish Thought. N.Y.: N.Y. University
Press, 1983. XIV, 327 p. Winner of the National Jewish
Book Award (Jewish Thought) for 1983. For a critical
review by Pamela Vermes, see JJS, 36:1 (Spring 1985):
135-37.

Kaufman, William E. ed. Contemporary Jewish Philosophies. N.Y.: Behrman, 1976. 276 p.

Kochan, Lionel. The Jew and his History. N.Y.:
MacMillan, 1977. 164 p. A study of Jewish historical
thought that rejects the position that Jewish stateless-
ness entailed the lack of Jewish history. (Cf. Dinur,
Baer, etc.).

Kohler, Kaufmann. Jewish Theology, Systematically and
Historically Considered. Reissue, N.Y.: MacMillan,
1928. XIII, 505 p. Rpt. N.Y.: Ktav, 1968. Kohler has
been described as the last giant of "classical Reform"
Judaism. Using "the viewpoint of historical research"
he attempted to remedy the lack of extensive work in
Jewish theology.

Kook, Abraham. Lights of Return. a trans. of Orot ha-
Teshuva by A.B.Z. Metzger. Jerusalem: Or Etzion, 1966.
Kook was Ashkenazic Chief Rabbi of Palestine from 1919
to 1935. A poet, mystic and pantheist, his thought
"bridged all abysses and sees reality and man in an all-

embracing view." Pub. in N.Y.: Yeshiva University, 1968.

Kook, Abraham. <u>Abraham Isaac Kook, The Lights of Penitence, The Moral Principles, Lights of Holiness, Essays, Letters, and Poems</u>. trans. and with Introd. by Ben Zion Bokser. Preface by Jacob Agus and Rivka Schatz. N.Y.: Paulist Press, 1978. Bibliography: writings on and by Kook, p. 389-392. See Dov Peretz Elkins, <u>Shepherd of Jerusalem</u>: <u>A biography of Rabbi Abraham Isaac Kook</u> (N.Y.: Shengold, 1975), and for a bibliography of Kook's works, see the comp by Naftali Ben-Manahem. <u>Books of Mosad Harav Kook</u>: <u>published during the years 1937-1970</u>. (Jerusalem: Mosad Harav Kook, 1970, Hebrew. 329 p.).

Landauer, Gustav. Discussed in sect. 3.

Langer, Jiri. <u>Nine Gates to the Hasidic Mysteries</u>. Discussed in Part 4, chap. 3,c. Langer's exotic identification with Eastern European Hasidism ("My brother had not come back from Belz, to home and civilization; he had brought Belz with him.") must be understood in the context of the split between enlightened and emancipated but assimilating German Jewry and the so-called "real" or <u>Ur</u> Jew of the unenlightened East.

Lapide, Pinchas E. <u>Israelis, Jews, and Jesus</u>. trans. from the Hebrew by Peter Heinegg. Foreword by Samuel Sandmel. Garden City, N.Y.: Doubleday, 1979. 156 p.

Lazare, Bernard. <u>Job's Dungheap; Essays on Jewish Nationalism and Social Revolution</u>. A trans. of parts of <u>Le Fumier de Job</u> (1928) and other writings by Harry

Lorin Binsse. Preface by Hannah Arendt. Portrait of Bernard Lazare by Charles Peguy. Lazare, neglected until very recently, took up the Dreyfus cause when most French Jews chose silence. He was a severe critic of the Jewish upper classes and of Jewish self-images. "The Jews look upon themselves always in relation to the Christians, never as themselves." The Jew as "pariah" will always "be useful as a scapegoat for the Christian nations." Lazare insisted that the "Jews will find no salvation except in themselves." The pariah must become a rebel and a champion of freedom for the oppressed people. Lazare died in 1903 at the age of 38.

Lewis, Bernard. History: Remembered, Recovered, Invented. (Gottesman Lectures, Yeshiva University, 1974). Princeton, N.J.: Princeton University Press, 1975. 111 p. Cf. Y. Yerushalmi (1982).

Libowitz, Richard Mordecai. Mordecai Kaplan and the Development of Reconstructionism (Studies in American religion, 9). N.Y., Toronto: The Edwin Mellen Press, 1983. 266 p. plates. Notes. "Selected Bibliography." pp. 259-266. Appendix A, B. No index. An introduction to Kaplan's thought that makes valuable use of Kaplan's diaries and personal papers. Libowitz demonstrates that Kaplan's basic points of view were formed before W.W. I and some years before Judaism as a Civilization (1928, as a paper, 1934), his first major book.

Maimon, Solomon. The Autobiography of Solomon Maimon. A trans. of Lebengeschichte, von ihm selbst geschrieben

(Berlin, 1793) with additions and notes by J. Clark Murray. With an Essay on Maimon's philosophy by Hugo Bergman. Oxford (East and West lib. bk.) Horowitz; N.Y.: Farrar, Straus, 1954. 207 p. illus. Maimon was born in Poland in 1753 and after an eventful and restless life was buried as a heretic in 1800. He impressed Kant and Mendelssohn and influenced the development of German Idealism. His work contains insight on Polish Jewry and the "court" of the great Maggid, disciple of Baal Shem Tov. See Noah J. Jacobs, "Solomon Maimon's Relation to Judaism." LBIY, 8 (1963): 117-135; and see Samuel Atlas (1964, cited above). According to Jacobs, Maimon's relationship to Judaism owed much to Spinoza, but Maimon (unlike Spinoza) respected and defended Jewish Law. Maimon was "haunted by a single vision to reaffirm the frail but enduring power of the human intellect...and to make all things, including Judaism, conform to reasonable principles." (pp. 134-135). On the technical philosophical level, Maimon affirmed the existence of general a priori principles but was skeptical about our knowledge of how they related to specific objects. Samuel Hugo Bergman has a study of Maimon, The Philosophy of Solomon Maimon (Jerusalem The Magnes Press, Hebrew University, 1967); see the recent insight, using the notion of Jewish self-hatred, in G. Gilman (1986, cited next sect.).

Margolies, Morris B. Samuel David Luzzatto. Traditionalist Scholar. Foreword by Gerson D. Cohen. N.Y.: Ktav, 1979. 253 p. Biblio.: p. 211-221. Indices. Appendix: Manuscript Sources and Trans. A thoroughly researched study of a versatile Italian scholar (1800-1865) who was "the great midwife of Judische Wissenschaft." (Cohen).

Martin, Bernard. ed. Contemporary Reform Jewish Thought. Chicago: Quadrangle, in coop. with the CCAR, 1968. 216 p. Cf., E. Borowitz (1984, cited above).

Martin, Bernard. ed. with Introd. Great Twentieth Century Jewish Philosophers; Shestov, Rosenzweig, Buber, with selections from their writings. N.Y.: Macmillan, 1970. 336 p. Select Biblio.: pp. 335-336. See Especially the Intorduction to the Shestov section and the selection from Shestov (who is not widely known in North America). Operating within the Pascal--Kierkegaard tradition--Shestov posits enmity between philosophy (Athens) and faith (Jerusalem); see his Athens and Jerusalem (trans. by Martin, Ohio University Press, 1966). "Human wisdom is foolishness before God...Whatsoever is not of faith is sin. As for the philosophy that does not dare to rise above autonomous knowledge and autonomous ethics...this philosophy does not lead man towards truth but forever turns him away from it." (Athens and Jerusalem, in Martin (1970, pp. 71-72)).

Maybaum, Ignaz. The Face of God After Auschwitz. Amsterdam: Polak and Van Gennep, 1965. 265 p.

Maybaum, Ignaz. Trialogue Between Jew, Christian and Muslim. (Littman lib. of Jewish civilization) London: Routledge & Kegan Paul, 1973. 179 p. In a sense, this is a contemporary dialogue with F. Rosenzweig.

Memmi, Albert. The Liberation of the Jew. trans. from the French by Judy Hun. N.Y.: Orion, 1966. 303 p.

Memmi was born in Tunisia; he escaped from a labor camp during the German Occupation. He has authored The Colonizer and the Colonized (ET, with an Introd. by Jean Paul Sartre, Beacon Press, 1967), a work favorably compared with F. Fanon. He has also written Portrait d'un Juif and Juifs et Arabes. He views Israel as the vanguard of Jewish liberation and the necessary form of reference for the Diaspora communities: "the national solution is not one of several; it is the only definitive solution..."

Mendelssohn, Moses. Jerusalem and Other Jewish Writings. ed. and trans. from the German by Alfred Jospe. N.Y.: Schocken Books, 1969. 179 p. Mendelssohn (1729-1786) was the first major modern Jewish philosopher in the pre-Kantian period of the German Enlightenment. This leader of German Jewry thought that conduct was the essence of religion, and law the determining principle of Judaism. The laws of Judaism are revealed but the truths of faith are one with the truths of reason which do not depend upon revelation: "...the religion of my fathers knows no mysteries which we have to accept on faith rather than comprehend." Mendelssohn was a great cultural mediator, bringing Jews into German culture and manifesting Jewish culture to Germans. He translated the Pentateuch into German, founded a Hebrew literary periodical, and started a Jewish Free School. In the treatise Jerusalem (1783) he makes a clear, cogent case for the separation of church and state. See the major biography by A. Altmann (1973, cited above).

Neusner, Jacob. History and Torah; Essays on Jewish Learning. N.Y.: Schocken, Books, 1965.

Neusner, Jacob.   Judaism in the Secular Age; Essays on Fellowship, Community and Freedom.   N.Y.: Ktav, 1970. 181 p.

Neusner, Jacob.   The Way of Torah; An Introduction to Judaism.   (The Life of Man series).   Belmont, CA.: Dickinson Press, 1970. 116 p. (pa.).   For more of Neusner's studies, see Part 2, chap. 2, a.

Neusner, Jacob.   comp. Understanding Jewish theology; Classical Issues and Modern Perspectives.   N.Y.: Ktav, 1973.

Neusner, Jacob.   ed. Take Judaism, for example; studies in the comparison of religions.   (Chicago studies in the history of Judaism).   Chicago: University of Chicago Press, 1983.   Contains high-merit essays.

Patai, Raphael and Jennifer Patai Wing.   The Myth of the Jewish Race.   N.Y.: Scribner, 1975. 350 p.   Argues (but why is it necessary?) against the notion of the Jews as a "separate race."

Petuchowski, Jakob J.   Ever Since Sinai; A Modern View of Torah.   N.Y.: Scribe Publications, 1961.

Petuchowski, Jakob J.   Heirs of the Pharisees.   N.Y.: Basic Books, 1970. 199 p.   By a "liberal" or "reform" philosophical theologian (Cf. R. Gordis, for the Conservative tradition, and E. Berkovits, for Orthodox apologetics).   Petuchowski argues the relevance of Pharisaism for Jewish religious thought of today and pleads for an end to the estrangement between "Orthodox" and "Reform."Plaskow, Judith.   "Christian Feminism and Anti-

Judaism." Cross Currents, 28:2 (Summer 1978): 306-309.
A critical analysis, by a Jewish feminist, of the "myth"
that attributes patriarchy to the ancient Hebrews and
Talmudic Rabbis. Traditional Jewish attitudes toward
women are not praiseworthy. "But Christian attitudes
are in no way essentially different." "The real tragedy
is that the feminist revolution has furnished one more
occasion for the projection of Christian failure onto
Judaism." (p. 309). Plaskow has written a feminist
critique of Reinhold Niebuhr and Paul Tillich, Sex, Sin
and Grace (University Press of America, 1980) and is co-
editor of Womanspirit Rising: A Feminist Reader in
Religion (Harper, 1979).

Polish, David. The Eternal Dissent; a search for
meaning in Jewish history. (Ram's horn bk.). N.Y.:
Abelard-Schuman, 1961. 228 p. An essay on Jewish survival.

Rosenbloom, Noah H. Luzzatto's Ethico-Psychological
Interpretation of Judaism. N.Y.: Yeshiva University,
1965. Includes a trans. of Luzzato's The Foundations of
the Torah.

Rosenbloom, Noah H. Tradition in an Age of Reform; The
Religious Philosophy of Samson Raphael Hirsch. Phila.:
JPS, 1976. 480 p.

Rotenstreich, Nathan. "Hegel's Image of Judaism."
Jewish Social Studies, 15 (1953): 33-52. Hegel failed
to grasp the fundamental dialectics in Judaism: "image
of God" vs. "dust and ashes." This is correct but Hegel
saw each religion, including Judaism, as having a
distinct rationality. They were "subordinate moments"
in the development of Christianity--the consummate

religion in which the truth of faith is one with the truth of philosophy. See Lectures on the Philosophy of History and esp. Vorlesungen über die Philosophie den Religion (Werke, Berlin, 1832, 1840); a new Eng. trans. by P.C. Hodgson, et al. is in progress, Vol. I (University of California Press, 1984). On this topic, see also: Y. Yovel, "Hegel's Concept of Religion and Judaism as the Religion of Sublimity." Tarbiz, 45 (1976): 301-326. Hebrew; and S. Avineri, "The Hegelian Position on the Emancipation of the Jews." Zion, 25 (1960): 134-136. Hebrew. A recent major historical study of Judaism in Hegelian and post-Hegelian thought is by Hans Liebeschutz, Das Judenthum im Deutschen Geschichtsbild von Hegel bis Max Weber (Tübingen: Mohr, 1967).

Rotenstreich, Nathan. Jews and German Philosophy. The Polemics of Emancipation. N.Y.: Schocken Books, 1984. 266 p. Notes. Biographical Index. Indices. An excellent work both for technical internal analysis of ideas and as an intellectual history of one form of the modern German and Jews and Jewish thought. Contains a balanced analysis of Nietzsche, interesting opinion on Schopenhauer; but the main focus is on Kant and Hegel's school and the Jewish reactions.

Rotenstreich, Nathan. The Recurring Pattern; Studies in Anti-Judaism in Modern Thought. N.Y.: Horizon, 1964. 135 p. Compare with E. Fackenheim (1973, cited above). For the systems of modern Jewish philosophy, see Rotenstreich, Jewish Philosophy in Modern Times. (N.Y., 1968).

Rothschild, Fritz A. "Abraham Joshe Heschel." In Modern Theologians: Christians and Jews. ed. by Thomas

E. Bird. Notre Dame, Ind.: University of Notre Dame Press, 1967. pp. 169-182.

Rubenstein, Richard L. After Auschwitz; Radical Theology and Contemporary Judaism. Indianapolis: Bobbs-Merrill, 1966. XXIV, 329 p. (Cited in Part 5, chap. 1, c:4).

Rubenstein, Richard L. The Religious Imagination; A Study in Psychoanalysis and Jewish Theology. Indianapolis: Bobbs-Merrill, 1968. XX, 246 p.

Rubenstein, Richard L. Morality and Eros. N.Y.: McGraw Hill, 1970. 205 p. Rubenstein asserts that "'Now' has become the decisive temporal category" in modern culture and that traditional faith is dead. "Judaism and Christianity are in the process of becoming neo-archaic, pagan religions in fact if not in name." Defines Deity as "Holy Nothingness" and concludes in a neo-Koheleth style that : "All we have is this world. Let us endure its wounds and celebrate its joys in undeceived lucidity."

Sandmel, Samuel. Two Living Traditions; Essays on Religion and the Bible. Detroit: Wayne State University Press, 1972. 366 p. The central theme (chap. 3) is on the relationship between Judaism and Christianity. Sandmel denies that Judaism has any place for systematic theology as is found in Christianity, although there are analogies between Oral law and Christian tradition.

Schechter, Solomon. Studies in Judaism. 3 vols. Vol. I, N.Y.: MacMillan, 1896, Vol. 2, Phila.: JPS, 1908,

Vol. 3. Phila.: JPS, 1924. O. VII, 336 p. (For more on Schechter, see Part 2, chap. 2, a).

Schechter, Solomon. Seminary Addresses and Other Papers. Cincinnati: Ark pub. Co., 1915. O. XIV. 253 p. Introd. by Louis Finkelstein. N.Y.: Burning Bush Press, 1960. XXVI, 253 p. (pa.); Rpt. (Religion in America) N.Y.: Arno Press, 1969. 253 p.

Schechter, Solomon. Studies in Judaism; A Selection. new paperback ed. N.Y.: Atheneum, 1970.

Schechter, Solomon. Studies in Judaism. Vol. 1, 1896. Rpt. Books for Libraries. Freeport, L.I.N.Y., 1970. XXV, 366 p.

Scholem, Gershom G. Major Trends in Jewish Mysticism. trans. from the German (in part) by George Lichtheim. (Hilda Stich Stroock lectures, 1938). N.Y.: Jewish Institute of Religion, 1941; Jerusalem-Talbieh, Palestine: Schocken Books, 1941. O. XIV, 440 p. rev. ed. N.Y.: Schocken Books, 1946. O., XIV, 454 p. Schocken paperback, 1961. For Scholem see also Part 2, chap. 2, c; Part 3, chap. 1, f:b: Part 4, chap. 2, b. On Scholem see S. Cain, "Gershom Scholem on Jewish Mysticism," Midstream, 17 (December 1970): 35-51 and the scholarly study by David Biale, Gershom Scholem...(1979, cited above, Part 4, chap. 2,b).

Scholem, Gershom G. On Jews and Judaism in Crisis; Selected Essays. ed. by Werner J. Dannhauser. N.Y.: Schocken Books, 1977. 306 p. Includes bibliographical references. Contains the important essay, "Martin

Buber's Conception of Judaism," pp. 126-71. Very high-level studies.

Scholem, Gershom G. From Berlin to Jerusalem: Memories of my Youth. trans. from the German by Harry Zohn. N.Y.: Schocken Books, 1980. 178 p.

Schorsch, Ismar. "The Philosophy of History of Nachman Krochmal." Judaism, 10 (1961): 237-245. Krochmal (1785-1840) was born in Brody in eastern Galicia. His papers were published by L. Zunz in 1851 under the title: Morei Nevukhei ha-Zeman (A Guide for the Perplexed of Our Time). Historical change is cyclical and every nation is an integrated whole (Cf. Vico, Herder). The God of the "eternal people" is Absolute Spirit and Jewish history is the working-out of the implications in the biblical image of God.

Schorsch, Ismar. ed. trans. and introd. Heinrich Graetz, The Structure of Jewish History and Other Essays. N.Y.: Ktav, Phila.: JPS, 1975. 325 p. Editorial notes and select bibliography are included. Schorsch's Introduction is entitled, "Ideology and History." Graetz (1817-1891) was a gifted and influential historian, biblical scholar and participant in the Wissenschaft des Judentum.

Schultz, Joseph P. Judaism and the Gentile Faiths: Comparative Studies in Religion. Rutherford, N.Y.: Fairleigh Dickinson University Press, 1981. 411 p. Index. Notes to each chapter. Biblio.: p. 376-396. Very interesting, based on secondary sources; generally done with care and avoids easy mechanical similarities. The first comprehensive work in Comparative Religion from a

Jewish perspective. Part 1: Judaism and the Non-Christian Faith. Part 2: Judaism and Christianity. Part 3: Judaism and Secular Challenge. Note, esp., the original essay on "Jonathan Edwards and the Hasidic Master of Habad."

Selzer, Michael. The Wineskin and the Wizard. N.Y.: MacMillan, 1970. 247 p. A reflective essay on East European Jewish culture and modern Jewish identity. Includes a critique of Jewish concern for normalcy and power: "For Judaism is the search for priorities in life, the refusal to accept phenomena as they are... the recognition that life is choice..." p. 203. For more on Selzer, see Part 2, chap. 1, sect. 7.

Shestov, Lev. Athens and Jerusalem. trans. from the Russian with an Introd. by Bernard Martin (b. 1905). Athens, Ohio: Ohio University Press, 1966. 447 p. Shestov argues that there is a basic incompatibility between Hebrew and Greek thought. Shestov (d. 1938) was professor of Russian philosophy in the University of Paris. See A Shestov Anthology, ed. with an Introd. by Bernard Martin (b. 1928). (Athens, Ohio: Ohio University Press, 1971, 328 p.). On the Athens-Jerusalem tension, see the brillant insight of Leo Strauss.

Shorris, Earl. Jews without Mercy. A Lament. N.Y.: Doubleday, Anchor, 1982. 191 p. An eloquent and angry attack on the "Jewish neoconservatives" who, for Shorris, are typified "by the half dozen middle-aged former leftists" (e.g., Norman Podhoretz, Midge Decter (who really irks him), Irving Kristol, Nathan Glazer) who think that capitalism is good for the Jews. Having joined the "Haves" the Jewish neoconservatives now "live on the right side of the aisle, in a place without a minyan." They are "new court Jews" who have replaced "the elegance of the Jewish love of mercy with the desire for power and the vulgarity of self-interest." "What has been lost by Israel under Begin, and by the Jewish neoconservatives...is the understanding of the Law as it relates to the ethics of the paradigmatic minority." The last phrase is untypical of Shorris' prose which is unacademic and simple, using personal experience and reminiscence (e.g., the vivid account of the trip with his son to Eastern Europe and Russia) to reinforce his "lament" (which becomes in the process a question about the nature of Jewish identity).

Silver, Abba Hillel. Where Judaism Differed; An Inquiry into the Distinctiveness of Judaism. N.Y.: MacMillan, 1956. 318 p.

Soloveitchik, Joseph B. "Confrontation." Tradition, 6:2 (Spring/Summer 1964): 5-29.

Soloveitchik, Joseph B. "The Lonely Man of Faith." Tradition, 7:2 (Summer 1965): 5-67. These two essays by Soloveitchik, a highly gifted, reflective Orthodox theologian, are Rpt. in Studies in Judaica in honor of Dr. Samuel Belkin...ed. by Leon D. Stitskin. (N.Y.: Ktav, Yeshiva, 1965). And now see his Halakhic Man, trans. by Lawrence Kaplan (Phila.: JPS, 1984). Won the 1985 National Jewish Book Award (Jewish Thought).

Spero, Shubert. Morality, Halakha, and the Jewish Tradition. N.Y.: Ktav and Yeshiva University Press, 1983. 381 p. Described as "the most comprehensive and erudite work written on the ethics of Judaism in this century." That claim seems a bit too strong but Spero's effort to bring "to bear the tools of philosophic analysis upon the moral teachings of Judaism" merits high praise.

Steinberg, Milton. A Partisan Guide to the Jewish Problem. Indianapolis: Bobbs-Merrill, 1945. O. 7-308 p. One of Steinberg's maxims was: "As a man thinks about ultimates, so he deals with immediates." Largely accepts the Reconstructionist image definition of Jewish civilization.

Steinberg, Milton. Basic Judaism: (a book about the Jewish religion, its ideals, beliefs and practices written for both Jews and non-Jews). N.Y.: Harcourt Brace, 1947. O. IX, 172 p. Steinberg was philosophically informed, sensitive, and knowledgeable in modern Protestant theology; he also wrote an important novel about a first-century Jewish heretic (Elisha ben Abuyah): As a Driven Leaf (Bobbs-Morril, 1933).

Steinberg, Milton. Anatomy of Faith. ed. with an Introd. by Arthur A. Cohen. N.Y.: Harcourt Brace, 1960. Toronto: Longmans, 1960. 304 p. A collection of his theological papers.

Steiner, George. Language and Silence; Essays on Language, Literature, and the Inhuman. N.Y.: Atheneum, 1967. 426 p. London: Faber, sub-title: Essays 1958-1966. 1967. 454 p. Steiner, a brilliant literary and cultural critic, argues that the horrors of modern history have stunned the imagination into silence.

Stitskin, Leon D. ed. Studies in Torah Judaism. N.Y.: Yeshiva University, Ktav, 1969. An Orthodox point of view is represented.

Strauss, Leo. Persecution and the Art of Writing. Glencoe: The Free Press, 1952. 204 p. Index. Consists of an Introduction and 3 previously published scholarly (and difficult) essays: "Persecution and the Art of Writing" (Social Research, 1941), "The Literary Character of The Guide for the Perplexed," (Essays on Maimonides, ed. by S.W. Baron, 1941), "The Law of Reason in the Kuzari" (PAAJR, 1949). The influence of per-section on literature leads to "writing between the lines." "The fact which makes this literature possible can be expressed in the axiom that thoughtless men are careless readers, and only thoughtful men are careful readers." (p. 25). Strauss' distinction between the esoteric and the exoteric is basic to his analysis of Maimonides. The Guide, dealing with the secrets of the Torah, "is addressed to the small number of people who are able to understand by themselves." (p. 94). It is also basic to his interpretation of the Treatise, i.e., the practical part of its teaching "must be completely understood by itself before its hidden teaching can be brought to light." (p. 201) The issue of the conflict-ing claims of philosophy and religion (Athens vs. Jerusalem) is tackled in the essay on Halevi's Kuzari and also in the essay on Spinoza.

Talmage, Frank E. ed. Disputation and Dialogue; Readings in the Jewish-Christian Encounter. Foreword by Edward A. Synan. N.Y.: Ktav, Amer. Anti-Defamation League, 1975. 411 p. Readings: from "Messiah and Christ" to the post-Holocaust era.

Talmond, Jacob L. The Unique and the Universal; Some Historical Reflections. N.Y.: Braziller, 1966. 320 p. An original essay on the interrelationship between modern Jewish and European history. See pp. 119-164 for an insightful analysis of the three theories of anti-Semitism that arose in the 1870's and 1880's; 1) it was an anomaly, 2) anti-Semitism was chronic (Zionist position), and 3) it was the result of capitalism (socialist position).

Talmond, Jacob L.   Israel Among the Nations. London: Weidenfeld & Nicolson, 1970; N.Y.: MacMillan, 1971. 199 p. Contains three perceptive essays on the responses of Jewry to revolutionary universalism and Zionist nationalism. "Jews between Revolution and Counter-Revolution." "Types of Jewish Self-Awareness: Herzl's "Jewish State" after Seventy Years (1896-1966)." "Israel Among the Nations: The Six-Day War in Historical Perspective." But there is a danger of over-generalizing or abstractionism here: there was or is no "Jewish" response per se to revolution and nationalism.

Talmond, Jacob L.   Myth of the Nation and the Vision of Revolution. The Origins of Ideological Polarization in the 20th Century. London: Secker & Warburg, 1981. 632 p. Talmond is best known for his The Origins of Totalitarian Democracy (London: Secker & Warburg, 1952; Heinemann, 1961; Sphere, 1970).

Taubes, Jacob. "The Issue Between Judaism and Christianity." Commentary, 16 (1953), Rpt. In Arguments and Doctrines...ed. by Arthur A. Cohen (1970, cited above), pp. 402-18. This is a penetrating essay although it needs revision in light of Vatican II and changes in Catholic and Protestant thought. "The controversy between the Jewish and the Christian religions points to the perennial conflict between the principle of law and the principle of love." (p. 418).

Tcherikower, Elias. "Jewish Martyrology and Jewish Historiography." YIVO Annual of Jewish Social Science, I (1946): 9-23. Very significant.

Waskow, Arthur I. Season of our Joy. A Handbook of Jewish Festivals. N.Y.: Bantam Books, 1982. XXIV, 240 p. (pa.) illus. with papercuts by Martin Farren and Joan Benjamin-Farren.

Werblowsky, R.J. Zwi. Beyond Tradition and Modernity: Changing Religions in a Changing World. London: University of London, The Athlone Press, 1976. A comparative analysis of modern Jewish history. See, esp., chap. 3, "Sacral Particularity: The Jewish Case, with a Digression on Japan."

Wyschogrod, Michael. The Body of Faith. Judaism as Corporeal Election. N.Y.: The Seabury Press, 1983. 265 p. Notes. Index. A contribution written with verve and clarity to contemporary Jewish philosophical theology. Wyschogrod has read the major modern thinkers and is especially influenced by M. Heidegger. He uses the Christian incarnational image to advance an anti-spiritualized view of Jewish covenant/election as "carnal." "Salvation is of the Jews because the flesh of Israel is the abode of the divine presence in the world. It is the carnal anchor that God has sunk into the soil of creation." (p. 256). Wyschogrod's major affirmations are: Jewish faith must be biblical, Deity

is transcendent and personal, the reality of election,
the centrality of the ethical (but not as autonomous,
the ethical is rooted in the covenant), the significance
of the mythological and the poetical (as against subsum-
ing Judaism in a universalistic rationalism). Judaism
is the "religion of the land of Israel," and "authentic
Judaism must be messianic Judaism." In this epoch of
global consciousness, Wyschogrod's work is a contribution to inter-faith dialogue. That is not the primary
intent of the work, however, and only those operating
within a definite circle of faith can existentially
respond to his confident theological assertions. Cf.
A.A. Cohen The Tremendum (1981, discussed in Part 5,
chap. 1. c:4).

Yerushalmi, Yosef Hayim. Zakhor; Jewish History and
Jewish Memory. (Samuel and Althea Stroum lect. in
Jewish studies). Seattle: University of Washington
Press, 1983. 144 p. Notes. Index. A succinct, eloquent
and brilliant work, resting upon deep mastery of Jewish
(and other) sources. In chap. 4, "Modern Dilemmas,"
Yerushalmi argues that there is a wide distance in the
modern era between Jewish historiography and Jewish
group memory (p. 93, passim) and he asserts that "Jewish
collective memory" has weakened (p. 86, passim). These
claims may be unsound. Jewish group memory appears to
have grown stronger. In this century, in response to
anti-Semitism and the Holocaust, there are many memorial
books, a wealth of Testamental literature, imaginative
literary responses to the Holocaust as well as critical
historiographical studies. See Part 5, chap. 3, sect.
e, f, f:1.

1. Major Modern Thinkers. Cohen, Buber, Heschel, Rosenzweig.
(Baeck and Kook are discussed in preceding section).

Cohen, Hermann. <u>Reason</u> <u>and</u> <u>Hope</u>: <u>Sections</u> <u>from</u> <u>the</u> <u>Jewish</u> <u>Writings</u> <u>of</u> <u>Hermann</u> <u>Cohen</u>. trans. from the German and ed. by Eva Jospe. N.Y.: W.W. Norton, 1971. 237 p. Buber's I – Thou schema is heavily indebted to Cohen, see <u>Religion</u> <u>der</u> <u>Vernuft</u> (p. 17).

Cohen, Hermann. <u>Religion</u> <u>of</u> <u>Reason</u>; <u>From</u> <u>the</u> <u>Sources</u> <u>of</u> <u>Judaism</u>. trans. from the German (<u>Die</u> <u>Religion</u> <u>der</u> <u>Vernuft</u> <u>aus</u> <u>den</u> <u>Quellen</u> <u>des</u> <u>Judentums</u>, 1919) by Simon Kaplan with a Preface and an Introd. by the translator and an Introductory essay by Leo Strauss. N.Y.: Ungar, 1972. 489 p. XLIII. "Annotations from Hebrew sources," comp. and supplemented by L. Rosenzweig in accordance with the author's notes, Indices: "References in the Text to Biblical Passages, "References in the Text to Rabbinical Works," Index of Proper Names, Index of Hebrew Words. Original subtitle: <u>Jewish</u> <u>philosophy</u> <u>of</u> <u>religion</u> <u>and</u> <u>a</u> <u>Jewish</u> <u>ethics</u>. When Cohen (1842-1918) authored this powerful work his thought had shifted from a neo-Kantian concept of religion as a historical presupposition for ethics to a theocentric position that viewed Judaism as the manifestation of the uniqueness of Deity and the power of the ethical idea. Cohen's basic notions include "correlation," the reciprocal relationship between man and Deity, and Deity and man (Paul Tillich developed this concept in his <u>Systematic</u> <u>Theology</u> (Vol. I, University of Chicago, 1959, esp. pp.

59-66, Cohen is not cited); monotheism as the incommensurability of Deity and finite existence, and messianism as the end of earthly injustice and the reign of Good.

Buber, Martin. At the Turning: Three Addresses on Judaism. N.Y.: Farrar, Straus & Young, 1952. 11-62 p. The central motif in the works of this great philosopher of religion was the "interhuman" dimension of dialogue between persons. For more on Buber, see Part 4, chap. 3: a, Part 2, chap. 1.

Buber, Martin. A Believing Humanism: My Testament, 1902-1965. trans. with an Introd. and Explanatory Notes by Maurice Friedman. N.Y.: Simon and Schuster, 1968. 252 p.

Buber, Martin. Between Man and Man. trans. by Ronald Gregor Smith. N.Y.: MacMillan, 1948. O. VIII, 210 p. MacMillan paperback ed. with an "afterword by the author (trans. by M. Friedman) on the dialogical principle." 1965. XXI, 229 p. "One must be able to say I, in order to know the Mystery of the Thou."

Buber, Martin. Daniel; Dialogues on Realization. trans. with an Introd. by Maurice Friedman. N.Y.: McGraw-Hill, 1965; Holt, 1964. 144 p. A poetical, philosophical essay originally published in 1913.

Buber, Martin. Eclipse of God: Studies in the Relation Between Religion and Philosophy. N.Y.: Harper & Row, 1952; London: Gollancz, 1953. 7-192 p. Harper pa. ed. 1957. Contains one of the best critiques of Sartre and Heidegger ever done, but sadly neglected.

Buber, Martin.   For the Sake of Heaven. trans. from
the German by Ludwig Lewisohn. 2nd ed. Phila: JPS, 1953,
N.Y.: Harper, 1953. 316 p.   A stately and beautiful
composition with rich, wise lines. "The Yehudi turned
to him and said: 'Greet your master from me in the words
of Koheleth, the Preacher, which is Solomon: 'At the end
of a matter the whole is heard.' In the end of things
all the levels and all mystic lore and all miraculous
practices count for nothing; only the whole counts. And
what is this whole? It is life in its simplicity. 'For
this,' as the Preacher says further on, 'is the whole
man.' We are bidden to be human, only human and nothing
other than human--simple human beings, simple Jews."
(pp. 240-241).

Buber, Martin.   Hasidism. trans. by Greta Hort, et al.
N.Y.: Philosophical Library, 1948. 208 p.

Buber, Martin.   Mamre, Essays in Religion. trans. by
Greta Hort.   Melbourne University Press,   Toronto:
Oxford University Press, 1946. XIII, 190 p.

Buber, Martin and J.L. Magnes. Two Letters to Gandhi.
(The Bond, Jerusalem. Pamphlets, I). Jerusalem: Rubin
Mass, 1939. 44 p. For discussion see M. Friedman, vol.
II, Martin Buber's Life and Work, The Middle Years,
1923-1945. (N.Y.: E.P. Dutton, 1983).

Buber, Martin.   Hasidism and Modern Man.   ed. and
trans. by Maurice Friedman. N.Y.: Horizon Press, 1958.
256 p.

Buber, Martin.   Israel and Palestine; The History of an Idea. trans. by Stanley Godman. N.Y.: MacMillan, 1952, East and West Library. XIV, 165 p. Rpt. with the title: On Zion; The History of an Idea. N.Y.: Schocken Books, 1972. Contains a new foreword by Nahum N. Glatzer.

Buber, Martin.   Kingship of God. trans. from the German (vol. I, 1932) by Richard Scheimann. 3rd enl. ed. N.Y.: Harper & Row, 1967. 228 p. This was Buber's first major work in Biblical studies and the foundation for his Moses and for The Prophetic Faith.

Buber, Martin.   The Knowledge of Man. A Philosophy of the Interhuman. ed. with an Introductory essay by Maurice Friedman. trans. by Maurice Friedman and Ronald Gregor Smith. N.Y.: Harper & Row, 1966. 184 p. (pa.)

Buber, Martin.   The Legend of the Baal-Shem. trans. from the German by Maurice Friedman. N.Y.: Harper, 1955; Schocken, 1969. 222 p. First pub. in Frankfurt in 1908.

Buber, Martin.   Moses; The Revelation and the Covenant. trans. by I.M. Lask. N.Y.: Harper & Row, 1958. 226 p. First pub. in Hebrew: Moshe (Jerusalem, 1945).

Buber, Martin.   On Judaism. ed. by Nahum N. Glatzer. N.Y.: Schocken, 1967. 242 p.

Buber, Martin.   I and Thou. trans. with a Prologue and Notes by Walter Kaufmann. N.Y.: Scribner's, 1970. This new translation of a great classic in religious philoso-phy has a prolix and slightly supercilious introduction.

Buber, Martin. Meetings. ed. and trans. with an Introd. and Bibliography by Maurice Friedman. La Salle, Ill.: Open Court, 1973.

Buber, Martin. The Origin and Meaning of Hasidism. ed. and trans. with an Introd. by Maurice Friedman. N.Y.: Horizon Press, 1960. paperback ed. 1962. Includes Hasidism and Modern Man. (1958).

Buber, Martin. Paths in Utopia. trans. by R.F.C. Hull with an Introd. by Ephraim Fischoff. London: Routledge, 1949, N.Y.: MacMillan, 1950. 152 p. Boston: Beacon paperback, 1958.

Buber, Martin. Pointing the Way; Collected Essays. ed. and trans. from the German by Maurice Friedman. N.Y.: Harper & Row, 1957; London: Routledge, 1957. 239 p.

Buber, Martin. The Prophetic Faith. trans. from the Hebrew by Carlyle Witton-Davis. N.Y.: MacMillan, 1949. 247 p. Note Buber's criterion for the true vs. the false prophet: "The false prophets make their subconscious a god whereas for the true prophets their subconscious is subdued by the God of truth..." (p. 179).

Buber, Martin. Tales of Angels, Spirits and Demons. trans. by David Antin and Jerome Rothenberg. N.Y.: Hawk's Well Press, 1958.

Buber, Martin. comp. Tales of the Hasidim, Vol. I, The Early Masters, Vol. 2, The Later Masters. trans. by

Olga Marx. N.Y.: Schocken Books, 1947, 1948. 335 p. 352
p. Paperback ed. 1961, 1971.

Buber, Martin. The Tales of Rabbi Nachman (retold by
Martin Buber). trans. from the German by Maurice
Friedman. N.Y.: Horizon Press, 1956. 213 p. Avon
Books, 1970. Scholars have asserted that these tales
influenced F. Kafka.

Buber, Martin. Right and Wrong; An Interpretation of
some Psalms. trans. by Ronald Gregory Smith. London:
SCM, 1952. 62 p.

Buber, Martin. Martin Buber and the Theatre, including
Martin Buber's mystery play Elijah. ed. and trans. with
three introductory essays by Maurice Friedman. N.Y.:
Funk and Wagnalls, 1970. 170 p.

Buber, Martin. Ten Rungs: Hasidic Sayings. trans. by
Olga Marx. N.Y.: Schocken Books, 1947, 1962, 1965 (pa.)
127 p.

Buber, Martin. Two Types of Faith. trans. by Norman
P. Goldhawk. N.Y.: MacMillan, 1952. 177 p. Harper
Torchbook, 1961. Contrasts Hebrew emunah "trust" with
Christian belief (trust as having to do with the total
person vs. "belief" as cognitive) and argues that Paul
transformed the teachings of Jesus into a faith-works
dualism. The contrast is useful but demands qualifica-
tion, e.g., belief in Christ for Paul was an
'existential' total relationship, not pistis as simply
intellectual assent.

Buber, Martin.   The Way of Man According to the
Teachings of Hasidism. (Cloister Press bk.) Chicago:
Wilcox and Follett, 1951. 5-46 p. N.Y.: Citadel Press,
1966.

Buber, Martin.   The Way of Response: Martin Buber.   ed.
by Nahum N. Glatzer. N.Y.: Schocken, 1966.

Buber, Martin.   Good and Evil. Two Interpretations: I,
Right and Wrong. trans. by Ronald Gregor Smith,   2,
Images of Good and Evil. trans. by Michael Bullock.
N.Y.: Scribners, 1953. 143 p. See, esp., chap. 4, vol.
1, "The Heart Determines (Psalm 73)," pp. 31-50. Psalm
73 expressed Buber's attitude toward death; he read that
Psalm at Rosenzweig's funeral and lines 22-24 (Heb.
text) were inscribed on Buber's tombstone, at his
request.

Buber, Martin.   The Writings of Martin Buber. sel. ed.
and Introduced by Will Herberg. N.Y.: Meridian-World;
Noonday Press, 1956. 351 p. (pa.).

Buber, Martin.   On the Bible. Eighteen Studies. ed.
by Nahum N. Glatzer. Introd. by Harold Bloom. N.Y.:
Schocken Books, 1968. There is a very close connection
between Buber's exegesis and his philosophy of the I-
Thou.

Buber, Martin.   "Autobiographical Fragments" and
"Replies to My Critics." In The Philosophy of Martin
Buber. ed. by Paul A. Schilpp and Maurice Friedman. La
Salle, Ill.: Open Court Press, 1967. pp. 3-39, 689-744.
See pp. 747-786 for "Bibliography of the Writings of
Martin Buber," comp. by M. Friedman; and see the enl.

bibliography in M. Friedman, Martin Buber: The Life of dialogue, 3rd rev. ed. (University of Chicago Phoenix Books, 1976); and see Moche Catane, Bibliography of Martin Buber's Works 1895-1957. (Jerusalem: Bialik Institute, 1958). There is a compilation by Margot Cohen and Rafael Buber, "Martin Buber. A Bibliography of his writings, 1897-1978." (Jerusalem: The Magnes Press, 1980), 160 p. Title index, arranged chronologically. Also of value is Haim Gordon's "Martin Buber's Life and Thought. Bibliographical Retrospect." Religious Studies Review, 4:3 (July 1978): 193-201.

Buber, Martin. Ecstatic Confessions. collected and Introd. by Martin Buber. ed. by Paul Mendes-Flohr, trans by Esther Cameron. N.Y.: Harper and Row, 1985. 160 p. Biblio.: p. 157-160. Orig. pub. as Ekstatische Konfessionen (Eugen Diederichs Verlag, 1909).

Selected Works on Buber.

Balthasar, H.U. von. Martin Buber and Christianity; A Dialogue between Israel and the Church. trans. from the German by Alexander Dru. N.Y.: MacMillan, 1962. 127 p. A Roman Catholic perspective.

Berkovits, Ekiezer. A Jewish Critique of the Philosophy of Martin Buber. N.Y.: Yeshiva University, 1962. A strong critique from an Orthodox point of view.

Bloch, Jochanan. Die aporie des Du. Probleme der Dialogik Martin Bubers [Phronesis. Eine Schriftenreihe. Band 2] Heidelberg: Verlag Lambert Schneider, 1977. 348

p.   Includes p. 9, Breslauce Corrigenda. A detailed
scholarly study.

Breslauer, S. Daniel. The Chrysalis of Religion, A
guide to the Jewishness of Buber's I and Thou. Nashville: Abingdon Press, 1980. 160 p. (pa.).

Cohen, Arthur A. Martin Buber. N.Y.: Hillary House,
1958. 112 p. By a very talented, independent-minded
theologian, and novelist. And see Cohen's "Martin Buber
and Judaism," LBIY, 25 (1980): 287-300.

Diamond, Malcolm M. Martin Buber, Jewish Existentia-
list. N.Y.: Harper & Row Torchbook, 1960; Oxford
University Press, 1960. 240 p. For Buber the Bible was
not Law but "...a record of the dialogical encounters
between Man and God..." (p. 92). For Buber's comments
on Diamond's interpretation (he thought that Diamond had
overstressed the conceptual element in his thought) see
M. Friedman (1983, cited below, p. 256).

Friedman, Maurice. Martin Buber's Life and Work.   3
vols. N.Y.: E.P. Dutton. Vol. I, The Early Years 1879-
1923 (1982), 455 p.; Vol. 2, The Middle Years 1923-1945
(1983), 398 p.; Vol. 3, The Later Years 1945-1965
(1983), 493 p. A richly detailed, lovingly done, biography that may remedy some of the unmerited neglect
that Buber has experienced within the Jewish community.

Friedman, Maurice. Martin Buber: The Life of Dialogue.
Chicago: University of Chicago Press, 1955; N.Y.: Harper
Torchbook, 1960; 3rd rev. ed. with new Preface and enl.
Bibliography. University of Chicago Phoenix Book, 1976.
And see the insightful essay by Friedman, "The Existen-

tialist of Dialogue" in <u>To Deny our Nothingness</u> (1979, cited below): "At the center of Buber's existentialism stands existential trust. This is the "holy insecurity" which is willing to go out to meet the unique person ...to accept the unique which is presented in each new situation..."

Gudopp, Wolf-Dieter. <u>Martin Buber's dialogischer Anarchismus</u>. Bern Herbert Lang; Frankfurt/M. Peter Lang, 1975.

Horwitz, Rivka G. <u>Buber's Way to I and Thou. An Historical Analysis and the First Publication of Martin Buber's Lectures "Religion als Gengenwart." (Phronesis. Eine Schriftenreibe</u>, Vol. 7) Heidelberg: Verlag Lambert Schneider, 1978.

Kohanski, Alexander. <u>An Analytical Interpretation of Martin Buber's I and Thou, with a biographical introduction and glossary</u>. Woodbury, New York: Barron's Educational Series, 1975. 176 p.

Kohanski, Alexander. <u>Martin Buber's Philosophy of Interhuman Relations: A Response to the Human Problematic of our Time</u>. Rutherford, N.J.: Fairleigh Dickinson University Press, 1982.

Moore, Donald J. <u>Martin Buber; Prophet of Religious Secularism, the criticism of institutional religion in the writings of Martin Buber</u>. Phila.: JPS, 1974. XXVII, 264 p.

Oliver, Roy. The Wanderer and the Way: The Hebrew Tradition in the Writings of Martin Buber. Ithaca, N.Y.: Cornell University Press, 1968.

Rollins, E. William and Harry Zohn. eds. Men of Dialogue; Martin Buber and Albrecht Goes. Preface by Maurice Friedman. Introd. by E.W. Rolline and Harry Zohn. N.Y.: Funk & Wagnalls, 1969. 288 p. Index. Essays, speeches and other writings by two 'men of dialogue.' The writer A. Goes (b. 1908) served as a chaplain in the Germany army. Goes read Buber during his theological studies and he and Buber met in 1953. Thus there developed a dialogue "important because of its representative significance for Protestant and Jew, Germany and Israel, scholar and poet." Includes three short novels by Goes, Unquiet Night (1950, autobiographical), The Burnt Offering, The Boychik. Includes Buber's important piece "The End of the German-Jewish Symbiosis" (1939), pp. 232-235. "The symbiosis itself is terminated and cannot return." Two short addresses and two short narratives describe Goes's encounters with Buber.

Rome, Sydney C. and Beatrice K. Rome. eds. with introductions. Philosophical Interrogations of Martin Buber (and others). N.Y.: Harper Torchbooks, 1970. 422 p. (pa.).

Schaeder, Grete. The Hebrew Humanism of Martin Buber. trans. from the German by Noah Jacobs. Detroit: Wayne State University Press, 1973. 503 p.

Schatz - Uffenheimer, Rivka. See Part 4, chap. 3.

Schilpp, Paul Arthur and Maurice Friedman. eds. The Philosophy of Martin Buber. (The Library of Living Philosophers, 12). La Salle, Ill.: Open Court Pub. Co. 1967. XX, 811 p. Contains contributions by thirty authors and Buber's replies.

Scholom, Gershom. See Part 4, chap. 3.

Streiker, Lowell D. "Martin Buber." In Modern Theologians: Christians and Jews. ed. by Thomas E. Bird. N.Y.: Association Press, 1967. pp. 1-17.

Streiker, Lowell D. The Promise of Buber. N.Y.: Lippincott, 1969. (pa.).

Susser, Bernard. Existence and Utopia; The Social and Political thought of Martin Buber. Rutherford, N.J.: Fairleigh Dickinson University Press, 1981. XIII, 218 p. Biblio.: p. 206-215. Index.

Tillich, Paul. "An Evaluation of Martin Buber: Protestant and Jewish Thought." In Theology of Culture. N.Y.: Oxford University Press, 1959. pp. 188-199. A very positive assessment.

Vermes, Pamela. Buber on God and the Perfect Man. (Brown Judaica Studies, 13). Chico. CA.: Scholars Press, 1980. Biblio.: p. 259-261. An incisive and searching analysis.

Wood, Robert E. Martin Buber's Ontology; an analysis of I and Thou. (Northwestern University studies in phenomenology and existential philosophy). Evanston, Ill.: Northwestern University Press, 1969. 139 p.

Abraham J. Heschel (1907-1972)

Heschel, Abraham J. "The Mystical Element in Judaism." In The Jews: Their History, Culture and Religion. 2 vols. ed. by Louis Finkelstein. N.Y.: Harper & Row; Phila.: JPS, 1949. Vol. I, pp. 602-623.

Heschel, Abraham J. The Earth is the Lord's; The Inner Life of the Jew in East Europe. N.Y.: Henry Schuman, 1950. Q. 109 p. with wood engr. by Ilya Schor.

Heschel, Abraham J. Man is Not Alone; A Philosophy of Religion. N.Y.: Farrar, Straus, and Young, 1951; Phila.: JPS, 1951. O. 305 p. Heschel was sensitive to the "ineffable"; the mystery "within and beyond things and ideas." (p. 127).

Heschel, Abraham J. The Sabbath; Its Meaning for Modern Man. N.Y.: Farrar, Straus, and Young, 1951. O. 118 p. with wood eng. by Ilya Schor. Rpt. with The Earth is the Lord's. N.Y.: Meridian Books, 1963. 109, 136 p. (pa.); Harper Torchbook, 1966. Heschel writes: "The Sabbath is the day on which we learn the art of surpassing civilization."

Heschel, Abraham J. Who is Man? (Stanford University, The Raymond Fred West memorial lectures, 1963) Stanford, Calif.: Stanford University Press, 1965. 119 p. Oxford, 1966.

Heschel, Abraham J. Man's Quest for God; Studies in Prayer and Symbolism. N.Y.: Scribner & Sons, 1954. 151 p.

Heschel, Abraham J.   "A Hebrew Evaluation of Reinhold Niebuhr."   In Reinhold Niebuhr; His Religious, Social, and Political thought.   Vol. 2 of The Library of Living Theology.   ed. by Charles W. Kegley and R.W. Bretall. N.Y.: MacMillan, 1956. pp. 391-410.

Heschel, Abraham J.   God in Search of Man; A Philosophy of Judaism.   Phila.: JPS, 1956; N.Y.: Farrar, Straus, and Cudahy, 1956. 437 p.   According to Heschel (1907- 1972), man has the power to seek God but not the power to find Him. (cf. G. Marcel, P. Tillich).   Judaism is "a link to eternity, kinship with ultimate reality." Judaism is the "sanctification of time, sanctification of history." (pp. 418, 422).

Heschel, Abraham J.   The Prophets.   N.Y.: Harper & Row, 1962.   2 vol. Harper Torchbook, ed. 1969. Vol. I, 235 p. Includes Indices.   Vol. II, 287 p.   Includes Indices and Appendix: "A Note on the Meaning of Pathos."   First pub. in German in Cracow by the Polish Academy of Sciences (Mémoires de la Commission Orientaliste, 22) 1936.   A monumental study: argues that the prophets provide the basic model for authentic spirituality.   Prophetic theology is a "theology of pathos."

Heschel, Abraham J.   Israel; An Echo of Eternity. N.Y.: Farrar, Straus & Giroux, 1969. 233 p.   Drawings by Abraham Rattner.

Heschel, Abraham J.   The Insecurity of Freedom; Essays on Human Existence.   N.Y.: Farrar, Straus & Giroux, 1966; Schocken, 1972. 306 p. (pa.).

Heschel, Abraham J.   A Passion for Truth. N.Y.: Farrar, Straus & Young, 1973. 336 p.

Heschel, Abraham J.   Between God and Man; An Interpretation of Judaism from the Writings of Abraham J. Heschel. sel., ed. and Introd. by Fritz A. Rothschild. N.Y.: Harper & Bros. 1959. 279 p.   N.Y.: The Free Press, 1959, 1965.   Includes a bibliography of Heschel's writings.   Heschel described his method as "depth theology."   The Bible, he wrote, was "not man's theology, but God's anthropology."   And the drama of Jewish history was the response to the Divine "pathos," the Divine call.   This view is quite close to that of Martin Buber; but Heschel, unlike Buber, had a mystical feeling for Jewish Law: "To perform deeds of holiness is to absorb the holiness of deeds."

Heschel, Abraham J.   Maimonides; A Biography. trans. from the German by Joachim Neugroschel.   Farrar, Straus and Giroux, 1982. 273 p.

Heschel, Abraham Joshua.   The Circle of the Baal Shem Tov. Studies in Hasidism (1985, cited above, Part 4: chap. 3,b).

Studies of Heschel.

Cherbonnier, Edmond.   "Heschel as a religious thinker."   Conservative Judaism, 23 (Fall, 1968): 25-39.

Rothschild, Fritz.   (1959 , cited above).

Sherman, Franklin. The Promise of Heschel. Phila.:
J.B. Lippincott, 1970. 103 p. (pa.). Outines major
themes in a succinct way.

Schneider, Herbert W. "On Reading Heschel's God in
Search of Man; a review article." The Review of
Religion, 21:1/2 (November, 1956): 31-38.

Franz Rosenzweig

On Jewish Learning. ed. by Nahum M. Glatzer. N.Y.:
Schocken Books, 1955. 128 p. Includes an English trans-
lation of "Zeit ists," "Bildung und Kein Ende," and "Die
Bauleute.

Rosenstock-Huessy, Eugen. ed. Judaism Despite Christianity; the "Letters on Christianity and Judaism" between
Eugen Rosenstock-Huessy and Franz Rosenzweig. University of Alabama Press, 1969. 198 p. N.Y.: Schocken
Books, 1971. (pa.). Very important and moving existential letters (also often very obscure) on the question
of the "theological existence today" of the Jew and the
Christian.

Rosenzweig, Franz. Briefe. sel. and ed. by Edith
Rosenzweig with the cooperation of Ernst Simon. Berlin:
Schocken Verlag, 1935.

The Star of Redemption. trans. from the 2nd ed. (1930)
by William W. Hallo. N.Y.: Holt, Rinehart, & Winston,
1971. 445 p. Written in 1921, Der Stern der Erlosung
was Rosenzweig's magnum opus. It was not, he said, "a
Jewish Book." According to Rosenzweig, faith was
encounter between God and the person: "There is no
essence of Judaism, that would be a concept. There is

only a "Hear, O Israel." "The Jew does not believe in something, he is himself the belief." (p. 343). Described by A.A. Cohen as "a mystical epistemology that devolves into a classic aggadic reading of Jewish liturgy and Law." (1981, p. 74).

Understanding the Sick and the Healthy; A View of World, Man, and God. ed. with an Introd. by Nahum N. Glatzer. N.Y.: Noonday Press, 1954. 106 p. Rosenzweig insisted that philosophy be rooted in concrete lived experience; thinking must be done "from the personal standpoint," and the Jewish thinker "must redefine Judaism in terms of the full development of "Jewish human beings!"

Studies of Rosenzweig.

Agus, Jacob B. Modern Philosophies of Judaism. N.Y.: Behrman, 1941. A good introduction, clearly written, is in chap. 3, pp. 131-209.

Clawson, Dan. "Rosenzweig on Judaism and Christianity; a critique." Judaism, 19 (Winter, 1970): 91-98.

Cohen, Carl. "Franz Rosenzweig." Conservative Judaism, 8 (November, 1951): 1-13.

Freud, Else-Hahel. Franz Rosenzweig's Philosophy of Existence; An Analysis of the "Star of Redemption." trans. from the German 2nd ed. 1959 (1933) by S.L. Weinstein and Robert Israel. The Hague: Nijhoff, 1979. An analysis of The Star within the context of

Schelling's positive philosophy and in terms of the notions of Creation, Revelation, and Redemption.

Glatzer, Nahum N. "Franz Rosenzweig, the story of a conversion." Judaism, I (1952): 69-79. Rpt. in Glatzer, Essays in Jewish Thought (University of Alabama Press, 1978), pp. 230-242.

Glatzer, Nahu N. Franz Rosenzweig; His Life and thought. N.Y.: Schocken Books, 1953. 400 p. illus. 2nd rev. ed. 1970. (pa.). 404 p. Includes biographical dates, a list of Rosenzweig's works, and a six-page bibliography. A valuable biography with selections from his writings.

Horwitz, Rivka G. "Franz Rosenzweig on Language." Judaism, 13 (Fall 1964): 393-406.

Lowith, Karl. "M. Heidegger and Franz Rosenzweig on Temporality and Eternity." Philosophy and Phenomenological Research, 3 (September 1942): 53-77; rev. version in Karl Lowith, Nature, History and Existentialism. ed. by A. Levison. Evanston, Ill.: Northwestern University Press, 1966. pp. 51-78. On a specialist philosophical level.

Rotenstreich, Nathan. "Common Sense and Theological Experience on the Basis of Franz Rosenzweig's Philosophy." Journal of the History of Ideas, 5 (1967): 353-360.

Schwarzschild, Steven S. "Franz Rosenzweig and Existentialism." Yearbook 62: The Central Conference of American Rabbis. Cincinnati: HUC Press, 1952.

Schwarzschild, Steven S.   "Franz Rosenzweig on Judaism and Christianity." Conservative Judaism, 10:2 (Winter 1956): 41-48.

Schwarzschild, Steven S.   Franz Rosenzweig, 1886-1929. (Makers of Modern Jewish History ser., 3) London: Hillel Foundation, 1961. 48 p.

Stahmer, Harold.   "Speak that I may see Thee!"; The Religious Significance of Language. N.Y.: MacMillan, 1968. 304 p. A penetrating examination of the sacramental dimension of language in the works of J.G. Hamann, Eugen Rosenstock-Huessy, F. Rosenzweig, M. Buber, and Ferdinand Ebner.

E. Social Critics and Criticism. The Jew as conscious pariah. The non-Jewish Jew. Jewish self-hatred and Jewish anti-semitism. Introductory Analysis.

> The best thing about religion is
> that it produces heretics. *Hebbel.*

The Jew as Pariah. In various ways the term pariah has been used of the Jews by M. Weber, B. Lazare and H. Arendt (her use was found distasteful by G. Scholem). The Jew-as-pariah notion is an abstraction and lacks precision, e.g., to talk about the Jew as pariah in the early modern period (Weber's pariah-capitalism) is very different from Arendt's use of the term for the modern Jew ("strangers everywhere") The image of the modern Jew as conscious pariah has some merit in pointing to a shared dimension among emancipation and post-emancipation intellectuals, e.g., S. Maimon, H. Heine, L. Borne, B. Lazare, F. Kafka, W. Benjamin, H. Arendt. This dimension is both a state of mind and a social fact, i.e., becoming estranged from Judaism as a religious community one finds acceptance by the mainstream culture problematical if not impossible.

The "non-Jewish Jew." Jewish Self-hatred. Jewish Anti-Semitism.
What does one mean by the non-Jewish Jew? One who identifies with Jewish civilization or peoplehood but rejects Judaism as a community of faith? A secular or atheistic Jew? A secular Zionist? These assertions can

all stand but there is a more fundamental level that we
want to propose. A non-Jewish Jew is a Jew through
negation, i.e., a Jew whose identity is conferred by the
Other. Trotsky is an example of the non-Jewish Jew
because his awareness of his Jewishness was primarily
related to the anti-Semitism of Stalin. The same can be
said of Marx, S. Weil and konfessionslos revolutionaries
like R. Luxemburg (1871-1919), and E. Goldman (1869-
1940), or I. Ehrenburg (see below, but hardly a
"revolutionary").

But Karl Marx would probably be the proto typical non-
Jewish Jew. His acts and writings were also a major
catalyst in the formation of the notion of Jewish self-
hatred. But regardless of the intensity and bitterness
of his attacks on Jews and Jewry (both the Sabbath Jew
(cf. Heine) and the Jew of commerce, or his personal
attacks on Lasalle) Marx was perceived as a Jew.

The phenomenology of the non-Jewish Jew illuminates the
role of negativity in identity formation. Identity has
a negative dimension, a condition of non-being, a situation of perceived difference. The non-Jewish Jew is a
Jew through the Look Sartre of the Other. The Jewish
Jew chooses the identity of Jew, defining himself or
herself as a Jew, regardless, finally, of the Other.
The difference imposed by the Other which initiated the
identity process has been sublimated into a higher form
of awareness. The non-Jewish Jew is a Jew through
negative apprehension. The identity of the Jewish Jew
does not cancel awareness of Otherness but the negativity of being perceived as Other is part of a process or
motion from negation to affirmation. Identity is not a
thing or a fixed state but positive identity is

concretized finally only through choice, not fate or
negation.

In discussing Jewish self-hatred one may begin by citing
Heine's comment about Jewishness as an "incurable
malady" (in "The New Jewish Hospital in Hamburg," 1842).
The term "malady" suggests a social-psychological answer
to the Jewish self-hatred problem.   19th-century
European cases of Jewish self-hatred may perhaps have
involved an internalization of the German Volkish or
French nationalistic critique that identified capitalism and modernity with the assimilated Jew.   This
Jewish self-hatred was then projected outward by Jews on
other Jews in a dualism of "good" vs. "bad" Jews. (On
this see the brilliant work by S.L. Gilman, 1986).
However, Jews since Pagan times have been the objects
of negative projection but only in a few cases has this
led to Jewish anti-Semitism.   Is a Jewish convert to
Christianity who urges the conversion of other Jews
motivated by Jewish self-hatred? Perhaps, but also he
or she may be motivated by theological conviction.   In
that case the self-hatred notion is simply reductive.
Jewish anti-Semitism may arise out of Jewish self-hatred
but it may also reflect theological and historical
contents that do not inhere in the notion of self-
hatred.   The analytical danger in the notion of self-
hatred is that it can dissolve the historically specific
into a general social-psychological analysis.   Jewish
self-hatred is a psychological condition that may or may
not be worked through and transcended. It may or may
not end in anti-Semitism. They are not the same.   To
link them requires psychological and biographical
evidence that might not be available or easy to inter-
pret. For example, were the rantings of S. Weil against

the Hebrew deity and the "fascism" of the ancient
Hebrews an expression of Jewish self-hatred? Is it not
more likely that it arose from a misreading of texts
mixed with fundamental ignorance?

In thinking about Jewish anti-Semitism one also must
distinguish theoretical-rhetorical anti-Semitism from
racialistic, conspiratorial anti-Semitism. Examples of
the latter are Otto Weininger (1880-1903), Geschlecht
und Charakter, 1903: ET, Sex and Character (1906), and
the lesser known "Jewish Aryan," A. Trebitsch (1887-
1921). In these two cases one is tempted to see an
extreme form of Jewish self-hatred expressing itself in
the racist categories of the day mixed with psychological categories.

The fine lines, shadings, ambiguous points between
Jewish self-hatred and Jewish anti-Semitism caution one
against an easy use of labels. For example, all of the
individuals named below have been called Jewish anti-
Semites or Jewish self-haters: K.Kraus (below, whom M.
Buber called a "Jew unhappy with himself"), T. Tuchosky
(see EJ entry, and F. Grunfeld, cited below), Jakob
Wasserman (1873-1933, who apparently deespised Ostjuden
and urged assimilation of the German Jew), Franz Werfel
(1890-1945), Ernst Toller (1894-1939).

A mechanical reading of their statements or actions
(e.g., conversion) could invite reductive use of the
anti-Semitic and/or self-hatred images; thus missing the
turmoil, confusion, and changes in their thought and
life. The concepts of Jewish self-hatred and Jewish
anti-Semitism must be kept under close critical
restraint.

Arendt, Hannah. The Jew as Pariah: Jewish Identity and Politics in the Modern Age. ed. with an Introd. by Ron H. Feldman. N.Y.: Grove Press, 1978. 288 p. (pa.). Part I: The Pariah as Rebel. Part II: Zionism and the Jewish State. Part III: The Eichmann controversy. Arendt, a commanding intellectual (b. 1906, Hanover; Ph.D. (philosophy) at Heidelberg, 1929, fled to Paris in 1933, NYC in 1944) chose the role of "conscious pariah." According to her, the status of social outsider for the Jew gave rise to two types of pariah, the conscious pariah and the parvenu. The former were "those who really did most for the spiritual dignity of their people...those bold spirits who tried to make of the emancipation of the Jews that which it really should have been--an admission of Jews as Jews to the ranks of humanity, rather than a permit to ape the gentiles or an opportunity to play the parvenu." ("The Jew as Pariah: A Hidden Tradition." (Apr. 1944) in The Jew as Pariah, pp. 66-67.). In this essay, Arendt selects Heine, Lazare, Chaplin, and Kafka as pariah types.

Arendt, Hannah. Rahel Varnhagen; The Life of a Jewish Woman. trans. by Richard and Clara Winston. rev. ed. N.Y.: Harcourt Brace Jovanovich, 1974 (1957). XX. 236 p. The biography of an early 19th-century socialite who kept a famous salon in Berlin. "Rahel had remained a Jew and pariah. Only because she clung to both conditions did she find a place in the history of European humanity." (p. 227). For more on these literary salons, see M. Meyer (1967, cited above), pp. 102-114; and H. Spiel, Fanny von Arnstein oder Die Emancipation. (Frankfurt, 1962).

Arendt, Hannah. <u>Men in Dark Times</u>. N.Y.: Harcourt, Brace and World, 1968. 272 p. The title is from a Brecht poem. A. Heibut describes the book as "a covert history of émigré intellectuals and artists." Includes an essay on Walter Benjamin, B. Brecht, Rosa Luxemburg, Isak Dinesen, two pieces on Jaspers, and an interpretation of Lessing: ("Let each man say what he deems truth, and let truth itself be commended unto God."). On Arendt, see Young-Bruehl (1982, cited below) and Hannah Arendt - a retrospective symposium," <u>Response, a contemporary Jewish review</u>, 39 (1980): 38-63. Essays by D. Biale, H. Feingold, S. Muller, J.M. Baron ("Personal Reflections").

Benjamin, Walter. <u>Illuminations</u>. trans. from the German (1955) by Harry Zohn. ed. with an Introd. by Hannah Arendt. N.Y.: Harcourt, 1968; Schocken Books, 1969, 280 p. See "Franz Kafka," pp. 111-140 and "Some Reflections on Kafka," pp. 141-145. Benjamin states that Kafka's work is an ellipse with two foci: mystical experience and the experience of the modern urban dweller. He quotes Kakfa, "We are nihilistic thoughts, sucidal thoughts that come into God's head...our world is only a bad mood of God, a bad day of His." (p. 116).

Benjamin, Walter. "Franz Kafka, zur 10. Wiederkehr seines Todestages." in <u>Gesammelte Schriften</u>, II. Frankfurt a.M.: Suhrkamp, 1955. Note his observation on thinking: "Thinking involves not only the flow of thoughts, but their arrest as well. Where thinking suddenly stops in a configuration pregnant with tensions, it gives that configuration a shock, by which it crystallizes into a monad." (pp. 262-3).

Benjamin, Walter.   Reflections: Essays, Aphorisms,
Autobiographical Writings. ed. with an Introd. by Peter
Demetz. trans. from the German by Edmund Jephcott.
N.Y.: Harcourt Brace Jovanovich, 1978. XLIII. 348 p.
Benjamin (1892-1940) was a gifted German Jewish scholar,
critic, literary alchemist and homme de lettres. Called
"the last intellectual" by Susan Sontag, (NY Review of
Books, Oct/ 12, 1978), Benjamin was a close friend of
Gershom Scholem. See Scholem's essay: "Walter Benjamin
and his Angel," in On Jews and Judaism in Crisis (N.Y.:
Schocken, 1976), and see Walter Benjamin: die Geschichte
u. Freundschaft (Frankfurt a.M.: Suhrkamp, 1957), trans.
by Harry Zohn, Walter Benjamin: The Story of a Friendship. Phila.: JPS, 1981. XI, 242 p. plates. Bibliographical references. Index.

Berlin, Sir Isaiah. "Benjamin Disraeli, Karl Marx and
the Search for Identity."   Midstream, 16 (August/
September 1970): 29-49. Berlin argues that the
rationalist ideals of Marx and the "mystical
conservatism" of Disraeli were both post-Emancipation
quests for personal identity.

Cahnman, Werner J. cited above, Part 3, chap. 2:a.

Canetti, Elias. The Human Province. trans. from the
German by Joachim Neugroschel. N.Y.: Seabury Press,
1978. 281 p. These fragments from his journals, 1942-
1972, reflect a widely-read and speculative mind.
Canetti (b. 1905) is known for his Crowds and Power
(Viking, 1962, 495 p.) and the brilliant, haunting,
nihilistic novel Auto-da-fe (London: Jonathan Cape,
1947; N.Y.: Knopf, under the title: Tower of Babel,
1947. trans. from the German (Die Blendung (The Decep-

tion, Vienna, 1935). Also: Canetti, The Tongue Set
Free: Remembrance of a European Childhood. trans. by J.
Neugroschel (N.Y.: Seabury Press, 1979, 268 p.), and see
The Torch in My Ear, trans. by J. Neugroschel (N.Y.:
Farrar, Straus and Giroux, 1982). According to Gilman
(1986, below, p. 326), this autobiography "serves as the
most detailed account existing in post-Holocaust letters
of the formation of a Jewish identity out of an
incorporation of the special language of the Jews."

Carlebach, Julius. Karl Marx and the Radical Critique
of Judaism. (Littman lib. of Jewish civilization).
London: Routledge & Kegan Paul, 1978. 466 p. Includes
annotated and general bibliography: 438-461. Carlebach
attempts to recreate the several social contexts in
which the "Jewish question" and the Marxian "solution"
emerged. He follows Sartre in recommending that the
Marxists "study real men in depth, not dissolve them in
a bath of sulphuric acid."

Carlebach, Julius. "The Forgotten Connection: Women
and Jews in the conflict between Enlightenment and
Romanticism," LBIY, 24 (1979): 107-38. A very important
essay; Weininger's (Sex and Character, 1903) connection
was that women and Jews could not think logically, had
no sense of humor, lacked depth; but the Jew was worse
than women because of a "want of reality" or identity
center. See the discussion in Gilman (1986, cited
below, pp. 244-248).

Clark, Ronald William. Einstein; The Life and Times.
N.Y.: World Pub. Co., 1971. 718 p. A detailed and solid
study.

Cuddihy, John Murray. The Ordeal of Civility; Freud, Marx and Levi-Strauss, and the Jewish Struggle with Modernity. N.Y.: Basic Books, 1974. 272 p. A lively and intelligent but overambitious study of the modernization process in terms of the question of Jewish assimilation, using comparative data on the modernizing elite of the new nations in relationship to the modernizing intelligentsia of the Jewish diaspora. The search for "culture" and a "civilized" language (derived from an Enlightenment model) defined the identity quest of the modern Jew. Uncivilized language and behaviour was represented in the image of the Ostjude.

Demetz, Peter. "Kafka, Freud, Husserl: Problem einer Generation." Zeitschrift für Religions und Geistesgeschichte. 7:1 (1955): 59-69.

Derrida, Jacques. "Edmond Jabès et la question du livre," and "Ellipse," In L'écriture et la différence (Paris, 1967), pp. 99-116, 429-436. From the Sephardic tradition, Derrida's central work is the brilliant but often obscure De la Grammatologie (Paris, 1967), trans. by Gayatri Chatravorty Spivak with an extensive and scholarly introduction (Baltimore: Johns Hopkins University Press, 1976), XC, 354 p. (pa.). See also: Glas (Paris, 1974), and "La question du style," in Nietzche aujourd'hui? (Paris, 1973), Derrida provides clue-ideas (although on a very high level of abstraction) for the development of a thematics of Jewish identity. For a perceptive (but difficult) study in the tradition of Derrida's "deconstructionism" (which is, put crudely: a margin-center thematic field shift, the marginal displacing the center and thus bringing a change in the values of a <u>corpus</u>) see Jeffrey Mehlman, <u>Legacies</u> of <u>Anti-Semitism</u> in <u>France</u> (Minn.: University of Minnesota. On four contemporary writers, Blanchot's contributions to <u>Combat</u>, Lacon on <u>Le</u> <u>salut</u> <u>par</u> <u>les</u> <u>juifs</u>, Giraudoux in <u>Pleins</u> <u>pouvoirs</u>, and Gide's statement on "Jewish literature" in the <u>Journal</u>, who have restored a lost pre-World War II (Hitler has eliminated anti-Semitism as an option for the French intellectual) anti-Semitic sensibility.

Deutscher, Isaac. <u>The</u> <u>Non-Jewish</u> <u>Jew</u> <u>and</u> <u>Other</u> <u>Essays</u>. ed. with an Introd. by Tamara Deutscher. N.Y.: Oxford University Press, 1968. 164 p. Describing himself as "an unrepentant Marxist, an atheist, an internationalist," Deutscher conceives the Jew as the prototype of the marginal radical. Generally speaking, the essays are not closely reasoned. (Cited in Part 5, chap. 3,g).

Fiedler, Leslie A. "Simone Weil: Prophet out of Israel, a Saint of the Absurd." <u>Commentary</u>, 2:1 (January 1951): 36-46. Fiedler, with excessive zeal, argues that Weil was a Jewish heretic who reflected aspects of Jewish tradition in her refusal to accept consolation in the face of terror, and in her affirmation of alienation as evidence of Divine love. "The absurdity, the absolutions, the incandescence of the prophets survive in Simone Weil, and for all her blemishes, their terrible purity." (p. 46). Perhaps, but Fiedler reduces Weil to a rather comic-absurd ("saint of the Absurd") literary figure.

Freud, Ernest L. ed. <u>Sigmund</u> <u>Freud</u>: <u>Letters,</u> <u>1873-1939</u>. new ed. trans. by Tania and James Stern. London: Hogarth Press, 1970. 464 p. illus. The standard 3-vol.

work on Freud is by Ernest Jones. It is ed. and abridged by Lionel Trilling and Stephen Marcus, The Life and Work of Sigmund Freud. (London: Hogarth, 1962). And see now the comprehensive biography by Ronald W. Clark, Freud, The Man and the Cause (N.Y.: Random House, 1980), p. 652. See also Marthe Robert, From Oedipus to Moses: Freud's Jewish Identity. trans. from the French (1974) by Ralph Manheim. (N.Y.: Doubleday Anchor Books, 1976. 229 p.). This is an analysis of Freud's "two-sided discomfort" as an acculturated Jew in a German-speaking world. On Freud and Judaism and on his reactions to anti-Semitism, see Earl A. Grollman, Judaism in Sigmund Freud's World. Foreword by Nathan W. Ackerman. (N.Y.: Appleton-Century, 1966. XXV, 173 p.). On his relationship to Judaism, Freud said: "It was only to my Jewish nature that I owed the two qualities that became necessary to me throughout my difficult life. Because I was a Jew I found myself free of many prejudices that restrict others in the use of the intellect: as a Jew I was prepared to be in the opposition and to renounce agreement with the 'compact minority.'" Also on Freud as a Jew, read Ernst Simon, "Sigmund Freud, the Jew." LBIY, 2 (1957): 270-305, and see the literature cited in S. Gilman (1986, below), pp. 428-429.

Gay, Peter. Freud, Jews and Other Germans; Masters and Victims in Modernist Culture. N.Y.: Oxford University Press, 1978. XXX. 289 p. Elegant and brilliant essays on the role of Jews, sometimes masters but usually victims, within modernist German culture. Gay claims that the German-Jewish symbiosis was a reality, but he avoids the needed hard analysis of what is German and what is Jewish in the artists and writers of the period.

Moreover he ignores Kafka and gives only passing mention of Benjamin and Scholem.

Gilman, Sander L. "Nietzsche, Heine, and the Otherness of the Jew." In Studies in Nietzsche and the Judaic - Christian Tradition. ed. by James C. O'Flaherty, et al. Chapel Hill: The University of North Carolina Press, 1985. pp. 206-225. An insightful essay, see bibliographical notes. "Nietzsche is thus not a philo-Semite but rather an anti-anti- Semite." (p. 210).

Gilman, Sander L. Jewish Self-Hatred. Anti-Semitism and the Hidden Language of the Jews. Baltimore: The Johns Hopkins Press, 1986. 461 p. Notes. Index. A learned and brilliant essay on "damaged discourse" and on the Jew as the Other.

Goldman, Emma. Nowhere at Home: Letters from Exile of Emma Goldman and Alexander Berkman. ed. by Richard and Anna Maria Drinnon. N.Y.: Schocken Books, 1975. XXVIII, 282 p. illus. See the solid biography by Richard Drinnon, Rebel in Paradise. A Biography of Emma Goldman. Boston: Beacon Press, 1961. 351 p. Goldman (b. 1869 (Kovno, Lith.) d. 1940) was an anarchist, free-thinker, "feminist," dynamic lecturer and radical-cause organizer. She wrote Living My Life (Knopf, 1931; Rpt. Dover, 1970, 2 vols.). After being deported, with A. Berkman, to Russia in 1919 she composed My Disillusionment in Russia. (London, 1925). Now also see Alice Wexler, Emma Goldman, An Intimate Life. (N.Y.: Pantheon Books, 1984. 339 p. plates. Epilogue, Notes, Biblio.: p. 319-327. Index). This is a sensitive and thoroughly researched account of the "all too human" (Goldman, of herself) personality behind the famous/infamous public images. And see Candace Falk, Love, Anarchy and Emma Goldman, A Biography. (N.Y.: Holt, Rinehart & Winston, 1984. 603 p. illus. plates. Notes, Biblio.: p. 575-585). Acknowledgements. Index). Uses letters (Ben Reitman) and other sources not available earlier; a major biography, mainly of Goldman's personal and intensely erotic life.

Grunfeld, Frederic V. Prophets Without Honour. A Background to Freud, Kafka, Einstein and Their World. N.Y.: Holt, Rinehart and Winston, 1979. 359 p. Notes. Biblio.: p. 323-334. Index. illus. A non-technical study, with copious translations, of a German-Jewish literature of the 1920's, some of which is not widely known; and a German-Jewish literature of the 30's and 40's written by émigrés, refugees and victims. Gertrude Kolmar perished in or on the way to Auschwitz, Walter Benjamin (her cousin) committed suicide, Sept. 27, 1940. See, especially, the discussion of Else Lasker-Schuler, Erich Muhsam, Ernst Toller (chap. 3), Kafka and Tucholsky (chap. 6), Walter Benjamin, Gertrude Kolmar (chap. 7), and Alfred Doeblin (virtually unknown except for the ET of Berlin Alexanderplatz) and H. Broch (discussed too briefly at the end of the book).

Heine, Heinrich. Der Rabbi von Bacharach (1840). In Heinrich Heine, Self-Portrait and other Prose Writings. sel., ed. and trans. with an Introd. by Frederic Ewen. Secaucus, N.J.: The Citadel Press, 1948. XII, 617 p. Biblio.: pp. 608-609. Heine (1797-1856) was the greatest lyric love poet of the 19th century and a gifted prose writer in the tradition of Lessing. He was a prominent member of the Verein (Society for the Culture and Academic Study of Judaism) but converted for career purposes in 1825. He regretted this action: "I make no secret of my Judisam, to which I have not returned, because I never left it." (1850). "Heine is the only German Jew who could truthfully describe himself as both a German and a Jew. He is the only outstanding example of a really happy assimilation in the entire history of that process." H. Arendt, "The Jew as Pariah..." In The Jew as Pariah (1978, cited above, p. 74). Always a romantic individualist, he said of himself: "Heine will and must always be Heine." (Heinrich Heine Briefe, I, p. 175, cited in M. Meyer (1967, cited above, p. 171)). See "Heine," EJ, 8, 270-275 and bibliography, H. Kohn, Heinrich Heine: The Man and the Myth (N.Y.: 1959). On Heine, see Israel Tabak, Judaic Lore in Heine; The Heritage of a Poet (Oxford University Press, and Johns Hopkins, 1948), XII, 338 p. See also Laura Hofrichter, Heinrich Heine. trans. from the German by Barker Fairley (Oxford: Oxford University Press, 1963), 175 p. And see the recent biography by Jefferey L. Sammons, Heinrich Heine; A Modern Biography (Princeton, N.J.: Princeton University Press, 1980), 425 p. Also of merit is Nigel Reeves' Heinrich Heine: Poetry and Politics (Modern Language and Literature Monographs). (Oxford Oxford University Press, 1974), 209 p. S.S. Prawer's Heine's Jewish Comedy, Oxford, 1983) is of first-rate importance; recent German works that deal with Heine's Jewish identity are Ludwig Rosenthal, Heinrich Heine als Jude (Frankfurt, 1973), Hartmut Kircher, Heinrich Heine und das Judenthum (Bonn, 1973) and Ruth L. Jacobi, Heinrich Heines judisches Erbe (Bonn, 1978).

Jay, Martin. The Dialectical Imagination. A History of the Frankfurt School and the Institute of Social

768

Research 1923-1950. Boston: Little, Brown and Co., 1973. 382 p. Includes Bibliography.

Kafka, Franz. Letters to Friends, Family, and Editors. trans. from the German by Richard and Clara Winston. N.Y.: Schocken, 1977. 509 p. Kafka, one of the greatest writers of this century, died of tuberculosis in 1924-- he was 40. The standard opinion has been that his emotional life, and especially with women, was a type of painful imprisonment. But it did not end so: in his last year he experienced a liberating love with a young Jewish woman Dora Dymant, the cook in a Jewish sanatorium. When he died, she cried: "My love, my love, my dearest!" See Nahum N. Glatzer, The Loves of Franz Kafka (Schocken Books, 1986).

Kafka, Franz. The Diaries of Franz Kafka, 1910-1913. Vol. I. trans. by Joseph Kresh. ed. by Max Brod. N.Y.: Schocken Books, 1948. 345 p. paperback ed. Schocken, 1965.

Kafka, Franz. The Diaries of Franz Kafka, 1914-1923. trans. by Martin Greenburg with the cooperation of Hannah Arendt. ed. by Max Brod. N.Y.: Schocken Books, 1949. 343 p. paperback. ed. Schocken, 1965.

Kafka, Franz. Letter to his Father. (Brief an Vater). trans. by Ernest Kaiser and Eithne Wilkins. N.Y.: Schocken Books, 1966. A paperback rpt. 127 p.

Kafka, Franz. I Am A Memory Come Alive; Autobiographical Writings. ed. by Nahum N. Glatzer. N.Y.: Schocken, 1974. 264 p. See also Elias Canetti, Kafka's Other Trial; the letters to Felice. trans. from the German by

Christopher Middleton (London: Calder and Boyars; N.Y.:
Schocken, 1974), 121 p. J.P. Stern has edited an antho-
logy of Kafka's writings, The World of Franz Kafka
(N.Y.: Holt, Rinehart & Winston, 1980), 263 p. plates.
The literature on Kafka is immense; for an excellent
critical study see Wilhelm Emrich, Franz Kafka, a criti-
cal study of his writings. trans. from the German by
Sheema Z. Buehne. (N.Y.: Ungar, 1968), 561 p. Includes
Bibliography. Kakfa's thought was rooted in the Hebrew
Bible: "Only the Old Testament has vision--say nothing
about it yet." And he was influenced by tenets in the
Kabbalah and Hasidism. See Gershom Scholem, Die
judische Mystik in ihren Hauptstromungen (Frankfurt,
1957), pp. 117 ff.

For studies that focus on Kafka as a Jew, see Helen
Milfull, "Franz Kafka--the Jewish Context." LBIY 23
(1978): 227-238. In this intelligent interpretation,
with good bibliographical references, Milfull argues
that Kafka was constantly concerned with his relationship to Judaism. She is critical of aspects of Brod's
interpretation, and makes interesting comments about
Benjamin and Scholem's views of Kafka. And see Clement
Greenberg, "The Jewishness of Franz Kafka. Some sources
of his particular vision." Commentary, 19:4 (1955): 32-
329; and noteworthy is Felix Weltsch's "The Rise and
Fall of the Jewish-German Symbiosis: The Case of Franz
Kakfa, LBIY, I (1956): 255-276. Weltsch was a publi-
cist and philosopher from Prague and a close friend of
Kafka's (see Kafka, Diaries). Weltsch has also written
Religion und Humor in Leben und Werk Franz Kafkas
(Berlin: F.A. Herbig, 1957).

Nahum N. Glatzer has written a fascinating short essay, "Franz Kafka and the Tree of Knowledge," in Essays in Jewish Thought (University of Alabama: University of Alabama Press, 1978, pp. 184-191). See Kafka's profound parable, "Before the Law." Fragmented human experience is constant witness to the tension between knowledge and life (peace, quietude, die Wahrheit des ruhenden, cf., Goethe, Faust, Bk. I). Kafka affirmed that the Tree of Life is somehow hidden within the Tree of Knowledge. As a metaphor for Wholeness this is correct; but within distorted (non-messianic) Existenz the discoveries are partial only and the at-one-ments fleeting. As the Buddhists affirm: "the world is a sorrowful bubble."

For Kafka and the theatre see the study by Evelyn Torton Beck, Kafka and the Yiddish Theater; Its Impact on His Work. Madison, Wisconsin: University of Wisconsin Press, 1971, 248 p. Biblio.: p. 228-237. Beck argues that Kafka's involvement with the Yiddish troupes that visited Prague in 1911-1912 awakened his interest in his Jewish heritage, and deeply influenced his writings: "...beginning with "The Judgment," the thematic and stylistic parallels between Kafka's work and the Yiddish plays are fairly insistent." (p. 210). See also Nicholas Howey, Who's Afraid of Franz Kafka: Art and Politics in the Czech Theatre (University Ala.: University of Alabama Press, 1974).

The standard biography is by Max Broad, Franz Kafka: A Biography. trans. from the German by G. Humphreys Roberts and Richard Winston. rev. 2nd ed. (N.Y.: Schocken Books, 1960, 267 p.). And now see the comprehensive study by Ronald Hayman, K: A Biography of Kafka (London: Secker & Warburg, 1982; N.Y.: Oxford University

Press, 1982), 349 p. Includes Bibliography, Notes, Index. The first full-scale biographical study written in English. But a more eloquent and reflective work is the biography by Ernst Pawel, The Nightmare of Reason. A Life of Franz Kafka (N.Y.: Farrar, Straus, Giroux, 1984. 466 p. Biblio.: p. 449-455. Index. plates.). The Bibliography on Kafka is estimated at about 15,000 titles in several languages.

Angel Flores has edited a collection of critical essays, The Kafka Problem (N.Y.: Octagon, 1963), 477 p. Includes Bibliography and list of Kafka's work in English. Among general interpretations one also may mention Marthe Robert, Franz Kafka's Loneliness. trans. from the French by Ralph Manheim (London: Faber, 1982; N.Y.: Harcourt Brace Jovanovich under the title: As lonely as Franz Kafka, 1982, 251 p.); Paul Goodman, Kafka's Prayer (N.Y.: Vanguard, 1947; Rpt. N.Y.: Stonehill Pub. Co., 1976), a searching argument with Kafka; and for a major new appraisal, with good insight on the intellectual climate of Prague, see Franz Kuna, Kafka: Literature as Corrective Punishment. (Bloomington, University of Indiana Press, 1974), 196 p.

Kohn, Hans. Karl Kraus - Arthur Schnitzler - Otto Weininger: Aus dem judischen Wien Jahrhundertwende. Tubingen: J.C.B. Mohr, 1962.

Kraus, Karl. In These Great Times. A Karl Kraus Reader. ed. by Harry Zohn with trans. by H. Zohn, et al. Manchester, Eng.: Carcanet Press Ltd., 1984. 263 p. Selected Bibliography. illus. See also H. Zohn, "A Crown for Zion: Karl Kraus and the Jews." WLB, 24 (1970): 22-26. Kraus (Vienna, 1874-1936) was a brilliant stylist, satirist, poet and dramatist. He founded the journal Die Fackel (The Torch) in 1899; his major drama was Die Letzten Tage der Menschheit (1919), pacifist in content, satirical and expressionistic in style and form. Kraus was dedicated to the purity of language; essentially apolitical he was mocking and satirical toward Heine, Zionism, and the Jewish press. He converted to Roman Catholicism in 1911 but then left the Church in 1923 in disgust over the Salzburg Festival. Kraus's last poem (Sept. 1933) was a response to the madness happening across the German border: "And silence reigns because the bedrock broke. No word redeems... The Word expired when that world awoke."

Landauer, Gustav. Skepsis und Mystik. Versuche im Anschluss an Mauthners sprachkritik. Berlin: Egon Fleischel & Co., 1903. Landauer was an influential intellectual anarchist and pacifist. He was admired by Scholem and was a close friend to Buber. On Landauer, see Maurice Friedman, Martin Buber's Life and Work, Vol. I (N.Y.: E.P. Dutton, 1981), chap. II. "Communal socialism and Revolution: Murder of Landauer," pp. 232-258; see also, Eugene Lunn, Prophet of Community: The Romantic Socialism of Gustav Landauer. (Berkeley, Ca.: University of California Press, 1973, 434 p.). "There is a memorializing essay on Landauer by Ernst Simon, "The Maturing of the Man and the Maturing of the Jew," in The Jew; Essays from Martin Buber's "Der Jude," 1016-1928. ed. by Arthur A. Cohen (University of Alabama: University of Alabama Press, 1980).

Lessing, Theodor. Der judische Selbsthass. Berlin: Judischer Verlag, 1930. This work popularized the "Jewish self-hatred" phrase. See S. Gilman (1986, cited above p. 393, <u>passim</u>, and bibliographical notes on Lessing.

Levi-Strauss, Claude. (b. 1908). Strauss is the leading exponent of structuralism. His massive <u>Mythologiques</u> appeared in 4 volumes, 1964, 1966, 1968, 1971. See Georges Charbonnier, <u>Conversations</u> <u>with</u> <u>Claude</u> <u>Levi-Strauss</u>, trans. from the French by John Weightman and Doreen Weightman (London: Jonathan Cape, 1969, 159 p.) and read the discussion in J. Cuddidy (1974, cited above).

Liptzin, Solomon. <u>Germany's</u> <u>Stepchildren</u>. Phila.: JPS, 1944. 298 p. Bibliographic Notes. Index. photos. See Part IV.

Maimon, Solomon. (Cited above, chap. 3:2)

Marx, Karl. <u>Marx</u> <u>and</u> <u>Engels</u> <u>on</u> <u>Religion</u>. 2nd ed. Foreign Languages Publishing House, 1963; N.Y.: Schocken Books, 1964 (pa.). Contains a fairly complete selection of Marx's (1818-1883) statements about religion. Marx's father was a Jewish lawyer who converted to Protestantism, for career reasons, when Marx was six years old. There is much controversy about Marx's attitude toward Jews and Judaism. It is clear that he identified Judaism with bourgeois capitalism (but as villain or ultimate victim?) for which he had no affection. Helmut Hirsch in his <u>Marx</u> <u>und</u> <u>Moses</u>: <u>Karl</u> <u>Marx</u> <u>zur</u> <u>"Judenfrage"</u> <u>und</u> <u>der</u> <u>Juden</u> ([Judenthum und Welt,2], Frankfurt am Main and Berne: Peter D. Lang, 1980) argues that Marx was not an "outspoken antisemite," but supported Emancipation, admired Spinoza and had many Jewish friends. On the other hand, Robert S. Wistrich in his essay "Karl Marx and the Jewish Question" (<u>Soviet Jewish Affairs</u>, 4:1 (1974): 53-60) argues that Marx's essays on the Jewish question reflected a desire to separate himself from his Jewish origins. Edmund Silberner in "Was Marx an anti-Semite?" (<u>Historia Judaica</u>, 11:1 (April 1949): 3-52) thinks that Marx was an unfortunately influential case of "Jewish self-hatred." According to Silberner, Marx held that Jews were the product of bourgeois society and Judaism an outgrowth of egoism. He maintained that the Jewish problem will disappear in a "humanely" emancipated society. Silberner concludes with the excessive-sounding statement that Marx's "aversion to the Jews was deeply rooted in his heart and mind, and lasted up to his very end." (p. 51). On Marx and Jewish self-hatred, see S. Gilmann (1986), pp. 188-208. Bracketing the biographical and psychological question of "Jewish self-hatred," the intellectual historian recognizes that Judaism for Marx was a mythological construct and symbol of modern bourgeois capitalist society. See also Murray Wolfson, <u>Marx Economist, Philosopher, Jew; Stages in the Development of a Doctrine</u>. (London: MacMillan, 1982, XX, 270 p.). Includes bibliography, notes, index. Also see Shlomo Avineri, "Marx and Jewish Emancipation," <u>Journal of the History of Ideas</u> (1964), 445-450; Eugene Kamenka, "The Baptism of Karl Marx." <u>Hibbert Journal</u>, 56 ((1958): 340-51.

Nedava, Joseph. <u>Trotsky and the Jews</u>. Phila.: JPS, 1972. 299 p. Notes. Biblio.: p. 279-290. Index. Describes Trotsky's ambivalence on Jewish identity and his later concessions to a temporary territorial solution to the Jewish problem. Trotsky was very aware of how Stalin exploited anti-Semitic attitudes. Trotsky's Jewishness "connoted a sort of moral counter-

balance to anti-Semitism." (p. 10). The standard bio-
graphy of Trotsky is the 3-volume study by Isaac
Deutscher (Oxford University Press, 1970). See also
Irving Howe, Trotsky (Brighton, Sussex: Harvester
Press, 1978), Robert S. Wistrich, Trotsky: Fate of a
Revolutionary (London: Robson Books, 1979, 235 p.), and
Ronald Segal, The Tragedy of Leon Trotsky. (London:
Hutchinson, 1979; Pantheon, 1980, 445 p. illus.).

Neusner, Jacob. "Jewish Self-Hatred." EJ: Decennial
Book. Jerusalem: Keter, 1982, 551 p. (with brief bibliography).

Rieff, Philip. "Fellow Teachers," Salmagundi, 20
(Summer/Fall, 1972). On "Jews of culture" vis a vis
"the ungospelled present."

Stambolian, George. Marcel Proust and the Creative
Encounter. Chicago: University of Chicago, 1972.
Although Proust was raised as a Catholic he "always
retained some Jewish sympathies, and it was he who
persuaded Anatole France to interfere in the Dreyfus
Affair." See "Proust," EJ, Vol. 13, p. 1257. Also the
image of the Jew occupies a strong place in his fiction.

Steiner, George. "One Definition of a Jew." Cambridge
Opinion, 39 (1964): 16-22. "But if the poison (the
Chosen People notion/image) is, in ancient past, Jewish,
so is the antidote, the radical humanism which sees man
on the road to becoming man. This is where Marx is most
profoundly a Jew (while at the same time arguing the
dissolution of Jewish identity)." p. 22. Cf. E.
Silberner (cited above).

Strauss, Leo. Persecution and the Art of Writing. Glencoe: The Free Press, 1952. 204 p. Discussed above, sect. d.

Weil, Simone. Past and Present Note Books. trans. from the French by Richard Rees. N.Y.: Oxford University Press, 1970; Eng. ed. under the title: First and Last Notebooks, Oxford University Press, 1970), 368 p. For a good introduction to Weil's life and thought, see Richard Rees, Simone Weil: A Sketch for a Portrait. Preface by Harry T. Moore. (Arcturus Books), (Carbondale & Edwardsville: Southern Illinois University Press, 1978), 205 p. and George Abbott White, ed. Simone Weil: Interpretations of a Life (Amherst: University of Massachusetts Press, 1981), 207 p. A collection of critical studies, those by White and S. Lynd focus on Weil as a political activist and thinker.

Weil, Simone. On Science, Necessity, and the Love of God. Essays collected, trans. and ed. by Richard Rees. London: Oxford University Press, 1968. 210 p. "Just as there is no tree like the Cross, so there is no harmony like the silence of God." ("Silence of God," p. 197). Weil's analysis of the Hebrew religion and her insights into Judaism were not simply exaggerations but were based on fundamental ignorance. Her connection of fascism with the ancient Romans and Hebrews was also quite preposterous. She had little knowledge of Judaism and no affection for it. Her parents regarded themselves as French only and she was not told until she was ten that their parents were Jewish. In her letter of 1942 to the Ministry of Education she denied all ties with Judaism. But about this letter, her biographer (in a fine book but one too closely identified with its subject) S. Petrement writes: "...she was mocking "The Statutory Regulations on "Jews" and the confused ideas on which all anti-Semitic racism rests."" Simone Weil. A Life. trans. from the French by Raymond Rosenthal (N.Y.: Pantheon, 1976), p. 392). On the question of personal Jewish identity and identification with the Jewish people, she accepted the then widespread notion of assimilation (a mistake but not anti-Semitism). She repudiated identification with any group. Her thought and range of sympathy was universalist (like E. Goldman, R. Luxemburg) and she regarded Jewish suffering as part of general human suffering, and not a special case. She was wrong but this error does not equal anti-Semitism or necessarily reflect Jewish self-hatred.

Weil died in August 1943; had she lived longer her empathy for the Jews would have increased. Probably. Her literal reading of the Hebrew Bible (she was not likewise naive in dealing with Greek texts) and her Marcion-type rantings against the Hebrew deity (probably rooted in the old Voltaire tradition) came at a very unfortunate time for the Jewish people. The gifted French philosopher, Henri Bergson, in his eighties and mentally a Roman Catholic, stood in line, refusing a dispensation, to register as a Jew and demonstrate his solidarity with the persecuted Jewish people. Also one thinks of the writer, A. Doeblin, who became a Catholic in 1941 but kept the conversion secret so as "not to attack my people in the rear."

Young-Bruehl, Elizabeth. Hannah Arendt, For Love of the World. New Haven, CT.: Yale University Press, 1982. XXV, 563 p. Biblio.: p. 535-547. A fascinating and rich "philosophical biography."

F. Literary Criticism and Creativity: Selected Works. (The principle of selection here is rather strange, indeed somewhat spotty and idiosyncratic. Yiddish works in translation, many not well-known, are included; memoirs and creative works by Jewish literary critics).

Abramovitsh, Sholem Yankev (Mendele Mokher Sefarmin). The Parasite. trans. from the Yiddish (Dos kleyne mentshele, 1879) by Gerald Stillman. N.Y.: T. Yoseloff, 1956. 174 p. This classic of Yiddish literature is rich in sharp-edged, sardonic imagery. See also: Naq, trans by Moshe Spiegel. N.Y.: Beechhurst Press, 1955. 223 p.; Fishke, the Lame, trans. by Gerald Stillman. Yoseloff, 1960. 221 p.

Abramovitsh, Sholem Yankev. "Victims of the Fire." trans. from the Yiddish ("Hanisrafim," 1897) by Elsa Teitelbaum. In Gems from Jewish Literature. comp. and ed. by Elsa Teitelbaum. N.Y.: Pardes, 1953. 223 p. pp. 28-41.

Abramovitsh, Sholem Yankev. The Travels and Adventures of Benjamin the Third. trans. from the Hebrew by Moshe Spiegel. N.Y.: Schocken Books, 1949. 124 p.

Abramovitsh, Sholem Yankev. "Shem and Japheth on the Train." trans. from the Hebrew ("Shem veYefet ba'agalah," 1890) by Walter Levi. In Modern Hebrew Literature. ed. by Robert Alter. N.Y.: Behrman House, 1975. pp. 10-38.

Abramovitsh, Sholem Yankev. Ale verk fun-Mendele Moykher Sformin (The Complete Works in Yiddish). new ed., 22 vols. Warsaw: Farlay Mendele, 1928. Called the "grandfather" of modern Yiddish literature, Abramovitsh (1835-1917) also wrote classics in Hebrew. See the discussion in Roskies (1984, cited above, chap. 3, "Broken Tablets and Flying Letters," esp. pp. 63-78.).

Agnon, Shmuel Yosef. A Guest for the Night. trans. from the Hebrew (Ore'ah nata lalun, 1938-39) by Misha Louvish. N.Y.: Schocken Books, 1968. 485 p. Agnon (1888-1970), a very gifted novelist and short-story-writer, was from a family of Polish Jewish rabbis, scholars, and merchants. He settled in Palestine in 1907; his first "Palestinian" story was called Agunot (1908, "Forsaken Wives"). His major works include Hakhnasat Kala (2 vols., 1919; The Bridal Canopy, 1937), 'Tmol shilshom (1945; The Day Before Yesterday), Bilvav yamin (1948, In the Heart of the Seas), Edo ve' Enam (1966, Two Tales). In 1938 he edited an anthology inspired by the High Holiday Days, Yamia nora'im (Days of Awe, 1948). On Agnon, see Arnold Band (1968, cited below), and David Aberbach, At the Handles of the Lock. Themes in the Fiction of S.J. Agnon (Oxford, 1984).

Agnon, Shmuel Yosef. Kol sipurav shel Shmuel Yosef Agnon (The Complete Works). 8 vols. Tel Aviv: Schocken Books, 1953-62, 1966. There are a variety of Agnon manuscripts and the other collection of his works is in 11 volumes, Kol sipurav shel Sh. Y. Agnon, Vol. 1-6, Berlin, 1931-35; Vols. 7-11 and Tel Aviv, 1939-52.

Aleichem, Sholom. Old Country Tales. trans. from the Yiddish by Curt Leviant. N.Y.: Putnam's, 1969. See the

subtle and instructive discussion of Aleichem in Roskies
(1984, chap. 7: "Laughing Off the Trauma of History."
esp. pp. 165-183).

Aleichem, Sholom.   The Tevye Stories and Others.
trans. by Julius and Frances Butwin.   N.Y.: Pocket
Books, 1965.

Aleichem, Sholom.   The Best of Sholom Aleichem.   ed. by
Irving Howe and Ruth R. Wisse.   Introd. by Ruth R.
Wisse.   Washington D.C.: New Republic Books, 1979.

Aleichem, Sholom.   Ale verk fun Sholem-Aleykhem.   28
vols. (The Complete Works).   N.Y.: Folks-fund Edition,
1917-1925.

Aleichem, Sholom.   The Adventures of Menahem-Mendl.
trans. from the Yiddish by Tamara Kahana.   N.Y.: Putnam,
1969. 22 p.

Aleichem, Sholom.   The Great Fair.   trans. from the
Yiddish by Tamara Kahana.   N.Y.: Collier, 1970. 273 p.

Aleichem, Sholom.   In the Storm.   trans. from the
Yiddish (In shturm, 1917) by Aliza Shevrin, with an
Introd.   N.Y.: Putnam's Sons, 1984. 7-16, 199 p.   The
setting is Russia in the period of Bloody Sunday and the
October 1905 pogrom that followed the retraction of the
constitution by Nicholas II.

Aleichem, Sholom.   Why Do the Jews Need a Land of Their
Own?   trans. from the Yiddish and Hebrew by Joseph
Leftwich and Mordecai S. Chertoff.   N.Y.: Hertz Press,
1984. 242 p.   Foreword by Abraham Lis and essay by J.

Klausner, "Sholom Aleichem the Zionist," pp. 13-19.
Contains stories, a very short novel "Messianic Times: A
Zionist Novel," and a collection of Menachem Mendel
letters, and political essays of a fervant Zionist
(Shivat Zion) tone, e.g., "Dr. Theodor Herzl," pp. 139-
153.

Alter, Robert. After the Tradition. Essays on Modern
Jewish Writing. N.Y.: E.P. Dutton, 1969. 256 p. A
collection of lucid and discerning essays (previously
published) divided into three parts; "Varieties of
Jewish experience," see especially "Sabbatai Zevi and
the Jewish imagination." (pp. 61-75). Modern writers,
Bellow and Malamud, Agnon and Wiesel, and part three
(over half the book) is on "The Israeli scene." Except
in a most general sense there is no conceptual continuity between the three sections. Alter is learned and
"gets things right." Reviewed by John Gross, Commentary, 47 (April 1968): 84.

Alter, Robert. ed. with introductions and notes.
Modern Hebrew Literature (Library of Jewish Studies).
N.Y.: Behrman House, 1975. 398 p. This anthology of
short traditional and experimental prose selections,
with critical prefaces, exhibits the diverse vitality in
modern Hebrew literature.

Alter, Robert. Defenses of the Imagination: Jewish
Writers and Modern Historical Crisis. Phila.: JPS,
1978. 262 p. Includes essays (all but three previously
published in Commentary) on U.Z. Greenberg, O.
Mandelstam, W. Benjamin, G. Scholem, S.Y. Agnon, Lea
Goldberg.

Ansky, S. (S.Z.Rappoport). "The Dybbuk." trans. and ed. by Joseph C. Landis. In The Great Jewish Plays. N.Y.: Horizon Press, 1966. Also pub., N.Y.: Liverright, 1926. 145 p. First performed in Warsaw, 1920; opened in New York, 1925. A famous and "perfect" Jewish folk play.

Ansky. S. Zikhroynes (Memoirs). In Gezamlte shriftn. Vol. 10-11. Vilna, Warsaw, New York, 1922.

Appelfeld, Aharon. See chap. 1, sec. F, 3.

Asch, Sholem. Kiddush Hashem. trans. from the Yiddish by Rufus Learsi. Phila.: JPS, 1946. A response-to-catastrophe novel set in the time of the Khmelnitsky massacres, 1648-49.

The Autobiography of Sholom Aleichem, ed. and trans by Curt Leviant. N.Y.: Viking Press, 1986. 262 p. Memoirs that cover his first 21 years, serialized in Der tog, the N.Y. Yiddish daily, 1915-16. The events in those 21 years were often sorrowful, difficult, somber.

Babel, Isaac. The Collected Stories. trans. from the Russian by Walter Morrison, with an Introd. by Lionel Trilling. N.Y.: Meridian, 1960. See, esp., "Red Calvary" (1926, ET, 1929). "In 'Red Calvary,' unquestionably a central work of modern fiction, Babel raised his conversion to the Cossack code of violence to a choice of universal significance." (Roskies, 1984, p. 160).

Babel, Isaac. You Must Know Everything: Stories, 1915-1937. trans. by Max Hayward. N.Y.: Farrar, Straus & Giroux, 1969.

Babel, Isaac. The Lonely Years, 1925-1939: Unpublished Stories and Private Correspondence. ed. by Nathalie Babel, trans. by Andrew R. MacAndrew. N.Y.: Noonday, 1964.

Babel, Isaac. The Forgotten Prose. ed. and trans. by Nicholas Stroud. Ann Arbor, Mich.: Ardis, 1978. 143 p. Babel (b. 1894) died in 1941 in a Siberian prison camp. He was "rehabilitated" after the death of Stalin in 1953. On Babel, see the insights of Roskies (1984, cited above, p. 160, passim) and see Arkady Lvov, "Babel the Jew," trans. by Sheila Gutter, Commentary, 75 (March 1983): 40-49.

Band, Arnold. Nostalgia and Nightmare: A Study in the Fiction of S.Y. Agnon. Berkeley, Ca: University of California Press, 1968. 563 p. Bibliographies. General Index, Index of Agnon's Works. An encyclopedic study and reference source. Emphasizes the comic dimension in Agnon.

Band, Arnold. "A History of Modern Hebrew Fiction." Prooftexts, I:1 (1981):

Baumgarten, Murray. City Scriptures: Modern Jewish Writing. Cambridge, Mass.: Harvard University Press, 1982. 185 p. The topic is the emergence of the Jew from ghetto to cosmopolitanism and the burden of the argument is to show the impact of urban life on Jewish literature. Discusses works by Amos Oz, Cynthia Ozick, Saul Bellow, I.B. Singer.

Bialik, Hayyim Nahman. Selected Poems of Hayyim Nahman Bialik. ed. & Introd. by Israel Efros. rev. ed. N.Y.: Bloch, 1965. XXXVII, 243 p. Bialik (1873-1934) was the leading modern Hebrew poet, his compositions are points of departure for modern Jewish poetry. His poetry was deeply influenced by early poverty, he being an orphan, and by intensive studies in classical Jewish literature. His reputation was established by "ha-Matnid" (The Talmud-Student) published in ha-Shiloah, ed. by his friend Ahad Ha'am. Bialik was deeply affected by the Kishinev pogrom of 1903 and in his "Upon the Slaughter," he challenged the image of Divine Justice. (trans. from the Hebrew by A.M. Klein, in Efros, ed. Selected Poems, ibidem, pp. 112-113; the Hebrew original is in Shirim (The Collected Poems), Tel Aviv: Dvir, 1966, pp. 152-153).

Bialik, Hayyim Nahman. "In the City of Slaughter." trans. from the Hebrew, "be-'Ir he-harega" (1904) by A.M. Klein, in Selected Poems. ibidem, pp. 114-128. The poem was translated into Yiddish by Bialik, "In shkhite-shtot" in Fun tsar un tsorn (Of Anguish and Anger), Odessa: Kadimah, 1906. pp. 7-22. "Arise and go now to the city of slaughter; Into its courtyard wind thy way..." As a result of this major poem, "Kishinev became a symbol of national ignominy--and of something more. For with one hand Bialik built the pogrom up into an archetype based on a support system of martyrdom, resurrection, retribution, confession, and mourning--while with the other hand he severed the link to God and called for His abdication." (Roskies, 1984, p. 91).

And in the brilliant chapter, "The Pogrom as Poem" (pp. 79-108), Roskies argues that in Bialik's poetry the pogrom becomes "prophetic indictment" that challenges tradition by "desacralizing history." Other major poems by Bialik include "Mete midbar" (The Dead of the Wilderness) and "ha-Berekha" (The Pool).

Bilik, Dorothy Seidman. Immigrant-Survivors: Post Holocaust Consciousness in Recent American Jewish Fiction. Middletown, Conn.: Wesleyan University Press, 1981. 216 p. An analysis of immigrant-survivor personages in recent works by I.B. Singer, B. Malamud and S. Bellow. Bilik argues that the dramatic integrity and force of these characters help American Jewish sensibility deal with the Holocaust.

Burnshaw, Stanley, Ted Carmi, and Ezra Spicehandler. eds. with an Introd. by Stanley Burnshaw. The Modern Hebrew Poem Itself. Sixty-Nine Poems in a New Presentation. N.Y.: Holt, Rinehart & Winston, 1965. 220 p. Appendix. Notes. Divided into three periods: European (1880-1924), Palestinian (1920-1947), Israeli (1948--). Poetry, Burnshaw thinks, is "that which is lost in translation." Therefore, the editors supply the "originals" and a transliteration, with a literal translation and a prose commentary. The focus is on hearing the poem. This is a valuable approach but only for those who have some knowledge of Hebrew. Reviewed by Baruch Hochman, Commentary, 40 (Oct. 1965): 188.

Cohen, Arthur A. An Admirable Woman. Boston: David R. Godine, 1983. 228 p. A tight and impressive novel, except for the excursus on H. Arendt, the general image behind the novel. See also Cohen's ambitious theological novel, In the Days of Simon Stern (cited above, Part 5, chap. I, f:3).

Davidson, Israel. Parody in Jewish Literature. N.Y.: Columbia University Press, 1907. 292 p. Indices. See chap. XIV: "Descriptive Bibliography of the Parodies, from the Beginning of the 19th Century to the Present Day." This classic study of Jewish satire (casting light on Jewish social history) builds on M. Steinschneider's "Purim und Parodie." Jewish parody reveals a close connection between tears and laughter; it has (like Jewish folklore) a moral aim.

Ehrenburg, Ilya. Memoirs, 1921-1941. Cleveland: World Press, 1964. 512 p. Vol. I of his six-volume memoirs (People, Years, Life) was published in London (1961) under the title: People and Life. Ehrenburg (1891-1967), the great survivor, was a very prolific writer, journalist, anti-Fascist propagandist, best known for his novel, The Thaw (1954, ET., 1955). The work brought him some measure of official censure (the 'thaw' being actually rather temporary). On Ehrenburg's life and writings see Anatol Goldberg, Ilya Ehrenburg. With Introd. Postscript and Additional Material by Erik de Maury (N.Y.: Viking, 1988, 312 p. Biblio.: p. 294-298. Appendixes (see, esp., Appendix 2, to Stalin on the Jewish Question in the USSR (1949). Index). There is a cloud over Ehrenburg's past (Goldberg is as sympathetic as one can be while still claiming "objectivity") because of his almost total submission to Stalin. He survived the horror of the anti-Jewish campaign in the late 40's (he lived in daily terror) because he was useful to Stalin and in a real sense he was a smoke-screen for Stalin's anti-Semitism. But he was not without courage, e.g., he refused (the only one of the 20 prominent Jewish intellectuals who were asked or rather told) to sign the document alleging the guilt of Soviet Jews for what became known as the 'Doctor's plot.' Of course, he rejected Zionism but he was assertive about his own Jewishness (cf. Pasternak) and his cosmopolitanism and his defense of modern art. "As long as there is a single anti-Semite left in the world, I shall proudly call myself a Jew." (True, this was said after the death of Stalin).

Eliot, George. Daniel Deronda. London: Harpers, 1876. Eliot's (1819-1880) last novel was on the "Jewish question." She attempted to portray Jews "as they really are," described Daniel Deronda as an "effort to contribute something to the ennobling of Judaism in the conception of the Christian community." She may have been successful in this worthy goal but her vision of Zionism contrasted, too simply, the Enlightening West and the despotic, degraded East. This contrast was all too common in the 19th century, e.g., Mill, Marx, Herzl, etc.

Fiedler, Leslie. The Collected Essays of Leslie Fiedler. 2 vols. N.Y.: Stein & Day, 1971. And see Fielder's (who is always brilliant but often perversely wrong) The Jew in the American Novel (N.Y.: 1959).

Fisch, Harold. The Dual Image; The Figure of the Jew in English and American Literature. 1959. rev. and exp. ed. N.Y.: Ktav, 1972. 149 p. Fisch attempts too much in a small space, and he fails to analyze with any rigour the relationship between the two sets of images he isolates, the image of the noble Biblical Jew vs. the negative modern image. The last chapter on the Israeli "catharis" is a piece of special pleading.

Fischer, Gretl. In Search of Jerusalem: Religion and Ethics in the Writings of A.M. Klein. Montreal, McGill-Queen's University. 1975. Klein was learned in Jewish sources and used poetry to protest Jewish persecution, see Hath not a Jew...1940, Poems, 1944, The Hitleriad, 1944. See Collected Poems (Toronto, 1974). For a collection of Klein's writings see Beyond Salvation (University of Toronto, 1982).

Foltin, Lore Barbara. ed. Franz Werfel, 1890-1945. Pittsburgh: University of Pittsburgh Press, 1961. 102 p. Critical essays.

Glickman, William M. In the Mirror of Literature. The Economic Life of the Jews in Poland as Reflected in Yiddish Literature 1914-1939. Preface by B.D. Weinryb. Foreword by Solomon Grayzel. N.Y.: Living Books, 1966. Includes notes and bibliography. An attempt through the use of fiction to reconstruct the daily life of the Polish Jews between the wars.

Haft, Cynthia. The Theme of Nazi Concentration Camps in French Literature. (New Babylon: Studies in the Behavioral Sciences, 12). The Hague: Mouton, 1973. 227 p. Appendix 1. Certain Linguistic Phenomena. a) of 'Kommandos. 'Biblio.: p. 213-225. Index of Authors. Haft believes that "...only by its entrance into literature can the phenomenon of concentration camps penetrate the individual and collective consciousness of men." (p. 10). The bibliography is very valuable but we are not told how many writers (except for the phrase "several hundred") confronted the camp experience or how many wrote about it without first-person experience compared to survivors. The base of scholarship is too narrow (only 6 non-French works cited), especially in respect to historical background (chap. 1) and interpretation (chap. 6). Haft says that the eye-witness accounts (temoignages) are generally inferior in literary quality and very few writers have created a masterpiece around the camp theme. She lists as those who have E. Wiesel, J. Semprun, C. Delbo, A. Schwarz-Bart. Part I of the Appendix on linguistic developments (distortions of language) is valuable.

Halkin, Simon. Modern Hebrew Literature; Trends and Values. N.Y.: Schocken Books, 1950. 238 p. Socio-historical in focus. Halkin describes his work as the first attempt to treat modern Hebrew literature "ideo-logically" rather than simply in literary terms. (Preface).

Halpern, Moyshe Leyb. "Never Again Will I Say" ("Keynmol shoyn vel ikh nisht zogn"). In Onions and Cucumbers and Plums. ed. by Sarah Z. Betsky (cited above). "There are people who perhaps would say/it is not polite to crowd around a dray/of onions and cucumbers and plums." Halpern was born in Zlotshev, East Galicia in 1886. He came to America in 1908, was active in the Yunge and worked as an editor and graphic artist.

Halpern, Moyshe Leyb. "A Night" (A nakht), 1919. trans. by Kathyn Ann Hellerstein, In Moyshe Leyb Halpern's 'In New York': A Modern Yiddish Verse Narra-tive. Ph.D. Dissert., Stanford University, 1980, pp. 416-536 (as cited in Roskies, 1984). And see the analysis of Halpern in Roskies (1984, cited above, 94-99). In his "A Night" Halpern depicts a universal landscape of violence and extremity. The poem "explored the impact of violence on the individual psyche; it viewed the pogrom in terms of broad historical categories; and it achieved all this in an innovative form that avoided a sequential narrative." Halpern's "apocalypse obeyed the logic of a nightmare..." (Roskies, p. 194, 226).

Halpern, Moyshe Leyb. In Nyu-york (In New York). N.Y.: Vinkl, 1919.

Hamburger, Michael. From Prophecy to Exorcism; The Premises of Modern German Literature. London: Longmans, Green & Co., 1965. Seven sharply insightful essays; Nietzche to the present, including a discussion of G. Grass. The theme is the attitude of the writer toward society, and the tensions between society and writers.

Handelman, Susan A. The Slayers of Moses: The Emergence of Rabbinic Interpretation in Modern Literary Theory. (SUNY series on modern Jewish literature and culture). Albany State University of New York Press, 1982. XXI, 267 p. Glossary, Notes. Bibliography. A very erudite, difficult but well-written study of alternative interpretative structures. Rabbinic methods of interpretation have emerged in modern secular form (e.g., in Freud, H. Bloom, J. Derrida). This approach/ theory assumes an open text, subject to reinterpretations and possessing multiple meanings. An opposite view of the text is held by the "patristics" or "Greco-Christians" as seen, for example, in Coleridge, N. Frye.

Harap, Louis. The Image of the Jew in American Literature; From Early Republic to Mass Immigration. Phila.: JPS, 1974. 586 p. Notes, Index. No bibliography. An exhaustive examination; from the Puritans to the end of the 19th century. Updates and corrects Solomon Liptzin's The Jew in American Literature (N.Y.: Bloch, 1966), 251 p.

Herzen, Alexander. My Past and Thoughts: Memoirs. trans. from the Russian by Constance Garnett. Abridged with a Pref. and notes by Dwight Macdonald. Introd. by Isaiah Berlin. London: Chatto and Windus, 1974. XLIV. 684 p.

Howe, Irving and Eliezer Greenberg. eds. A Treasury of Yiddish Stories. N.Y.: Viking, 1954. 630 p. With drawings by Ben Shahn.

Howe, Irving and Eliezer Greenberg. Voices from the Yiddish: Essays, Memoirs, Diaries. Ann Arbor: University of Michigan Press, 1972. 332 p. Glossary. The editors describe this volume as "a few characteristic voices from one of the most vibrant and humane of modern cultures." Themes range from shtetl life to the future of Yiddish; writers include I. Peretz, A. Heschel.

Howe, Irving. A Margin of Hope: an intellectual Autobiography. N.Y.: Harcourt, 1982. 352 p. Memoirs of a gifted literary critic, democratic socialist, and founder of the journal Dissent.

Kalechofsky, Roberta. ed Echad. An Anthology of Latin American Jewish Writings. Marblehead, Mass.: Micah Publications, 1980. 282 p. Expresses something of the cultural spectrum of Jewish life in Latin America. Includes an interesting essay by Jaime Alazrayhi. "Borges and the Kabbalah."

Knopp, Josephine Z. The Trial of Judaism in Contemporary Jewish Writing. Urbana, IL.: University of Illinois Press, 1974. 164 p. Bibliographical footnotes. Index. Argues that the Jewish novel is a coherent genre; the contention hinges upon her notion of Mentshlehkhayt.

Leftwich, Joseph. comp. and trans. The Way We Think; A Collection of Essays from the Yiddish. 2 vols. N.Y.: Thomas Yoseloff, 1969. 841 p.

Leivick, H. "The Golem," in The Dybbuk and Other Great Yiddish Plays. trans. by Joseph C. Landis. N.Y.: Bantam, 1966, pp. 223-356. A play by an American-Yiddish poet (b. 1888, White Russia) who "was in many respects the forerunner of the Holocaust survivor" (Roskies, 1984, cited above, p. 102). In "The Golem," Leivick explores the destructive powers of redemption.

Leivick, H. "On the Roads of Siberia," trans. by Cynthia Ozick, in A Treasury of Yiddish Poetry. ed. by Irving Howe and Eliezer Greenberg. N.Y.: Holt, Rinehart & Winston, 1969. p. 118. "Even now/on the roads of Siberia/you can find/a button,/a shred of one of my shoelaces,/a belt,/a bit of broken cup,/a leaf of Scripture."

Leivick, H. "Forever" ("Eybik"), trans. by Sarah Zweig Betsky, in Onions and Cucumbers and Plums, 46 Yiddish poems. trans. and ed. by Sarah Zweig Betsky. Detroit: Wayne State University Press, 1958, 2nd printing with new Preface, 1981.#37. "The world grasps me in hands that wound,/and bears me to fire, and bears me to auto-da-fe;/I burn and I burn, and I am not consumed./I rise up again and go on my way."

Manger, Itzik. The Book of Paradise: The Wonderful Adventures of Shmuel-Aba Abervo. trans. from the Yiddish by Leonard Wolf. N.Y.: Hill and Wang, 1965. "At the edge of the abyss even laughter becomes desperate" (1939), quoted in Roskies (1984, p. 128, original Yiddish, p. 328, n. 41).

Manger, Itzik. "Love" (Libshaft"), "Saint Balshemtov" ("Sankt Bes''t), "The Ballad of the Holy Evening Bread" ("Di balade fun dem heylikn ovnt-broyt"), "Cain and Abel" ("Keyn un Hevl"), "Hagars Last Night at Abraham's," ("Hogors letste nakht bay Avronmen"), "...like the smoke of chimney is the love of a man." "The Binding of Isaac" ("Ekeydes Yitskhok"), "At the Crossroad" ("Oyfn Sheydveg"). Numbers 14, 19, 22-26 in Onions and Cucumbers and Plums, cited above. This very gifted poet was born in 1901 in Czernowitz, Bukovina. The image of Jesus and of Christianity occurs in several of Manger's poems, e.g., "The Binding of Isaac." See Janet Hadda, "Christian imagery and dramatic impulse in the Poetry of Itsik Manger," Michigan Germanic Studies, 3:2 (1977): 1-12. According to Roskies (1984, p. 273), the horror of the Holocaust caused Manger (and Sutzkever) to expunge "the glowing references to Jesus and Gentiles from their earlier poetry..."

Mintz, Alan. Hurban... (cited above, chap. 1,f).

Miron, Dan. A Traveler Disguised: A Study in the Rise
of Modern Yiddish Fiction in the Nineteenth Century.
N.Y.: Schocken Books, 1973. 347 p. illus., Bibliography.
Index. A major, instructive, scholarly study of Yiddish
fiction. An exact, precise analysis of S. Abramovitz
(the "traveller disguised") and S. Aleichem is presented, the Hebrew-Yiddish conflict is discussed and Yiddish
fiction is related to it.

Miron, Dan. "Rediscovering Haskalah Poetry." Prooftexts, I:3 (1981): 292-305. On socioeconomic context.

Miron, Dan. "Folklore and Antifolklore in the Yiddish
Fiction of the Haskala." in Studies in Jewish Folklore,
ed. by Frank Talmage. Cambridge, Mass.: Association for
Jewish Studies, 1980. pp. 219-249.

Neugroschel, Joachim. ed. and trans. The Shtetl: A
Creative Anthology of Jewish Life in Eastern Europe.
N.Y.: Richard Marek, 1979. 572 p. Contains very
valuable selections and material but no notes and no
bibliography.

Ozick, Cynthia. Art & Ardor; Essays. N.Y.: Knopf,
1983. 305 p. A collection of insightful, often
original, essays on writers, culture, Judaism. See,
esp., "Literary Blacks and Jews" (on the famous Irving
Howe-Ralph Ellison exchange), "Cultural Impersonation,"
(an impressive discussion of John Updike and an appreciative interpretation of Mark Harris' The Goy (N.Y.:
Dial, 1970), "The Fourth Sparrow: The Magisterial Reach
of Gershom Scholem," a somewhat flaccid and excessive
tribute, "Toward a New Yiddish," a lecture delivered in
Rehovoth, Israel in the summer of 1970 and pub. in

Judaism (Summer 1970) under the title: "America: Toward Yavneh." This contains a sharp attack on American pluralism and a plea for Jewish literary culture. "The problem of Diaspora in its most crucial essence is the problem of aesthetics." (p. 165). A very abstract-sounding statement but it is part of an argument for Jewish specificity (Covenant and conduct) and a repudiation of the religion of Art. See also "Literature as Idol: Harold Bloom," and "Out of the Flames: The Recovery of Gertrud Kolmar" (first pub. as a Foreword to Dark Solioquy: The Selected Poems of Gertrud Kolmar).

Peretz, I.L. Selected Stories. ed. with an Introd. by Irving Howe and Eliezer Greenberg. N.Y.: Schocken Books, 1975. (pa.) 159 p. Glossary. Peretz was the major writer of Yiddish culture in Poland. The "voice dominating these stories is ironic, ambivalent, skeptical..." They are wisdom stories "expressing" the Jewish mind engaged in self-reflection, self-argument, self-criticism, but most of all self-discovery." (pp. 18-19). "Bontsha the Silent" (pp. 70-77) is his most famous story.

Peretz, I.L. Stories and Pictures. trans. from the Yiddish by Helena Frank. Phila.: JPS, 1906. Originals in: Ale verk fun Y.L. Perets, ed. by S. Niger. II Vols. N.Y.: CYCO, 1947. Peretz (1852/51-1915) brought the standard of Yiddish literature to a high level, achieving a neoclassical form in the 1890's. His "Travel Pictures" (in Stories and Pictures, ibidem) deal with the myth and reality of the shtetl. His visionary drama, The Golden Chain, on the timeless chain of Jewish tradition, ends with: "And so we stride--our souls ablaze." Peretz also wrote in Hebrew. His Yiddish is described as taut and concise; he is credited with founding the Yiddishist movement. Unlike Solomon Aleichem he was opposed to political Zionism.

Peretz, I.L. "The Dead Town" (1895-1900), trans. by Irving Howe, in A Treasury of Yiddish Stories. ed. by Irving Howe and Eliezer Greenberg. N.Y.: Viking, 1954. pp. 205-213.

Pinsker, Stanford. The Schlemiel as Metaphor. Carbondale: Southern Illinois University Press, 1971. Read together with R. Wisse (1971, below).

Rosenberg, Isaac. The Collected Works of Isaac Rosenberg: Poetry, Prose, Letters, Paintings and Drawings. ed. with an Introd. and notes by Ian Parsons. Foreword by Siegfried Sassoon. Oxford University Press, 1979. 320 p. Indices. This very gifted English-Jewish poet and painter was killed on the Western Front in 1918 at the age of 28.

Rosenfeld, Isaac. An Age of Enormity: Life and Writing in the Forties and Fifties. ed. and Introduced by Theodore Solotaroff. Foreword by Saul Bellow. Cleveland: World Pub. Co., 1962. 347 p. Rosenfeld, an incisive literary critic in the 1940's and early 1950's, died in 1956. In these essays he discusses Kafka, S. Weil, Sartre and the "enormities" of modern culture. "Terror is today the main reality because it is the model reality."

Samuel, Maurice. The World of Sholom Aleichem. N.Y.: Knopf, 1943. A sensitive study of the greatest of Jewish humorists and a literary mirror of Russian Jewry.

This is not a literary or biographical study but a gracefully written social history of Aleichem's world, esp. of the town of Kasrielevky, "the townlet of the tiny folk." The Kasrielevkiites had no name for religion "because for them it was simply equated with being human." This fact "distinguishes the world of Sholom Aleichem from every other world that has ever been reproduced by a regionalist writer." (p. 54) For an appreciation of S. Aleichem, see Alfred Kazan, Contemporaries (Boston: Little Brown, 1962).

Samuel, Maurice. Little Did I Know: Recollections and Reflections. N.Y.: Knopf, 1963. An autobiography. In Little Did I Know, Samuel promises a work on Yiddish. This appeared in 1971; In Praise of Yiddish (N.Y.: Cowles Book Co., XIV, 283 p. Index) is a very compelling and eloquent inside account of Yiddish, full of illustrative anecdote, folklore, personal memories.

Shapiro, Lamed. "In the Dead Town." 1910. trans. from the Yiddish (In der toyter shtot) by David G. Roskies, Mosaic (Cambridge, Mass.) 12 (1971): 10-23.

Shapiro, Lamed. The Jewish Government and Other Stories. ed. and trans. from the Yiddish by Curt Leviant. N.Y.: Twayne, 1971. 186 p.

Shapiro, Lamed. "White Chalah." 1919. trans. from the Yiddish (Vayse Khale) by Norbert Guterman, in Howe and Greenberg, eds. A Treasury of Yiddish Stories. N.Y.: Viking, 1954. pp. 325-353. Shapiro's pogrom stories--"a landscape of extremity"--subvert the traditional images of God and man, and universalize violence. In the terrifying images in "White Chalah"--which depicts violence against Jews from the point of view of Gentiles--"man reverts to beast, the Judeo-Christian heritage is replaced by a cult of human sacrifice, nature revokes its life-giving capacities, and the beast of the apocalypse reigns supreme." (Roskies, 1984, p. 155, see pp. 146-157.) On Shapiro, (1878-1948) see Esther Frank, "An Analysis of Four Short Stories by Lamed Shapiro," Working Papers in Yiddish and East European Jewish Studies, 28 (November 1978): 18-27.

Shmeruk, C. "Yiddish Literature in the U.S.S.R.." in The Jews in Soviet Russia since 1917. ed. by Lionel Kochan. London: Oxford University Press, 1970, and see Y.A. Gilboa, "Hebrew Literature in the U.S.S.R., ibidem.

Schnitzler, Arthur. My Youth in Vienna. Foreword By Frederic Morton. trans. from the German by Catherine Hutter. N.Y.: Holt, Rinehart & Winston, 1970. 304 p. illus. The memoirs (b. 1862) of this physician, play- wright and novelist are useful as a source for middle- class Austrian Jewry. See the centennial commemorative volume, ed. by Herbert W. Reichert and Herman Salinger, Studies in Arthur Schnitzler (Chapel Hill: University of North Carolina Press, 1964, 116 p.), and Reinhard Urbach, Arthur Schnitzer. trans. from the German by Donald Daviau. [World dramatists]. (N.Y.: Ungar, 1973), 202 p. illus.

Schultz, Bruno. The Street of Crocodiles. trans. from the Polish (Cinnamon Shops, 1934) by Celina Wieniewska. N.Y.: Walker and Co., 1963. 159 p. C. Ozick (1982, cited above) called Schultz "one of the most original literary imaginations of modern Europe." This is a haunting novel of recollection, fantasy disruption and metamorphic change. Schultz was shot by an SS officer in 1942 in his hometown of Drogobych.

Schultz, Bruno. _Sanatorium under the sign of the Hourglass_. trans. from the Polish (1937) by Celina Wieniewska. N.Y.: Walker and Co., 1978. Translator's preface. 178 p.

Schwartz, Delmore. _In Dreams Begin Responsibilities and Other Stories_. ed. with an Introd. by James Atlas. Foreword by Irving Howe. N.Y.: New Directions, 1978. VII–XXI, 202 p. The eloquent lead story was published in 1937 in the first issue of _Partisan Review_. Included: "In Dreams...," "America! America!," "The World is a Wedding," "New Year's Eve," "The Commencement Day Address," "The Track Meet," "The Child is the Meaning of This Life," "Screeno." In general terms these stories express "the pathos and comic hopelessness of the conflict between immigrant Jewish families and their intellectual children..." (I. Howe). _In Dreams Begin Responsibilities_ was the title of Schwartz's first book (New Directions, 1938).

Schwartz, Delmore. _Selected Poems, Summer Knowledge_. N.Y.: New Directions, 1938, 1950.

Schwartz, Delmore. _Summer Knowledge; New and Selected Poems, 1938-1958_. Garden City, N.Y.: Doubleday & Co., 1959. 240 p. Won the 1959 Bollingen prize for poetry. Among Schwartz's poems, read: "In the Naked Bed, in Plato's Cave" (1939), "For the One Who Would Take Man's Life in His Hands" (1938), "Dogs Are Shakespearean, Children Are Strangers" (1938) "The Heavy Bear Who Goes

with Me" (1938), "The Winter Twilight, Glowing Black and
Gold" (1959), "The Mind Is an Ancient and Famous
Capital" (1959). A fictional portrait of Schwartz is
drawn by Saul Bellow in Humboldt's Gift (N.Y.: Viking,
1976); and see the excellent biographical study by James
Atlas, Delmore Schwartz, The Life of an American Poet
(N.Y.: Farrar, Straus, Giroux, 1977; Toronto: Ryerson,
1977, 418 p. Includes Index and bibliographies). For
Atlas' assessment of Bellow's picture of Schwartz, see
pp. 332-334, passim. Schwartz's characteristics "became
identified with a whole temper: that of the alienated
Jew, the radical, the poete maudit, the modern intellectual hero." X. Now see: Letters of Delmore Schwartz.
select. and ed. by Robert Phillips. (Princeton, N.J.:
Ontario Review Press, 1984. 334 p.). On July 25, 1943
he wrote to Dwight Macdonald, "Eliot never...nor tried
...nor made, nor was motivated by the alienation which
only a Jew can suffer, and use, as a cripple uses his
weakness, in order to beg." (p. 185). There is little
in this collection on Schwartz in relation to his Jewish
heritage but note his awareness of and suffering from
anti-Semitism (late 30's, early 40's, p. 62-63, 182),
and read the powerful and moving critique of Pound's
"race prejudice." "Without ceasing to distinguish
between past activity and present irrationality, I
should like you to consider this letter as a resigna-
tion: I want to resign as one of your most studious and
faithful admirers."

Silberschlag, Eisig. From Renaissance to Renaissance.
Hebrew Literature from 1492-1970. Vol. One. N.Y.:
Ktav, 1973. 431 p. Bibliographical epilog. Notes. Index.
Very learned in Hebrew and western literatures, rich,
dense sentences and critical acuteness. See, esp., the
original essay on "...Hebrew Literature in America."

pp. 249-328. Jewish literary creativity usually comes at the end of a long period of philosophical developments, e.g., Philo and Hellenism, Maimonides. "For Jewish originality consists of a genius for adaptation." (p. 7).

Silberschlag, Eisig. Hebrew Literature in the Land of Israel, 1870-1970. (From Renaissance to Renaissance, Vol. 2) N.Y.: Ktav, 1977. 427 p. Notes, Bibliographical comment, Index. A major scholarly study of Hebrew literature. These hundred years have witnessed a literature that reflects the great events of the century but "the liberating power of genius is missing." The eternal themes "have not been invested with articulation that has a ring of the eternal." Silberschlag concludes: "A new Torah has not yet come out of Zion." (p. 319).

Silberschlag, Eisig. Saul Tschernichowsky, Poet of Revolt. With trans. by Sholom J. Kahn, et al. Ithaca: Cornell University Press, 1968. 209 p. illus. This brilliant poet (1875-1943) was a contemporary of Bialik but they had little in common. Tschernichowsky was deeply influenced by Greek culture and Hellenism. His basic genres were the idyll, in which he celebrated Jewish rural life, the sonnet and the ballad. He was a translator of vast scope, e.g., the Finnish, Kalevala, Greek, English, German. He wrote powerful angry poems on medieval Christian persecution, "Baruck of Mayence," "The Dead of Dortmund."

Sinclair, Clive. The Brothers Singer. London: Allison and Busby Ltd., 1983. An exciting study of the Singer brothers and the virtually unknown sister, Ester

802

Kreitman who wrote Yiddish novels (<u>Esther</u>, trans. M. Kreitman, London, 1946, rpt. Virago, 1983).

Singer, Isaac Bashevis. <u>In My Father's Court</u>. N.Y.: Farrar, Straus, Giroux, 1966. 307 p. Singer's memories, intense and poetic, of his childhood in 10 Krochmalna St., Warsaw. For a fascinating account of arguments between his older brother, Isaac, and his mother, see "A Boy Philosopher," pp. 207-212. The Yiddish title is <u>Beth Din</u> (first pub. in the <u>Jewish Daily Forward</u>) and the concept behind the Rabbinical court "is that there can be no justice without godliness, and that the best judgment is one accepted by all the litigants with good will and trust in divine power." (Author's Note).

Singer, Isaac Bashevis. <u>Selected Short Stories of Isaac Bashevis Singer</u>. ed. by Irving Howe. N.Y.: Modern Library, 1966. There is now a rather large literature on Singer, see Marcia Attentuck, ed. <u>The Achievement of Issac Bashevis Singer</u>. (Carbondale: Southern Illinois University Press, 1969), and see the recent biography by Paul Kresh, <u>Isaac Bashevis Singer. The Magician of West 86th Street</u>. (N.Y.: The Dial Press, 1979. 441 p. Biblio.: p. 421-427. Index.). And see <u>An Isaac Bashevis Singer Reader</u>. N.Y.: Farrar, Straus, 1971. 560 p. (pa.).

Singer, Isaac Bashevis and Ira Moskowitz. <u>A Little Boy in Search of God: Mysticism in a Personal Light</u>. trans. from the Yiddish by Joseph Singer. Garden City, N.Y.: Doubleday, 1976. Q. 209 p. illus. A memoir with drawings by Moskowitz.

Singer, Israel Joshua. Of a World That is No More. trans. from the Yiddish by Joseph Singer. N.Y.: Vanguard Press, 1971. 253 p. I.J. Singer (1893-1944) was the older brother of I.B. Singer and his inspiration. This memoir, written in the 1940's, is informative about the society of Polish Jewry before 1939.

Wisse, Ruth R. The Schlemiel as Modern Hero. Chicago: The University of Chicago Press, 1971. Includes an Appendix, on the etymology of schlemiel (Jewish underworld slang and the Hebrew word schlimazl, luckless), Biblio.: p. 127-130. Aspects of Jewish history in modern times is mirrored in the image of the schlemiel, master of irony: "God will provide, if only god would provide until He provides!" Cf. S. Pinsker (above).

Wisse, Ruth R. ed. with Introd. and notes. A Shtetl and other Yiddish Novellas. N.Y.: Behrman House, 1973. 364 p. Includes I.M. Weissenberg's "A Shtetl," trans. by Ruth R. Wisse.

Wisse, Ruth R. "Die Yunge and the Problem of Jewish Aestheticism." JSS, 38 (1976): 265-276.

Wisse, Ruth R. "Die Yunge: Immigrants or Exile?" Prooftexts, Vol. 1:1 (January 1981): 43-61.

Yudkin, Leon I. Escape into Siege: A Survey of Israeli Literature Today. (Littman Library of Jewish Civilization). London: Routledge & Kegan Paul, 1974. 197 p.

Zweig, Stephen. The World of Yesterday; An Autobiography. N.Y.: Viking Press, Toronto: MacMillan, 1943. O. XIV. 455 p. This trans. of Die Welt von Gestern (1942)

is a source for Jewish life in Vienna. Zweig claimed
that "most, if not all that Europe and America admire
today as an expression of a new, rejuvenated Austrian
culture, in literature, the theatre, in the arts and
crafts, was created by the Viennese Jews." Zweig (1888-
1942) was "esteemed as a great storyteller biographer,
and humanitarian spirit." See the review by Hannah
Arendt, "Portrait of a Period" (Oct. 1943) in The Jew as
Pariah (1978, cited above), pp. 112-121. Arendt
comments on Zweig's concern with honor: "For honor never
will be won by the cult of success or fame, by cultiva-
tion of one's self nor even by personal dignity. From
the "disgrace" of being a Jew there is but one escape--
to fight for the honor of the Jewish people as a whole."
(p. 121).

JEWISH STUDIES